RESEARCH HANDBOOK OF EMPLOYMENT RELATIONS IN SPORT

Research Handbook of Employment Relations in Sport

Edited by

Michael Barry

Professor and Head, Department of Employment Relations and Human Resources, Griffith University, Australia

James Skinner

Director, Institute for Sport Business and Professor of Sport Business, Loughborough University London, UK

Terry Engelberg

Associate Professor, College of Healthcare Sciences, Division of Tropical Health and Medicine, James Cook University, Australia

Edward Elgar
PUBLISHING

Cheltenham, UK • Northampton, MA, USA

Published by
Edward Elgar Publishing Limited
The Lypiatts
15 Lansdown Road
Cheltenham
Glos GL50 2JA
UK

Edward Elgar Publishing, Inc.
William Pratt House
9 Dewey Court
Northampton
Massachusetts 01060
USA

A catalogue record for this book
is available from the British Library

Library of Congress Control Number: 2016931789

This book is available electronically in the **Elgar**online
Business subject collection
DOI 10.4337/9781783470464

MIX
Paper from
responsible sources
FSC   FSC® C013056
www.fsc.org

ISBN 978 1 78347 045 7 (cased)
ISBN 978 1 78347 046 4 (eBook)

Typeset by Servis Filmsetting Ltd, Stockport, Cheshire
Printed and bound in Great Britain by TJ International Ltd, Padstow

Contents

Contributors

Jack Anderson

Jack Anderson is a Professor of Law at Queen's University, Belfast, Northern Ireland. Jack has published widely on the topics of sports law including monographs such as *The Legality of Boxing* (2007) and *Modern Sports Law* (2010) and an edited collection *Landmark Cases in Sports Law* (2013). He is currently Editor-in-Chief of the *International Sports Law Journal* published jointly by the Asser Institute at The Hague and Springer-Verlag. Jack has lectured internationally on the topic of sports law including at the National Sports Law Institute, Marquette University, Milwaukee; the Australian National University, Canberra; the Australian Research Council's Centre of Excellence in Policing and Security, Brisbane; University of Cambridge; German Sports University, Cologne; and the China University of Political Science and Law, Beijing. He has also delivered papers and workshops relating to sports law for Interpol, FIFA and the International Rugby Board. Jack contributes regularly to the media in Britain and Ireland on sports law matters and, being a Fellow of the Chartered Institute of Arbitrators (FCIArb), he is also a member of a number of sports dispute resolution tribunals in the UK and Ireland.

Michael Barry

Michael Barry is Professor and Head of the Department of Employment Relations and Human Resources at Griffith University, Australia. Michael's main research interests are in the areas of employee voice and engagement, international and comparative employment relations, and employer associations. Michael is currently working on a large, funded study of employee–employer relations and workplace challenges in the US, Australia and the UK.

Peter Bouris

Peter Bouris is a PhD student at the University of Toronto's Centre for Industrial Relations and Human Resources. He originally hails from Buffalo, New York, USA. As a lifelong fan of sport, one of his discipline interests is collective bargaining power dynamics in North America's major sports leagues. He also is currently doing work involving interest arbitration and labour organizing strategy and strength.

Christine Coupland
Christine Coupland is Professor of Organizational Behaviour at the Loughborough University School of Business and Economics, UK. Her research interests centre on issues of career, identity and language, drawing upon theoretical perspectives from organization studies and constructionist social psychology. Her most recent research focuses on the career paths of elite professional rugby players. She serves on the editorial board of the *Journal of Organizational and Occupational Psychology*. She is currently Senior Editor for *Organization Studies* and regularly convenes research streams at the British Academy of Management conference.

Craig A. Depken II
Craig A. Depken II is a Professor of Economics in the Belk College at UNC Charlotte, USA. His research interests include sports economics, industrial organization, real estate economics and finance. He is currently Co-editor of *Contemporary Economic Policy*.

James B. Dworkin
James B. Dworkin is currently the Chancellor of the Purdue University North Central (PNC), Indiana, USA campus, which is part of the Purdue University system. Prior to coming to PNC, James served as Associate Dean of the School of Management and the Krannert Graduate School of Management on the Purdue West Lafayette Campus. He has been with Purdue since 1976. He received his BA in Economics (with high honours) and MA in Industrial Relations from the University of Cincinnati and his PhD in Industrial Relations from the University of Minnesota. He is a member of the National Academy of Arbitrators. He has taught many courses in industrial relations and negotiations both at the undergraduate and graduate levels. He has written one scholarly book, *Owners versus Players: Baseball and Collective Bargaining*, as well as 99 professional articles and reviews. His first children's book, *The Dog and the Dolphin*, was published in July of 2014. His professional research interests include professional sports and collective bargaining. He continues to serve as an active arbitrator, fact-finder and mediator. James is the recipient of the 'Sagamore of the Wabash' award from Indiana Governor Michael Pence. He has received many other awards, including the 'Special Boilermaker Award' from the Purdue University Alumni Association, and was recognized by *Northwest Indiana Business Quarterly* as an Outstanding Community Leader in 2012.

Terry Engelberg
Terry Engelberg is an Associate Professor in the College of Healthcare Sciences at James Cook University, Australia. She has a background in

social psychology and in sport science and was a small business owner in the health and fitness sector before entering academia. She has published on topics such as sexual harassment, organizational commitment and doping in sport for leading journals and books. She is also a certified athletics coach and a certified fitness instructor for children and young adolescents. She is a former recipient of an Australian Sports Commission (ASC) Sport Leadership Grant for Women. Terry has previously conducted seven major studies on anti-doping in Australia (six for the Australian Government's Anti-Doping Research Program, and one for WADA). She is currently undertaking a project on detecting doping, funded by the inaugural International Olympic Committee (IOC) anti-doping fund (with Stephen Moston).

Simon Gardiner
Simon Gardiner is Professor of International Sports Law at Leeds Becket University, UK and has worked at a number of universities in the UK and in Australia including Middlesex University and Griffith University in Queensland. Simon has been an active researcher in the area of sports law for over twenty years and has an international reputation. His particular research interests include sports governance and the regulation of sports-related corruption, racism in sport and the construction of national identity and athlete mobility in sport. He has been involved in funded research projects and consultancy for a range of sports bodies and has worked with the European Union concerning a number of projects. He is lead author and editor of the UK's principal student-targeted textbook, namely Gardiner et al., *Sports Law*, that is due to be published in its fifth edition in 2016.

Rafael Gomez
Rafael is a Professor of Employment Relations at the University of Toronto, Canada. In 2015 he assumed the Directorship of the Centre for Industrial Relations and Human Resources, at the University of Toronto. In 2015 he also co-authored the book *Small Business and the City: The Transformative Potential of Small Scale Entrepreneurs*.

Berndt Keller
Berndt Keller is Professor Emeritus of Employment Relations at the University of Konstanz, Germany. He is the author and editor of several books and numerous articles on German and European employment relations. He was co-editor of *Industrielle Beziehungen*/The German Journal of Industrial Relations and was a member of the Executive Committee of the International Labor and Employment Relations Association. His present research interests include the consequences of European

integration, atypical forms of employment, employment relations in the public sector, and union mergers.

Lisa Pike Masteralexis
Lisa Pike Masteralexis is the Associate Dean of Administration for the Isenberg School of Management at the University of Massachusetts-Amherst, USA. For 17 years she served as Department Head of the Mark H. McCormack Department of Sport Management and an Associate Professor of Sport Law and Labor Relations in Sport. She is an editor of *Principles and Practice of Sport Management* (5th Ed.) plus author of numerous sport law articles. She holds a JD from Suffolk University School of Law and a BS in Sport Management from the University of Massachusetts-Amherst. She is a member of the Massachusetts and US Supreme Court Bars, a certified player agent with the Major League Baseball Players Association, and a principal in DiaMMond Management Group, an athlete management firm.

Greg Maynes
Greg Maynes is a Lecturer in Economics including Macro-Economics and Development Economics in the School of Economics, Finance and Marketing, RMIT University, Australia. His recent research has included the process of human capital investment and the impact of education on economic development.

Heather Mitchell
Heather Mitchell, PhD, M. App. Sci., B. App. Sci. (Maths), Dip. C.E., graduated with her PhD in Mathematical Statistics in 1997, after which she commenced as a Lecturer in RMIT University's School of Economics, Finance and Marketing. She retired in 2013 and is now an Honorary Professor in the school. She has over 30 publications in refereed journals including *Biometrika* and the *Journal of Banking and Finance*. Before academia she worked as a civil engineer for the Melbourne and Metropolitan Board of Works (MMBW).

Stephen Moston
Stephen Moston has extensive experience in the field of forensic psychology and has conducted major research studies for bodies such as the Royal Commission on Criminal Justice, UK Home Office, Metropolitan Police, and has most recently worked with members of the Queensland Police Service on projects relating to police investigative processes. He has a strong interest in anti-doping issues, particularly in the forensic identification and detection of athletes committing doping violations. He has previously conducted seven major studies on anti-doping in Australia (six for the Australian Government's Anti-Doping Research Program,

and one for WADA). He is currently undertaking a project on detecting doping, funded by the inaugural International Olympic Committee anti-doping fund (with Terry Engelberg).

James A.R. Nafziger
James A.R. Nafziger is the Thomas B. Stoel Professor of Law and Director of International Law Programs, Willamette University College of Law, USA. He also serves as Honorary President of the International Association of Sports Law and is a member of the Board of Advisors of the National Sports Law Institute. His several books and numerous articles on sports law include *International Sports Law*, the first book in that field; *Handbook of International Sports Law* (with Stephen F. Ross); and *Transnational Sports Law*. Professor Nafziger has also taught sports law at Marquette University, as the Boden Visiting Professor, and the University of Barcelona.

Matt Nichol
Matt Nichol is an Assistant Lecturer in the Department of Business Law and Taxation at the Monash Business School, Monash University, Australia. He is currently undertaking a PhD on the regulation of labour in professional baseball in the US, Japan and Australia at the Adelaide Law School, University of Adelaide. Matt has been involved in Australian baseball as a player, coach and administrator for 30 years. Recently he has worked with the Melbourne Aces of the Australian Baseball League in a variety of roles, including as a liaison for professional players from Japan's Saitama Seibu Lions.

Rodney Paul
Rodney Paul has a PhD in Applied Economics from Clemson University, USA. His research interests in the economics and finance of sports include attendance modelling, market efficiency and sports gambling markets, television ratings in sports, competitive balance and uncertainty of outcome. He is currently Full Professor in the Department of Sport Management in the David B. Falk College of Sport and Human Dynamics at Syracuse University.

Peter Schuwalow
Peter Schuwalow is a Lecturer in Economics including Sports Economics in the Department of Economics, Monash University, Australia. Recent research has included the history of labour market regulation in professional sports and the economic value of professional sport.

James Skinner
James is the Director of the Institute for Sport Business, Professor of Sport Business and Associate Dean Enterprise at Loughborough

University London, UK. His research and consultancy interests are in
leadership, culture and change in sport; doping in sport; and sport and
social capital. In conjunction with colleagues he has received external
research funding from the Australian Research Council, the World
Anti-Doping Agency, the Australian Federal Government's Anti-Doping
Research Program, the Australian Sports Commission and London Sport.
His current research is examining policy mechanisms and frameworks to
apply a uniform approach to athlete regulation and conduct.

John Solow
John Solow is Professor of Economics, Tippie College of Business, the
University of Iowa, USA. Professor Solow received his BA in Economics
from Yale University and his MA and PhD in Economics from Stanford
University. He joined the Iowa faculty in 1981. His research interests include
sports economics, antitrust law and economics, and public policy, and his
work has been published in the *American Economic Review*, the *Journal
of Public Economics* and the *Journal of Sports Economics*, among others.
He has worked at the Federal Energy Administration and the Electric
Power Research Institute, served as a consultant to the US Departments
of Energy and Justice, Mid-American Energy, Qwest Telecommunications
and numerous law firms, and has been a Visiting Scholar at Stanford
University, the University of Auckland and Monash University.

Mark Stewart
Mark Stewart is a Senior Lecturer in the School of Economics, Finance
and Marketing at RMIT University, Australia. His publications have
appeared in journals including the *Journal of Sports Economics*, the
International Journal of Sports Finance and *Applied Economics*. Mark has
also previously worked as a professional athletics coach and currently
holds the part-time position of National Junior Coach (Pole Vault) for
Athletics Australia.

Klaus Vieweg
Klaus Vieweg is Director of the Institute of Law and Technology, Chair
for Civil Law, Law of Information Technology, Law of Technology,
and Business Law at the Law School of Friedrich-Alexander University
Erlangen-Nuremberg, Germany. He is Vice President of the German
Sports Law Association, Honorary Vice President of the International
Association of Sports Law (IASL), Co-founder of The Hague International
Sports Law Academy (HISLAC) and Member of the German Court of
Arbitration for Sports. His main areas of research are national, European
and international facets of law of associations and federations, sports law,
tort law, property law, law of technology and business law.

Peter von Allmen

Peter von Allmen is a Professor of Economics at Skidmore College, USA and currently serves as Department Chair. Previously, he served as a Fellow of the American Council on Education and is currently the President of the North American Association of Sports Economists. He received his BA from the College of Wooster and his PhD from Temple University. His central research focus is on the economics of sports. In addition to his primary research, he is the co-author of *The Economics of Sports* (with Michael Leeds), now in its fifth edition.

Andrew Weinbach

Andrew Weinbach is Professor at Wall College of Business, Coastal Carolina University, USA. He has published widely on major sporting codes in North America, with a particular emphasis on gambling behaviour.

Roger Welch

Roger Welch was a Principal Lecturer, and is now a Visiting Research Fellow, at the University of Portsmouth, UK. He has written extensively on collective and individual employment rights and on employment law in the context of professional sport. He is an original and ongoing co-author of *Sports Law*, published by Routledge, and the lead author of *Employment Law*, published by Pearson in its Living Law series.

1. Sidelined: employment relations in professional sports
Michael Barry, James Skinner and Terry Engelberg

INTRODUCTION

This book aims to address an area of research that remains greatly under-developed in sport management. There is no scholarly research hand-book that we are aware of that examines the interconnection between Employment Relations (ER) and sport. There are books that look at sport and related areas such as human resource management (HRM), behavioural economics, international law and psychology. While some of these volumes incorporate aspects of ER, none of them deal with ER in great depth. Remarkably, some large research volumes do not include any specific treatment of ER issues. As well as providing an in-depth treatment of ER issues in sports, this handbook is broad in its coverage. The book is explicitly international in that it includes issues and concepts relevant to sporting codes in various countries, and it also draws on an international field of scholars and includes case studies from different codes of sport in a number of countries.

The study of ER incorporates aspects of industrial relations (IR), such as labour law, collective bargaining and industrial disputes, and HRM, including recruitment, training and development, and performance and reward management. While years ago these were treated as separate and distinct fields of research, there has been an increasing emphasis on integration. It is important to acknowledge, however, that there are some core differences between these approaches to ER. The traditional IR view sees an inherent divergence between the interests of workers and managers which can create conflict and lead to industrial disputes such as those examined in this volume. While there are many areas of cooperation, there is as one author puts it a 'structured antagonism' in ER (Edwards, 1986). HRM, which was previously known as personnel management, operates from a perspective that views the interests of both parties as being closely aligned around the goals of the firm, and so conflict is more aberrant than inherent. In this handbook we employ the abbreviation ER because we try to capture both approaches, although there will be differences in emphasis

1

within the topics we cover. For example, a chapter on bargaining or disputes will have more of an IR emphasis compared to a chapter on player or coach career development which will be more aligned with the core principles of HRM.

EMPLOYMENT RELATIONS AND SPORTS

According to Kahn (2000), the sports industry is the perfect laboratory for labour market research. A wealth of data is available in sports for workers and supervisors over the life of their careers, including exact measures of performance and remuneration. Despite this, the academic field of ER has taken only a mild interest in the sports industry, both historically and in recent years. We find it curious that sport has remained on the backburner for ER scholars, for we argue that the ER aspects of sport have become increasingly relevant and interesting for scholarly research. In the ER literature, interest in sports has remained concentrated on a few particular issues, such as the analysis of the share of total sporting revenue that players receive and how this is distributed among players (e.g. Booth, Brooks & Diamond, 2012; Dabscheck, 2011; Ducking, Groothuis & Hill, 2014), with little attention paid to many other areas, such as governance, institutions and regulation, or indeed the nature of work itself. Equally, sports academics have not drawn extensively on the field of ER despite the growing importance of ER to the way sport is organised, conducted and governed. The sports management literature has looked at some HRM issues, such as the development of volunteers (Engelberg, Skinner & Zakus, 2014), job satisfaction (Taylor, Doherty & McGraw, 2015), gender participation in sports (Hanlon, Morris & Nabbs, 2014), diversity (Adair, Taylor & Darcy, 2010), governance (Yeh & Taylor, 2008; Ordway, 2014) and the working conditions of female coaches (Allen & Shaw, 2013).

Our contention is that sport is both interesting and unusual as an area of ER analysis in that developments in sport run counter to important ER trends in most other industries and sectors. This deserves greater interest than what ER scholars have so far shown. For example, across different codes and countries, there has been marked industrial disputation in professional sports (Ahlburg & Dworkin, 1991) during an era of greatly decreased disputation in most other industries. Professional sport has witnessed major strikes and lockouts and these have delayed and even led to the cancellation of sporting seasons. The public interest in these disputes has been enormous, and employers have sometimes responded (with mixed success) by engaging replacement players. As demonstrated in this volume, these disputes have had a major impact on some of the most prominent codes, particularly in North America (Staudohar, 1996).

As sport has been professionalised, the conflict of interest over what ER scholars refer to as the 'wage/effort' bargain has increasingly come to the fore. Underlying much of the tension between players, teams and sporting organisations (those bodies that govern sporting codes) are efforts by players to obtain a greater share of the revenue derived from their work (Dabscheck, 2010). The increasing professionalism of sport has also coincided with a push for greater organisation of players' collective interests, which makes sports a fertile ground for ER scholars to examine employee representation.

Thus, while a litany of research has demonstrated that there has been a strong trend towards de-unionisation across most industries in almost all Organisation for Economic Co-operation and Development (OECD) countries, leaving unions with a difficult task of engaging in organisational renewal to retain their relevance (e.g. Fairbrother & Yates, 2003), in sports there has been something of an opposite trend, with a greater development and influence of player associations, and a concerted push for collective agreement making. In some sports, star players have led campaigns to increase minimum payments in collective agreements for professional players who, considering the short average length of a career, earn fairly modest salaries. Indeed, there can be a marked disparity in sports between the highest paid athletes and other professional players who in the same or other codes earn incomes little better than average wages (Dabscheck, 2011).

Efforts to improve the terms and conditions of lower paid athletes have produced increased collectivism in sport, which makes this industry an important case study for researchers interested in union organising and union revitalisation, and how workers collectively agitate for a larger share of the spoils of competition in the face of employer opposition (Becker & Von Nesson, 1985; Dabscheck, 1996; Korr, 1991; Voight, 1991). According to one study, sporting unions develop behaviours consistent with non-sporting unions as they mature, by seeking to institutionalise in bargaining agreements a component of seniority-based pay while also seeking reductions in productivity-based wage differentials that can otherwise result from competitive bidding for talented players (Hill & Jolly, 2012).

In order to examine the employment relationship in sports we also need to understand the unique power that resides in bodies that regulate sporting competitions. In other industries, regulatory bodies do not ordinarily have the same capacity as they do in sports to sanction individuals or organisations (Healey, 2012). Governing bodies of sport may impose penalties on players, coaches or on teams themselves. These penalties can be severe, including stripping teams of competition points or indeed sporting titles, as well as imposing bans on individuals for behaviours that are deemed to constitute bringing the game into disrepute (Macdonald & Booth, 2007). For example, Macdonald and Booth note that clubs in Australia's major sporting codes sought to 'illegally' pay players outside the salary cap and suffered the consequences through the imposition of large fines, the loss of draft selections and by being stripped of competition points and even competition titles. An important point to note here is that regulators are able to impose sanctions, not only on teams but also on individuals, that can have career-limiting effects, and yet the regulatory bodies are not themselves parties to the employment relationship.

Another key area of interest for ER scholarship is occupational health and safety (OHS), and in few other industries are concerns around OHS as evident as in sport. The debate over concussion has drawn a great deal of public interest, particularly in the United States where class action litigation between former football players and the National Football League (NFL) resulted in a huge out-of-court settlement (Fainaru-Wada & Fainaru, 2013). The implications of this case have been felt widely across other codes of heavy contact sports. Player associations have been vocal, as have codes themselves in pushing for improved safety standards, including by altering some of the rules around how contact is made and by imposing new rules around recovery from concussion. The changes that are being implemented to protect players reflect a growing awareness in sports, as in other industries, of the general principle that employers have a primary duty of care in OHS. However, surprisingly, just as we have claimed there has been a paucity of ER research on sports, so too has there has been little academic and practitioner analysis of the application of OHS to professional sports (Windholz, 2015). OHS law imposes a responsibility on clubs as employers, and codes themselves as regulators, to provide a safe working environment in what are inherently dangerous places of work. While it is absurd to think that risk can be eliminated from contact sports, the principles of OHS demand that risk be managed and minimised as far as it is practicable to do so. OHS risk also arises from issues beyond the contact made between rival players, such as from fan violence (pitch invasions) or from players being injected with substances to enhance performance, perhaps unwittingly, such as has unfolded in a long saga in the Australian Football League (Gowthorp, Greenhow & O'Brien, 2016). While sports are subject to anti-doping regulations, as will be explored in this volume, these cases also raise OHS matters that pertain to the rights of the parties under the contract of employment – where breaches could result in resignation, termination or legal remedy – and therefore go to the nexus between ER and professional sport.

Sport is also noteworthy in how economic and regulatory considerations intersect with ER, around the mode of recruitment, to produce an idiosyncratic labour market. In some codes, initial employment is governed by an external draft system which restricts the capacity of employers to recruit their preferred players (Dabscheck & Opie, 2003). Drafts determine that players are required to work for a specific employer and might need to relocate across the country to undertake work. Under transfer systems, players can also be sent from one location to another sometimes with very little notice. Drafts are generally designed to equalise competition – that is, they are created for sporting reasons – but nevertheless they also function as a model of recruitment, which makes employment in sport rather unique from an ER perspective. Player salaries can also be impacted by systems that try to equalise competition through the capping of player payments. Caps restrict wealthy clubs from monopolising the most talented players, but also constrain the capacity of employees either individually or collectively to obtain a higher share of the revenue of sports through their agents or through collective bargaining agreements (Booth, Brooks & Diamond, 2012). These effects are tempered, to some degree, by rules in some codes that allow experienced players to become 'free agents' who can offer their services to other teams; however, if overall salary caps apply then free agency may still not lead to dramatically higher salaries or allow the richer teams to obtain all the premium talent (Sandy, Sloane & Rosentraub, 2004).

Taking these economic considerations into account the labour market for sports players can be characterised as a 'bilateral monopoly' whereby the bargaining power for lesser players resides primarily with the clubs while the highest-quality players have some, or perhaps significant, market power (Pedace & Hall, 2012). However, bargaining power is constrained by sporting systems that are themselves predicated on the need to produce 'competitive balance'. Fundamentally, as Dabscheck (2011:59) points out, 'the very nature of the way sport is organised is akin to a cartel rather than a competitive market'. This is because there is little imperative in sports for an employer to force other employers (teams) out of competition. Generally speaking, sporting contests should also produce relatively even outcomes if they are to promote the greatest interest among supporters (and, therefore, the highest revenue), and so there is a strong imperative for schemes that bring balance to the contest (Macdonald & Booth, 2007; see also Sanderson & Siegfried, 2003 for a review of different schemes).

Finally, sport as a workplace environment is often questioned for the lack of workplace rights and the masculine practices that shape it (Schull,

Shaw & Kihl, 2013; Shaw, 2012). An emerging challenge for sport organisations is to work within the parameters of modern anti-discrimination and harassment legislation. Practices such as shouting, swearing, bullying, intimidation and public humiliation are still seen by some as the way to discipline athletes in professional sport. Perhaps the most publicised incident of this behaviour occurred when Sir Alex Ferguson allegedly lost his temper and threw a boot that hit England Captain David Beckham. It may have been coincidence that following frenzied media speculation and a level of public dissatisfaction over the incident, Beckham subsequently left Manchester United for Real Madrid. Similarly, the sexual harassment of women in the workplace continues to be an area of specific concern for sports organisations. The unacceptable treatment of women and the unsatisfactory way it is often handled by sport administrators has resulted in considerable publicity, incited community debate and could lead to long and unnecessary legal disputes (Cense & Brackenbridge, 2001).

The above discussion provides a rationale for the need to examine the unique ER environment that surrounds sport. The purpose of this edited research volume is to explore how sport is organised and run, bringing into consideration legal, regulatory and economic considerations, and to understand the implications and outcomes this has for the labour market and for the relationship between players, managers and clubs. Contributions to this volume will demonstrate what the ER field can learn from sport and shed light on what remains an interesting but neglected area of ER analysis. ER issues related to the sports industry, which will be included in chapter contributions to the volume, include:

1. the concepts of competitive advantage and competitive balance, and implications for corporate governance and regulatory structures, leagues, the role of employment and labour law in the employment of athletes, sports officials and coaches, and the implications of labour market controls on performance and job security;
2. the economic and legal aspects of player transfer and salary regulations including player drafts, transfer fees and salary caps;
3. collective bargaining agreements and the key principles of effective negotiation;
4. the development and role of player associations and unions for athletes and sports officials;
5. the role of sports agents, professional development programmes for athletes and sports coaches, and programmes to prepare athletes for their post-playing careers;
6. the management of anti-discrimination/harassment issues and drug testing programmes and policies.

STRUCTURE OF THE BOOK

In exploring these issues the handbook is divided into four parts. Part I explores the regulation of professional sports. It begins by examining this context at a macro level through considering how a major sporting code (European football) is regulated across multiple countries. In Chapter 2, Berndt Keller examines the emerging supranational modes of sports governance given the recent transformation of professional football. Keller notes that at the European Union level, one major instrument for establishing supranational forms of governance is social dialogue (SD), a focal element and core pillar of the European Social Model. SD takes place at the macro and sectoral level. Throughout the 1990s SD at macro level was more prominent whereas sectoral social dialogues (SSDs) have dominated since the early 2000s. SSDs are considered to be more flexible and more appropriate for the regulation of sector-specific issues, in this case, issues relating to sport. It is his analysis of SSD that is central to the chapter. Keller argues that recent developments in the European sports sector fit into the long-term trends of SSD establishment and institutionalisation in the sport sector. He suggests the likelihood of the ongoing 'Europeanization' of the sports sector is dependent on agreed principles of good governance and a continued evolution of a system of co-regulation.

In Chapter 3, John Solow and Peter von Allmen begin the discussion on labour-market controls. They outline how labour markets in North American professional team sports are noticeably different from labour markets in other industries and are also different between sports. Solow and von Allmen discuss the idiosyncratic nature of these markets and provide an overview of the long-term employment relationships stemming from employment contracts. The authors outline how these contracts have an impact on players' performance incentives, job security and risk allocation. For example, some players may be bargaining for guaranteed salaries, while in other cases, players may be negotiating for salaries contingent upon measurable performance. This situation makes it hard for scholars to draw overarching conclusions.

In Chapter 4, Matt Nichol reviews the business of professional baseball in the United States. He highlights that for the first time in 2013, Major League Baseball (MLB) revenues were expected to exceed US$8 billion, representing a growth of 264 per cent since 1994. Noting that the underlying product that creates these revenues is the playing of a professional baseball game by 30 Major League clubs, his chapter focuses on MLB's system of labour regulation. The system raises two interrelated questions that form the basis of his analysis: (1) how is the MLB labour market regulated and (2) how does this regulatory system fit within general regulatory theory? Through this analysis he concludes that the regulation of MLB provides insight into how internal and external systems of labour regulation interact and, in the context of regulation dominated by internal regulatory actors, provides an understanding of when external regulatory intervention is needed and the circumstances in which external regulatory actors like the state, the courts and the National Labour Relations Board will intervene in the affairs of MLB.

Lisa Pike Masteralexis extends our discussion of regulation to the regulation of player agents in Chapter 5. Masteralexis discusses the regulatory framework of sports agents in the modern sports industry. Historical developments, plus factors that led to the emergence and rapid growth of the sports agent industry are reviewed to better understand challenges that regulators face in the current competitive industry landscape. As is discussed, the sport industry has grown exponentially since the 1970s and so too has the sport agent business. However, despite the emergence of a complex and multi-tiered regulatory system, both public and private, agent misbehaviour and the subordination of the best interests of the athlete have become widespread. In response to the current regulatory framework and the ethical and legal violations of sports agents that persist, Masteralexis provides recommendations for future research to improve the effectiveness of the current regulatory framework.

Part II examines the traditional mechanisms of ER, including collective bargaining, arbitration and industrial action in professional sports. Examining professional sports highlights the continuing relevance and importance of the institutions of ER. The part begins with the chapter by James B. Dworkin on the evolution of collective bargaining in sports (Chapter 6). In this chapter Dworkin examines the history of collective bargaining through a focus on seven individuals who had an enormous impact on the development of collective bargaining in professional baseball. The chapter then examines the state of collective bargaining in the four major sports in the United States: baseball, basketball, football and ice hockey. He concludes by looking into the future and identifies ten trends we are likely to observe.

In Chapter 7, Jack Anderson examines the contractual relations between individual sports participants and their employing club. The chapter opens with an outline of the contractual 'web' of agreements involving parties such as agents, advisers and sponsors as well as national and international sporting federations. Anderson outlines key issues of contract law, namely the sports participant's 'capacity' to contract, which is of particular interest where the participant is of a young age. He then assesses the content of a hypothetical 'standard' sports contract. To illustrate these points, Anderson addresses the standard Football Association of England

Premier League (FAPL) contract. The chapter concludes on issues relating to the termination of contract, and particularly where a player seeks to end a contract prematurely in order to facilitate a transfer to another club. The intriguing debate here is between the desire, on the one hand, to promote contractual stability in a sport and the need, on the other hand, to respect players' legal rights to employment mobility.

Craig A. Depken II's chapter provides insight into industrial action in professional sport, with a focus on strikes and lockouts (Chapter 8). Identifying that the number of strikes in the United States has been falling over the past several decades he notes that several high-profile work stoppages in North American professional sports provide an opportunity to discuss the history of the mechanics associated with the sports labour market in North America. In doing this he explains why work stoppages in professional sport appear to be more common in the late twentieth and early twenty-first century than in the decades of the late nineteenth and first three-quarters of the twentieth century. Depken suggests that this situation may change as many North American sports franchises in the early twenty-first century have the potential to regularly earn positive profits. He suggests almost all could enjoy increasing value over time amid increasing popularity of their sport and the discovery of more revenue streams in the future. Moreover, the extent to which these new revenue streams could reduce financial disparity across teams within a league might help discourage work stoppages that can arise from stalemate negotiations caused by inter-team disputes. Under these circumstances Depken suggests that if owners and players can avoid lost seasons such as that suffered by the National Hockey League (NHL) in 2004, they will likely be dividing increasing revenues.

This part concludes with a chapter by Peter Bouris and Rafael Gomez (Chapter 9). The authors provide an explanation of why owners and professional athletes would abrogate an entire season and forfeit the most lucrative period of playoff operations if, in the end, they eventually reached a deal. They use a behavioural ER model to describe the two season-ending labour disputes in MLB and the NHL that occurred in 1994 and 2004 respectively. Their argument is that both events were instigated by one party (ownership), and with bargaining positions that were strengthened by strategies of credible pre-commitment such as deliberately negotiating substandard television revenue deals and punishment or retaliation (in the form of playoff/season abrogation) for perceived past wins by the union. Subsequent labour peace and tempered player demands (in baseball) and the acceptance of a salary cap (in hockey) were the long-term payoffs achieved by ownership, this suggesting that ownership's ultimate goals were achieved. The authors argue that most popular observers failed to recognise these features of the negotiated settlements and instead blamed both parties as needlessly greedy. These observations suggest that ownership achieved a double-sided win: effectively constraining public sympathy towards players while dictating the terms upon which bargaining has been conducted over the past two decades.

Part III explores contemporary issues in the management of professional sports. The part highlights how contemporary issues, such as transitioning from professional sport to life after sport, the management of discrimination, sexual harassment and anti-doping, are issues sporting organisations need to address. Christine Coupland's work in Chapter 10 begins this part.

Coupland provides a discussion of the nature of the careers of sport professionals, that is, the careers of athletes who make a living by playing sport. As such, her discussion centres on the notion of sport as work and the application of work career theories to professional sport careers. This is particularly important as sporting careers can either end abruptly through injury or slowly through deterioration. Coupland contends that sport scholars can learn from vocational career theories and research. An application of this approach is the study of working individuals with fractured or fragmented career paths and difficult career transitions, to the understanding of the inevitable end of the professional sports career.

In Chapter 11, Greg Maynes, Heather Mitchell, Peter Schuwalow and Mark Stewart continue the discussion on sporting careers, and argue that with the increasing demands on professional sports players, they must now devote themselves exclusively to one sport. This suggests that the choice of sport needs to be made at a relatively young age, usually towards the end of high school. This chapter examines this choice of sport from an economic supply and demand perspective using statistical techniques to compare the competitiveness of different sports with the number of opportunities there are to become a professional sportsman or sportswoman. They note that such a comparison between the demand and supply of sportsmen and women can also be used to determine if some sports offer more professional opportunities than others. They argue that although ability and passion are essential in sporting success, when a person has these in near equal measure in more than one sport, economic considerations can help make a more informed decision.

In Chapter 12 Klaus Vieweg and James A.R. Nafziger draw our attention to the issue of discrimination in sport and its relationship to the law. Identifying that discrimination in the sports arena is one of the most serious issues of sports law, they suggest that in recent years measures to combat discrimination in sports have been fundamental as the law has tried to keep pace with new issues and developments. While acknowledging that anti-discrimination laws govern sports universally, the authors suggest they do so somewhat haphazardly as gaps exist in the applicable laws and regulations, as well as in their enforcement at both international and national levels. They argue that an emerging theme of international sport law involves responses to acts of national, racial and gender discrimination in particular. Their chapter surveys these critical and emerging legal issues involving discrimination against athletes, with an emphasis on the applicable law drawn primarily from examples in the United States, Germany and the European Union.

Terry Engelberg and Stephen Moston's chapter also examines the issue of unacceptable workplace practices, with specific reference to sexual harassment (Chapter 13). They contend that sexual harassment is a form of sex discrimination that affects both men and women in a variety of organisational and educational contexts. They argue that, in the sport context specifically, inappropriate sexualised or sexist attitudes and behaviour are frequently perceived as 'part of sport' and are either condoned or ignored as problematic. Their review of research on sexual harassment and sexual abuse in general in sport organisations and contexts relating to sport (e.g. sport journalism) suggests that women in particular are negatively affected by sexual harassment, but at the same time they appear more accepting of harassing attitudes and behaviour. Sporting organisations may add to the problem by dismissing the issue of sexual harassment as 'not relevant to the business of sport'. This position, as Engelberg and Moston conclude, is damaging to the sport industry and serves to undermine employment relationships.

In Chapter 14 James Skinner, Terry Engelberg and Stephen Moston describe how drug use in sport, in one form or another, has been a regular part of sporting history. However, in the mid-twentieth century, confronted with a growing recognition that performance enhancing drug use was linked to the deaths of elite athletes, governments and sporting organisations began to develop a coordinated anti-doping policy. This included the creation of an independent agency, the World Anti-Doping Agency (WADA), to lead the anti-doping agenda. Despite strong in-principle support for WADA and its goals, anti-doping policy has been a source of considerable tension, as it seeks to balance the difficulty of detection with the day-to-day lives of athletes. Athletes, it is argued, must accept unique workplace conditions, such as the need to specify their whereabouts even when they are not competing. Furthermore, in a reversal of the burden of proof, athletes falsely accused of doping must effectively prove that the charges against them are false.

Part IV explores how economic considerations impact the regulation of professional sports and what implications this has for sporting codes and for players, including how the restriction of labour movement may restrict career opportunities. Simon Gardiner and Roger Welch's chapter on player trades, free agents and transfer policies in professional sport begins this part (Chapter 15). They note that for a typical employee, the relationship with the employer, including how and when that relationship can be terminated, is regulated by the contract of employment. Similarly, employment contracts also have an important role to play for professional sportsmen and women, but in some team sports, internal sporting rules operate to act as a player restraint and provide significant control on the part of the employer over the employee player. Highlighting that player restraints can be characterised, first, as those that specifically restrict freedom of movement from one club to another, and that, second, restraints on player movements can occur indirectly, by restraints on wages through mechanisms such as salary caps in North America and in Europe, to a lesser extent, through Financial Fair Play rules, they posit it is necessary to understand how employment contractual relationships interrelate with transfer systems and the requirement for a player to be registered with a specific club. To explain the relationship they illustrate how transfer systems work and their relationship with European law, in particular the role that has been played by the European Commission and rulings of the Court of Justice of the European Union and international sporting bodies such as the Fédération Internationale de Football Association (FIFA). They conclude by discussing how transfer systems may be further regulated in the future.

In Chapter 16 Rodney Paul and Andrew Weinbach explain that the terms 'competitive balance' and 'uncertainty of outcome' are often used interchangeably, but their methods of calculation are distinct. The authors compare the differences and similarities in these measures by using recent data on the National Basketball Association (NBA) and NFL. Paul and Weinbach argue that the two measures are closely related in the NBA, but are quite different in the NFL. While competitive balance was shown to worsen in the NFL, uncertainty of outcome has remained generally unchanged. This illustrates the importance of understanding which measure sports fans actually use when making decisions. This understanding will also provide the opportunity for leagues and teams to better implement policies to improve their product.

In the final chapter, Chapter 17, we return to the work of Gardiner and Welch. Focusing on the issue of player quotas, the authors chart the response to the Bosman ruling within football and the continuing use of player quotas for non-EU players. The focus of the chapter is on the reintroduction of player quotas within Europe as a result of the Union of European Football Associations' (UEFA's) 'home grown player rule', which requires a specified number of players in a squad to have been developed by the club, or within the same football association, for a specified number of years as youth players. They discuss why player quotas have been incrementally reintroduced into football and other team sports and evaluate their legality in the context of the Bosman ruling and EU discrimination law.

CONCLUSION

This research handbook fills a gap that exists in the management of sport literature by examining professional sports with a particular emphasis on the employment relationship. In four parts the handbook discusses first the regulatory context of professional sports at cross-national, national and sporting code levels, second the history, evolution and current ER institutions and practices in major sporting codes with an emphasis on how conflict between players, clubs and codes is managed, third a number of important contemporary issues in the management of sports and sporting careers, and fourth how economic imperatives, such as the need to ensure balance in competition, interact with the employment relationship to produce a unique labour market in professional sports. We hope the handbook encourages further publications in this field and acts as a catalyst for greater research in the area of ER and sport. As professional sports continues to grow as an industry, extending its reach into new markets with varying economic, cultural and social environments, it is essential that we continue to critically evaluate the ER practices that accompany this growth.

REFERENCES

Adair, D., Taylor, T.L. and Darcy, S.A. (2010). 'Managing ethnocultural and "racial" diversity in sport: Obstacles and opportunities', *Sport Management Review*, 13 (4), 307–312.
Ahlburg, D.A. and Dworkin, J.B. (1991). 'Player compensation in the N.F.L'. In P.D. Staudohar and J.A. Mangan (eds), *The Business of Professional Sports*, Urbana, IL: University of Illinois Press, pp. 61–70.
Allen, J.B. and Shaw, S. (2013). 'An interdisciplinary approach to examining the working conditions of women coaches', *International Journal of Sports Science and Coaching*, 8 (1), 1–17.
Becker, N. and Von Nesson, P. (1985). 'Sport and restraint of trade: Playing the game the courts' way', *Australian Business Law Review*, 13, 180–197.
Booth, R., Brooks, R. and Diamond, N. (2012). 'Player salaries and revenues in the Australian football league 2001–2009: Theory and evidence', *Economic and Labour Relations Review*, 23 (2), 39–54.
Cense, M. and Brackenbridge, C. (2001). 'Temporal and developmental risk factors for sexual harassment and abuse in sport', *European Physical Education Review*, 7 (1), 61–79.

Dabscheck, B. (1996). 'Playing the team game: Unions in Australian professional team sports', *Journal of Industrial Relations*, 38, 600–628.

Dabscheck, B. (2010). *The Linkage between Player Payments and Benefits to Revenue Sharing in Australian Sport*, Australian Athletes' Inc. and Braham Dabscheck, Australia.

Dabscheck, B (2011). 'Player shares of revenue in Australia and overseas professional team sports', *Labour and Industry*, 22 (1–2), 57–82.

Dabscheck, B. and Opie, H. (2003). 'Legal regulation of sporting labour markets', *Australian Journal of Law*, 16 (2), 2–25.

Ducking, J., Groothuis, P. and Hill, J. (2014). 'Minimum pay scales and career length in the NBA', *Industrial Relations*, 53 (4), 617–635.

Edwards, P.K. (1986). *Conflict at Work*, Oxford: Blackwell.

Engelberg, T., Skinner, J. and Zakus, D. (2014). 'What does commitment mean to volunteers in youth sport organisations?', *Sport and Society: Cultures, Commerce, Media, Politics*, 17 (1), 52–67.

Fainaru-Wada, M. and Fainaru, S. (2013). *League of Denial: The NFL, Concussions, and the Battle for the Truth*, New York: Crown Archetype.

Fairbrother, P. and Yates, C. (2003). *Trade Unions in Renewal: A Comparative Study*, Routledge: London.

Gowthorp, L., Greenhow, A. and O'Brien, D. (2016). 'An interdisciplinary approach in identifying the legitimate regulator of anti-doping in sport: The case of the Australian Football League', *Sport Management Review*, 19 (1), 48–60.

Hanlon, C., Morris, T. and Nabbs, S. (2014). 'Program provider's perspective: Recruitment and retention strategies for women in physical activity programs', *Sport Management Review*, 17 (2), 133–144.

Healey, D. (2012). 'Governance in sport: Outside the box', *Economic and Labour Relations Review*, 23 (3), 39–60.

Hill, J. and Jolly, N. (2012). 'Salary distribution and collective bargaining agreements: A case study of the NBA', 51 (2), 342–363.

Kahn, L. (2000). 'The sports business as a labor market laboratory', *Journal of Economic Perspectives*, 13 (3), 75–94.

Korr, C.P. (1991). 'Marvin Miller and the new unionism in baseball'. In P.D. Staudohar and J.A. Mangan (eds), *The Business of Professional Sports*, Urbana, IL: University of Illinois Press, pp. 115–134.

Macdonald, R.D. and Booth, R. (2007). 'Around the grounds: A comparative analysis of football in Australia'. In B. Stewart (ed.), *The Games Are Not the Same: The Political Economy of Football in Australia*, Carlton, Victoria: Melbourne University Publishing, pp. 236–331.

Ordway, C. (2014). 'Women filling the sports governance gap', *Play by the Rules Magazine*, April.

Pedace, R. and Hall, C. (2012). 'Home safe: No-trade clauses and player salaries in Major League Baseball', *Industrial Relations*, 51 (3), 627–644.

Sanderson, A. and Siegfried, J. (2003). 'Thinking about competitive balance', *Journal of Sports Economics*, 4 (4), 255–279.

Sandy, R., Sloane, P. and Rosentraub, M. (2004). *The Economics of Sport: An International Perspective*, Basingstoke, UK: Palgrave Macmillan.

Schull, V., Shaw, S. and Kihl, L. (2013). '"If a woman came in . . . she would have been eaten up alive": Analyzing gendered political processes in the search for an athletic director', *Gender and Society*, 27 (1), 56–81.

Shaw, S. (2012). 'Managing gender equity in sport'. In D. Hassan and J. Lusted (eds), *Managing Sport: Social and Cultural Perspectives*, London: Routledge, pp. 186–200.

Staudohar, P.D. (1996). 'Competition and pay for National Hockey League players born in Québec', *Journal of Sports Economics*, 5, 186–205.

Taylor, T.L., Doherty, A. and McGraw, P. (2015). *Managing People in Sport Organizations: A Strategic Human Resource Management Perspective*, 2nd edn, Milton Park, UK: Routledge.

Voight, D.Q. (1991). 'Serfs versus magnates: A century of labor strife in Major League Baseball'. In P.D. Staudohar and J.A. Mangan (eds), *The Business of Professional Sports*, Urbana, IL: University of Illinois Press, pp. 95–114.

Windholz, E.L. (2015). 'Team-based professional sporting competitions and work, health and safety law: Defining the boundaries of responsibility', *Australian Business Law Review*, 43 (4), 303–328.

Yeh, C.M. and Taylor, T. (2008). 'Issues of governance in sport organisations: A question of board size, structure and roles', *World Leisure Journal*, 50 (1), 33–45.

PART I

THE REGULATION OF
PROFESSIONAL SPORTS

2. The regulation of professional football at the European Union level: towards supranational employment relations in the football industry?
Berndt Keller

INTRODUCTION*

In Europe football (or soccer, as it is called in parts of the Anglo-Saxon world) is the uncontested number one of all sports. Its professionalized segment constitutes a "growth industry" and is the most popular spectator sport but has experienced serious financial problems in some countries despite considerable revenue growth (UEFA, 2011).

Regulation of this highly commercialized industrial sector still takes place primarily at national level but with growing influence from the supranational level (Gammelsæter & Senoux, 2011a). Since the 1990s, the European Union (EU) has had a gradually increasing impact on a variety of not only economic sectors and policy fields, but also sports in general and professional football in particular (Niemann et al., 2011a). More recently, the Lisbon Treaty (2009) recognizes explicitly the specific nature of sport and its autonomy but enhances the formal options of European authorities (Article 165). Furthermore, the White Paper on Sport (European Commission, 2007) represents an important stage of the sector-specific processes of Europeanization. It indicates the official view of the Commission and its strategic plans for the future governance of sports in the EU. The Commission recommends that private corporate actors should participate in the future regulation of the sports sector and encourages once again the establishment of social dialogue structures. In its recent Communication on "Developing the European Dimension in Sport" (European Commission, 2011), the Commission presents its concept, which has to be compatible with European economic law.

In this chapter we elaborate on the emerging supranational modes of sports governance with special consideration of the recent transformation of professional football. Throughout the chapter we argue, in contrast to other authors, from an employment relations perspective and analyze our specific case in a broader, somewhat comparative perspective of European employment relations, especially working conditions. We do not provide another analysis in a purely legal perspective (Branco Martins, 2004; Colucci & Geeraert, 2011) and do not describe again the early stages and protracted history in great detail (Branco Martins, 2004; Gábriš, 2010; Theodorou, 2013). After some introductory remarks on institutional characteristics, we first elaborate on the corporate actors. Then, we analyze the first outcome of their activities and present a preliminary assessment. Next, we discuss in great detail various issues and problems of transposition and implementation of EU regulation at national and club level. An outlook concludes the chapter.

SOME INSTITUTIONAL AND PROCEDURAL CHARACTERISTICS

At EU level, one major appropriate instrument for establishing supranational forms of governance is social dialogue (SD), a focal element and core pillar of the "European Social Model" (or the "social dimension of the internal market" in Jacques Delors' famous terms of the early 1990s). SD comprises an institutionalized set of procedural arrangements and can be utilized to establish supranational governance structures in a broad range of policy fields, especially social policy, in an encompassing sense. In our perspective, SD constitutes a characteristic feature of employment relations and refers to the changing relationships between "both sides of industry."[1] The principles of this EU-specific mode of regulation, that is considered an effective instrument for common solutions of bilateral problems, have also been tested in the sports sector.

Some remarks on institutional characteristics are necessary to aid understanding:

SD takes place at the macro or interprofessional as well as the sectoral level. Throughout the 1990s the SD at macro level was more prominent (Falkner, 1998) whereas sectoral social dialogues (SSDs) have dominated since the early 2000s. They are considered to be more "flexible" and more appropriate for the regulation of sector-specific issues. For the purposes of our analysis SSDs are of primary interest.

The corporate representatives of employees and employers at supranational level are called social partners in more recent Euro jargon. In our case, individual clubs are employers and professional players are their employees.[2] Both are directly or indirectly represented by their national organizations, employers' associations, and unions, whose unequivocal identification sometimes creates difficulties, a problem we refer to later on. In legal terms, employment law is applicable when both sides agree on contracts for individual players.

SD can be of tri- or bipartite nature; for instance, it may include or exclude European authorities, especially the Commission. SSDs are usually bilateral arrangements between the social partners who have been granted broad opportunities of regulation. Their scope of autonomous action relates to all stages of the policy cycle from agenda setting to implementation of outcomes. Thus, SSDs are not top-down processes but initiatives towards self-regulation. For our purposes, only the bipartite variant is of relevance.

The Commission encourages the establishment and supports the activities of SSDs but is not necessarily and not always a corporate actor itself (Article 152 TFEU[3]). Its Directorate General Employment, Social Affairs and Inclusion (DG EMPL) provides organizational and financial support (among others, travel and hotel expenses, simultaneous translation, technical equipment). In our case, two DGs, EMPL as well as Education and Culture (EAC), are involved. The DG EMPL takes the lead and is, therefore, of primary interest for our analysis.

The outcomes of activities can refer to the relationship between the social partners themselves or to their relationships and cooperation with others, especially EU institutions. The latter, external alternative intends to initiate EU policies or to influence their introduction through lobbying activities. In our case, the outcome to be dealt with later refers exclusively to the internal relationship.

All in all, there are more than 40 SSD committees.[4] Their number has increased not only but especially since the Commission initiated a major restructuring of all formerly existing heterogeneous forms in the late 1990s (Commission Decision 98/500/EC). The ambitious goal of this major institutional reform, which we refer to later, was the voluntary conclusion not only of more outcomes in general but especially of more outcomes of binding character. We deal exclusively with the more recent stage of development.

The first necessary prerequisite for the establishment of SD is the assessment of the representativeness of European peak organizations that claim to represent their national member associations (European Commission, 1993). Since the mid-1990s, their organizational structures have been officially examined by the Commission.[5] All applicants have to fulfill certain criteria in order to be officially accepted as social partners. Associations of management and labor should:

1. "be cross industry or relate to specific sectors or categories and be organized at European level;
2. consist of organizations, which are themselves an integral and

recognized part of Member State social partner structures and with the capacity to negotiate agreements, and which are representative of all Member States, as far as possible;
3.   have adequate structures to ensure their effective participation in the consultation process" (European Commission, 1998).

In arbitrary cases of smaller and/or competing associations the Commission prefers a highly "flexible" interpretation of its established criteria, pursues a strategy of inclusion instead of exclusion, and accepts problematic applicants. This preference for pluralist instead of exclusive representation avoids conflicts at an early, preparatory stage of SSD development without, however, later on facilitating the implementation of outcomes. From the supranational associations' point of view, their official recognition by the Commission adds to their legitimacy vis-à-vis their members, European institutions, and the public. Furthermore, it enhances the effectiveness of SD. Social partners have privileged access to European institutions and a higher official status than pure interest groups.

The vertical dimension of SSD refers to transposition procedures from the European to the national level and, therefore, needs special attention. Article 155 TFEU defines two choices: "Agreements concluded at Union level shall be implemented either in accordance with the procedures and practices specific to management and labour and the Member States or . . . at the joint request of the signatory parties, by a Council decision on a proposal from the Commission."

Throughout the 1990s, the latter option was utilized in a limited number of Directives that had to be transposed by the Member States (parental leave 1996, part-time work 1997, and fixed-term work 1999). Since the early 2000s, in times of more emphasis on the autonomy and bipartism of the social partners, it has been of less importance (among others, telework 2002, work-related stress 2004, harassment and violence at work 2007, inclusive labor markets 2010). At sectoral level, the Commission has always acted as a neutral agent and facilitator of outcomes and, in the vast majority of instances, has refrained from any active interference. In our case, the first option will be of exclusive relevance.

All SD outcomes are categorized according to their legal status, for instance, their more or less binding character for the signatory parties. A typology officially proposed by the Commission (European Commission, 2004) distinguishes various types of "new generation texts":

1.   agreements implemented in accordance with Article 155 TFEU, either by Council decision or by the procedures and practices specific to management and labor in the Member States;

2. process-oriented texts such as frameworks of action, guidelines and codes of conduct, and policy orientations;
3. joint opinions, declarations, and tools;
4. procedural texts laying down the rules for bipartite dialogue between the parties and the rules of procedures for the SSD committees;
5. follow-up reports on the implementation and reporting of so-called "new generation" texts.

We focus and elaborate on the first cluster because the hard outcome of our SSD belongs to this comparatively rare category. Two sub-forms are to be distinguished. In the 1990s, agreements at macro level were initiated by the Commission, negotiated by the social partners, and implemented by a Council decision and a following Directive. In the 2000s, autonomous agreements at sectoral level were initiated, concluded, and implemented by the social partners themselves. Because of the characteristics of the outcome our analysis is restricted to the latter group.

Last but not least, existing research on SSDs (Pochet et al., 2009) indicates that there are various monitoring instruments and procedures for later stages of the policy cycle:

1. written surveys of members;
2. annual or periodic reports;
3. plenary meetings, oral or written reports;
4. presentation of good practice;
5. conferences and websites;
6. new texts and initiatives.

All these soft follow-up procedures comprise fundamental weaknesses (Keller & Weber, 2011). It remains to be seen if they will be of relevance in our case.

CORPORATE ACTORS: THE SOCIAL PARTNERS IN PROFESSIONAL FOOTBALL

Within the sports sector there are at present two SSDs at different stages of development. The more heterogeneous one for the "sport and active leisure industry including not-for-profit sport, professional sport and active leisure" has been in its test phase since late 2012 (Pierre & Buisine, 2013); the more homogeneous one for "professional football" was officially inaugurated in mid-2008. Our primary interest is on the second, more advanced SSD, without completely neglecting the first that is still in its early stage. All in all, these recent developments in the sports sector do not constitute an exception but fit into the general, long-term trends of SSD establishment and institutionalization in an increasing number of sectors.

The Social Partners

The necessary "Study on the Representativeness of the Social Partner Organizations in the Professional Football Players Sector" was completed in early 2006 (Université Catholique de Louvain, 2006). The identified and officially recognized social partners are described below (Colucci & Geeraert, 2011; European Commission, 2008).

The International Federation of Professional Footballers (FIFPro),[6] "the worldwide representative organization for all professional football players," is the federation of national associations. FIFPro Division Europe, one of its continental divisions, organizes more than 28000 players in 20 EU Member States.[7] FIFPro is an independent professional union but has close ties with UNI Europa, the major European industry federation of national private service sector unions.

The Association of European Professional Football Leagues (EPFL)[8] represents high-level national leagues from 17 EU Member States with more than 600 clubs. EPFL consists of 30 "Member Leagues and Associate Members."[9]

The European Club Association (ECA) "is the sole, independent body directly representing individual football clubs at European level."[10] It replaces the G14 and the European Club Forum, both dissolved at the beginning of 2008.[11] At present, ECA has around 200 major clubs as ordinary or associated members (to be precise 214 members from 53 associations in early 2014).

The former G14, a European Economic Interest Group, consisted of a strictly limited, self-recruited number of major clubs (Fligstein, 2008). Members insisted on their autonomy and aimed at more efficient interest representation towards their national leagues and the international associations UEFA (Union of European Football Associations) and FIFA (Fédération Internationale de Football Association) (Mittag, 2007, pp. 212–213). At a certain point of time, the G14 clubs even threatened the use of their economic power and the foundation of a "breakaway" supranational league, the European Super League (Szymanski & Kuypers, 1999, pp. 301–308), which was supposed to exclusively consist of big clubs. This threat of "exit" (Hirschman, 1970) does not exist any longer, and the foundation of a European professional league constitutes an unrealistic idea. Finally, the G14 transnational grouping disbanded.[12] Nowadays, its former members receive considerable payments from their national associations when players play on national teams and, therefore, face additional risks of injury.

Another exemption has to be explicitly mentioned. UEFA is the continental confederation and the European branch of FIFA (Olsson, 2011).[13] UEFA, the governing body of European football, is an "associate party in the Committee" but not a social partner officially recognized by the Commission: ". . . since this organization does not consider itself as a representative of employers or industrial relations actor, it is not to be seen as a competitor of any of the sector-related European organisations" (Adam, 2013). Nevertheless, all social partners agreed that the UEFA President chairs the SSD meetings. Thus, UEFA participates in all stages of the policy cycle, from problem definition to processes of decision making and implementation procedures. Furthermore, ECA and UEFA have "very close ties" (García, 2011, p. 39).

Characteristic Features and Peculiarities

Due to characteristics of the sports sector, especially the small overall number of clubs, the number of members belonging to each organization is small in comparison with other sectors; density ratios are high because of mandatory membership. The foundation dates of associations on the employers' side (EPFL 2005, ECA 2008 in contrast to FIFPro 1965) are closely related to the project of launching a SSD. These dates indicate the emerging shift in EU governance of football and the internal distribution of power between organizations.

The existence of more than one social partner on one side, especially the employers', or sometimes even on both sides, is not unusual for the general SSD structure. Some organizational fragmentation reflects the simultaneous existence of common as well as differing interests, if not even some inter-organizational rivalry and competition (for example between small and big companies within an industry or companies with different fields of specialization). All in all, more employer than union federations are engaged in SSD activities (European Commission, 2010a, Annex 1).

The employers' associations follow distinct principles of organizing and, therefore, strategic action: EPFL constitutes the federation of national associations; ECA is the supranational association of the limited number of very large clubs and exclusively represents their (primarily financial) interests (corresponding to their sporting performance and, accordingly, their budgets). ECA organizes only a minority but the most powerful section of professional clubs. Only two thirds are based within the EU, a specific composition of membership we have to come back to later on. All in all, ECA directly represents the specific, rather homogeneous interests of a comparatively small group of highly successful clubs whereas EPFL indirectly represents the more general and heterogeneous interests of a larger group of smaller clubs and national leagues.

Our empirical evidence of SSD research (Keller & Weber, 2011; Pochet et al., 2009) indicates that organizing is frequently more complicated on the employers' than on the employees' side. The main reason is that negotiations at EU level require the European federations to be mandated by their national affiliates and, thus, lead to a certain loss of (national) autonomy and (probably some financial) resources. Therefore, interests remain limited at national and especially at supranational level. Furthermore, if employers organize at all at EU level they usually prefer voluntary instead of binding outcomes.

Competition has a horizontal as well as a vertical dimension. It takes place not only at national but also at supranational level. The UEFA Champions League is the most important European club competition. The UEFA Cup constitutes a second competition of less commercial importance, less public interest and prestige. Both competitions have to be regulated by rules to be established at supranational level. However, individual clubs are not only opponents who compete for victories and national as well as European championships. They also share common interests in keeping some sort of competitive balance in their processes of joint production. Consequently, forms of cooperation and competition have to be carefully balanced and their problems simultaneously solved by procedural regulation. Therefore, long-term league characteristics are to be pursued by some sort of collective instead of purely individual action; leagues have to produce not only individual but also collective goods (Olson, 1965, 1982). Differences of interest regarding the distribution of available resources (among others, distinctly increasing revenues from the sale of media rights on domestic as well as foreign markets) are manifest, and national solutions differ considerably, as the example of individual versus collective marketing systems of TV broadcasting rights indicates (Brand & Niemann, 2006, pp. 134–136).

The labor market of professional football is vastly segmented and more internationalized or even globalized than the majority of others. In 1995, the famous Bosman ruling by the European Court of Justice (ECJ) confirmed the freedom of movement, one of the fundamental principles of European integration, also for professional football players and, thus, abolished nationality quotas for club teams (Fligstein, 2008; García, 2011; Olsson, 2011). Through this massive legal intervention, the ECJ initiated a major transformation of traditional, rather rigid nation-specific transfer systems, enforced their liberalization, and kicked off more cross-border mobility of players.[14]

THE OUTCOME – A PRELIMINARY ASSESSMENT

First, the Commission co-financed some preparatory projects, and various activities of a working group took place. Then, the mentioned "Study on Representativeness" was finished in early 2006. Next, a two-year test phase constituted the transition from informality to formality. Finally, the "Sectoral Social Dialogue Committee on Professional Football" was officially launched in 2008. In close cooperation with the Commission, the social partners formulated their own rules of procedure, established a Steering Committee and agreed on a first work program 2008–09.[15]

Their SSD is one of the youngest among more than 40 SSDs and belongs to the group of "third generation committees" (Degryse & Pochet, 2011, p. 147). It constitutes a recent establishment and not the continuation of a formerly existing one. In comparison with other, not only major industrial but also service sectors it constitutes a latecomer; reasons include the complexity and specificity of the sports sector. "Regarding labour relations, the sector's roots in non-profit organisations and volunteering have slowed the emergence of social dialogue in most Member States" (European Commission, 2010b, p. 64).

The Outcome

So far, the only but important achievement is the "Autonomous agreement regarding the minimum requirements for standard player contracts in the professional football sector." It defines "minimum requirements" to be offered and introduced in all individual cases. Contracts must be in writing and signed by both sides. They should define the club's financial as well as the player's obligations.

The club's financial obligations include among others (Article 6.2):

(a) "salary (regular; monthly, weekly, performance based);
(b) other financial benefits (bonuses, experience reward, international appearances);
(c) other benefits (non-financial ones such as car, accommodation, etc.);
(d) medical and health insurance for accident and illness (as mandatory by law) and payment of salary during incapacity (definition to be determined including its consequences with regard to salaries paid);

(e)   pension fund/social security costs (as mandatory by law or collective bargaining agreement);

(f)   reimbursement for expenses incurred by the Player."

The player's obligations include (Article 7.2):

(a)   "to play matches to the best of his best [sic] ability, when selected;

(b)   to participate in training and match preparation according to the instructions of his superior (e.g. head coach);

(c)   to maintain a healthy lifestyle and high standard of fitness;

(d)   to comply with and act in accordance with Club officials' instructions (reasonable; e.g. to reside where suitable for the Club);

(e)   to attend events of the Club (sporting but also commercial ones);

(f)   to obey Club rules (including, where applicable, Club disciplinary regulations, duly notified to him before signing the Contract);

(g)   to behave in a sporting manner towards people involved in matches, training sessions, to learn and observe the laws of the game and to accept decisions by match officials;

(h)   to abstain from participating in other football activities, other activities or potentially dangerous activities not prior approved by the Club and which are not covered by Clubs insurance;

(i)   to take care of the property of the Club and to return it after termination of the Contract;

(j)   to immediately notify the Club in case of illness or accident and to not undergo any medical treatment without prior information to the Club's doctor (except in emergencies) and to provide a medical certificate of incapacity;

(k)   to undergo regularly medical examination and medical treatment upon request of the Club's doctor;

(l)   to comply with the terms of any association, league, player's union and/or club anti-discrimination policy;

(m)   not to bring the Club or football into disrepute (e.g. media statements);

(n)   not to gamble or undertake other related activities within football."

Furthermore, the Agreement also contains individual sections on anti-doping, action against racism, and disciplinary procedures. In case of minors the contract must be signed by the parent or guardian. Youth players have the right to follow mandatory school education in accordance with national law.

The Agreement was signed in April 2012, shortly after the official SSD establishment. In comparative perspective with other SSDs this specific sequence of events is unusual. It is to be explained by the fact that preparatory discussions took place not only during the former informal stages, but also in the different projects of working groups. The conclusion of the Agreement indicates that both sides have not only been interested in a pure exchange of information, but that forms of mutual understanding and the gradual development of trust and relations of cooperation have developed.

A Preliminary Assessment

From a general SSD perspective, it comes as no surprise that the Agreement defines only "minimum requirements" to be introduced into players' contracts throughout Europe. These basic standards can be improved on a purely voluntary, but by no means enforceable basis. In general, because of the legal institutional characteristics of SSDs, agreements can only be concluded on topics of parallel interests, whereas all issues of opposing interests are excluded because of the purely voluntary nature. Therefore, potential topics are "soft" and consensual, definitely not "hard" or non-consensual; especially wages are explicitly excluded (according to Article 153 TFEU).

Nowadays, the Commission itself is more skeptical about consequences than it used to be throughout the 1990s: "Autonomous agreements are very well adapted to regulate and improve certain aspects of working conditions, but they cannot guarantee uniform outcomes, binding status and full coverage in all countries" (European Commission, 2009, pp. 126–127). SSD outcomes always constitute the smallest common denominator and define, as already indicated, exclusively minimum standards. To be acceptable they must simultaneously provide some distinct "value added" for both sides.

Sport has not only economic but also social and cultural dimensions that have been officially recognized (Council of the European Union, 2011) and could become topics of SSD. SSDs actually deal with a broad range of issues that extend far beyond employment questions in a strictly limited sense (Pochet et al., 2009). The Agreement exclusively defines some minimum obligations of individual players and their clubs and, thus, selected aspects of the employment relationship, but does not deal with others. We come back to this issue.

Nowadays huge differences in professional players' salaries consist of three dimensions: first, they exist within individual teams between the vast majority of normal players and a limited number of excessively numerated superstars, who are not only well-known celebrities but have considerable market power. Second, major differences exist between the small number of top clubs[16] and all others. Third, pay inequality exists between (the first and second, in some cases also third) national divisions. All these significant differences will not be reduced let alone eliminated – they are not at all mentioned in the Agreement. Some social partners' expectations of "harmonization" and the establishment of unified standards or at least some "convergence" of national standards and "raising" of working conditions in the European football industry (European Commission, 2014, p. 41) constitute nothing but wishful thinking; the emergence of a vertically integrated European system of employment relations is highly unrealistic. The Agreement constitutes, as a prototypical negotiated compromise, not more than the point of departure to overcome existing forms of regulatory minimalism.

The Agreement will not erode national standards or lead to a race to the bottom and leave already existing standards basically untouched. It does not constitute an instrument of strict deregulation or liberalization. Any development towards some kind of convergence and a level playing field for social partners is unrealistic or, at least, constitutes a long-lasting process.

An additional caveat concerns the fundamental but frequently missing explicit distinction between SSD and collective bargaining. SSDs are by no means to be confused with collective bargaining (de Boer et al., 2005; Keller, 2005). At least until now, they do not even constitute an early stage towards the development of a European system of collective bargaining. The official statement that the "parties regard this Agreement as an outcome of collective bargaining at European level between the Social Partners" ("Whereas" in the Agreement, p. 3) is hardly correct, or at least decidedly exaggerated, in an employment relations perspective.

By definition, collective bargaining includes the option of strikes and/or lockouts. Industrial action as a means for solving distributional conflicts is, however, legally excluded from the potential range of SSDs (Article 153 TFEU).[17] According to empirical evidence, SSDs have a broad notion and are only appropriate for purposes of mutual information and consultation as well as joint initiatives addressed to third parties; collective bargaining has a more precise notion and includes the implementation as well as the later enforcement of outcomes. So far, this option exists exclusively at national level, and professional football does not constitute an exception. Various attempts to establish appropriate legal institutional prerequisites for a transnational system of collective bargaining have failed (Ales et al., 2006) – and they are unlikely to be set up in the future (Keller, 2007).

Finally, another important feature, the formal status of the Agreement, has to be emphasized. We presented already the official typology of outcomes with varying legal status and, therefore, binding character. The database of joint texts provided by the Commission as well as independent studies show that autonomous agreements are, in contrast to joint opinions, declarations, and tools, very rare outcomes (Pochet et al., 2009, pp. 20–21; European Commission, 2012, p. 59). They deserve special attention because of their binding consequences for the signatory parties. In any case, further activities of member associations are required at national and company, in our case club, level, in order to implement the Agreement.

LASTING PROBLEMS: TRANSPOSITION AND IMPLEMENTATION

Most SSD research has focused on the early stages of the policy cycle (agenda setting, policy formulation) and dealt with the formulation and conclusion of policies. However, we know from recent research that the later stages (implementation, restructuring/termination) are indispensable and of utmost importance for the final outcome (Falkner et al., 2005). Therefore, these lasting effects cannot be ignored. In theoretical terms, the implementation has to be explicitly distinguished from the formulation and conclusion (Keller & Weber, 2011). In substantive terms, the initial official intent can be (rather) different from the final outcome.

This general empirical evidence is especially true for the EU system of multi-level governance. All SSDs comprehend not only a horizontal but also a vertical dimension (Léonard et al., 2011). Their outcomes have, first, bridged the sizeable gap between the European and the national level and, then, the gap between the meso (or sectoral) and the micro (or company, in our case club) level. Therefore, processes and procedures of transposition and implementation should be explicitly distinguished. National legal institutional characteristics as well as diverging interests and power relations of social partners at European and national level permit for considerable discretion in interpreting and applying EU norms (Keune & Marginson, 2013). Later on, there is the already mentioned supplementary need to develop and utilize various monitoring instruments and follow-up procedures. They are of major importance for overall sustainability as well as long-term effectiveness and require not only the existence of common interests but also the input of additional resources. Both social partners face not only inter- but also complex intra-organizational negotiations as well as legal institutional constraints at national level.

General Problems

Autonomous agreements are signed at EU level. Therefore, they constitute only framework regulations which first have to be transposed to the national level or, in our example, to the national associations and leagues.[18] Later on, agreements have to be implemented at the individual club level. Attempts at implementation do not take the above-mentioned legal route. The voluntary option definitely prevails: the associations, and not the Commission or its Directorates General, are in charge of all procedures. In our case, the Commission confirmed even officially that the Agreement will have to be implemented by the private activities of the signatory parties (European Commission, 2013, pp. 18, 205). Both social partners "have committed themselves to autonomously implementing the agreement by using the most appropriate legal instruments as determined by the relevant parties at the national level in the EU and in the remaining countries of the UEFA territory" (European Commission, 2013, p. 206).

The problem is that the European federations on both sides of the industry are based (more or less) on voluntary, not mandatory membership.[19] They need at least ad hoc or, if possible, general mandates to be authorized to negotiate on behalf of their constituencies. However, they are hardly able to exert sufficient pressure on their national member organizations, first, to secure their commitment and close cooperation to formulate policies and negotiate outcomes despite heterogeneous interests and, later on, to guarantee their proper implementation (Léonard et al., 2011). In other words, autonomous agreements define only broad frameworks without being strictly binding for the signatory parties – and without indicating any sanctions for only partial or even non-compliance in individual cases. Therefore, the Agreement explicitly clarifies that specific national legislation applies to the contract.

Existing differences in institutional characteristics at national level[20] lead to high levels of heterogeneity in the processes as well as results of implementation; the examples of autonomous agreements concluded in other sectors illustrate that, most likely, a variety of instruments will be used (BusinessEurope et al., 2011). Furthermore, empirical evidence of other SSDs indicates the existence of varying levels of commitment. One side, usually the employees, is more interested in strict forms of implementation whereas the other prefers more flexibility (Keune & Marginson, 2013). Our case fits into this pattern of hard versus soft forms: from the beginning, FIFPro preferred a binding agreement whereas, at first, EPFL and ECA refused any binding status of outcomes (Parrish, 2011).

Collective agreements on players' contracts exist in some EU Member States, such as France and the Netherlands, but by far not in all (Université Catholique de Louvain, 2006). Collective regulation takes place in only less than one half of Member States, whereas individual regulation dominates in others (Colucci & Geeraert, 2011). In employment relations terms, there are multi- as well as single-employer agreements. As a consequence, specific institutional traits of national systems, such as levels of centralization and coordination, differ significantly, and this diversity has a major impact on the processes and results of implementation.

The Agreement proposes, without however indicating details, that "in case a national collective bargaining agreement exists, the Agreement shall be implemented in the national collective bargaining agreement" (Annex 8 of the Agreement). For all other cases a specific "European Professional Football Social Dialogue Taskforce" is to be established. It is supposed to consist of experts and to coordinate implementation and enforcement procedures at national level according to a precisely indicated schedule. If single employer agreements predominate, the frequent existence of standard or model employment contracts could serve as a point of departure and reference and ease difficulties of implementation. The limited number of clubs could also facilitate the solving of emerging problems.

The official assessment is, as usual, fairly optimistic: "The agreement is a significant achievement for the EU social dialogue in the professional football sector" (European Commission, 2013, p. 206). And: "The agreement, its implementation and monitoring is not only an expression of the autonomy of the social partners but also of the autonomy of sport as recognized in the Lisbon Treaty" (European Commission, 2013, p. 206). These confident statements have been made too early because the final results of implementation processes are not available yet.[21] Therefore, the officially proclaimed rather positive impact of the Agreement cannot, or at least not yet, be confirmed on an empirical basis.

Recent research on other SSDs illustrates that, first of all, the perceived relevance of the addressed topic, already existing national regulation, and the quality of national SD, have a major impact on the final outcome (Weber, 2013). Therefore, as in comparable cases, these purely voluntary processes of implementation will be rather selective and uneven despite the common efforts of the official social partners as well as UEFA. The empirical impact of the Agreement on initiating change and producing some added value will vary to a considerable degree at national level. The interests and activities of some members of national associations, or to be more precise of the major ones, are more influential in these processes than others. There will also remain considerable discrepancies according to regions within Europe, especially in the Eastern countries. In other words, the mentioned introduction of minimum standards has differing effects because of major variations in national standards. There is definitely no room for any one-size-fits-all solution.

Furthermore, there exist significant differences between different layers of professional football. In the second, especially as they exist in a number of countries, and the third leagues (Annex 6 of the Agreement for details), there is an unknown percentage of foreign players not only from Central and Eastern European but also from Latin American and African countries. In overall quantitative terms: "In 2005, it was estimated that there were more than 34.000 professional football players and more than 1.700 professional football clubs" (European Commission, 2010b, p. 65). The Agreement is supposed to be applied in all leagues "with full-time and/or part-time professional football players under contract" (Annex 6 of the Agreement).

Especially on the employers' side, organizational structures as well as legal and factual competences of associations differ to a considerable degree not only across but also within countries (Gammelsæter & Senoux, 2011b). The sizeable grey zone between professional leagues and their players has so far hardly been dealt with. In other words, the Agreement contains an implicit bias in favor of the first national divisions – and an obvious neglect of others. This is the case despite the fact that the minor leagues employ a higher number of players who face more difficulties than their first division counterparts in negotiating their working conditions. The reason is that the overall revenues are significantly smaller (resulting, primarily, from ticketing, transfers, sponsoring, merchandising, and media rights). Therefore, the minor leagues will have to cope with more serious difficulties when they have to implement the Agreement.

Regional Problems Within EU Member States

The indicated diversity of employment relations in general and SSD in particular has always existed but has significantly increased as a lasting consequence of the Eastern enlargement when ten new members joined the EU in 2004. "Whereas culture of social dialogue is well rooted in most Western countries, trade unions and the system of collective bargaining can be looked at with suspicion in post-communist regimes" (Léonard et al., 2011, p. 265). The necessary but still "missing link" is sector-level bargaining coordination (Ghellab & Vaughan-Whitehead, 2003).

Differential impacts of EU regulation for EU Member States are a frequent phenomenon in various policy fields. Our case fits into this general pattern. In professional football, as in other sectors, SSD outcomes will have less far-reaching consequences in the Western, old Member States than in the Central and Eastern, new ones. The Commission has officially recognized that

> Issues related to enlargement and the integration of new actors have remained high on the agenda of most committees, in particular in relation to capacity-building projects for new Member States and candidate countries carried out in some sectors . . . although further efforts seem warranted to assess and enhance

the effective impact in terms of participation of representatives from the new Member States and reinforcing social dialogue at local and company level in the New Member States. (European Commission, 2010b, p. 10)

In Western European leagues, especially in the economically most successful, and therefore most resourceful, "big five" (France, Germany, Italy, Spain, UK), but also in others (such as the Scandinavian countries), the minimum standards have already been accomplished during the lasting processes of professionalization and extensive economization of professional football. Therefore, the social partners concluded that there is no need for action in some countries (Annex 8 of the Agreement). The Commission has also recognized this obvious discrepancy and stated officially: "The agreement has been accompanied by a joint letter stipulating that in a certain number of countries the standard of contractual protection is already above the standards provided for in the autonomous agreement and, consequently, no further action is required" (European Commission, 2013, p. 206).

More heterogeneity of national framework regulation, and sometimes even non-regulation, exists in Central and Eastern European countries (Siekmann, 2004). They seem "to have embraced a liberal market model in the post-communist era and . . . approached a more non-interventionist stance . . ." (Gammelsæter & Senoux, 2011a, p. 279). There are divergent interests and specific obstacles that have to be coped with. FIFPro has explicitly indicated abuses of contracts in these leagues:

Among these are: incentives and bonuses only paid in the event of good performance, to be determined by the club; no contract guarantee during illness and/or injuries; a net salary of which only 10 percent is guaranteed; penalties from 10% to 100% of salary and bonuses unilaterally determined by the club management; the club can reduce the level of the incentive premiums and bonuses during the term of the contract, etc. (Colucci & Geeraert, 2011, p. 64).

The social partners definitely foresaw the enormous difficulties of transposition because of missing national structures for implementation and insufficient mechanisms of vertical coordination between the supranational and national level. They tried to contribute to the urgently needed capacity building at national level. In late 2012, the Steering Committee established a "Working Group on implementation of the 'Autonomous Agreement'" whose objective is "to make the minimum requirements a reality throughout the whole UEFA territory, whilst respecting the principle of subsidiarity." Its primary tasks include raising awareness of national member organizations, representatives of individual clubs, and players' unions, as well as other potential stakeholders, such as governments, and adding to capacity building and mutual learning at national level.

According to its biannual work program (2013–14), the working group undertakes a series of "visits to individual countries," first, in order to identify country-specific issues and, later on, to support and monitor the processes and progress of implementation. In early 2013, the social partners organized three kick-off meetings whose primary purpose was to inform their national member organizations about the Agreement and potential procedures of implementation. Furthermore, they drew a table "on the identification of problems country by country" and organized roundtables in target countries as well as regional roundtables for national representatives "to facilitate the exchange of best practice and experience between national social partners and football authorities." Then, the social partners successfully submitted a project application "on the implementation of the autonomous agreement" to be financed by EU funds and managed by DG EMPL (European Commission, 2014, pp. 24, 41).[22] At the end of the project period the Commission not only expects but insists on a summarizing evaluation report to be submitted and published by the European social partners on the results and assessments of their implementation activities in EU Member States. According to its work program (2014–15), the working group is supposed to play a crucial role at later stages in monitoring the progress of implementation results and applying follow-up procedures.

Regional Problems Outside of the EU

Last but not least, there is another remarkable, in comparison with all other SSDs, exceptional characteristic feature of this Agreement. The social partners publicly announced their ambitious intention to implement it not only in the (at present 28) EU Member States but to extend it to all other (all in all 53) UEFA members (European Commission, 2013, p. 206).[23] The social partners' organizations on both sides have members not only in the EU but also "in the rest of the UEFA territory." The officially indicated reasons include, among others, the reputation of professional football, raising standards for players and clubs, and legal stability. The underlying motives for the ambitious plan "to make the minimum requirements a reality throughout the whole UEFA territory" are the membership domain and geographical spread.

Therefore, this Agreement is supposed to cover a much broader territory than all other SSD outcomes. Its overall impact in non-EU Member States will be more encompassing – if appropriate implementation can be managed at all. In contrast to EU Member States, UEFA is and, for reasons of efficiency, must constitute a more important corporate actor in extending and completing activities of implementation. This is an urgent task despite the fact that, as indicated above, UEFA is not an officially recognized social partner but an associate party. It has to be pointed out that UEFA decided voluntarily to get involved in the conclusion of the Agreement despite the existence of other, exclusively self-determined options for supranational regulation.[24] UEFA obviously expected some value added despite the anticipation of implementation problems. Thus, both systems of regulation, autonomy and some soft EU interference, are of complementary, not necessarily competing or even opposing, nature for the emerging system of European football governance.

This unusual, ambitious plan towards more encompassing "Europeanization" will lead to additional problems of implementation. There exists a certain moral obligation, and obviously some goodwill on both sides – not more and not less. Anyhow, proper implementation "throughout the whole UEFA territory" will need lots of scarce resources as well as more time than originally expected. The already indicated, weak EU procedures will be even more difficult to apply in non-EU Member States where significant differences in standards of national regulation as well as organizational structures of social partners exist. Thus, the voluntary route of implementation that could be exclusively taken by the social partners themselves does not constitute a realistic alternative but needs external support. Again, the SD task force is supposed to support implementation processes. Its members visit individual countries and consult with national associations and social partners, the important stakeholders who are in charge of all follow-up processes. The overall impact of the task force is limited and rests on voluntary forms of cooperation.

Some procedures in accordance with international contract law are the only alternative. They require, however, the existence of mandates on both sides in order to authorize supranational federations to negotiate on behalf of their national constituencies and to legitimize outcomes. Otherwise, any binding effects of an agreement could not be guaranteed and potential sanctions in cases of complete or partial non-compliance would be invalid. In any case, binding consequences of implementation would, by definition, be constrained to the present members of national associations. This necessary legal precondition creates additional problems because the existence of sufficiently high density ratios cannot be taken for granted in all countries.

Interestingly enough, these legal as well as practical difficulties of implementing and monitoring the Agreement in non-EU Member States are not mentioned in the official work program that is, by definition, valid for Member States only. Thus, all implementation processes will be wide open for differing interpretation and strategic maneuvering by associations at national level. Even non-compliance could be an option for some national stakeholders – if not even a potential opportunistic strategy. In such cases, there are no effective instruments for sanctioning deviant behavior.

Finally, national legal institutional characteristics lead to a characteristic sequence of implementation. Its procedures are to be finished within an indicated period (of usually two to three, in our case not more than three, years) after an agreement was signed. Delays usually happen at least in some countries. In our case, the fastest group consists of associations in the old Member States, to be followed by the new ones. All others will need more time – and more scarce resources.

IS THERE A FUTURE FOR THE SSD IN PROFESSIONAL FOOTBALL?

Important but Neglected Topics

Recent research and official reports conclude that the "productivity" and "effectiveness" of SSDs vary significantly (European Commission, 2010b). The empirical evidence indicates that the first SSD outcome might constitute the triggering event for others but might as well remain the only one for quite some time. There is no automatism or guarantee for any kind of linear upward development. In any case, SSDs constitute long-term projects as well as commitments for all participants. The Committee in professional football is currently focusing on:

1. "strengthening the social partners' capacity to shape future developments regarding employment in the professional football sector and to articulate European levels of social dialogue;
2. implementing the autonomous agreement: career funds;
3. contractual stability/respect of contracts" (European Commission and DG EMPL, 2014).

At present, issues of bilateral interest are discussed in working groups of the committee, "Contractual Stability and Respect of Contracts" and "Career Fund." Especially the establishment of "career funds" constitutes an important issue because of professional footballers' inevitability to initiate a second career, in comparison with other employees, at a comparatively early age. FIFPro is more in favor of such funds than the employers' associations that do not strictly argue against them but doubt the usefulness of standards defined at European level. Controversial issues are not only the feasibility but also the portability of funds.

It remains to be seen if this SSD will reach a stage of stability and maturity that is, according to the officially formulated benchmarks, supposed to mean "fewer documents overall but more binding agreements" (European Commission, 2013, p. 230). As examples of other SSDs indicate, soft outcomes of less or no binding obligations for the social partners, such as recommendations, joint opinions and declarations, are more likely to be concluded than binding agreements.

So far not SSD but other arenas of interest intermediation have been of relevance for solving urgent problems. The future of this SSD depends on the identification of additional common interests and the establishment of a sustainable balance of power. Various issues of common concern and increasing impact at European level exist but their inclusion in the SSD agenda requires the explicit approval of all social partners. There is a broad range of potential activities and relevant contributions, if not primary competence.[25] All listed issues require coordinated action by individual clubs, national leagues, and European federations.

Some urgent, but sensitive problems of the integrity of football at supranational level, such as effective doping prevention and sanctions, spectator violence and hooliganism, as well as emerging counter activities such as "Football against racism in Europe," are only briefly mentioned but hardly tackled in the Agreement.

Since the 1990s, the number of agents and their activities for numerous players has increased in ongoing processes of Europeanization and domestic professionalization. The Agreement ignores these important more recent actors of the football business. Their frequent, controversially disputed, sometimes even dubious activities remain not only unregulated but even untouched despite the existence of a typical principal agent problem.

Other important issues include intellectual property rights of athletes and the selling of media, especially television rights.[26] Their impact on individual clubs' budgets and collective mechanisms of (ideally more solidaristic) financial redistribution have hardly been dealt with. Related issues are the increasing revenues of some clubs but ailing ones of many others and, therefore, growing imbalances within leagues that need to be minimized in order to re-establish some kind of financial stability.

Furthermore, an overarching policy of "financial fairplay" according to recent UEFA concepts (UEFA, 2012) exists but has not been completely implemented. It is important to realize that the financial difficulties of major football clubs have not been caused by the consequences of the Great Recession (among others, falling output, increasing unemployment, especially youth unemployment) but are the results of clubs' long-term policies and their failure.

One integrated part is the binding introduction and implementation of sustainable systems of professional club licensing and strict financial discipline in order to support principles of corporate governance and to avoid huge financial losses or, in the worst possible case, even insolvency. Necessarily, these measures have to include procedures of reinforcement, such as financial penalties or even exclusion from international competition or relegation of individual clubs.

The future maximal impact of private (and even international financial) investors in the already highly commercialized growth industry needs also to be regulated. These potential stakeholders are getting more and more interested in clubs and want to be not only sponsors but in some prominent cases even owners. At national level these plans sometimes require changes in the legal structure of clubs.

Last but not least, different problems of a criminal nature, such as fraud and match fixing or illegal gambling by individuals as well as betting activities by internationally organized syndicates, definitely exist in at least some, not only Eastern European leagues. These problems need to be solved in order to save the integrity and credibility of sports.

Outlook

A new balance towards principles of good governance in policy making could be reached by the continued evolution of a more or less sophisticated system of co-regulation between the rule setting by private actors and EU-specific regulation (Fligstein, 2008). The SSD in professional football could provide a semi-legal framework for keeping the shifting balance between former national autonomy and exclusive self-regulation by private associations versus emerging more frequent intervention of EU authorities (Parrish, 2011). In the multi-level policy arena it has to respect the fundamental principle of subsidiarity (Article 5 TFEU) as well as the existing enormous degrees of national diversity.

Furthermore, SSDs frequently serve other purposes than the conclusion of autonomous agreements. Lobbying not only national governments but also EU institutions with regulatory competence, first of all the Commission, constitutes a well-documented joint activity of social partners. It aims at the advancement of common interests by using various instruments and alternate channels of influence (de Boer et al., 2005).

The SSD in professional football is the first within the ongoing "Europeanization" of the sports sector. Therefore, it could take the lead in these processes of substantial and procedural change because it is more advanced than its potential counterparts in all other major sports. Football could benefit from its first mover advantage and act as the driving force for others. In the introduction we mentioned the SSD for the sport and active leisure industry whose establishment is officially supported by the Commission (European Commission, 2011, p.12).[27] In comparative perspective, it is not unusual that several SSDs exist within a specific sector. Such a sub-division frequently facilitates the conclusion of outcomes because specific features of sub-sectors can be more adequately respected.[28]

Some associations of other national professional leagues, first of all basketball and ice hockey, announced their interests in establishing their own SSDs that must pay attention to their specificities. The Commission indicated in its White Paper on Sports that it would encourage and support further "joint requests" by potential social partner organizations (European Commission, 2007, p.19). However, such SSDs should not be too numerous and not be completely independent from each other, but should be divisions of an overarching structure. The formulation of minimum requirements for individual contracts could be of even more importance than in professional football.

All in all, further steps towards the incremental and evolutionary development of the so far not yet existing "European Model of Sport" are to be expected. More recently the Commission issued its Communication "Developing the European Dimension in Sport" (European Commission, 2011) that explicitly encourages the establishment of SSDs and elaborates on their expansion in the sports sector even far beyond its highly professional segments.

NOTES

*   Authors frequently get by with a little help from some colleagues and friends. In my case, I would like to thank Ellen Durst, Ulrich Mückenberger, Werner Nienhüser, Sabrina Weber and Uwe Wilkesmann for valuable suggestions and profound critique.
1. Since the early 1990s the European Commission has issued a number of Communications in order to clarify its understanding of various emerging issues. The changing official views are indicated in a series of articles in Eurofound (2013a).
2. They are in strictly legal terms not self-employed.
3. TFEU refers to the Treaty on the Functioning of the European Union.
4. For a complete updated list see European Commission (2012, Annex 1).
5. See Eurofound (2013b) for an updated summary of existing studies of representativeness.
6. http://www.fifpro.org/.
7. For a complete member list http://ec.europa.eu/social/main.jsp?catId=521&langId=en &agreementId=5241, Annex 3.
8. http://www.epfl-europeanleagues.com/index.htm.
9. http://ec.europa.eu/social/main.jsp?catId=521&langId=en&agreementId=5241, Annex 1.

10. For a complete list of ordinary and associate members http://ec.europa.eu/social/main.jsp?catId=521&langId=en&agreementId=5241, Annex 2.
11. http://www.ecaeurope.com/.
12. The protracted power struggle between G14, UEFA and the Commission is analyzed in detail by Grant (2006).
13. http://www.uefa.org/.
14. To read more on recent issues of mobility and transfers of players see Dalziel et al. (2012); KEA & CDES (2013).
15. All official documents are available via the home page of DG Employment, Social Affairs & Inclusion http://ec.europa.eu/social/main.jsp?catId=480, then select "Professional football."
16. There are only two in the Primera División in Spain, five or six in the Premier League in the UK, and two or three in the Bundesliga in Germany.
17. Strikes happened in some highly professionalized national leagues, such as Italy or Spain, but not in others, such as Germany.
18. Political interference in the national arrangements of football differs significantly across EU Member States. In our case, the vast majority of governments will not act as interlocutors.
19. The German Professional Football Players Association, Vereinigung der Vertragsfußballspieler e.V. (VDV), constitutes a major exception. This occupational union is established at national level but is not a regular member of FIFPro at European level. Thus, German professionals are not, or at least not directly, represented at EU level.
20. The organizational and legal governance structures of professional football in selected countries are described in detail in Gammelsæter and Senoux (2011b) and Niemann et al. (2011b).
21. The selected, completely different cases of Cyprus and Italy are analyzed in Theodorou (2013).
22. After the Commission approved the mentioned funding proposal by the social partners for implementation processes these funds are, by definition, exclusively available for EU Member States as well as candidate countries but not for all others. Reimbursement of travel expenses and subsistence allowances is possible.
23. In the 1990s the only other exception was the extension of SD outcomes to members of the European Economic Area (especially Norway and Iceland) that were not EU members.
24. Especially UEFA can also make use of other instruments, such as lobbying, to pursue its interests (García, 2007).
25. A list of potential topics is provided by Gábriš (2010), and there is the Commission's compilation of "challenges and perspectives" (European Commission, 2010b, p. 64). In a position paper ECA presents its view on key issues, including "structured dialogue" (ECA, 2011). Present problems of sports are already mentioned in the White Paper on Sports (European Commission, 2007) and now officially listed (European Commission, 2011).
26. At national level this financial topic is regulated either on a collective, centralized basis, as in Germany, or marketed by individual clubs, as in Spain. At supranational level central forms of marketization dominate.
27. The social partners are the European Association of Sport Employers (EASE) and UNI Europa Sport (Pierre & Buisine, 2013). The results of the study of representativeness were published in mid-2013 and are available at http://www.eurofound.europa.eu/docs/eiro/tn1105058s/tn1105058s.pdf. EASE presents its point of view at www.easesport.org/cat.php?id=1168.
28. The transport (sub)sectors with their separate SSDs based on different carriers are a well-known example (Keller, 2005).

REFERENCES

Adam, G. (2013), 'Representativeness of the European social partner organisations: Sport and active leisure industry', accessed 14 March 2014 at http://www.eurofound.europa.eu/eiro/studies/tn1105058s/tn1105058s_4.htm.

Ales, E., S. Engblom, T. Jaspers, S. Laulom, S. Sciarra, A. Sobczak, and F. Valdés Dal-Ré (2006), *Transnational Collective Bargaining: Past, Present and Future*, Final report, Brussels.

Branco Martins, Roberto (2004), 'Social dialogue in the European professional football sector: A European legal football match heading for extra time', *International Sports Law Journal*, (3–4), 17–29, http://www.asser.nl/default.aspx?site_id=11&level1=13910&level2=13947&level3=&textid=36312.

Brand, Alexander and Arne Niemann (2006), 'The Europeanization of German football', in Alan Tomlinson and Christopher Young (eds), *German Football: History, Culture, Society*, London, UK: Routledge, pp. 127–142.

BusinessEurope, CEEP, ETUC, and UEAPME (2011), *European Social Dialogue: Achievements and Challenges Ahead: Results of the Stock-Taking Survey amongst National Social Partners in the EU Member States and Candidate Countries. Final Synthesis Report – May 2011*, accessed 14 March 2014 at http://resourcecentre.etuc.org/linked_files/documents/IP3%20-%20Study%20-%20European%20Social%20Dialogue%20achievements%20and%20challenges%20ahead%20-%20EN.pdf.

Colucci, M. and A. Geeraert (2011), 'Social dialogue in European professional football', *International Sports Law Journal*, (3–4), 56–67, http://www.playthegame.org/fileadmin/documents/AGGIS_article_-_social_dialogue_in_european_professional_football.pdf.

Council of the European Union (2011), 'Resolution of the Council and of the Representatives of the Governments of the Member States, meeting within the Council, on a European Union Work Plan for Sport for 2011–2014' (2011/C 162/01).

Dalziel, M., P. Downward, R. Parrish, G. Pearson, and A. Semens (2012), 'Study on the assessment of UEFA's "home grown player rule". Negotiated procedure EAC/07/2012', accessed 14 March 2014 at http://ec.europa.eu/sport/library/documents/f-studies/final-rpt-april2013-homegrownplayer.pdf.

De Boer, R., H. Benedictus, and M. van der Mer (2005), 'Broadening without intensification: The added value of the European social and sectoral dialogue', *European Journal of Industrial Relations*, 11 (1), 51–70.

Degryse, C. and P. Pochet (2011), 'Has European sectoral social dialogue improved since the establishment of SSDCs in 1998?', *Transfer*, 17 (2), 145–158.

ECA (2011), 'ECA position paper. The clubs' perspective on the major issues impacting European football', accessed 12 March 2014 at http://www.ecaeurope.com/Global/ECA%20Position%20Paper.pdf.

Eurofound (2013a), 'European industrial relations dictionary', multiple accesses January–March 2014 at http://www.eurofound.europa.eu/areas/industrialrelations/dictionary/.

Eurofound (2013b), 'European sectoral social partner organisations and their representativeness', accessed 12 March 2014 at http://www.eurofound.europa.eu/eiro/representativeness.htm.

European Commission (1993), 'Communication concerning the application of the agreement on social policy presented by the Commission to the Council and the European Parliament' (COM (93) 600 final), Brussels.

European Commission (1998), 'Commission Decision of 20 May 1998 on the establishment of Sectoral Dialogue Committees promoting the dialogue between the social partners at European level' (98/500/EC), Brussels.

European Commission (2004), 'Partnership for change in an enlarged Europe: Enhancing the contribution of European social dialogue' (COM(2004) 557), Brussels.

European Commission (2007), 'The White Paper on Sport' (COM(2007) 391 final), Brussels.

European Commission (2008), 'Footballers and employers launch new EU forum for social

dialogue – IP/08/1064 01/07/2008', accessed 10 March 2014 at http://europa.eu/rapid/press-release_IP-08-1064_en.htm.
European Commission (2009), 'Industrial relations in Europe 2008', Brussels: European Commission.
European Commission (2010a), 'Commission staff working document on the functioning and potential of European sectoral social dialogue' (SEC(2010)964), Brussels.
European Commission (2010b), 'European sectoral social dialogue: Recent developments', Luxembourg: European Commission.
European Commission (2011), 'Developing the European dimension in sport' (COM(2011) 12 final), Brussels.
European Commission (2012), 'Social Europe guide – Volume 2: Social dialogue', Luxembourg: European Commission.
European Commission (2013), 'Industrial relations in Europe 2012', Luxembourg: European Commission.
European Commission (2014), 'EU social dialogue liaison forum – Newsletter No. 6', accessed 8 March 2014 at http://ec.europa.eu/social/main.jsp?langId=en&catId=329&newsId=2027&furtherNews=yes.
European Commission and DG EMPL (2014), 'Sectoral social dialogue – professional football', accessed 8 March 2014 at http://ec.europa.eu/social/main.jsp?catId=480&langId=en&intPageId=1848.
Falkner, Gerda (1998), *EU Social Policy in the 1990s: Towards a Corporatist Policy Community*, New York, USA: Routledge.
Falkner, Gerda, Oliver Treib, Miriam Hartlapp, and Simone Leiber (2005), *Complying with Europe: EU Minimum Harmonisation and Soft Law in the Member States*, Cambridge: Cambridge University Press.
Fligstein, Neil (2008), *Euroclash: The EU, European identity, and the future of Europe*, Oxford: Oxford University Press.
Gábriš, T. (2010), 'European social dialogue in sports', accessed 6 March 2014 at http://papers.ssrn.com/sol3/papers.cfm?abstract_id=1635604.
Gammelsæter, Hallgeir and Benoit Senoux (2011a), 'Understanding the governance of football across Europe', in Hallgeir Gammelsæter and Benoit Senoux (eds), *The Organisation and Governance of Top Football across Europe: An Institutional Perspective*, New York and London: Routledge, pp. 268–291.
Gammelsæter, Hallgeir and Benoit Senoux (eds) (2011b), *The Organisation and Governance of Top Football across Europe: An Institutional Perspective*, New York and London: Routledge.
García, B. (2007), 'UEFA and the European Union: From confrontation to cooperation', *Journal of Contemporary European Research*, 3 (3), 202–223.
García, B. (2011), 'The influence of the EU on the governance of football', in Hallgeir Gammelsæter and Benoit Senoux (eds), *The Organisation and Governance of Top Football across Europe: An Institutional Perspective*, New York and London: Routledge, pp. 32–45.
Ghellab, Youcef and Daniel Vaughan-Whitehead (eds) (2003), *Sectoral Social Dialogue in Future EU Member States: The Weakest Link*, Budapest: ILO.
Grant, W. (2006), 'Two tiers of representation and policy: The EU and the future of football', accessed 6 March 2014 at http://aei.pitt.edu/7888/1/grant-w-10i.pdf.
Hirschman, Albert (1970), *Exit, Voice, and Loyalty. Responses to Decline in Firms, Organizations, and States*, Cambridge: Harvard University Press.
KEA and CDES (2013), 'The economic and legal aspects of transfer of players', accessed 4 March 2014 at http://ec.europa.eu/sport/library/documents/f-studies/cons-study-transfers-final-rpt.pdf.
Keller, B. (2005), 'Europeanisation at sectoral level: Empirical results and missing perspectives', *Transfer*, 11 (3), 397–408.
Keller, Berndt (2007), 'An optional framework for transnational collective bargaining: Old wine in new bottles or a major breakthrough?', in Otto Jacobi, Maria Jepsen, Berndt Keller, and Manfred Weiss (eds), *Social Embedding and the Integration of Markets: An*

Opportunity for Transnational Trade Union Action or an Impossible Task?, Düsseldorf: HBS, pp. 179–192.

Keller, B. and S. Weber (2011), 'Sectoral social dialogue at EU level: Problems and prospects of implementation', *European Journal of Industrial Relations*, **17** (3), 227–244.

Keune, M. and P. Marginson (2013), 'Transnational industrial relations as multi-level governance: Interdependencies in European social dialogue', *British Journal of Industrial Relations*, **51** (3), 473–497.

Léonard, E., E. Perin, and P. Pochet (2011), 'The European sectoral social dialogue: Questions of representation and membership', *Industrial Relations Journal*, **42** (3), 254–272.

Mittag, Jürgen (2007), 'Die Europäische Union und der Fußball. Die Europäisierung des Profifußballs zwischen Bosman- und Simutenkow-Urteil', in Jürgen Mittag and Jörg-Uwe Nieland (eds), *Das Spiel mit dem Fußball. Interessen, Projektionen und Vereinnahmungen*, Essen: Klartext, pp. 203–218.

Niemann, Arne, Borja García, and Wyn Grant (2011a), 'Introduction: The transformation of European football', in Arne Niemann, Borja García, and Wyn Grant (eds), *The Transformation of European Football*, Manchester: Manchester University Press, pp. 1–19.

Niemann, Arne, Borja García, and Wyn Grant (eds) (2011b), *The Transformation of European Football*, Manchester: Manchester University Press.

Olson, Mancur (1965), *The Logic of Collective Action*, Cambridge: Harvard University Press.

Olson, Mancur (1982), *The Rise and Decline of Nations: Economic Growth, Stagflation, and Social Rights*, New Haven and London: Yale University Press.

Olsson, Lars-Christer (2011), 'Decisive moments in UEFA', in Hallgeir Gammelsæter and Benoit Senoux (eds), *The Organisation and Governance of Top Football across Europe: An Institutional Perspective*, New York and London: Routledge, pp. 17–31.

Parrish, R. (2011), 'Social dialogue in European professional football', *European Law Journal*, **17** (2), 21–229.

Pierre, J. and S. Buisine (2013), 'Social dialogue in the sports sector at EU level', *Transfer*, **19** (4), 581–595.

Pochet, Philippe, Anne Peeters, and Evelyne Léonard (2009), *Dynamics of European Sectoral Social Dialogue*, Luxembourg: European Foundation.

Siekmann, R.C.R. (2004), 'Promoting the social dialogue in professional football in the new EU member states', *International Sports Law Journal*, (3–4), 31–33.

Szymanski, Stefan and Tim Kuypers (1999), *Winners and Losers: The Business Strategy of Football*, London and New York: Viking.

Theodorou, D. (2013), 'The social dialogue in professional football at European and national level (Cyprus and Italy)', Master thesis, Tilburg University, accessed 2 March 2014 at http://arno.uvt.nl/show.cgi?fid=129334.

UEFA (2011), 'The European club footballing landscape: Club licensing benchmarking report Financial year 2010', accessed 2 March 2014 at http://www.uefa.org/MultimediaFiles/Download/Tech/uefaorg/General/01/74/41/25/1744125_DOWNLOAD.pdf.

UEFA (2012), 'The European club licensing benchmarking report: Financial year 2011', accessed 28 February 2014 at http://www.uefa.org/MultimediaFiles/Download/Tech/uefaorg/General/01/91/61/84/1916184_DOWNLOAD.pdf.

Université Catholique de Louvain, Institut des Sciences du Travail (2006), 'Study on the representativeness of the social partner organizations in the professional football players sector', Research Project No VC/2004/0547. Research project conducted on behalf of the Employment and Social Affairs DG of the European Commission, accessed 28 February 2014 at http://www.uclouvain.be/cps/ucl/doc/trav/documents/FOOT_ENGLISH_Resumee_draft.pdf.

Weber, Sabrina (2013), *Sektorale Sozialdialoge auf EU-Ebene. Supranationale und nationale Perspektiven*, Baden-Baden: Nomos.

3. Performance expectations, contracts and job security
John Solow and Peter von Allmen

INTRODUCTION

In this chapter we discuss the idiosyncratic nature of labor contracts in North American professional baseball (Major League Baseball – MLB), football (National Football League – NFL), ice hockey (National Hockey League – NHL), and basketball (National Basketball Association – NBA). Labor markets in North American professional team sports are quite different from those in other industries and to a lesser extent even from those of professional sports leagues elsewhere in the world. Specifically, our goal is to provide an overview of the long-term employment relationships that frequently result from such contracts, most importantly as they impact performance incentives, job security, and risk allocation.

In the four major professional team sports, we see profound differences in the employer–employee relationship compared to most industries. Briefly, they fall into three main categories, which we summarize here and discuss in greater detail below. First, instead of an agreement between two parties (or three in the case of a union or player association), there are four primary parties and two levels of negotiations involved. The league and player association negotiate a collective bargaining agreement (CBA) that establishes the parameters within which individual player contracts can be negotiated, and the team and the player (and his or her agent) negotiate the terms of the player's individual contract subject to the restrictions set forth in the CBA. Second, salaries are typically guaranteed *ex ante* as opposed to paid *ex post*. If we use the term "remuneration" to refer to "an amount of money paid to someone for the work that person has done" (Merriam Webster online dictionary, 2014), in the case of professional sports, athletes typically do not receive remuneration. Instead, they receive payments that are guaranteed for productivity not yet realized. As we discuss below, this substantially complicates the principal–agent problem. Third, teams and players often agree to long-term contracts that stipulate (and in many cases guarantee) salaries for many years into the future, perhaps well beyond the expected productive career of the player. While there are important differences in the structure of such contracts across sports, long-term contracts carry potential risks for both parties, making the payment of a risk premium an interesting empirical question.

THE PECULIAR NATURE OF US PROFESSIONAL SPORTS CONTRACTS

The popular press often makes reference to overall employment conditions by referencing the labor market. The reality is that there are countless individual markets in the United States. These markets may be highly localized, as in the case of unskilled labor, or national (or even international) in the case of highly specialized talent. Yet for all these differences, there are some important commonalities. In a typical employer–employee relationship not governed by collective bargaining, profit maximizing employers hire labor in the relevant market by agreeing to terms of compensation that cover both pecuniary and non-pecuniary aspects. These relationships are not guaranteed but open-ended, and remain in place until one party or the other terminates them. In the absence of a union, there are just two parties involved: the firm and the worker. The usual assumption is that employee choices reflect utility maximization, with an objective function strongly though not solely influenced by income. Workers and firms may operate under an implicit contract that generates expectations for both parties.[1]

For a variety of reasons, labor market institutions in the major US professional sports and the contracts between players and teams that they generate are far more idiosyncratic than these simple arrangements would suggest. For one thing, the potential for principal–agent problems looms large in sports. Principal–agent problems can arise when the agent's productivity (in this case, the player's performance) depends on his or her chosen level of effort, and effort is costly to monitor or even unobservable and therefore cannot be used to determine compensation in the contract. Assuming that there is disutility associated with increased work effort, workers prefer to reduce effort when possible, which is inconsistent with the firm's profit maximizing goals. When the agent's output is a deterministic function of effort, compensation can be conditioned on the level of output through some pay for performance method such as piece rates, bonuses or commission, or straight salary per period.[2] If, however, the agent's output depends on both effort and random factors beyond the agent's control, a contract that conditions pay on performance makes the agent face the risk resulting from the uncertainty. If the principal is less risk averse than the agent, a reasonable assumption in many settings including professional sports, a trade-off arises between aligning incentives and sharing risk optimally.

When workers are easily monitored through their own output, such as when they individually produce a physical product or quantifiable service, piece rates are often employed. As Lazear (1986) notes, commissions are a form of piece rates; that is, workers receive commissions based on actual sales or output, such as in the insurance industry. When output is difficult or impossible to quantify, firms generally offer salary-per-period subject to some measurable performance standard. Such arrangements may also include the opportunity for the worker to earn periodic bonuses. Bonuses are somewhat of a hybrid form of compensation. If a bonus is based on an individual achieving a specific performance target, such payments resemble piece rates. However, those targets may be only loosely linked to actual output in a given period and the ability to earn them is often not entirely under the control of the individual who receives them (as in revenue targets for a group or division within a company).

While sports are frequently blessed with a plethora of measures of player performance, in many cases it is difficult to separate the contributions of an individual player from that of his or her teammates. Thus, while it is a straightforward thing to measure, say, the scoring efficiency of a basketball player, that performance is likely to depend on the performance of her teammates, which influences the defensive schemes (e.g. double-teams, zone versus player-on-player) chosen by the opposing team. Similarly, while passing efficiency ratings for quarterbacks are easily calculated, the ability of a quarterback to gain yardage by completing passes depends a great deal on the ability of the offensive line to give him time to find an open receiver and deliver the ball, the ability of the receivers to get open and catch the ball, and even the ability of the running backs to provide a threat that keeps the defense uncertain as to whether plays will involve a run or a pass. As we discuss further below, the problem of employee interdependence is very common in sports, though bonuses are still a frequently seen feature in player contracts.

All four of the major professional sports leagues in the United States involve a union which negotiates on behalf of the players. In a typical unionized environment, the union serves as a third party in the negotiation process and contracts are explicit rather than implicit. Through collective bargaining, unions and firms set a variety of parameters that typically include wages, health and safety regulations, work rules, benefits, disciplinary procedures, and working conditions. Unions are charged with maximizing the welfare of the membership. While this can be a complex process, especially when workers have widely divergent preferences, maximizing income is certainly an important aspect of this process. In the typical unionized setting, workers do not negotiate directly with their employer, but simply sign a contract that embodies the parameters that the union and firm have negotiated.

Again, labor relations in professional sports do not fit this simple model. For one thing, the players' union does not negotiate with individual teams on behalf of that team's players, but instead negotiates with the collective ownership of all of the teams (the league) together on behalf of all current and even future players. Moreover, the CBAs that come out of these negotiations do not set the pay scale for most veteran players (the terms of the CBA may, however, determine the pay for entry level players who, per the CBA, are not free to negotiate with multiple potential employers for the best deal). What the CBA does establish is the framework within which the negotiations between the player and his or her team take place; what variables, if any, can be used to condition pay; the extent to which payment is guaranteed; and so forth. Within these parameters, veteran players who are not currently under contract negotiate individually through their agents with teams about such things as contract length, the amount and timing of payment, and other terms allowed by the CBA.

In the next section, we discuss the primary characteristics of sports labor markets as outlined above. Then, we describe individual contract outcomes, with specific attention to risk allocation. Then, we discuss the impact of collective bargaining on the negotiation process. Finally, we offer suggestions for future work and conclusions.

INDIVIDUAL CONTRACT NEGOTIATIONS

As we noted above, there are four parties involved in the negotiation of a contract: the player, the team, the league, and the player association. We will now discuss the role and incentives of each, with particular attention to the contracting process and outcome. In general, we can think of the contracting process as occurring on two levels. The league and the player association establish the parameters under which individual contracts are written. The team and player then negotiate within this framework in pursuit of their own objectives. We explain the role and incentives of each party in greater detail below.

The Player

When new players enter the league, their ability to negotiate favorable contract terms is highly restricted as each league maintains some version of the well-known reserve clause that places the property rights for the players' services squarely in the hands of the teams.[3] For most players, the road to free agency is through accumulated service time. In this section, unless otherwise noted, we focus our attention on players who are free to negotiate new contracts with any team (i.e. free agents). One way to look at this is as the result of a Nash bargaining process, in which the player and the team seek to maximize their share of the surplus generated by bringing together the player's talents and the talents of the other players under the control of the team.[4]

Virtually all players are represented by an agent or player representative, who acts on behalf of the player in negotiations with the team. There is very little existing literature on sports agents in the economics literature. This lack of work is most likely because agents' fees are relatively modest[5] and because their incentives in the contract negotiation process are thought to be so closely aligned with those of the player that their actions cannot be parsed out from the incentives of the player.[6] This may, however, be fertile ground for future research.

Athletes are employees and so expend effort in exchange for compensation. The existing literature contains few theoretical papers in which utility functions are made explicit.[7] Typically, empirical papers implicitly assume that players maximize income in exchange for effort. If effort were observable (or inferable) we might expect to see contracts that specify pay as a function of effort. As noted earlier, however, effort is difficult to observe directly and difficult to infer from performance due both to inherent randomness and the contributions of other players. Instead, considering first a one-year contract, salary (S) can be conditioned on some measure of performance (p), which in turn would depend on the player's talent (τ), effort (e), and a random variable (ε) that captures the inherent randomness involved:

$$S = s(p(e,\tau,\varepsilon))$$

If, as is often the case, tying salary to actual performance is not allowed under collective bargaining and salary must be set in advance of the season, then salary will be based on expected performance, which can be expected to depend on talent and historical performance, but not on effort or the random events of the coming season.

$$S = s(\mathrm{E}[p_t|t, p_{t-1}, p_{t-2}, \ldots])$$

In the case of a multi-year contract of length n, the player must also evaluate the expected future payments under the contract. Let φ_t denote the probability of being paid in year t; φ_t could reasonably be expected to depend on the player's observed history of performance and the anticipated pay that the player would receive under the contract if he or she are allowed to continue with the team, as well as the player's age, history of injuries, and so forth. In that case, the value of the contract would be:

$$V = S_1(p_1, \beta_1, \varphi_1) + \sum_{x=2}^{n} \beta^{x-1} \varphi_x S_x(p_x(e_x, \tau_x, \varepsilon_x))$$

where β is the discount factor. Valuing the contract in this way allows for all sorts of dynamic complexities; for example, how effort in earlier years affects the probability of being paid in subsequent years, whether effort in earlier periods affects talent in subsequent years, player ageing, or whether there is a serial correlation in the random variable that captures inherent randomness in performance. We do not take those up, but note there is much fertile ground for research here.

Players are assumed to maximize their utility over the length of their careers, a time window not known to either the team or the player:[8]

$$U = \sum_{i=1}^{m} u_i$$

where u_i is a concave utility function that includes as arguments contract salary value, other benefits (B), and effort for the ith contract:

$$u_I = u(V_I, B_I, e_I)$$

The marginal utility of all inputs are assumed to be positive except e, as more effort decreases utility. Although benefits are an important determinant of utility, they are in large part stipulated in the CBA.

If players are risk averse regarding their future productivity, they may opt to accept wages that are below what they could earn in the one-year spot market for talent in order to secure additional years of guaranteed income. As we discuss further below, an individual player's bargaining power is a function not only of his or her expected future productivity but also of the bargainable rents available to the team in the form of fixed revenues.[9]

If income per year is guaranteed for the life of the contract, as in MLB, $\varphi_t = 1$ for $t = 2$ through n. Even so, however, the length of the contract (n) is an important term of the contract which must be negotiated. Such players may continue to elicit high effort, but the current contract is independent of this level.

If players must earn a roster spot every year in order to receive their salary beyond the first year, $\varphi_t < 1$ and the player's maximization problem is more complex. This is most relevant in the NFL where other than the signing bonus and stipulated rookie contracts, players must earn a position on the team each year to receive their negotiated salary. In the NFL, the portion of compensation that is guaranteed has risen from just 15 percent in 1992 to 57 percent in 2011, due largely in part to favorable changes in free agency rules and the attending increased competition for talent (Breer, 2012). It is no surprise that players prefer guaranteed compensation to wages that can only be earned if the player makes the roster in that year. What is less clear is the extent to which they are willing to accept a contract with a lower expected value to secure a longer stream of guaranteed payments.

The Team

The team acts in two roles. First, each team is a member of its league which, acting jointly as a cartel, bargains with the player association to set the rules for individual players' contract negotiations. Second, it acts independently when negotiating and hiring individual players within that framework. For the moment, we focus on the latter; in this context, the individual team is engaged in (off-field) competition with other teams. Teams prefer higher profits and profits are positively related to team quality. While there are exceptions – most notably those driven by revenue sharing – it is generally true that wins (W) are positively related to revenue (R) and profits (Π) and that performance is positively related to wins (Burger & Walters, 2003; Solow & Krautmann, 2007). Hence:

$$W = w(p(e, \tau, \varepsilon))$$

and

$$\Pi = R(W(p(e, \tau, \varepsilon)), Z_R) - C(S, Z_C)$$

where Z_R represents factors that affect revenues unrelated to short-run variations in team quality, such as city population and income, recent previous team performance, and having a new stadium; and Z_C are other costs beyond the team's salary bill. Here, e, τ, ε and S should be thought of as vectors of effort, talent, luck, and salary with elements for each team member.

Thus, teams demand talent as part of the revenue function. In some instances, the aggregate supply of talent may be fixed (perfectly inelastic supply), so that the only way for a team to acquire additional talent comes at the expense of other teams in the league.[10] Even if another source of talent is available (say, from leagues in other countries), the supply of talent is likely to be highly inelastic, as it becomes increasingly difficult to acquire players capable of playing at the professional level. If wins are positively related to revenue, then the team has an incentive to minimize cost subject to producing the desired (expected) number of wins.

It is common in the principal–agent literature to assume that the employers are risk neutral (Holmstrom & Milgrom, 1991), either because they can diversify away risk by employing a number of agents or because their stockholders can diversify away risk by holding stock in a portfolio of companies. In the sports setting, however, roster limitations mean that teams can have at best a limited number of players at any position, and team owners are not permitted to diversify their risk by owning shares in several teams in the same sport. As a result, team owners are likely to be risk averse as well.[11] This manifests itself, for example, in teams preferring shorter contracts to longer ones, even at the cost of paying more on a per season basis, when contracts are guaranteed. A longer guaranteed contract places more of the risk that a player's ability declines rapidly or that the player is seriously injured and unable to perform on the team, while a shorter contract makes the player bear more of that risk. This is discussed at greater length below.

This general framework allows for the possibility of principal–agent problems, where the incentive of the player to trade off effort for compensation does not align with the team's goal of eliciting maximum effort, and for compensation to be based on performance so as to realign those incentives. Shirking may manifest itself as actual reduced effort during contests. However, it is more likely to take the form of:

1. reduced intensity and dedication with which the athlete devotes himself to his off-season conditioning program;
2. failing to prepare optimally for each game during the season by skipping practice sessions, weight training, and film sessions;
3. staying out late carousing instead of returning home or to the hotel to get adequate sleep;
4. other similar types of behavior (Berri & Krautmann, 2006).

Finally, performance at the professional level requires a high degree of focus and concentration, which takes effort that a player may fail to exert.

Collective Bargaining

The collective bargaining process establishes the ground rules and parameters of how, when, and to what extent negotiation can take place. For every player contract, the CBA parameters impact risk allocation, options for incentives, and job security. For example, rules about guarantees of compensation in the event of injury mitigate risk for the player, while rules regarding failure to report for required team activities (e.g. practice) mitigate risk for the team. More recently, for example, CBAs have put additional stress on player safety, such as the elimination of two-a-day workouts and reduced contact in practice in the NFL (Volin, 2013). Below we discuss the various parties in the collective bargaining process and their influence on the contractual landscape.

The Leagues

The leagues function as cartel managers.[12] They are powerful and complex organizations which, although run by and for the teams, make decisions based on league-wide maximization criteria. Strategies implemented to pursue such criteria may be at variance with those that any individual team might choose and so (as in all cartels) frequently adopt policies that inevitably lead to internal tension. For example, policies related to revenue sharing promote overall financial stability. While such a strategy benefits all teams in a global sense, it requires the league management to take actions that systematically advantage one team over another and may adversely impact the otherwise desirable link between profit maximization and win maximization. Policies designed to promote financial stability can adversely affect fan demand if not carefully managed from a public relations standpoint. While the need for competitive balance is sometimes invoked in defense of rules that limit labor markets, the maintenance of monopsony power and the stability it brings is often a more plausible explanation. There is considerable theoretical literature devoted to showing when redistributive policies within sports leagues (such as revenue sharing, salary caps, and luxury taxes) have no impact on the equilibrium league balance (the so-called "invariance principle"),[13] and Solow and Krautmann (2007) show that revenue sharing in MLB had no impact on winning percentages but significantly lowered average salaries between 1996 and 2001.

Through collective bargaining with the player associations (e.g. the Major League Baseball Players Association (MLBPA), the Professional Cricketers Association (PCA), and so forth), leagues also set team level parameters such as salary caps, floors, contract length limits, draft structures, trade rules, and more, which affect incentives, risk sharing, and job security. As we discuss below, the four major league player associations vary substantially in their ability to combat attempts to limit the free movement of labor. Ultimately, league rules limit teams' ability to hoard talent and provide disincentives to inflate salaries (which happens to a limited degree in the MLB and to a lesser extent in the NBA because of the imperfect "soft" cap).

The Player Association

The player association serves as a countervailing force to the owners' monopsony power. Before the rise of the Marvin Miller era MLBPA, player associations were loosely organized, lacked unity of purpose, and were largely ineffective against well-organized owners and leagues. When Miller took over the MLBPA, he succeeded in turning the tide and significantly improved outcomes for players, most notably defeating the reserve clause, leading to free agency in the mid-1970s. Although the National Basketball Players Association (NBPA), National Football League Players Association (NFLPA), and National Hockey League Players' Association (NHLPA) have made great strides in working for players' rights, and players in all leagues enjoy free agency, the MLBPA has consistently proved to be the model player association as MLB remains the only league without a salary cap.

The history of the four player associations is rich and complex, and our discussion here is limited to their role in establishing contract parameters. As with any union, the goal of the player association is to maximize the welfare of its members. As noted above, operationalizing this goal is complex as there are a number of dimensions to player welfare both at the individual and aggregate level. They include bargaining for larger rosters, fewer rounds of the player entry draft (allowing more players to enter the league with some measure of bargaining power), higher maximum salaries, higher minimum salaries, player safety issues, and more. The one thing that player associations generally do not engage in that most unions do is the negotiation of specific worker wages or pay grades. The negotiation of players' wages are left to the team and the player (and his or her agent) subject to the agreed upon parameters of the CBA. So while the union works to create a more favorable environment for individual contract negotiation, they do not negotiate contracts between teams and players.

Leagues and player associations do bargain over which revenue streams will be shared with players, the percentage that is shared, and allowable expenses that teams may deduct in the determination of revenue. Table 3.1 shows for each of the four leagues the percentage of revenues dedicated to players in the four major leagues.

Common to all four agreements are minimum contract values. Such minima create a modest level of income certainty for players. Additionally, player contracts in the NBA, NHL, and NFL are in varying degrees

Table 3.1   Percentage of revenues dedicated to player salaries

League	Total salaries as a percentage of revenue current CBA
NBA	49–51% of basketball related income depending on revenues*
NFL	Varies by source of revenue. Player share must exceed 47% over the 10-year life of the current CBA**
NHL	50%***
MLB	No rule. 47% in 2013****

Sources: *Coons (2014); **NFL (2012); ***NHL (2013); ****Brown (2014).

Table 3.2   Average, minimum, and maximum salaries in the NBA, NFL, NHL, and MLB, 2014 or 2014–15

League	Minimum	Average	Maximum
NBA*	$507,336	$4.19 million	$20.64 million (35% of cap for 10+ year veterans)
NFL**	$420,000	$2.06 million	No individual maximum
NHL***	$550,000	$2.14 million (2013/14)	20% of team salary cap
MLB****	$500,000	$3.84 million	No individual maximum

Sources: *NBA: minimum: Coons (2014); average: Basketball-reference.com (2014); **NFL: minimum: Belzer (2014); average: http://www.spotrac.com/nfl/; ***NHL: minimum: http://www.capgeek.com/faq/new-cba; average: http://www.spotrac.com/nhl/; ****MLB: minimum: http://mlb.mlb.com/pa/info/faq.jsp#minimum; average: Petchesky (2014).

governed by individual player maximum annual salaries through draft-slot-determined salaries and negotiated maximum compensation rates for veterans. These, of course, limit player negotiating power and mitigate team risk at the individual player level. Table 3.2 shows the current (2014) average and minimum salaries in the four major leagues as well as maximum values where relevant.

Contract Parameters

Restrictions on contracts vary greatly by league, but set significant limits on the universe of options available to the team and player. These include the structure of the entry draft, the player reservation and free agency process, salary restrictions on new and established players, allowable bonuses, contract length, payment guarantees, team salary caps, and more.

With few exceptions (e.g. international players in MLB and players not selected in the draft) players enter the industry through the reverse order entry draft. The number of rounds varies from sport to sport from a low of two in the NBA to unlimited in MLB. Though the draft is so commonplace that we tend to take it for granted, it is a very unusual way for firms and workers to form matches for two reasons. First, teams do not compete for players and players do not offer services to teams in a simultaneous bidding format as in most markets. Instead, teams simply choose new players serially. Second, once drafted, a player gives up his or her right to negotiate with any other employer until he or she achieves free agency. So while being drafted may insulate the player from the risk of unemployment in the short run (as in the NBA, where first round draft picks are guaranteed contracts), it also prevents the player from offering his or her services on the open market. There is an extensive literature on the effects of this profound monopsony power on player wages, beginning with Rottenberg (1956) and Scully (1974). We do not review that here other than to note that while numerous and varied in the specifics of their empirical approaches, economists typically find that fully reserved players are paid less than half of their marginal revenue product.[14]

In general, the first contract that a player signs (his or her rookie contract) leaves little room for bargaining between the team and the player. Rookie contracts in the NBA are highly prescriptive, specifying a very narrow wage band for each year of a two-year (with team option for a third) contract. First round picks sign contracts for between 80 and 120 percent of the stipulated annual wage; this is set by draft position. As a result, protracted negotiations with newly drafted players are almost non-existent simply because there is almost nothing to negotiate (Jessop, 2012). In the NHL, the CBA stipulates a salary range and contract length based on the age of the player when drafted (with a maximum of three years for the youngest players). The restrictions decrease as the age of the drafted player increases. At the upper limit, players over 25 are not subject to the entry level system restrictions (NHLPA, 2012). The NFL system is nearly the same as the NBA, as salaries (including bonuses) are determined by draft order. Contracts are all set at four years and are fully guaranteed for top picks, with guarantees declining later in the draft (Brandt, 2014). As Brandt (2014) notes, this has both shifted dollars towards veterans and limited teams' exposure to risk by limiting the pay of untested new players. In MLB, most new players make at least or very close to the league minimum and receive modest increases in years two and three. For players who find quick success at the major league level, the value of their performance may well exceed their salary. However, as a group, players have agreed to such a possibility in exchange for certainty of pay for untested talent. From the team perspective, all of these salary restrictions limit downside risk for teams. The more conservative and prescriptive are the salary limits, the less the team risks in being stuck with a long-term contract for which they receive no productive contribution to team revenue.

In professional football, the impact of the most recent NFL–NFLPA agreement was profound. In the draft before the most recent agreement, quarterback Sam Bradford signed a six-year, $78 million contract, with $50 million guaranteed. Just one year later, under the new CBA, Cam Newton signed a four-year contract worth just $22 million (all guaranteed). Thus, the new CBA reduced the guaranteed payout to a top quarterback prospect by more than 50 percent and reduced the contract length by two years (Smith, 2011).

Once players attain free-agent status, they are able to negotiate more favorable contracts for two important reasons. First, and most importantly, they are free to negotiate with all teams in the league simultaneously, creating a market that much more closely resembles the competitive markets for talent in other industries. Second, they are no longer bound by the restrictive terms of rookie contracts. The increase in player bargaining power has the potential to substantially increase the risk borne by the team. In MLB, there are no salary caps on individuals or teams, which puts elite players in a very powerful position. Long-term contracts are common, especially for high revenue teams, as they try to ensure a stable roster of talented players. For example, following an extraordinarily productive early career that contributed to a successful team (and ultimately a World Series in 2008), Philadelphia Phillies first baseman, Ryan Howard, signed a $125 million contract extension in 2010 (fully guaranteed as are all MLB contracts). Howard's productivity has since plummeted, leaving the team in a very difficult position. During the 2014 season, he was benched at times in favor of substitutes. At the time he was still owed $25 million for two additional seasons, with a team option for an additional year. While there is no evidence that Howard is not still doing his best to perform, the combinations of age and injuries have resulted in productivity far below the value of his contract (Sportrac, 2015).

In the NBA, the CBA continues to place important constraints on the contracting process by establishing not only veteran minimums but also individual player maximums. When it comes to signing highly productive veterans, this not only saves teams money, but importantly, in the context of our discussion here, it reduces the risk that the player will underperform relative to his contract. In the NHL, no player may earn more than 20 percent of the salary cap and contracts may not exceed seven years (eight when a team re-signs its own players). In the NFL, there are no individual maximum limits on contracts, though the team must manage its talent acquisition in the context of a hard salary cap and a large roster size.

Given the prospect for principal–agent problems noted earlier, it is perhaps surprising how loosely player salary is tied to measures of performance. The various CBAs do allow bonus payments to different extents. It is best here to distinguish between signing bonuses, which are not tied to performance, and performance bonuses, which are. All four major sports leagues allow the former, which are guaranteed. The leagues differ greatly on the extent of the latter. The extreme case is the MLB, where pay based on performance is not permitted. Rule 3(b)(5) of the Major League rulebook states that no player (in the major or minor leagues) may receive a bonus for any individual skill related performance measure (such as batting average or pitching earned rate average), nor may they receive a bonus for end of season standings.[15] However, they may earn bonuses based on playing time (e.g. plate appearances or innings pitched). Bonuses for receiving end of season awards, such as the Silver Slugger for hitting, the Golden Glove for fielding, or the league Most Valuable Player award, are allowed and occasionally negotiated, but the amounts of the payment are very small compared to annual salary.

At the other extreme, the NHL CBA stipulates that players may receive individual bonuses payable by teams for ice time, various measures of offensive productivity, and plus/minus rating (a measure designed to capture overall effectiveness). There are nine types of such Category "A" bonuses for forwards, ten for defensemen, and eight for goaltenders, and the league sets maximum bonus values for both each measure and the aggregate for the category. The league also maintains Category "B" bonuses which are earned for performance relative to the league (such as the league scoring trophy). While players may earn substantial bonuses here, they do not represent part of the employer–employee contract as we normally think of it as they are paid by the league rather than the team. However, teams may opt to supplement the league awards, in which case either side may use this as a risk allocation/incentive mechanism.[16]

In the NFL, teams often pay signing bonuses, which are prorated across the life of the contract for cap purposes, but serve as guaranteed income paid in advance. The prevalence of guaranteed signing bonuses has increased markedly in recent years and is an important component of the increase in the guaranteed portion of NFL salaries (Breer, 2012). Performance and playing time bonuses are permitted and count against the salary cap if they are likely to be earned (e.g. the player exceeded that level of performance in the previous year). The NFL CBA lists specific categories of bonuses based on team and individual performance that are allowable and specifically prohibits others (NFL–NFLPA Collective Bargaining Agreement, 2011, pp. 96–101).

Finally, in the NBA, teams may offer signing bonuses though they may not exceed 15 percent of the contract value. While not stipulated in the CBA, Coons (2014) notes that base values of NBA contracts are in practice almost all fully guaranteed.[17] Teams and players may also opt to include non-guaranteed performance or incentive clauses.[18] Multi-year contracts are permitted, up to a maximum length of five years. Thus, as with most other sports, teams and players have the ability to share risk and create incentives using contract length and a combination of guaranteed and non-guaranteed payments.

Players, of course, have every reason to prefer guaranteed contracts; performance-based pay and incentive clauses place the risk of injury, declining talent, or bad luck squarely on the player. In addition, players should be concerned that their ability to perform or earn contractual bonuses is partly in the hands of management. One can imagine the player who needs one more goal, home run, or touchdown to earn a large bonus being worried that management will hold them out of the game in order to avoid the risk of having to pay them, particularly late in a season if the ultimate success of the team is not at stake. Given this managerial advantage and the prospect of principal–agent problems and shirking, it is a little surprising that leagues are seemingly so willing to give up the opportunity to use performance-based pay and incentive clauses. One possible explanation is that measurable performance statistics do not always align with what is required in game situations to win games. Faced with salaries that are tied to performance statistics, players have an incentive to maximize or pad those statistics, whether that is what is best for the team in a given situation or not. A player who can earn a large bonus by hitting a given number of home runs has an incentive to swing for the fence on marginal pitches, the player who gets paid according to how many points he or she scores has an incentive to take shots rather than pass to teammates, and a player whose salary depends on how many yards are gained has an incentive to fight for yardage rather than go out of bounds and stop the clock.

Contract Terms and Risk

Earning one's income playing professional sports is inherently risky. Even in non-contact sports such as baseball or basketball, career ending injuries do occur and injuries that result in moderate to long spells of disability are common. In sports such as football and ice hockey, the severity of injuries is much greater. Even if a player is still able to compete, the accumulation of minor injuries can leave them unable to do so at a level that warrants a contract. Even productive players may fall victim to the whim of a new coach with a system incompatible to that particular player's skill set. As a result, players prefer guaranteed salaries; the lower the share of the contract that is guaranteed, the greater the risk to the player. Some players in MLB, the NBA, the NHL, and the NFL could earn a salary that approximates the salary earned in the US league by playing in another country (most notably hockey but also to a certain extent basketball), but for most, their reservation wage outside the league is nowhere near their salary in the US league. In the absence of a CBA, the relatively low reservation wage would dramatically weaken the players' bargaining position. Thus, though it receives much less attention than the salary cap, a critical function of the CBA is to establish a minimum salary.

Contracts that guarantee wages for an entire season are inherently risky too, but for the team, contracts that guarantee income for multiple seasons are riskier still. If the ability to pay performance bonuses is limited, teams and players are left to negotiate a wage based on their own estimated productivity and the probability that it will be realized. If the player's career is on a strong upward trajectory and his or her market power is on the increase (i.e. he or she is approaching free agency), the team may have to accept more of the risk by offering a guaranteed long-term contract (Maxcy, 2004).

As previously noted, new and less experienced players are systematically disadvantaged in the contracting process. As a vestige of earlier agreements that allowed veteran players access to free agency at the entry point to the league, the allocation of talent is according to a pre-determined process (the draft), and drafted players have no bargaining rights. Thus, inter-team competition for talent is virtually non-existent, and we observe the well-known result that players suffer monopsonistic exploitation (see, for example, the references cited in note 14). As a result, the risk to the team of a reserved player failing to meet expectations is relatively small. Such players are generally not offered long-term guaranteed contracts and so in addition to being paid below their expected Marginal Revenue Product (MRP), can be released if they fail to produce.

Once players attain free agency, however, competition among teams for talent may be intense. Teams may be willing to pay the entirety of expected MRP and commit to long-term contracts that extend well beyond the point at which the player's productivity begins to decline. In the case of a guaranteed contract, as is typical in the MLB (which are all guaranteed) and the NBA (according to Penn (2011) about 90 percent of NBA contracts are guaranteed), the risk to the team of an injured, ageing, or otherwise underperforming player is borne by the team once the contract is signed (Penn, 2011). In contrast, only the signing bonus portion of NFL contracts is guaranteed. Combined with the short average career length in the NFL (3.5 years), professional football players' income security is far lower than their NBA or MLB counterparts (Porter, 2012). In the NHL, contracts are guaranteed, creating the same risk–reward dilemma as in MLB. Teams must offer lucrative long-term contracts to players to attract talent, but then also bear the resulting risk of decreased productivity and injury. Interestingly, maximum contract lengths are set in the NHL as part of the CBA. By capping the maximum contract length at seven years (eight if re-signing with the same team), the teams reduce risk at the back end of the contract. While employed at the individual team level, the structure that creates this limit is set at the league level with the player association.

EMPIRICAL EVIDENCE

Since professional sports are blessed with an abundance of performance and pay data and detailed knowledge about contract parameters, there is a large and growing literature on the incentives provided by the long-term contracts of professional athletes. That literature, however, presents a very mixed picture. The typical study examines a player's performance either in the season immediately following the signing of a new long-term contract, or in the player's last season of an existing contract. Shirking is inferred if a player's performance falls off in the year following the new contract. While some studies have found evidence of shirking after a player signs a long-term contract (Marburger, 2003; Scoggins, 1993; Stiroh, 2007), others have not (Krautmann, 1990; Maxcy, 1997; Maxcy, Kratmann, & Fort, 2002). Further adding to the confusion is a series of papers which find conflicting evidence of shirking depending on the methodology used to study the phenomenon (Barth, 2013; Berri & Krautmann, 2006; Krautmann & Donley, 2009). More recently, Perry (2006), Krautmann and Solow (2009), and Congdon-Hohman and Lanning (2013) also find strong evidence that players' performance responded positively to impending free-agent contract negotiations. Sorting out the offsetting incentive effects of guaranteed pay and impending contract renewal are critical to explaining some of the confusion in the empirical shirking literature; a finding that athletes do not shirk may be explained by a true lack of effect or the confluence of strong but opposing incentives.

Conlin (1999) focuses on information asymmetries in the negotiation process and finds evidence of a separating equilibrium in the NFL. Particularly relevant for our discussion here is his finding that higher quality players engage in longer contract negotiations that result in more lucrative contracts. The empirical model was estimated using data from before the institution of rookie wage scale salaries set by draft order that effectively ended the practice of protracted holdouts by rookies. As discussed above, recent changes that, as of 2011, instituted draft slotted salaries work to insulate teams against the risk associated with holdouts.

Maxcy (2004) finds that high performing players in MLB are more likely to have long-term contracts and that as market power shifts from the team to the player (as he or she approaches and attains free-agent status) the probability of a long-term contract increases significantly. As Maxcy notes, this implies that teams are more willing under such circumstances to offer long-term contracts to protect against the risk of losing a highly productive player with a strong upside potential. These results are consistent with Kahn (1993), who found that players who were free agents or in their last year of arbitration eligibility "appear to 'spend' their greater bargaining power" on longer guaranteed contracts (p. 163).

Given the dramatic changes in the institutional arrangements in recent collective bargaining, we see much fertile ground for future empirical work. Reconsiderations of the important work of Maxcy, Conlin, and others will have the benefit of changes in the landscape across CBAs.

CONCLUDING REMARKS

Sports leagues provide a great opportunity to develop and test economic models in labor, industrial organization, game theory, and other fields of economics. They have an abundance of data, and a great deal is often known about the institutional details of the markets involved. Once the analyst begins to look beneath the surface, however, it becomes clear that, as always, the devil is in the details. The markets for athletic talent in professional sports are remarkably idiosyncratic in their institutional features. They involve multiple levels of bargaining, with the outcome of the bargain between the league and the players' union determining the contract space within which individual players can bargain with individual teams, and the former can and do differ greatly from sport to sport. These outcomes in turn color the latter negotiations. As a result, players in some cases are bargaining for guaranteed salaries while in others they are negotiating for salaries that will be conditioned on measurable indicators of performance. Some are negotiating for a guaranteed term of contract while others are uncertain whether they will still be employed in the subsequent year. Some teams are negotiating under constraints on aggregate spending, while others are not. The end results have important implications for incentives, performance, and risk bearing. Accordingly, it is difficult to draw overarching conclusions, but the door is open for further analysis that provides a richer and deeper understanding of bargaining, incentives, and performance.

NOTES

1. There is an extensive literature on the economics of implicit contracts, which we do not review here. Interested readers might begin with reading Sherwin Rosen's 1985 survey in the *Journal of Economic Literature* (Rosen, 1985).
2. See Edward P. Lazear (1986). Several authors have investigated the shirking hypothesis in sports labor markets. We do not review that literature here, but interested readers should see, for example, Krautmann and Donley (2009) and Berri and Krautmann (2006) for examples of work in major league baseball and basketball.
3. The reserve clause was first used in Major League Baseball (MLB) in the 1880s. As originally construed, it effectively transferred all property rights to the players' services from the player to the team by preventing the player from negotiating with any other team, granting teams extensive monopsony power. Though it was limited by the advent of free agency in the 1970s, MLB, the NBA, the NHL and the NFL still restrict the movement of players when they enter the league.
4. Solow and Krautmann (2011) present a model of such bargaining when the player's threat point is determined by negotiating with a set of teams and each team's threat point is given by the value and cost of the best available alternative player.
5. According to Belzer (2013), agent fees are 3 percent in the NFL, 4 percent in the NHL or NBA and 5 percent in baseball. In some cases, maximum fees are set by rule, in others there is no maximum and agents can use fees to compete for players. Brandt (2012) states that in the NFL, agent fees may not exceed 3 percent and agents may charge "less than 1 percent to entice a player to sign."
6. There are a few relatively recent examples of attempts to determine if some agents are more productive than others. For example, see Berri, Leeds, and von Allmen (2015).
7. For examples of work in which the authors do specify a utility function, see Conlin (1999), Brown et al. (2006), Maxcy (2004), and Marburger (2003).
8. Our specification here is left in general form, intended to give the reader a sense of the important drivers of player utility. See Marburger (2003), Maxcy (2004) and Conlin (1999) for examples of empirical models derived from specific functional forms.
9. See Berri, Leeds, and von Allmen (2015) for a detailed explanation of the bargaining model. For readers interested in the transition of contract type that immediately followed the defeat of the reserve clause in MLB, Lehn (1982) contains an extensive discussion and analysis of the changes to the bargaining landscape.
10. For example, see Berri et al. (2005) for an exploration of this phenomenon in the NBA.
11. For an extensive discussion of this point, see Maxcy (2004).
12. For a more complete discussion on this point, see Scully (1995).
13. See Szymanski (2003) for an excellent review of much of this literature.
14. For examples of work on the impact of monopsony power on wages, see Scully (1974); Zimbalist (1992); Krautmann, von Allmen, and Berri (2009).
15. With thanks to Steve Walters and Ned Rice for this information.
16. For complete details on NHL bonus rules, see Exhibit 5 of the NHL CBA.
17. See question 64 in Coons (2014).
18. See Section VII(3)(b) in the NBA CBA.

REFERENCES

Barth, D. (2013), 'Estimating effort shirking with endogenous contract lengths', Hamilton College working paper, accessed 16 February 2016 at http://people.hamilton.edu/documents/BarthD_NBA_Effort_Shirking.pdf.

Belzer, J. (2013), 'The world's most powerful sports agents', accessed 31 July 2013 at http://www.forbes.com/sites/jasonbelzer/2013/07/31/the-worlds-most-powerful-sports-agents/.

Berri, D.A., S. Brook, B. Frick, A.J. Fenn, and R. Vicente-Mayoral (2005), 'The short supply of tall people: Competitive imbalance and the National Basketball Association', *Journal of Economic Issues*, **39** (4), 1029–1041.

Berri, D.A. and A.C. Krautmann (2006), 'Shirking on the court: Testing for the incentive effects of guaranteed pay', *Economic Inquiry*, **44** (3), 536–546.

Berri, D.A., M. Leeds, and P. von Allmen (2015), 'The distribution of economic rent in the NBA', *International Journal of Sport Finance*, **10** (1), 5–25.

Brandt, A. (2012), 'An agent's life isn't all glamour', accessed 12 November 2012 at *ESPN.com*.

Brandt, A. (2014), 'The new age of rookie contract negotiations', accessed 23 July 2014 at mmqb.si.com/2014/05/22/nfl-rookie-contract-negotiations/.

Breer, A. (2012), 'NFLPA says players have benefitted from new CBA', accessed 3 August 2012 at http://nfl.com/news/story/090000d5d8293f393/article/nflpa-says-players-have-benefitted-from-new-cba.

Brown, M. (2014), 'MLB's billion dollar TV deals, free agency, and why Robinson Cano's deal with The Mariners isn't "Crazy"', at Forbes.com at http://www.forbes.com/sites/maurybrown/2014/01/07/mlbs-billion-dollar-tv-deals-free-agency-and-why-robinson-canos-deal-with-the-mariners-isnt-crazy/.

Brown, S., L. Farrell, M.N. Harris, and J.G. Sessions (2006), 'Risk preference and employment contract type', *Journal of the Royal Statistical Society*, **169** (4), 849–863.

Burger, J.D. and S.J.K. Walters (2003), 'Market size pay and performance: A general model and application to Major League Baseball', *Journal of Sports Economics*, **4** (2), 108–125.

Congdon-Hohman, J. and J. Lanning (2013), 'Do workers change effort and output in response to incentives? Evidence from Major League Baseball', College of the Holy Cross Working Paper 1304.

Conlin, M. (1999), 'Empirical test of a separating equilibrium in National Football League contract negotiations', *Rand Journal of Economics*, **30** (2), 289–304.

Coons, L. (2014), 'NBA salary cap FAQ', accessed 25 July 2014 at http://www.cbafaq.com/salarycap.htm.

Holmstrom, B. and P. Milgrom (1991), 'Multitask principal–agent analyses: Incentive contracts, asset ownership, and job design', *Journal of Law, Economics, and Organization*, **7** (Special Issue: Papers from the Conference on the New Science of Organization, January 1991), 24–52.

Jessop, A. (2012), 'The structure of NBA contracts', accessed 28 June 2012 at http://www.forbes.com/sites/aliciajesop/2012/06/28/the-structure-of-nba-rookie-contracts/.

Kahn, L.M. (1993), 'Free agency, long-term contracts and compensation in Major League Baseball: Estimates from panel data', *Review of Economics and Statistics*, **75**, 157–164.

Krautmann, A.C. (1990), 'Shirking or stochastic productivity in Major League Baseball?', *Southern Economic Journal*, **56**, 961–968.

Krautmann, A.C. and T.C. Donley (2009), 'Shirking in Major League Baseball: Revisited', *Journal of Sports Economics*, **10** (3), 292–304.

Krautmann, A.C. and J.L. Solow (2009), 'The dynamics of performance over the duration of Major League Baseball long-term contracts', *Journal of Sports Economics*, **10** (1), 6–22.

Krautmann, A.C., P. von Allmen, and D. Berri (2009), 'The underpayment of restricted players in North American sports leagues', *International Journal of Sport Finance*, **4**, 75–93.

Lazear, E. (1986), 'Salaries and piece rates', *Journal of Business*, **59** (3), 405–431.

Lehn, K. (1982), 'Property rights, risk sharing, and player disability in Major League Baseball', *Journal of Law and Economics*, **25**, 273–279.

Marburger, D.R. (2003), 'Does the assignment of property rights encourage or discourage shirking', *Journal of Sports Economics*, **4** (1), 19–34.

Maxcy, J. (1997), 'Do long-term contracts influence performance in Major League Baseball?', in W. Hendricks (ed.), *Advances in the Economics of Sport*, Greenwich, CT, USA: JAI Press, pp. 157–176.

Maxcy, J. (2004), 'Motivating long-term employment contracts: Risk management in Major League Baseball', *Managerial Decision Economics*, **25**, 109–120.

Maxcy, J., A.C. Krautmann, and R. Fort (2002), 'The effectiveness of incentive mechanisms in Major League Baseball', *Journal of Sports Economics*, **3** (3), 246–255.

Merriam Webster online dictionary (2014), accessed 12 July 2014 at http://eee.merriam-webster.com/dictionary/remuneration.

NFL (2012), 'NFL clubs approve comprehensive agreement', 21 July 2011, updated 26 July 2012, at http://www.nfl.com/news/story/09000d5d820e6311/article/nfl-clubs-approve-comprehensive-agreement.

NFL–NFLPA Collective Bargaining Agreement (2011), accessed 8 November 2014 at http://nfllabor.files.wordpress.com/2010/01/collective-bargaining-agreement-2011-2020.pdf.

NHL (2013), *NHL/NHLPA Proposed CBA – Summary of Terms, January 12, 2013*, at http://www.nhl.com/nhl/en/v3/ext/CBA2012/NHL_NHLPA_Proposed_CBA_-_Summary_of_Terms_FINAL_-_Jan._12,_2013%20(1).pdf.

NHLPA (2012), 'Collective bargaining agreement between the National Hockey League and the National Hockey League Players' Association – September 16, 2012–September 15, 2022', accessed 25 July 2014 at www.nhl.com/nhl/en/V3/ext/CBA2012/NHL_NHLPA_2013_CBA.pdf.

Penn, T. (2011), 'NBA players have the best deal', accessed 3 November 2011 at http://espn.go.com/espn/commentary/story/_/id/7181583/even-concessions-nba-players-best-deal-pro-athletes.

Perry, D. (2006), 'When does a pitcher earn an earned run?', in Jonah Keri (ed.), *Baseball between the Numbers*, New York, NY, USA: Basic Books.

Porter, A. (2012), 'How far does an NFL contract really go?', accessed 21 February 2012 at http://bleacherreport.com/articles/1074216-how-far-does-an-nfl-contract-really-go.

Rosen, S. (1985), 'Implicit contracts: A survey', *Journal of Economic Literature*, **23** (3), 1144–1175.

Rottenberg, S. (1956), 'The baseball players' labor market', *Journal of Political Economy*, **64**, 242–258.

Scoggins, J. (1993), 'Shirking or stochastic productivity in Major League Baseball: Comment', *Southern Economic Journal*, **60**, 239–240.

Scully, G. (1974), 'Pay and performance in Major League Baseball', *American Economic Review*, **64**, 915–930.

Scully, G. (ed.) (1995), *The Market Structure of Sports*, Chicago, IL, USA: University of Chicago Press.

Smith, M.D. (2011), 'Cam Newton, Panthers agree to four-year, $22 million contract', accessed 29 July 2011 at http://profootballtalk.nbcsports.com/2011/07/29/cam-newton-panthers-agree-to-four-year-22-million-contract/.

Solow, J. and A.C. Krautmann (2007), 'Leveling the playing field or just lowering salaries: The effects of redistribution in baseball', *Southern Economic Journal*, **73** (4), 947–958.

Solow, J. and A.C. Krautmann (2011), 'A Nash bargaining model of the salaries of elite free agents', *Journal of Sports Economics*, **12** (3), 309–316.

Sportrac (2015), 'Ryan Howard, Current Contract', accessed 23 April 2015 at http://www.spotrac.com/mlb/philadelphia-phillies/ryan-howard/.

Stiroh, K. (2007), 'Playing for keeps: Pay and performance in the NBA', *Economic Inquiry*, **45** (1), 145–161.

Szymanski, S. (2003), 'The economic design of sporting contests', *Journal of Economic Literature*, **41** (4), 1137–1187.

Volin, B. (2013), 'Now more than ever, we realize the NFL owners won', accessed 21 July 2013 at http://www.bostonglobe.com/sports/2013/07/20/nfl-owners-destroyed-players-cba-negotiations/ia3c1ydpS16H5FhFEiviHP/story.html.

Zimbalist, A. (1992), 'Salaries and performance: Beyond the Scully model', in Paul M. Sommers (ed.), *Diamonds Are Forever: The Business of Baseball*, Washington, DC, USA: Brookings Institute.

APPENDIX

salary	(*S*)
performance	(*p*)
talent	(*τ*)
effort	(*e*)
random variable	(*ε*)
probability of being paid	φ_t
year	*t*
discount factor	β
utility function	u_i
other benefits	(*B*)
value of the contract	*V*
length of the contract	(n)
wins	(*W*)
revenue	(*R*)
profits	(Π)
factors that affect revenues	Z_R
other costs beyond the team's salary bill	Z_C

4. Making sense of labor regulation in Major League Baseball: some insights from regulatory theory
*Matt Nichol**

INTRODUCTION

The business of professional baseball in the United States dates back to the 1870s, and the current business activities of Major League Baseball have now transformed it into a lucrative industry. For the first time, in 2013 Major League Baseball revenues were expected to exceed US$8 billion, representing a growth of 264 percent since 1994 (Brown, 2013). The underlying product that creates these astronomical revenues is the playing of a professional baseball game that involves the 30 Major League clubs. This chapter will focus on players, the workers who provide the spectacle of a Major League game of baseball.[1] Unionism and collective bargaining has seen the players enjoy a larger slice of the financial successes of baseball and negotiate many labor controls in Major League Baseball's Basic Agreement,[2] a collective agreement enforceable under the National Labor Relations Act of 1935 (NLRA).[3]

Collective bargaining saw the minimum wage of a Major League player rise to US$500 000 in 2014 (Basic Agreement 2012, article VI.A.(1)), while the average income of a Major League player is now US$3.44 million (CBS Sports, 2014). Baseball's elite players can receive contracts that exceed one hundred million dollars, as evidenced by the highest contract ever given to a pitcher, Clayton Kershaw's seven-year US$215 million contract with the Los Angeles Dodgers (Matsuzeweski, 2014). The growth in player salaries saw the total payroll for all Major League teams on Opening Day 2014 exceed US$3 billion, and the highest Opening Day payroll was the Dodgers' US$241 million (USA Today, 2014).

Major League Baseball's labor system raises two interrelated questions that form the basis of this chapter: how is the player labor of Major League Baseball regulated, and how does this regulatory system fit within general regulatory theory? The regulation of labor in Major League Baseball now operates in a modern world of regulation that encompasses a range of regulatory actors, who perform various regulatory activities and functions in what can be described as a regulatory terrain (Gahan & Brosnan, 2006,

p. 129), or regulatory space (Parker et al., 2004, p. 7). The composition of a regulatory terrain is fundamentally influenced by how the concept of regulation is constructed. Regulation can be viewed narrowly as a system of government endorsed rules, or expanded to cover all mechanisms of social control that influence behavior (Freiberg, 2010, pp. 2–3). Government rules are traditionally formulated as 'command and control' regulation, whereby the state identifies a social or economic problem that requires regulatory intervention through state sanctioned rules (Cooney, 2006, pp. 192–193). Non-compliance is punished by discretionary and non-discretionary penalties (Ayres & Braithwaite, 1995, p. 38). However, the expansion of the concept of regulation has seen an increase in the number of approaches to regulation, and now includes various models of self-regulation and meta-regulation (Baldwin et al., 2012, pp. 137–157). The result is the decentralization of the 'control' function of regulation and an increase in the number of private regulatory actors (Baldwin et al., 2012, p. 8).

Operating within this regulatory paradigm is the regulatory space of Major League Baseball. This chapter will analyze how the regulation of Major League Baseball has resulted in internal regulatory actors controlling the regulation of labor. These regulatory actors are the owners of Major League clubs, the league through the institution of Major League Baseball, the players and the players' labor union, the Major League Baseball Players Association (MLBPA). Since the emergence of the MLBPA in the late 1960s, these regulatory actors have negotiated the key aspects of Major League Baseball's current system of labor regulation through multiple rounds of collective bargaining agreements and a labor war that lasted nearly 30 years. The formal regulatory rules and processes of Major League Baseball's labor system are located in its constitution, internal rules and the current Major League Basic Agreement. These regulations are aptly described by Christine Parker et al. as intentional activity aimed at controlling, ordering or influencing the behavior of other people through the setting of standards, monitoring compliance and enforcement (Parker et al., 2004, p. 1). Yet baseball's internal regulatory system does not operate without external influence and, as will be seen, interacts with the external regulation of courts and the state.

Understanding the regulation of labor in Major League Baseball is important due to the size of its combined Major and Minor League workforce, its status, the standard of competition and the high remuneration received by players. The system of labor sees Major League clubs contract over 9000 players to play in both the Major and Minor Leagues, in turn creating the world's largest professional baseball labor market. How labor is regulated in this complex system influences the working life of thousands of professional athletes, and its regulatory practices influence other major professional sports in the United States and foreign professional baseball leagues. This chapter aims to enhance the understanding of labor regulation in Major League Baseball by drawing on general theories of regulation and literature on the nature and function of labor law, thereby allowing an assessment of how the regulation of labor in Major League Baseball sits within general practice and the relevant literature.

This chapter will start by establishing a framework of labor regulation in Major League Baseball by examining the labor system's structure, key regulations and regulatory actors. In order to provide a complete picture of this regulatory landscape, Part B will examine how Major League Baseball regulates and controls the labor supply of professional baseball in North America through an analysis of the regulation of labor in the Minor Leagues. Part C will then assess Major League Baseball's labor system by applying regulatory theory and labor law literature. This chapter will conclude by drawing on these theories to examine how the historical interaction between Major League Baseball's internal and external regulatory actors has influenced its system of labor regulation.

A. THE REGULATION OF LABOR IN MAJOR LEAGUE BASEBALL

Professional baseball can be differentiated from the ranks of amateur baseball and semi-professional baseball. Inside the labor system of Major League Baseball operates a classification system that gives the National League and American League the status of Major Leagues, and lower level affiliated leagues the status of Minor Leagues. Part A will analyze how Major League Baseball's labor system is internally regulated through formal rules and other relevant regulatory practices.

The Structure of Major League Baseball

The 30 Major League clubs are located in large cities across the United States (and Toronto in Canada) (Figure 4.1). Fifteen clubs compete in both the National League and the American League. Each league is then separated into three geographic divisions: East, Central and West (Major League Constitution, article VIII, section 1; Major League Rules, rule 1 and attachment 52). The Major League Rules[4] allocate each club a geographic territory for their home stadium and operations (Major League Rules, rule 1 and attachment 52). Spring training commences in February and the 162-game regular season starts

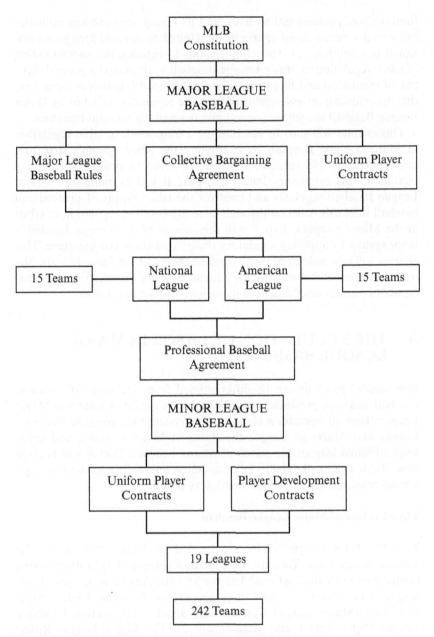

Figure 4.1   The structure of Major League Baseball

at the beginning of April and ends in September when the multi-round playoff series starts. The season officially ends with the conclusion of the World Series Championship in October (Major League Constitution, article IX). Therefore, a Major League Baseball player works as a professional baseball player for between seven and nine months a year, and some players participate in winter leagues in Mexico, Venezuela, Australia and throughout the Caribbean.

The Major League Constitution[5] is an agreement that binds the owners of all 30 Major League clubs (Major League Constitution, article I), who are now comprised of a mix of wealthy individuals, consortiums of wealthy individuals and corporations (Nathanson, 2010, pp. 603–609). Even though the Major League Constitution was introduced in 1921, the American and National Leagues continued to formally operate as separate legal entities until their merger in 2000 (Broshius, 2013, p. 59). Under the Major League Constitution, Major League Baseball's executive governance structure consists of the Office of the Commissioner of Baseball and the Executive Council (Major League Constitution, articles II and III). As the chief executive officer, the Commissioner of Baseball is appointed by the clubs (Major League Constitution, article II, section 9) and enjoys broad regulatory powers by being required to administer the league in the best interests of baseball. In addition, the Commissioner has executive responsibility for labor relations (Major League Constitution, article II, section 2) and general administrative matters through the maintenance of the Major League Regulations (Major League Constitution, article XI, section 3).

The Labor of a Major League Baseball Club

A game of baseball has nine specialized positions on the field.[6] Each player has a fixed position in the batting lineup and the American League allows a designated hitter to bat for the pitcher. The entire workforce of a Major League club is comprised of 'reserved' players on the 40-man roster, also known as the 'reserve list' (Figure 4.2). Reserving a player permits a club to control the contractual rights to players for a period of six years of service (Major League Rules, rule 2(a)(b)(1)(A)). From the 40-man roster an active roster of 25 players is selected to play in official games (Major League Rules, rule 2(c)(2)(A)). The remaining 15 players are assigned to a Minor League club until at least 1 September. Thus, 750 players make up the entire workforce in Major League Baseball, and each season the total Major League workforce can increase to a maximum of 1200 players when rosters may be expanded to a maximum of 40 players after 1 September (Major League Rules, rule 2(c)(2)(A)). The active and reserve

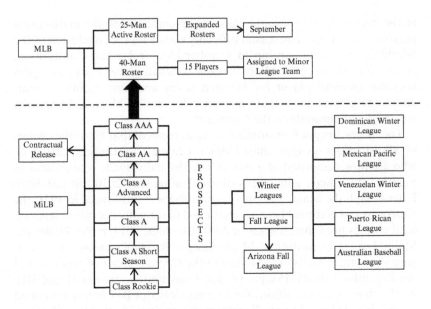

Figure 4.2   Major League Baseball's labor system

rosters also serve the purpose of establishing the membership of the bargaining unit for the purposes of collective bargaining (Basic Agreement 2012, article II), a group that continues to diversify as 28 percent of Major League players were born outside the United States in 2012 (ESPN, 2012).

The Major League labor system functions to allow clubs to add and remove players from its active roster and reserve list. Roster changes may be in response to the immediate or long-term needs of the active roster, and relevant factors include injury, poor performance, personnel requirements, the playoff race, the availability of a player from a rival club, or more recently, for the purposes of roster management. An internal method of meeting such needs is to utilize a club's Minor League labor by recalling a player on the 40-man roster or selecting the contract of a non-rostered player. Alternatively, a Major League club can obtain labor externally by trading Major or Minor League players (or cash), or a combination of players, to another Major League club in exchange for a player or cash. During the course of a 162-game season, over a period of six months, a Major League club makes hundreds of roster transactions, producing a labor system across all 30 Major League clubs that annually produces thousands of roster transactions.

The Modern Reserve System and Controlling Major League Baseball Labor

The reserve system is the cornerstone of Major League Baseball's labor regulation (Edmonds, 2012) and is contained in the regulatory matrix of the Major League Rules, the Basic Agreement 2012 and uniform player contracts. The modern reserve system gives a Major League club the right to reserve players contracted in both the Major and Minor Leagues. Players on a club's reserve list cannot transfer to another club unless they are traded, claimed by another club through Major League Baseball's internal contracting system, unconditionally released from their contract, or they become a free agent.[7]

The rules and procedures of the modern reserve system are now located in Article XX.A of the Basic Agreement 2012, which individual players agree to in the 'renewal' clause in paragraph 10(a) of the Major League Uniform Player's Contract.[8] Unless a contracted player qualifies as a free agent, on or before 2 December each year a club can retain the reservation rights to a player by tendering a contract to a player for the following year. If the parties do not agree to a contract before 2 March, the club can renew the contract for one year on the same terms as the previous contract, except in regards to salary. Thus, until the player becomes a free agent after six years of service, the Major League club can renew a player's contract from year to year (Major League Uniform Player's Contract 2012, paragraph 10(a)). Once both parties sign a contract, the contract is sent to the Commissioner's Office for approval, and upon the Commissioner approving the contract, the contract becomes valid (Basic Agreement 2012, p. 288). The role of the Commissioner is necessary to protect against cheating and other undesirable practices that may arise in a system of self-regulation.

Labor Controls and the Salary System in Major League Baseball

The United States Court of Appeal, in describing the internal regulation of salaries in American professional sport, states that 'a mix of free agency and reserve clauses combined with other provisions is the universal method by which leagues and player unions set individual salaries in professional sports'.[9] Free agents are excluded from the renewal clause, and it is a status given to players that was first recognized as a formal right in salary arbitration in 1975, when arbitrator Peter Seitz rejected the long-held argument of owners that the reserve clause operated in perpetuity.[10] Serving the six-year qualification period to become a free agent[11] extinguishes a club's right to reserve a player and allows the player to negotiate a contract with any club. In certain circumstances a player's new club must provide compensation to the player's former club (Basic Agreement 2012, article XX.B.(4)), leading some clubs to trade for pending free agents to obtain a draft selection as compensation.[12] The operation of contract procedures in the Basic Agreement also gives a player free agent status if the club or player terminates the contract, the club fails to tender the player a contract or renew the contract by the deadline, or if a player's contract is assigned outright by the club (Basic Agreement 2012, article XX.A.(2)(3)).

In Major League Baseball player salaries are influenced by whether a player is a reserve player, arbitration eligible or a free agent. Reserve players have little Major League experience, are usually in their first three years of Major League service and typically earn the collectively bargained minimum wage of US$500000 (Basic Agreement 2012, article VI.A.). Some clubs provide incremental wage increases to players in their second and third years in the Major Leagues. Arbitration eligible players use the uncertainty of salary arbitration to negotiate salaries closer to market value. The Basic Agreement governs eligibility for salary disputes, and arbitration eligible players generally require between three and six years of Major League service. Some players qualify after two years as 'super two' players if they meet specific active roster service requirements (Basic Agreement 2012, article VI.E.(1)(a)(b)). The arbitral system in Major League Baseball is called 'final offer' arbitration, where the player and the club each submit a salary for the player and the arbitrators choose one of the offers (Primm, 2010, pp. 87–88). Finally, free agent players can negotiate their salary on the market, and most of these players choose their employer for the first time in their professional baseball career.

Trading and Assigning Players: Major League Baseball's Internal Contract System

The interconnected regulations of the Major League Rules, the Basic Agreement and the Major League Uniform Player's Contract govern the movement of labor in Major League Baseball. Underpinning the movement of labor between clubs is the right of clubs to assign a Major League player's contract to another club (Major League Rules, rule 9). An assignment is usually called a trade because players are traded from one team to another. Multiple clubs and players (as well as cash) may be involved in a transaction, even players to be named in the future. Players agree to this system when they sign the Major League Uniform Player's Contract, and can negotiate to limit or eliminate this right by special covenant (Major League Uniform Player's Contract 2012, paragraph 6(a)).

However, the Basic Agreement restricts the rights of clubs to assign the contract of two types of veteran players. Clubs must receive a player's written consent to assign a contract if the player has five or more years of Major League service. For players with ten or more years of Major League service, the last five being with the one club, clubs also require the player's written consent to assign his contract. But if such a player waives his right to prevent assignment of his contract when entering a multi-year contract, he can use the '10–5' rule and negotiate a 'no-trade' clause that designates a maximum of 16 clubs that his contract can be assigned to (Basic Agreement 2012, article XIX.A.(1)(2); Major League Rules, rule 9(d)(e)).

Trading Players and the Waiver System

In addition to the assignment system, player movement also occurs through the waiver system (Major League Rules, rule 10) and the use of different types of assignment waivers. The operation of the waiver system determines a club's current and future rights to reserve a player and the ability of a player to work in the Major Leagues. The product of the waiver system is an internal contracting system that regulates the movement of labor within a Major League club and also allows workers to move to one of the other 29 Major League clubs. Central to this system is an 'optional assignment waiver', which allows a player on the active roster to be optioned to a Minor League club, while the Major League club retains the right to recall the player (Major League Rules, rule 10(a)(4)). Clubs can exercise three options on a player without forfeiting their right to reserve the player (Major League Rules, rule 10(3)(A)(B)). But creating a position on the active or 40-man roster may require moving a player from the 40-man roster who has no remaining options. In such cases the player must be designated for assignment, a decision which involves substantial risk as the player's contract can be claimed by any other Major League club during the ten-day waiver period. Unclaimed players are either assigned to a Minor League club or unconditionally released (Major League Rules, rule 2(k)).

A similar waiver process exists for players who are unconditionally released (Major League Rules, rule 10(a)(5)) or have their contract assigned 'outright' to a Minor League club (Major League Rules, rule 10(a)(5)(b)(2)). Furthermore, 'trade assignment waivers' facilitate the trading of players during the trade period from 31 July to the end of the season (Major League Rules, rule 10(a)(2)(b)(1)). The Major League Rules outline the general procedures for waivers and for specific types of waivers (Major League Rules, rule 10(c)). Not only does the waiver system allow clubs to move players to Major and Minor League clubs, it prevents

Major League clubs from stockpiling young talent and peripheral Major League players.

Enforcing the Major League Baseball Labor System

Players contracted by Major League clubs who breach the internal labor rules and attempt to play for another professional club face two punitive penalties. All Major League players agree in their uniform contract to allow their club to obtain an injunction (not damages for breach of contract) to prevent transfers that violate the labor controls in the contract and the Major League Rules (Basic Agreement 2012, article 4(a)). In addition, a player's right to work in professional baseball is denied as clubs place players on a 'blacklist', an enforcement mechanism that is strengthened via the 'tampering prohibition', a rule that requires clubs to receive the express written consent from a player's club to negotiate the present or future employment of a reserved player (Major League Rules, rule 3(k); Kurlantzick, 2009).

Unionism in Major League Baseball and the National Labor Relations Act

Unionism in Major League Baseball has played a central role in the evolution of the internal system of labor regulation. Major League players formed a number of short-lived labor unions in 1885, 1914 and 1946, but unionization did not take root in Major League Baseball until the establishment of the MLBPA in 1954. Major League labor regulation would forever be influenced by the union's decision in 1966 to appoint Marvin Miller, a former steel industry union economist and negotiator, as chief executive officer. Miller educated players on their rights as workers and, most importantly, actively used the protections and procedures of American labor law. The MLBPA negotiated Major League Baseball's first collective bargaining agreement in 1968, which included arbitration to deal with grievances, minimum salaries and pension payments. Then, in 1969, the National Labor Relations Board (NLRB), the statutory body responsible for administering and enforcing the NLRA, held that baseball's antitrust exemption (to be examined below) did not extend to labor law as Congress intended the NLRA to apply to the labor of Major League Baseball.[13]

Part of Miller's legacy was his use of the NLRA to secure legislative protections for the operation of Major League Baseball's player labor system. The NLRA gives workers the rights to organize and join unions, and prohibits employees and employers from engaging in unfair labor practices (NLRA 1935, sections 7 & 8). American courts have held that the NLRA requires collective bargaining on 'mandatory subjects',[14] and therefore players and owners must negotiate on matters such as wages and hours. Collective bargaining also involves 'permissive subjects' of bargaining, like individual bargaining rights and salary arbitration, but parties are not obligated to negotiate on such matters.[15] However, the NLRA is unable to protect all players employed by Major League clubs. Collective bargaining in Major League Baseball only covers the work of current and future Major League players, and excludes Minor League players (Basic Agreement 2012, article I). The MLBPA is the sole and exclusive bargaining unit for current and future Major League players (Basic Agreement 2012, article II). The Basic Agreement gives players the right to appoint a player agent, accredited by MLBPA, to negotiate salary and special covenants in their uniform contract (Basic Agreement 2012, article IV).

Regulatory Actors

Internal regulatory actors dominate the regulation of labor in Major League Baseball and include Major and Minor League clubs, players, the MLBPA, the institution of Major League Baseball and the Office of the Commissioner of Baseball. These regulatory actors have enforcement agents, or 'street level bureaucrats', who give the system of labor regulation idiosyncrasies when using discretion to enforce regulation (Piore, 2011, pp. 389–390). Internal enforcement agents include a team's manager, coaches, the general manager, front office staff, scouts, and the baseball operations and labor relations departments in Major League Baseball. Not only are internal regulatory actors involved in creating and enforcing regulations, they can also be the target of regulations, for example, players and clubs.

Major League Baseball's internal regulatory system of labor also engages with external regulatory actors, traditionally, the state and the courts. Although rare in Major League Baseball, the state can use statute to directly regulate labor. The most common method of state regulation in Major League Baseball is through labor law by way of the NLRA and the NLRB. Likewise, courts tend to sit on the outer periphery of the regulation of labor in baseball. But the enforcement of law by the courts, and even the threat of litigation by internal stakeholders or legislative intervention by the state, possesses regulatory force in this system of labor regulation. Labor relations in professional sport now include another important regulatory actor, player agents, who are governed by the MLBPA (MLBPA, 2010) and perform the roles of identifying potential clubs for players and negotiating a player's salary and duration of employment.

B.   MAJOR LEAGUE BASEBALL'S LABOR SUPPLY

Major League clubs source the majority of their labor from the Minor Leagues, a hierarchical structure of leagues classified on the general standard of competition. Most players contracted by Major League clubs are assigned to a Minor League club. Major League clubs use the Minor Leagues for player development, to identify prospective Major League players, and to provide training and games for rostered Major League players who are either not on the active roster or returning from injury.

The Contractual Relationship between Major and Minor League Baseball

Players signed to a Minor League contract by Major League clubs play in the network of Minor Leagues spread across the United States under the umbrella organization of the National Association of Professional Baseball Leagues (NAPBL), commonly known as Minor League Baseball or MiLB (Major League Rules, attachment 52). The Professional Baseball Agreement (incorporated into the Major League Rules) governs the relationship between the NAPBL, Major League Baseball and the respective member clubs. The relationship between a Major League club and its Minor League clubs is set out in rule 56 of the Major League Rules and an agreement between the two clubs called the Player Development Contract (PDC) (Major League Rules, rule 56, attachment 56). As most Minor League clubs are independently owned (Smith, 2013), the majority of Major and Minor League clubs enter a PDC. Thus Minor League Baseball is commonly referred to as 'affiliated baseball', and is distinguished from the independent professional baseball leagues (Independent Professional Baseball Federation, 2014).

Under the Major League Rules, Major League clubs must maintain the player lists for all of their Minor League clubs, and are the exclusive source of players, managers, coaches and trainers for their Minor League affiliates. Major League clubs can transfer players through their network of clubs, a power derived from their right to direct, transfer or assign a player, and the player's contract, to any team in its Minor League system, a Major League club or a winter league club (Major League Rules, rule 56(g)(3)). Players formally consent to this system by signing the Minor League Uniform Player's Contract[16] (Minor League Uniform Contract 2008, paragraph XVII). In exchange for controlling the key personnel decisions of a Minor League club, Major League clubs are responsible for the salaries of these workers (Major League Rules, rule 56(a)(g)).

The Minor League Labor System

The Minor League network is comprised of 242 clubs that compete in 19 leagues, and has over 7000 players. The Minor Leagues are commonly described as a 'farm system' as each year the annual crop is cut, and then harvested, producing the fertilizer to grow the next year's talent. To obtain a position on a Major League 40-man roster, most Minor League players must progress through a series of hierarchically structured Minor League teams. These teams are in various leagues that are classified as Class Rookie, Class Short-Season A, Class A, Class A-Advanced, Class AA and Class AAA (Major League Rules, rule 51(a)). Major League clubs generally maintain a network of seven or eight Minor League teams, consisting of over 200 contracted players (Broshius, 2013, p. 62). Reserve lists for teams range from 35 players at Class Rookie to 38 players at Class AAA (Major League Rules, rules 2(b)(1)(B)–(E)), and active rosters are made up of between 24 and 35 players (Major League Rules, rule 2(c)(2)(B)–(F)). Some 'prospects' may be invited to instructional leagues like the prestigious Arizona Fall League, or offered an opportunity to play in affiliated winter leagues in Latin America or Australia (Major League Rules, rule 18(a)).[17] All players are contractually required to maintain 'first class' physical condition (Minor League Uniform Contract 2008, paragraph XII).

Major League clubs are permitted to reserve a Minor League player for seven years (Major League Rules, attachment 3; Minor League Uniform Contract 2008, paragraph VI.A.). One year of Minor League service is credited as 30 days on a Minor League club's active or disabled lists (Major League Rules, rule 5(b)(1)), and Minor League free agents may sign a Minor or Major League contract with any Major League club. As a dual system of Minor and Major League free agency exists, if a player makes a Major League roster, the free agency qualification period begins again. Consequently the 30 Major League clubs use the reserve system to control the labor of over 7000 non-unionized workers. Exacerbating the effects of a non-unionized workforce is the high percentage of foreign Minor League players: 46 percent of Minor League players are born outside the United States, many of whom are from non-English speaking countries in Latin America (ESPN, 2012).[18]

One in ten contracted players in the farm system will make a Major League roster, and of these players, 1 in 50 will play more than six years of Major League Baseball (Szuchman, 1996, p. 281). William Gould analogizes a player's progression through the Minor Leagues to an apprenticeship, an apprenticeship that almost every current Major League player has served (Gould, 2013, p. 7). For Major League clubs the operation of a

Minor League system is expensive and, at minimum, represents an annual cost of US$20 million (Zimbalist, 2010, p. 23).

The Recruitment of Minor League Players

Major League clubs select amateur players in the United States, Canada and Puerto Rico in the 40 rounds of the Major League Rule 4 draft. Eligible players must be in high school, college or junior college, and include foreign students. Clubs can sign undrafted players (Major League Rules, rule 3(a)(2)(3), 4(a)(b)(i)), while international amateurs are signed as non-drafted international free agents. In an effort to regulate the rapid growth in international scouting, the Basic Agreement 2012 established an International Talent Committee to explore the introduction of an internal amateur Major League draft and implemented a signing bonus and taxation system for international players. In a designated signing period, clubs who exceed their allocated signing bonus pool are taxed an amount of money and lose the ability to sign amateurs for designated signing bonuses in the next signing period, both of which are calculated by the amount they exceed their allotment (Basic Agreement, 2012, attachment 46, article II.A).

Professional players represent a small percentage of the total number of foreign players recruited in the Major and Minor Leagues. These players transfer through protocols contained in private agreements that Major League Baseball has with Nippon Professional Baseball (NPB), the Korean Baseball Organization (KBO), the Chinese Professional Baseball League in Taiwan and the Mexican League (Major League Rules, rule 18(f)(g)(h); Basic Agreement 2012, attachment 46,I. D.10, 11). Also, some professional players defect from Cuba to pursue a career in Major League Baseball.

The rights of young entry-level players are formed when they sign a uniform Minor League contract (Major League Rules, attachment 3). A drafted player must sign a contract, or sit out of professional baseball for 12 months until the next draft (Major League Rules, rule 4(a)(h)). Most draftees and international amateurs are presented with a 'take it or leave it offer', a system reinforced by the new Rule 4 Draft taxation system on signing bonuses. Each draft selection in the first ten rounds is allocated a signing bonus, and, in 2014, the overall number one draft selection was allotted a bonus of US$7.9 million. The signing bonuses for the first 56 draft selections in the first three rounds was not less than US$1 million, and selections in round ten were allotted signing bonuses of US$100 000 (Baseball America, 2014). The draft therefore creates a Minor League system that consists of a few rich players called 'bonus babies', while the majority of players drafted in the later rounds receive signing bonuses between US$1000 and US$2500 and are labeled 'penniless players' (Broshuis, 2013, pp. 63–64).

The Minor League Wage System

Major League Baseball recommends to its clubs the wages for Minor League players, and players only receive income during the course of the season (Minor League Uniform Contract 2008, paragraph VI.B.). The monthly salary for each Minor League classification is set out in a player's uniform contract (Minor League Uniform Contract 2008, addendum C). Incomes start at approximately US$1100 per month for Class Rookie and Short-Season A, increase to US$1250 per month at Class A, then US$1500 per month at Class AA, and peak at US$2150 per month at Class AAA.[19] Many Minor League players in the lower leagues earn less than US$7500 per year, and some earn as little as US$3000.[20] Players with previous Major League experience or who are on a 40-man roster earn a Minor League minimum wage of US$81500 (Basic Agreement 2012, article VI.A.(2)). Therefore, Minor League players who receive a large signing bonus may need to use this money to supplement their income during the season and in the offseason.

The Minor League system of wages largely exists due to the exemption of Minor League labor from American antitrust law created by the Curt Flood Act of 1998[21] and the non-unionization of Minor League workers. The inequities inherent in the Minor League labor system are being aired by a number of former Minor League players, who in 2014 filed a class action against Major League Baseball and their respective former Major League clubs in the United States District Court (Matter, 2014; Rothman, 2014). The plaintiffs claim that their employment in the Minor Leagues breached the federal minimum wage and overtime provisions in the Fair Labor Standards Act (FLSA),[22] and that the unpaid training they performed in the offseason breached the labor laws of the state of their residence.[23] The financial threat posed by this action has seen Minor League Baseball begin to lobby Congress for a statutory exemption from the FLSA for Minor League teams (Leventhal, 2014).

Regulatory Actors in Minor League Baseball

The Minor Leagues greatly expand the number of regulatory actors identified in Part A and add complexity to the internal regulation of labor in Major League Baseball. These additional internal regulatory actors include over 242 clubs, 19 Minor Leagues, the NAPBL and over 7000 non-unionized players, many of whom are represented by agents. Intrinsically shaping the regulatory activities of these internal actors are the external regulatory activities of Major League Baseball and its 30 clubs.

C.   THE LABOR OF MAJOR LEAGUE BASEBALL AND REGULATORY THEORY

The Function of Modern Regulation

Major League Baseball's regulation of labor is an example of the growing complexity and multidisciplinary regulatory approach experienced in mainstream regulation. Based on the intended effect of regulation on the behavior of a regulatory target, Robert Baldwin et al. (2012) classify regulation based on its purpose as 'red light' or 'green light' regulation. Red light regulation restricts or prohibits certain types of behavior and, naturally, green light regulation promotes or facilitates certain behavior (Baldwin et al., 2012, pp. 2–3). Many of the labor regulations examined in this chapter possess elements of the green light function. For example, a reserve list allows a club to maintain lists of protected players under contract. But when viewed as part of the entire system of Major League labor controls, the reserve list operates with the active list, the right of assignment, waivers and free agency, to produce a distinctly red light system of labor regulation designed to control the mobility and cost of labor.

Identifying the general functions of regulation raises the question of who performs the regulatory function. Gahan and Brosnan (2006) answer this question by identifying the common models of regulation as direct regulation by the state, indirect regulation by the state and non-state regulation (Gahan & Brosnan, 2006, p. 132). The above analysis of labor in Major League Baseball demonstrates that the state sometimes directly intervenes in the regulation of Major League labor through the regulatory activities of the NLRB. Part C will explore the state's indirect regulation of labor in Major League Baseball via Congress, and even the President of the United States. The regulation of labor by Major League Baseball's internal regulators can be classed as non-state regulation, that is, all forms of social or economic influence (Baldwin et al., 2012, p. 3). The interaction between the internal and external regulation of labor in Major League can be viewed through a 'multifocal regulatory lens', and as this chapter will now highlight, the lens can be adjusted to narrowly examine baseball's internal regulators or, more broadly, to examine external modes of regulation (Parker et al., 2004, pp. 2–7).

Regulatory Theory and Labor Regulation

In order to examine regulatory theory and the regulation of Major League labor, it is necessary to establish a construct of labor regulation. The labor regulatory paradigm has involved a major structural transition in recent decades, shifting from the traditional 'standard employment relationship' of full-time, ongoing employment that emanated in the years after World War II (Tham, 2007, pp. 123–125) to new flexible forms of work. The fundamental form and function of this new paradigm is interconnected with external developments like globalization, technology, privatization and the general weakening of unions (Hartog, 2002, p. 830). The changing nature of work and employment practices has resulted in labor law scholars like Richard Mitchell and Christopher Arup expanding the scope of labor law beyond the narrow parameters of the power imbalance between employee and employer.

Mitchell and Arup (2006) promote the 'law of labour market regulation', a regulatory paradigm that recasts the 'employee' as a 'worker', or an 'active labour market participant', a person who moves through periods of unemployment and unpaid work through the course of their life, and a suitable description of the work life of a professional baseball player. The 'workplace' is expanded to the 'world of work' (Mitchell & Arup, 2006, pp. 3–4) and aptly describes the world of Major Leagues, Minor Leagues, winter leagues, player drafts and trades. The world of work is an interdisciplinary world comprised of 'hard' and 'soft' law regulatory techniques (Howe, 2011, p. 299) that, in the context of baseball, allows the identification of 'hard' regulations in the Major League Rules, Basic Agreement and uniform contracts, and the 'soft' regulations of informal rules and normative practice on Major League fields and in clubhouses.

Autopoietic Systems of Labor Regulation

Autopoietic theories of law are useful for understanding how the system of labor regulation in Major League Baseball has evolved and developed. Teubner uses autopoietic theories of law to assess legal systems as analogous to political or economic systems, all of which are composed of self-constructed rules of internal order and operate as functional autonomous systems. Autopoietic systems of law involve the law reproducing itself by reference to its own structures and operations. In this regard, Teubner argues autopoietic systems are operationally closed, but cognitively open, as they respond to external factors and other autopoietic systems (Deakin & Rogowski, 2011, pp. 230–231).

Teubner's general theory of legal autopoiesis can be adapted to labor law and regulation. According to Deakin and Wilkinson, over time, societal and economic changes influence the form, operation and regulation of labor markets (Deakin & Wilkinson, 2005, p. 3). Ralf Rogowski expands this construct of autopoiesis to include modern sociological systems theory and post-structuralist approaches to law, thereby creating a reflexive theory of labor law where self-referencing and self-production produces an autopoietic system of labor law that attempts to protect its own autopoiesis (Deakin & Rogowski, 2011, p. 230; Rogowski & Wilthagen, 1994, pp. 6–7). Autopoietic theories can be applied to Major League Baseball.

Major League Baseball's Autopoietic System of Self-Regulation

Major League Baseball's autopoietic system of labor regulation can be categorized as an internal system of non-state regulation that involves voluntary self-regulation by an industry (Ayres & Braithwaite, 1995, pp. 101–102). Over time this system has been implicitly and explicitly endorsed by the regulatory actions of the government and the courts, providing an example of what Anthony Ogus argues is the lack of a clear dichotomy between public regulation and self-regulation. Ogus conceptualizes regulation on a spectrum based on a system's legislative constraints, the role of insiders and outsiders in performing the regulatory function, rules that may be voluntary, binding or codes of practice, and external accountability (Ogus, 1995, pp. 98–100). Systems of self-regulation can be criticized on the basis of insufficient public oversight, evaluation and accountability (Cooney, 2006, p. 195).

The criteria identified by Ogus in assessing a regulatory system places Major League Baseball at an extreme end of the regulatory spectrum. Over a number of decades, regulatory inaction by the state and courts has allowed a system of regulation to evolve that empowers baseball's internal regulatory actors with a high degree of autonomy and monopolistic power. The reluctance of these external regulators to directly intervene in baseball's labor system, as will be seen below, is intimately connected to the evolution of the modern system of labor regulation in Major League Baseball. The minimal role of external regulation encouraged, and promoted, the development of baseball's internal labor system as players (and eventually owners) used labor law mechanisms such as collective bargaining, leading to the gradual realignment of regulatory power between owners and players. The modern mix of regulations in the Major League

Rules, the Basic Agreement and uniform player contracts attempts to exclude or limit the ability of players and clubs to seek external regulatory intervention. In the event there is a challenge to the system, internal regulatory actors attempt to use labor law to validate baseball's labor control and practices.

Internal Enforcement of Major League Baseball's Autopoietic System of Labor Regulation

Modern approaches to regulation frequently utilize an 'enforcement pyramid'[24] and allow the effectiveness of a regulatory system to be assessed according to its level of responsiveness to the structure of an industry, the motivations of regulated actors and the objectives of regulated enterprises and unions. Enforcement pyramids adopt a 'tit-for-tat' approach to regulation whereby non-compliance results in the escalation of the state's response through the levels of the enforcement pyramid (Ayres & Braithwaite, 1995, pp. 4–5, 19).[25] An enforcement pyramid can be two-dimensional, or three-dimensional, if quasi-regulators such as unions operate alongside the state and the corporation (Baldwin & Black, 2008, p. 65).

The structure of the enforcement pyramid in Major League Baseball differs from the pyramids in the above theories in several ways. Notably, labor is regulated through a number of contracts that create a system of voluntary self-regulation. Therefore, the courts cast a shadow over Major League Baseball's enforcement pyramid due to the ever-present threat that players or clubs may challenge an agreement between player and club, or an agreement between clubs. Even though the role of the courts and government in this enforcement pyramid is typically passive, with direct regulation by the government reactive to regulatory activities within baseball, the threat that the courts can be used to determine the enforceability of the labor controls contained in the various contracts that regulate labor in Major League Baseball possesses a strong regulatory effect. Another important difference is the number of dimensions in the enforcement pyramid. Major League Baseball, Major League clubs, the NAPBL, Minor League clubs and the MLBPA all perform enforcement activities.

Perhaps the operation and enforcement of regulation in Major League Baseball more closely resembles risk-based regulation. This regulatory approach assesses the level of risk posed by a regulated person or firm to the regulator's objectives. In the case of professional baseball, the key labor risks are the free movement of labor and the unregulated price of labor. In risk-based regulation, regulatory resources are targeted at the highest risks, requiring ongoing evaluation of new regulatory risks and challenges (Baldwin & Black, 2008, pp. 66–67). Collective bargaining in Major League Baseball allows risks to be identified and targeted at the end of the term of each bargaining agreement.

D.   THE EVOLUTION OF MAJOR LEAGUE BASEBALL'S AUTOPOIETIC SYSTEM OF LABOR REGULATION

So far this chapter has examined the current regulation of labor in Major League Baseball and assessed this system using regulatory theory. This chapter will now examine how the interaction between internal and external regulation of labor in Major League Baseball has shaped the evolution of its autopoiesis. Key regulatory events in this regulatory interaction will now be examined.

The Reserve System, the Courts and Contract Law

As previously discussed, professional baseball's reserve system allows a club to protect a designated number of players from playing for another club through the reserve clause in a player contract and the maintenance of a reserve list. Arthur Soden created the reserve system in 1879, and as the system is designed to suppress wages, and control the movement of labor, it did not take long for the reserve system to create unrest among players (Edmonds, 2012, pp. 40–47). Supported by the National Brotherhood of Professional Base Ball Players, professional baseball's first union, players successfully challenged the reserve system using contract law in several cases in 1890. A number of American courts accepted the players' arguments that the reserve clause lacked fairness, mutuality and certainty, and that the agreements were the product of a power imbalance between player and club.[26]

The ability of players to use contract law to challenge the legality of the reserve system was short lived. In 1902, the Pennsylvania Supreme Court in *Philadelphia Ball Club v Lajoie*[27] applied the principles from the British case of *Lumley v Wagner*[28] to hold that the contract of a professional baseball player was a 'special contract of service' for an exclusive period of time. Instead of requiring specific performance, or awarding damages for breach of contract, the court found Nap Lajoie's skills to be so unique that his loss would cause irreparable harm, and issued an injunction to prevent him from changing teams.[29] The decision in *Lajoie* established a powerful precedent and, as seen in Part A, is now incorporated into the uniform contract of Major League (and Minor League) players.

The Reserve System, the Courts and American Antitrust Laws

The *Lajoie* decision and the general anticompetitive nature of Major League Baseball's labor system saw the first use of antitrust law to test the reserve system in 1914. In *American League Baseball Club of Chicago v Chase*[30] the Supreme Court of New York ruled that the Sherman Antitrust Act of 1890[31] did not apply to Major League Baseball because the business of baseball was not interstate trade or commerce. However, the Court held that baseball's regulatory system promoted a monopoly that contravened the common law and impeded personal liberty. Therefore, the New York Supreme Court overturned a lower court's decision to issue an injunction that prevented Chase from changing leagues (Irwin, 1991, p. 290).[32] Then, in 1922, the antitrust challenge to professional baseball's labor system progressed to the Supreme Court of the United States, who unanimously held that baseball was not interstate trade or commerce in *Federal Baseball Club of Baltimore Inc v National League of Professional Baseball Clubs*[33] and therefore created a judicial exemption from antitrust law for Major League Baseball.

The business of Major League Baseball fundamentally changed in the years after *Federal Baseball* with the development of a national system of Minor Leagues, and national radio and television broadcasting (Pierce, 1958, p. 567). But these developments were to have no impact on the Supreme Court. Antitrust litigation followed the creation of the Mexican League in 1946, and Major League Baseball blacklisted former Major League players from playing in the Major Leagues after returning from Mexico (Pierce, 1958, p. 573).[34] In 1953, as part of three cases heard simultaneously,[35] not only did the Supreme Court affirm *Federal Baseball* in *Toolson v New York Yankees*,[36] the Court ruled that it had no jurisdiction to apply antitrust law to Major League Baseball as the matter required legislative intervention by Congress.[37] Then, in 1972, *Flood v Kuhn*[38] was the final antitrust case concerning Major League's reserve system. A 5–3 majority of the Supreme Court acknowledged that *Federal Baseball* was incorrect, but refused to overturn the decision by again denying its own jurisdiction, this time on the basis of precedent and *stare decisis* (Goldman, 2008).[39]

The Reserve System and Congress

Over the years spanning the antitrust cases, and in response to the decisions of the courts, Congress examined the regulation of labor in Major League Baseball in the context of baseball's antitrust exemption. After the Mexican League led to two antitrust cases that were settled before trial,

Gardella and *Martin*, Congress investigated the baseball antitrust exemption in 1951 and 1952. Both the Senate and the House of Representatives introduced various bills, none of which were passed by Congress (Pierce, 1958, p. 573),[40] a decision largely influenced by the desire of Congress to see if the courts would hold the reserve clause to be a reasonable restraint of trade (Broshius, 2013, p. 68). Unfortunately, the Supreme Court once again refused to review the reserve system in *Toolson*, and in response, 1954 saw more hearings and proposed laws but still no laws were passed.[41] When the Supreme Court held that professional American football was subject to antitrust law in 1956,[42] further Congressional activity occurred between 1957 and 1965 (Edmonds, 1994, pp. 637–644), but antitrust law was not changed in relation to Major League Baseball.

By the time *Flood* was decided in 1972, the Supreme Court had ruled that antitrust laws applied to legitimate theater,[43] boxing,[44] ice hockey,[45] American football, basketball[46] and golf.[47] *Flood* instigated more Congressional inquiries in 1975.[48] As the labor battles between Major League Baseball and the MLBPA intensified in the 1980s, Congress held a number of inquiries,[49] introduced several bills to repeal baseball's antitrust exemption,[50] and conducted hearings and debates on these bills. Ultimately the law remained unchanged (Edmonds, 1994, pp. 648–650). Prior to the 1994 strike, Congressional activity on baseball's antitrust immunity took place in 1993, resulting in proposed bills and subcommittee hearings but no new law (Edmonds, 1994, p. 653).[51]

The Reserve System, Labor Law and Baseball's Internal Labor War

The unwillingness of the American courts to deem Major League Baseball's system in violation of antitrust law led to the players and their union using labor law to challenge the reserve system. Collective bargaining and industrial action were the mechanisms used to achieve their aims. Not long after Major League Baseball's first collective agreement in 1968, the MLBPA called its first strike in 1972 and, in the same year, the new collective agreement added an independent arbitrator to the dispute resolution process. Subsequently, salary arbitration saw the recognition of free agency in 1975, a labor control that was the subject of bargaining in 1976. Over the ensuing decades, free agency became central to collective bargaining (Goldberg, 2008, pp. 22–23, 43–44), in part because after *Flood* owners had not expected salary arbitration and free agency to coexist. This period marked the beginning of a series of ugly and ongoing labor disputes that would last nearly three decades and include six strikes, three lockouts and, as will now be seen, the cancellation of the season and the World Series in 1994 (Gould, 2004, pp. 67–78).

The labor disputes reached a climax in 1994. Owners had fought the spiraling costs of player labor since the recognition of free agency in 1975, and their solution was a salary cap. During collective bargaining negotiations in 1994, owners proposed a player salary cap and the elimination of salary arbitration, and, in exchange, free agent eligibility would be reduced from six to four years. Players rejected this proposal, and then offered to owners to decrease salary arbitration eligibility and increase the minimum salary. Owners rejected the players' proposal. The players then went on strike in the middle of August in 1994 and, in response, the owners cancelled the season and the World Series in September. The situation escalated further on 22 December 1994 when the owners eliminated salary arbitration and free agency for some players. On the same day, the owners rejected another proposal by the MLBPA, and then declared negotiations at an impasse under the NLRA. Owners then attempted to unilaterally end salary arbitration and implement their own system of free agency (Gould, 2007, p. 986).

The seriousness of the standoff between players and owners resulted in involvement by the White House. In January 1995, President Clinton appointed W. J. Usery, a former Labor Secretary, to mediate the dispute. Meanwhile, Congress refused to directly intervene, and some members once again reviewed baseball's antitrust exemption (Gould, 2007, pp. 990–991). At this time the state was already involved as the MLBPA had filed with the NLRB an unfair labor practices complaint against owners and the league,[52] claiming that the owners' actions represented a refusal to bargain in good faith, and that impasse had not been reached. In March 1995, the NLRB determined that the owners had not followed the procedures of the NLRA and voted to seek an injunction against Major League Baseball and club owners. The United States District Court found that impasse had not occurred, and therefore the owners' changes to salary arbitration and free agency were unlawful as unilateral changes in work rules. The injunction was granted,[53] and the decision upheld by the United States Court of Appeals (Gould, 2007, pp. 988, 993–994).[54] Owners were forced to reinstate the expired collective agreement, players and owners returned to the negotiation table, and the end of the strike delayed the start of the 1995 season (Wollett, 2008, pp. 62–64).

Collective Bargaining, the State and Partial Repeal of Major League Baseball's Antitrust Exemption

The 1995 and 1996 seasons were played without a collective bargaining agreement, and the terms of the expired agreement governed relations between the owners and players (Roberts, 1999, p. 416). Subsequent collective bargaining led to a new agreement for the 1997 season, and although a salary cap was not agreed to, the compromise that was reached was a 'luxury tax' that penalized the clubs with the five highest payrolls (Dryer, 2008, p.271). The taxation system has now evolved, and in 2015 and 2016, clubs who exceed a total payroll of US$189 million are taxed, and the money redistributed to other clubs in accordance with the revenue sharing agreement (Basic Agreement 2012, article XXIII.B.(2)). This period of collective bargaining saw Major League Baseball and the MLBPA agree to lobby Congress to repeal the antitrust exemption, and the two parties proposed a bill to Congress that was passed as the Curt Flood Act of 1998 (Staudohar, 2002, p. 16; Dryer, 2008, p. 271; Roberts, 1999, pp. 415–416).[55]

However, the Curt Flood Act only partially repealed Major League Baseball's judicial antitrust exemption: the legislation only applies American antitrust law to the employment of Major League players (Curt Flood Act, 1998, sections 2 & 3). But by 1998 labor law and the NLRA were firmly entrenched as the state's regulation that externally governs Major League Baseball's player labor system. Section 3 of the Curt Flood Act is notable for excluding from antitrust law Minor League players, the National Association of Professional Baseball Agreement, the Professional Baseball Agreement between Major and Minor League Baseball, sports broadcasting and Major League franchises.

The Reflexive Autopoietic System of Labor Regulation in Major League Baseball

The formal regulation of labor in Major League Baseball has evolved to incorporate the Major League Constitution, the Major League Rules, the Basic Agreement and uniform player contracts. Owners, Major League Baseball, the players and the MLBPA protect this autopoietic labor system through the creation of what Joo Cheong Tham describes as a 'regulatory pivot' (Tham, 2007, pp. 123–125), a regulatory paradigm where labor law insulates, validates and protects baseball's autopoietic labor system and its privileged Major League players and clubs. Reinforcing this regulatory pivot is the Curt Flood Act, the antitrust exemption cases in the Supreme Court of the United States and the exclusion of Minor League players from the MLBPA.

The evolution of Major League Baseball's regulation of labor has created a highly reflexive autopoietic system. Evidence of the reflexive nature of this autopoietic system is the Curt Flood Act. In the aftermath of the cancelled World Series in 1994, it was not Congress but Major League Baseball and the MLBPA who drafted what Congress would pass as the Curt Flood Act in 1998. While this law partially repealed baseball's antitrust exemption and applied American antitrust law to the labor of Major League Baseball players, it protected Major League Baseball's autopoietic system of labor regulation by excluding Minor League players and clubs from American antitrust law. In fact, the Curt Flood Act went beyond labor to protect matters related to broadcasting and Major League franchises from competition law. Even if the decision in *Federal Baseball* was to be fully repealed, American antitrust law would have a negligible regulatory impact on the labor of Major League Baseball, as collective bargaining is excluded from antitrust law through a non-statutory exemption[56] and statutory exemption (Clayton Act 1915, sections 6 & 20; Norris-LaGuardia Act 1932, section 4; NLRA 1935, sections 151–169).[57]

CONCLUSION

The internal regulation of labor in Major League Baseball involves a highly reflexive autopoietic system that is dominated by the powerful regulatory actors of the league and the players' union, respectively representing the owners and players. It is quite remarkable that in the wake of the cancelled season and World Series in 1994, Major League Baseball and the MLBPA cooperated to lobby Congress to partially repeal baseball's antitrust exemption, although the motivation was to protect baseball's internal autopoietic system of regulation. The regulation of Major League Baseball provides insight into how internal and external systems of labor regulation interact, and in the context of regulation dominated by internal regulatory actors, provides an understanding of when external regulatory intervention is needed, and the circumstances in which external regulatory actors like the state, the courts and the NLRB will intervene in the affairs of Major League Baseball.

NOTES

*   The author would like to thank Professor Andrew Stewart and the referee for their feedback on earlier drafts, and Professor Rosemary Owens and Professor Kent Anderson for their direction and feedback on relevant sections of my PhD.
1.   Other workers in professional baseball include the manager, coaches, medical and training staff, clubhouse staff, a club's 'front office' of administrators and umpires.
2.   The current agreement, at the time of writing, is the '2012–2016 Basic Agreement', effective from 12 December 2011 and referred to in this chapter as the Basic Agreement 2012 (available at http://mlb.mlb.com/pa/pdf/cba_english.pdf).
3.   (49 Stat. 449) 29 U.S.C. sections 151–169.
4.   The Major League Rules referred to in this chapter are those as published in 2008 by the Office of the Commissioner of Baseball.

5. Originally adopted in 1921 and subsequently amended.
6. The positions are pitcher, catcher, first base, second base, third base, shortstop, left field, center field, right field.
7. During each offseason Major League clubs acquire a small number of eligible Major and Minor League players through the Rule 5 Selection Meeting: Major League Rules, Rule 5, 6.
8. The Major League Uniform Player's Contract, effective from 12 December 2011 and referred to in this chapter as the Major League Uniform Player's Contract 2012, can be found in Schedule A of the 2012–2016 Basic Agreement.
9. *Silverman v Major League Baseball Player Relations Committee*, 67 F.3d 1054, 1061–1062 (2d Cir. 1995).
10. *National & American League Professional Baseball Clubs v Major League Players Association*, 66 Lab. Arb. Rep. 101, 102 (1975) (Seitz, Arb.). The right of an arbitrator to review the reserve system was affirmed in *Kansas City Royals Baseball Corp v MLBPA*, 532 F.2d 615 (8th Cir. 1976).
11. One year of Major League Baseball service is credited as 172 days on the active roster: Basic Agreement 2012, article XXI.A.
12. A club who signs a 'qualified free agent' provides compensation in the form of their first draft selection in the next draft if the player declines a qualifying offer by their club and signs with another club: Basic Agreement 2012, article XX.B.(4)(a)(b).
13. *American League of Professional Baseball Clubs v Association of National Baseball League Umpires*, 180 NLRB 190 (1969).
14. *Labor Board v Borg-Warner Corp.*, 356 U.S. 342 (1958).
15. *Silverman*, 67 F.3d 1054 (2d Cir. 1995).
16. The chapter references the contract in attachment 3 of the Major League Rules published in 2008 and is referred to hereafter as the Minor League Uniform Players Contract 2008.
17. Official winter leagues in the offseason include the Arizona Fall League and winter leagues in Venezuela, the Dominican Republic, Mexico and Australia: Australian Baseball League (2013).
18. Foreign players contracted by Major League clubs have been from countries including Canada, the Dominican Republic, Venezuela, Puerto Rico, Cuba, Mexico, Nicaragua, Aruba, Canada, Japan, South Korea, Curacao and Australia: ESPN (2012).
19. *Senne, Liberto, Odle and Others v Office of the Commissioner of Baseball, Major League Baseball and Others*, Case 3:14-cv-00608-JCS (N.D. Cal, 201 February 7), Complaint (*Senne v MLB*, Complaint), paragraph 98.
20. Ibid. paragraph 101.
21. Pub.L. 105–297 (105th Cong. 1998).
22. 29 USC § 201 (1938).
23. *Senne v Major League Baseball*, Complaint, paragraph 164, 176–177.
24. One of the leading approaches to regulation that uses an enforcement pyramid is Ayres and Braithwaite's 'responsive regulation': Ayres and Braithwaite (1995, pp. 4–5). Robert Baldwin and Julia Black slightly modified this theory to create 'really responsive regulation': Baldwin and Black (2008, pp. 69–74). Another variation of responsive regulation is 'smart regulation', an approach that identifies similarities and incompatibilities between different regulatory instruments: Baldwin and Black (2008, p. 65).
25. Persuasion is at the base of the pyramid and regulatory responses can escalate to warnings, civil penalties and criminal penalties: Ayres and Braithwaite (1995, pp. 35–36).
26. *Metropolitan Exhibition Company v Ward*, 9 N.Y.S. 779, 785 (Sup. Ct. 1890), *Philadelphia Ball Club v Hallman*, 8 Pa. C. 57, 58 (C.P. 1890) and *Metropolitan Exhibition Company v Ewing*, 42 F. 198 (C.C.S.D. N.Y. 1890). In *American Association Base-Ball Club v Picket*, 8 Pa. C. 232 (C.P. 1890) the Pennsylvania County Court ruled against the player: Vander Velde (1992, pp. 823–824).
27. 202 Pa. 210 (Pa. 1902) ('Lajoie').
28. [1852] De G.M. and G. 687.

29. *Lajoie*, 202 Pa. 210, 217–221 (Pa. 1902).
30. 149 N.Y.S. 6 (N.Y.S. 1914) ('Chase').
31. 2 July 1890, ch. 647, 26 Stat. 209 (15 U.S.C. § 1–7).
32. *Chase*, 149 N.Y.S. 6, 16–17 (N.Y.S. 1914).
33. 259 U.S. 200 (1922) ('Federal Baseball').
34. In 1948 two players that were blacklisted after they played in the Mexican League,
     Gardella and Martin, lodged antitrust cases against Major League Baseball, but both
     Gardella v Chandler, 172 F.2d 402 (2d Cir. 1949) and *Martin v National League Baseball
     Club*, 174 F.2d 402 (2d Cir. 1949) were settled before trial.
35. The other cases were *Kowalski v Chandler*, 202 F.2d 413 (1953) and *Corbett v Chandler*,
     202 F.2d 428 (1953).
36. 346 U.S. 356 (1953) ('Toolson').
37. *Toolson*, 346 U.S. 356, 356–357 (1953).
38. 407 U.S. 258 (1972) ('Flood').
39. *Flood*, 407 U.S. 258, 282 (1972).
40. H.R. 4229, H.R. 4230, H.R. 4231, 82d Cong., 1st Sess. (1951), S. 1526, 82d Cong.,
     1st Sess. (1951) and *Organized Baseball: Report of the Subcommittee on the Study of
     Monopoly Power of the Committee on the Judiciary*, H.R. REP. No. 2002, 82d Cong.,
     2d Sess. 50–57 (1952).
41. *Hearings on S.J. Res. 133 Subjecting Professional Baseball Clubs to Antitrust Laws
     before the Committee on the Judiciary*, 83d Cong., 2d Sess. (1954).
42. *Radovich v National Football League*, 358 U.S. 445 (1957) overturned *Radovich v
     National Football League*, 231 F.2d 620 (9th Cir. 1956) ('Radovich').
43. *United States v Shubert*, 348 U.S. 22 (1956).
44. *United States v International Boxing Club*, 348 U.S. 236 (1955).
45. *Peto v Madison Square Garden Corp*, 1958 Trade Cases, 69, 106 (S.D.N.Y. 1958).
46. *Haywood v National Basketball Association*, 401 U.S. 1204 (1971).
47. *Deesen v Professional Golfers' Association*, 358 F.2d 165 (CA9). cert. denied, 385 U.S.
     846 (1966).
48. *Hearings on the Rights of Professional Athletes and H.R. 2355 and H.R. 694 before the
     Subcommittee on Monopolies and Commercial Law of the House Judiciary Committee*,
     94th Cong., 1st Sess. (1975).
49. *Hearings on Antitrust Policy and Professional Sports before the Subcommittee on
     Monopolies and Commercial Law of the House Judiciary Committee*, 97th Cong., 1st &
     2d Sess. (1982), *Hearings on the Professional Sports Team Community Protection Act
     before the Senate Judiciary Committee*, 98th Cong., 2d Sess. (1984) and *Hearings
     on Professional Sports Team Community Protection Act before the Subcommittee
     on Commerce, Transportation, and Tourism of the House Energy and Commerce
     Committee*, 98th Cong., 2d Sess. (1984).
50. The bills included the Sports Franchise Relocation Act, H.R. 823, 97th Cong., 1st Sess.
     (1981) and the Professional Sports Stabilization Act of 1982, H.R. 6467, 97th Cong., 1st
     Sess. (1981).
51. *Hearings on Baseball's Antitrust Immunity before the Subcommittee on Antitrust,
     Monopolies and Business Rights of the Senate Judiciary Committee*, 102d Cong., 2d
     Sess. (1992) and *Hearings on Baseball's Antitrust Exemption before the Subcommittee on
     Economic and Commercial Law of the House Committee on the Judiciary*, 103d Cong.,
     1st Sess. 2 (1993).
52. The MLBPA's first application to the NLRB claiming unfair labor practices was in
     1981. The United States District Court refused to issue an injunction against Major
     League owners: *Silverman v Major League Baseball Player Relations Committee*, 516 F.
     Supp. 588, 598 (S.D.N.Y. 1981).
53. *Silverman v Major League Baseball Player Relations Committee*, 880 F. Supp. 246
     (S.D.N.Y.1995).
54. *Silverman v Major League Baseball Player Relations Committee*, 67 F.3d 1054
     (2d Cir. 1995).

55. The delayed Congressional action on Major League Baseball's antitrust exemption can be contrasted to its actions on the use of performance enhancing drugs by Major League players: Showalter (2007); Mitchell (2007).
56. *National Football League v Mackey*, 543 F.2d 606, 615 (8th Cir. 1976) and *Brown v Pro Football Inc*, 116 S. Ct. 2116, 2121 (1996).
57. Where labor controls are the product of collective bargaining, the only option available to Major League players is to dissolve and decertify the union. Individual players could then initiate legal action under antitrust law. The player unions in the National Basketball Association and the National Football League recently adopted this course of action: Grow (2013, pp. 476–477).

REFERENCES

Australian Baseball League (2013), *Australian Baseball League Media Guide 2013–14*, accessed 12 May 2014 at http://web.theabl.com.au/content/page.jsp?ymd=20131120&content_id=6 4078512&sid=1595&vkey=league3.
Ayres, I. and J. Braithwaite (eds) (1995), *Responsive Regulation: Transcending the Deregulation Debate*, New York, USA: Oxford University Press.
Baldwin, R. and J. Black (2008), 'Really responsive regulation', *Modern Law Review*, **71** (1), 59–94.
Baldwin, R., M. Cave and M. Lodge (2012), *Understanding Regulation: Theory, Strategy, and Practice*, Oxford, UK: Oxford University Press.
Baseball America (2014), '2014 draft: Assigned pick values for top 10 rounds', *Baseballamerica.com*, accessed April 2014 at http://www.baseballamerica.com/draft/2014-draft-assigned-pick-values-for-top-10-rounds/.
Broshius, G. R. (2013), 'Touching baseball's untouchables: The effects of collective bargaining on Minor League Baseball players', *Harvard Journal of Sports and Entertainment Law*, **4**, 51–103.
Brown, M. (2013), 'Major League Baseball sees record revenues exceed $8 billion for 2013', accessed 13 December 2013 at http://www.forbes.com/sites/maurybrown/2013/12/17/major-league-baseball-sees-record-revenues-exceed-8-billion-for-2013/.
CBS Sports (2014), 'MLB salaries, average player salaries', *CBS Sports.com*, accessed 10 April 2014 at http://www.cbssports.com/mlb/salaries/avgsalaries.
Cooney, S. (2006), 'Exclusionary self-regulation: A critical evaluation of the AMMA's proposal in the mining industry', in C. Arup, P. Gahan, J. Howe, R. Johnstone, R. Mitchell and A. O'Donnell (eds), *Labour Law and Labour Market Regulation: Essays on the Construction, Constitution and Regulation of Labour Markets*, Sydney, Australia: Federation Press, pp. 187–201.
Deakin, S. and R. Rogowski (2011), 'Reflexive labour law, capabilities and the future of social Europe', in R. Rogowski, R. Salais and N. Whiteside (eds), *Transforming European Employment Policy: Labour Market Transitions and the Promotion of Capability*, Cheltenham, UK and Northampton, MA, USA: Elgar Publishing, pp. 229–254.
Deakin, S. and F. Wilkinson (2005), *The Law of the Labour Market: Industrialization, Employment and Legal Evolution*, Oxford, UK: Oxford University Press.
Dryer, R. T. (2008), 'Beyond the box score: A look at collective bargaining agreements in professional sports and their effect on competition', *Journal of Dispute Resolution*, **1**, 267–292.
Edmonds, E. P. (1994), 'Over forty years in the on-deck circle: Congress and the baseball antitrust exemption', *Thurgood Marshall Law Review*, **19**, 628–661.
Edmonds, E. (2012), 'Arthur Soden's legacy: The origins and early history of baseball's reserve system', *Albany Government Law Review*, **5**, 38–89.
ESPN (2012), 'Percentage of foreign players rises', accessed 5 April 2012 at http://espn.go.com/mlb/story/_/id/7779279/percentage-foreign-major-league-baseball-players-rises.

Freiberg, A. (2010), *The Tools of Regulation*, Sydney, Australia: Federation Press.

Gahan, P. and P. Brosnan (2006), 'The repertories of labour market regulation', in C. Arup, P. Gahan, J. Howe, R. Johnstone, R. Mitchell and A. O'Donnell (eds), *Labour Law and Labour Market Regulation: Essays on the Construction, Constitution and Regulation of Labour Markets*, Sydney, Australia: Federation Press, pp. 127–146.

Goldberg, J. B. (2008), 'Player mobility in professional sports: From the reserve system to free agency', *Sports Lawyers Journal*, **15**, 21–57.

Goldman, R. M. (ed.) (2008), *One Man Out: Curt Flood versus Baseball*, Kansas, USA: University of Kansas Press.

Gould, W. B. (2004), 'Labor issues in professional sports: Reflections on baseball, labor, and antitrust law', *Stanford Law and Policy Review*, **15** (1), 61–97.

Gould, W. B. (2007), 'The 1994–95 Baseball strike and national labor relations board: To the precipice and back again', *West Virginia Law Review*, **110**, 983–997.

Gould, W. B. (2013), 'Bargaining, race, and globalization: How baseball and other sports mirror collective bargaining, law, and life', *University of San Francisco Law Review*, **48**, 1–42.

Grow, N. (2013), 'Decertifying players unions: Lessons from the NFL and NBA lockouts of 2011', *Vanderbilt Journal of Entertainment and Technology Law*, **15** (3), 473–505.

Hartog, H. (2002), 'Stone's transitions', *Connecticut Law Review*, **34**, 821–832.

Howe, J. (2011), 'The broad idea of labour law: Industrial policy, labour market regulation, and decent work', in G. Davidov and B. Langille (eds), *The Idea of Labour Law*, New York, USA: Oxford University Press, pp. 295–314.

Independent Professional Baseball Federation (2014), accessed at http://www.independent-professionalbaseballfederation.com/.

Irwin, R. L. (1991), 'A historical review of litigation in baseball', *Marquette Sports Law Journal*, **1**, 283–300.

Kurlantzick, L. (2009), 'The tampering prohibition and agreements between American and foreign sports leagues', *Columbia Journal of Law and the Arts*, **32** (3), 271–331.

Leventhal, J. (2014), 'MiLB opposes players, supports MLB in lawsuit', accessed 11 December 2014 at http://www.baseballamerica.com/minors/milb-opposes-players-backs-mlb-lawsuit/.

Major League Baseball Players Association (2010), *MLBPA Regulations Governing Player Agents* (amended in 2013), accessed 15 June 2014 at http://mlbplayers.mlb.com/pa/info/agent_regulations.jsp.

Matsuzeweski, E. (2014), 'Yankees give Tanaka fifth richest pitcher-deal in MLB history', accessed 23 January 2014 at http://www.bloomberg.com/news/2014-01-22/yankees-tanaka-agree-to-155-million-contract-fox-sports-says.html.

Matter, D. (2014), 'Minor leaguer-turned-lawyer targets MLB in lawsuit', accessed 25 June 2015 at http://www.stltoday.com/sports/baseball/minor-leaguer-turned-lawyer-targets-mlb-in-lawsuit/article_713f4d65-e981-5565-a4a2-2e36ed1e627c.html.

Mitchell, G. J. (2007), *Report to the Commissioner of Baseball of an Independent Investigation into the Illegal Use of Steroids and Other Performance Enhancing Substances by Players in Major League Baseball*, accessed 17 February 2016 at http://files.mlb.com/summary.pdf.

Mitchell, R. and C. Arup (2006), 'Labour law and market regulation', in C. Arup, P. Gahan, J. Howe, R. Johnstone, R. Mitchell and A. O'Donnell (eds), *Labour Law and Labour Market Regulation: Essays on the Construction, Constitution and Regulation of Labour Markets*, Sydney, Australia: Federation Press, pp. 3–20.

Nathanson, M. (2010), 'Truly sovereign at last: C.B.C. redefinition of the concept of baseball', *Oregon Law Review*, **89**, 581–621.

Ogus, A. (1995), 'Rethinking self-regulation', *Oxford Journal of Legal Studies*, **15**, 97–108.

Parker, C., C. Scott, N. Lacey and J. Braithwaite (2004), 'Introduction', in C. Parker, C. Scott, N. Lacey and J. Braithwaite (eds), *Regulating Law*, Oxford, UK: Oxford University Press, pp. 1–12.

Pierce, S. R. (1958), 'Organized professional team sports and the anti-trust laws', *Cornell Law Review*, **43** (4), 566–616.

Piore, M. J. (2011), 'Flexible bureaucracies in labor market regulation', in G. Davidov and B. Langille (eds), *The Idea of Labour*, New York, USA: Oxford University Press, pp. 385–404.

Primm, A. (2010), 'Salary arbitration induced settlement in Major League Baseball: The new trend', *Sports Law Journal*, **17**, 73–116.

Roberts, G. R. (1999), 'A brief appraisal of the Curt Flood Act of 1998 from the Minor League Perspective', *Marquette Sports Law Journal*, **9**, 413–437.

Rogowski, R. and T. Wilthagen (1994), 'Reflexive labour law: An introduction', in R. Rogowski and T. Wilthagen (eds), *Reflexive Labour Law: Studies in Industrial Relations and Employment Regulations*, Boston, USA: Kluwer, pp. 1–19.

Rothman, L. (2014), 'Former Minor League Baseball players file class action suit against MLB', accessed 11 March 2014 at http://time.com/16344/minor-league-baseball-class-action-suit/.

Showalter, B. D. (2007), 'Steroid testing policies in professional sports: Regulated by Congress or the responsibility of leagues?', *Marquette Sports Law Review*, **17** (2), 651–678.

Smith, C. (2013), 'Minor League Baseball's most valuable teams', accessed 17 July 2013 at http://www.forbes.com/sites/chrissmith/2013/07/17/minor-league-baseballs-most-valuable-teams/.

Staudohar, P. D. (2002), 'Baseball negotiations: A new agreement', *Monthly Labor Review*, December, 15–22.

Szuchman, D. M. (1996), 'Step up to the bargaining table: A call for the unionization of Minor League Baseball', *Hofstra Law Review*, **14**, 265–312.

Tham, J. C. (2007), 'Towards an understanding of standard employment relations under Australian labour law', *Australian Journal of Labour Law*, **20**, 123–158.

USA Today (2014), 'MLB salaries', accessed 22 May 2014 at http://www.usatoday.com/sports/mlb/salaries/2014/team/all/.

Vander Velde, L. S. (1992), 'The gendered origins of the Lumley doctrine: Binding men's consciences and women's fidelity', *Yale Law Journal*, **101** (4), 775–782.

Wollett, D. (2008), *Getting on Base: Unionism in Baseball*, New York, USA: iUniverse Inc.

Zimbalist, A. (2010), 'Reflections on salary caps and salary shares', *Journal of Sports Economics*, **11** (1), 17–28.

5. Regulating player agents
Lisa Pike Masteralexis

INTRODUCTION

The need for agents to assist professional athletes has grown as their earning potential, salaries, and marketing opportunities have increased. Salaries have grown as athletes have accessed teams' and leagues' growing revenue streams, particularly media revenues. Additionally, unionization enabled athletes, through players' associations, to engage in collective bargaining and to arm agents with data and salary information. As the business of sports has found its way into the news, business managers, athletes, and fans alike have come into more analytical information to inform athletes of their market value. Armed with this information, agents teach athletes to better understand their market value and navigate complex league rules, contracts, and collective bargaining agreements. Athletes have become increasingly reliant on agents or intermediaries to negotiate playing contracts and off-the-field marketing opportunities. The spike in the number of agents fighting for a piece of the billion dollar player representation market in North America, however, far exceeds the number of athletes available as clients. In 2014, the four major North American sports leagues – Major League Baseball (MLB), the National Basketball Association (NBA), the National Football League (NFL), and the National Hockey League (NHL) – combined had over 1900 player agents (Pugh Interview, 2014a; Pugh Interview, 2014b). In the European Union, it is estimated that there are at least 3600 agents representing athletes in 32 different sports (European Commission, 2009). In the European Commission's "Study on Sports Agents in the European Union" the international nature of the profession was noted. Thus, the number of sports agents in the global sport of football dwarfs all others. The Fédération Internationale de Football Association (FIFA), which until May 2015 certified agents, listed 6861 football agents in its worldwide registry (FIFA, 2014). Other international regulatory bodies include the International Association of Athletics Federations (IAAF), which currently has 282 certified agents (IAAF, 2015), and the Fédération Internationale de Basket-ball (FIBA), which counts 498 certified agents among its ranks (FIBA, 2016).

The number of agents seeking clients has grown at a disproportionate rate compared to the number of athletes needing representation. Consider it a product of competition, similar to what the players represented by these agents face on the field, pitch, court, or ice. According to Shropshire and Davis (2003):

> Because of the lucrative fees many agents receive, the level of competition among sports agents to provide services and to obtain that first client has become extraordinary. As with any industry, as the field of competitors for a limited number of clients has increased, so have the cutthroat methods of competition. (p. 50)

This competition, coupled with the rise in the earning power of athletes, has led to patterns of misbehavior and underhanded dealings by agents, despite legislative and governing bodies' best efforts to curtail such acts through state and federal legislation, rules, regulations, and policies (Masteralexis, Masteralexis, & Snyder, 2013). With such a large number of agents competing for limited clients, is there a best set of practices to keep agents in line or for leagues or governing bodies to limit or eliminate those cutthroat methods? Whether in North American leagues or internationally through nations and federations such as FIFA, FIBA, IAAF, and the International Rugby Board (IRB), regulating agent behavior has proven onerous and often ineffective. In fact, due to FIFA's estimation that unlicensed agents conduct 30 percent of player transfers worldwide, it has stopped regulating agents as it has instead adopted the FIFA Regulations on Working with Intermediaries, which will supersede its agent regulations and transfer the responsibility of regulating player representatives to national associations and clubs (Rudd, 2013).

In the United States, state and national governments took notice of the disturbing trend and passed reactionary measures. Before the Uniform Athlete Agents Act (UAAA) was enacted in 2000 by the US Uniform Law Commission (Edelman, 2013) numerous states passed various statutes regulating agents. Through this process 42 states have adopted the UAAA. Despite that, Congress still saw fit in 2004 to pass the Sports Agent Responsibility and Trust Act (SPARTA), a piece of legislation meant not to override UAAA, but to act as supplemental legislation in concert with state-level laws (Willenbacher, 2004). According to Sobel (2009), "sports agents today must maneuver through a maze of conduct governing regulations" (pp. 1–3).

Similarly, in Europe a maze of regulations exist across five countries (Bulgaria, France, Greece, Hungary, and Portugal), four international federations (FIBA, FIFA, IAAF, and IRB), and numerous national federations (European Commission, 2009) and even leagues, such as the German Ice Hockey League (European Commission, 2011). Further, most

European countries have laws or regulations involving job placement (European Commission, 2009). European sports agents are viewed more as intermediaries placing employees in jobs, whereas in North America agents are viewed as business managers and legal and/or financial advisors.

Part A of this chapter reviews prior literature written on the topic of sports agent regulation and discusses the suggestions that have been proffered to improve the regulatory framework of the sports agent industry. Part B discusses the history and the factors that have led to the emergence and rapid growth of the sport agent industry. The modern industry landscape will be discussed within the context of the current regulatory framework. Part C examines the legal framework of labor regulations for agents, including the regulation of player agents in North American sports leagues and international governing bodies such as FIFA, FIBA, IAAF, and World Rugby (formerly IRB), as well as provides a historical review of legislation and practices instituted in the attempt to regulate the sports agent market. It will also identify the differences between the North American system and those in European-based sporting bodies, and the role of attempted regulatory acts. Finally, Part D concludes with a discussion of future research and how it could be used to build a better system of sports agent regulation.

A.   LITERATURE REVIEW

According to Edelman (2013), the main purpose of agency law is to "ensure that agents act in the best interests of their principals, and not for their own personal gain" (p. 147). The regulatory framework that has developed to carry out this purpose in the sports agent industry is a complex and multi-tiered regulatory system consisting of public regulation through federal law (SPARTA) and state law (the UAAA and common law), as well as the regulations of private organizations, including union/player associations regulations, various levels of involvement by professional sports leagues, National Collegiate Athletic Association (NCAA) bylaws, university policies, and bar association ethics rules. Despite the many layers of regulations, "agent misconduct might be worse than ever" (Deubert, 2011, p. 22).

The financial growth of the sports industry has led to an increasingly competitive landscape, which has contributed to a rise in agent misconduct. Agents have been responsible for ethical and legal violations, including improper client solicitation and fraud. Agents have subordinated the best interests of their clients due to financial conflicts of interest, and incompetence has grown due to the entrance of unqualified agents into the industry. Karcher (2006) asserts that "everyone, including players, heads of the players associations, and even many agents, universally agrees" that agent behavior has become a problem and it is common for agents to display a "[l]ack of competence, client stealing, and overly aggressive negotiating tactics" (p. 739). According to Deubert (2011), the competitive landscape has a chilling effect on adherence to regulations because "[i]n such a competitive environment, with a general lack of enforcement, agents who choose to follow the rules are at a competitive disadvantage" (p. 23).

A number of flaws in the regulatory system have led to ineffective agent regulation, including the lack of consistent and uniform regulations, ineffective regulatory penalties, inconsistent enforcement of penalties, and the placement of a disproportionate burden of regulatory oversight on unsophisticated student-athletes. Various suggestions have been made to address the shortcomings of the regulatory system. Willenbacher (2004) and Edelman (2013) advocate for increased federal regulation. Willenbacher (2004) recommends increasing federal regulation through amendments to SPARTA, including the implementation of a national licensing or registration program for agents that would increase national uniformity, and the enactment of more stringent penalties to deter violations, including revocation or suspension of an agent's license. Edelman (2013) recommends that Congress enacts a new federal regulation that draws from three statutes that govern fiduciary relationships: the Muhammad Ali Boxing Reform Act (regulation of boxing managers), Investment Advisers Act (regulation of investment advisors), and the Miller-Ayala Athlete Agents Act (regulation of agents). According to Edelman (2013), the new law should do a better job of applying three themes that are "conspicuously omitted from most sports agent laws": principal protection, universality, and minimizing conflicts of interest (p. 184). To the contrary, Mills (2012) argues that increased federal regulation is unnecessary because better utilization of the existing statutory and common law framework would be sufficient.

Masteralexis et al. (2013) and Payne (2011) recommend that Congress create an overarching regulatory body that enables the industry to regulate itself. According to Masteralexis et al. (2013), Congress should promote industry self-regulation through the creation of a Sport Agent Oversight Board (SPAAB) that is modeled after the Public Company Accounting Oversight Board of the Sarbanes-Oxley Act of 2002. Reputable industry professionals would run the SPAAB as an independent non-profit corporation. The SPAAB would strengthen enforcement of agent regulations, including SPARTA and the UAAA, and ensure consistent ethical standards nationwide. The SPAAB would accomplish these goals through its chief duties, which will be "to certify sports agents who intend to conduct business in the U.S., establish quality control and ethical standards for those agents, conduct inspections of sports agent firms, conduct investigations and disciplinary proceedings and impose appropriate sanctions and enforce compliance with agent laws and regulations" (Masteralexis et al., 2013, p. 98). Similarly, Payne (2011) advocates for the establishment of a Sports Agent Licensing and Oversight Commission (SALOC) that "would provide a centralized mechanism to (1) enforce the registration disclosure requirements of the UAAA; (2) establish a single application process and fee; (3) monitor registered agents; and (4) bring suits, both criminal and civil, against non-registered agents who violate the law" (p. 684). According to Payne (2011), the establishment of the SALOC should be part of a multi-faceted solution that also includes "statutory causes of action for student-athletes, relaxation of NCAA amateurism regulations, and better reciprocity between the various regulatory bodies" (p. 683).

According to Karcher (2006) and Nahwrold (1999), various private associations should play a greater role in agent oversight. Karcher (2006) recommends that players unions assume a greater role in athlete representation and advocates for the creation of "[a]n internal player management agency giving players the option to retain a full-time salaried agent employed by the union, combined with revisions to the unions' existing agent regulations imposing an alternative fee structure and a complete ban on solicitation" (p. 780). According to Karcher (2006), the results of such a system "would substantially reduce the incentive for agents to engage in 'harmful' competition, and would ensure that players are paying their agents a reasonable fee, but would still maintain the player's autonomy in selecting his own agent" (p. 780). Nahwrold (1999) recommends fighting agent incompetence through the requirement that agents possess a law degree, restricting entry into the agent industry and allowing state bar associations to police agent conduct.

Internationally, sport federations usually manage the regulation and organization of the sport free from government intervention. In Europe, for example, agents are far removed from sporting rules and play. Their actions representing players impact on aspects of sport regulated by the European Union such as unethical behavior, criminal behavior, competition, and the free movement of workers (athletes and agents) across states. For this reason, the European Commission has commissioned studies on sports agents and what forms, if any, regulation should take in the European Community. The results encouraged delegation to sport federations to work in harmony with public authorities (European Commission, 2009). It will be interesting to see what model prevails now that FIFA has deregulated agents in football in favor of national federations. FIFA's deregulation may open the door for EU-level regulation as nation by nation regulation may cause differences across jurisdictions leading to unfair barriers to entry and confusion due to a lack of uniformity throughout the European Community.

B.   EMERGENCE AND GROWTH OF THE SPORTS AGENT INDUSTRY

Athletes' reliance on sports agents has become commonplace in professional sport. Athletes have fought for more leverage in negotiations and better financial opportunities. As they have faced increasing complexities in their lives and as sport has merged with entertainment, agents have emerged as key advisors influencing their every move.

What Is an Agent?

The movie "Jerry Maguire" provided a dramatized example of what it means to be an agent, but what exactly is the definition of an agent? Merriam-Webster's Dictionary defines an agent as "a person who does business for another person; a person who acts on behalf of another." Ruxin (2004) notes that the term "sports agent" may cover a broad range of relationships, including friend, lawyer, teacher, or coach, and is similar to a talent agent in the entertainment business.

Unsurprisingly, sports leagues and players unions have more in-depth definitions of player agents. For example, the Major League Baseball Players Association's (MLBPA) Agent Regulations define a "Player Agent" as an individual who is "certified by the MLBPA and authorized thereby to engage in certain conduct as more fully described in Sections 3(A) and 3(B)" (MLBPA, 2015, p.4). Conduct and duties include: negotiation, administration, or enforcement of player agreements and rights; and recruitment and maintenance of players as clients. Additionally, the MLBPA offers two types of certification: a general certification and a limited certification. In 2014, there were 426 General Certified Agents and 217 Limited Certified Agents (Pugh Interview, 2014a). The key difference between general and limited certified agents is limited certified agents are "not authorized to engage in representing or advising individual Players in negotiations, etc., as more fully described in Section 3(A)" (MLBPA, 2015, p. 5).

While the MLBPA clearly defines the term "agent" in its regulations, other professional sports leagues, such as the NBA, have elected to delineate the actions its "agents" can take. According to regulations issued by the National Basketball Players Association (NBPA), these actions include:

> The providing of advice, counsel, information or assistance to players (including rookies) with respect to negotiating their individual contracts with clubs and/or thereafter enforcing those contracts; the conduct of compensation negotiations with the clubs on behalf of individual players; and any other activity or conduct which directly bears upon the player agent's integrity, competence or ability to properly represent individual NBA players and the NBPA in individual contract negotiations. (NBPA, 1991, p. 4)

Prior to enacting sweeping agent regulation changes in 2014, FIFA defined a player agent as "a natural person who, for a fee, introduces players to clubs with a view to negotiating an employment contract or introduces two clubs to one another with a view to concluding a transfer agreement, in compliance with the provisions set forth in these regulations" (FIFA, 2007, p. 4). After introducing the legislation, which goes into effect on 1 April 2015, FIFA struck the word "agent" from its vernacular and replaced it with "intermediary." The updated regulations streamlined the definition of an intermediary to read as "[a] natural or legal person who, for a fee or free of charge, represents players and/or clubs in negotiations with a view to concluding an employment contract or represents clubs in negotiations with a view to concluding a transfer agreement" (FIFA, 2014, p. 4). With the many types of advisors that athletes and professional sports entities rely upon, a universal definition of an agent is hard to find.

The History of Agents

Early on in sport business, agents were only occasionally a part of the landscape. In 1925, C.C. "Cash and Carry" Pyle, a theater promoter, helped negotiate a $3000 per game contract for Red Grange, Chicago Bears' star running back. Pyle also secured Grange an additional $300000 in movie rights (Masteralexis et al., 2013). Babe Ruth, baseball's pre-eminent superstar of the 1920s and 30s, took financial advice from sports cartoonist Christy Walsh. In 1966, Hollywood agent Bill Hayes orchestrated a joint holdout of Los Angeles Dodgers pitchers Sandy Koufax and Don Drysdale. While they did not achieve the three-year, one million dollar contracts that they sought, they obtained raises of $30000–40000, which increased their contracts to $125000 and $115000, respectively, and demonstrated the value of leverage to their colleagues (Helyar, 1995). Despite these success stories, agents were the exception not the rule. Even star players were frequently threatened or retaliated against for selecting someone to represent their interests in contract negotiations.

In 1960, however, a handshake deal between aspiring agent Mark H. McCormack and golf superstar Arnold Palmer revolutionized the agent–athlete relationship and the earning power of individual sport athletes (Steinbreder, 1996). McCormack's company, IMG, quickly grew into the industry standard for athlete representation and ushered in a new era of the one-stop shop for athlete representation. Influenced by IMG's structure, sports agents are responsible for much more than contract negotiations, including the procurement of endorsement contracts, financial management, and other off-field tasks. This allows agents' clients to focus solely on their athletic pursuits (Fraley & Harwell, 1989).

Following IMG's success, entertainment agencies began hiring sports agents and merging with sports agencies that already possessed valuable sports portfolios, to build super agencies that intertwined entertainment and sport, helping to expand opportunities for their athlete-clients. In fact, in December 2013, IMG was sold to William Morris Endeavor (WME) for $2.3 billion, merging the large sport business with an entertainment one. The combination of two powerful talent and acquisition agencies will create challenges for competitors that are not super agencies such as IMG-WME and Creative Artists Agency (CAA). CAA Sports manages nearly $5.4 billion in contracts – $2.9 billion of which is housed in CAA's American football wing (Belzer, 2013). To compete with such behemoths, agents may resort to overly aggressive client recruitment and retention tactics – yet another reason for regulation.

Emergence of the Agent Industry through Growth of Players Unions, Collective Bargaining, and Free Agency

While the McCormack/Palmer partnership showed what agents could do for clients in individual sports, the agent–athlete relationship for players in team sports began to blossom in the mid-1970s, a decade that brought about many changes in negotiations and the strength of players associations. Due to the strong historical connection between North American sport and the reserve clause, which perpetually bound a player to a team, agents like Pyle and Walsh served little importance from the 1920s through the late 1960s. When the MLBPA elected Marvin Miller, a longtime labor advocate and chief economist of the Steelworkers Union, as its executive director on 1 July 1966, it seemed to be a mere footnote in the association's history (Edmonds, 2010). Miller, though, initiated sweeping reforms that culminated in baseball's first collective bargaining agreement in 1968 (1968 MLB CBA), which eventually opened the door for players to challenge the reserve clause and institute free agency.

The 1968 MLB CBA permitted players to use agents for contract negotiations, but that did not lead to immediate wide-sweeping changes across MLB. Because the reserve clause was still in effect, player movement between teams was limited to trades or players not tendered a contract for the next season. After the 1968 MLB CBA was completed, negotiators became a more prominent part of contract decisions; however, during this time, the reserve clause's strength was not in question and players had little use for agents.

In 1974, an arbitration decision allowed Jim "Catfish" Hunter to become a free agent because of a breach of contract by Oakland Athletics owner Charles O. Finley. Hunter eventually signed a five-year, $3.75 million contract with the New York Yankees (Staudohar, 2002). Due to the 1968 MLB CBA's introduction of arbitration, Hunter was able to use the arbitration process to solve his grievance against Finley and achieve free agent status.

Although Hunter was the first MLB player to achieve free agent status, it was arbitrator Peter Seitz's ruling in the landmark Messersmith–McNally arbitration decision on 23 December 1975 that truly opened the door to free agency and the unfettered use of agents. When Seitz ruled in favor of Messersmith and McNally, effectively ending the reserve clauses' perpetual hold over players, it fundamentally changed contract negotiations in professional sports. The results were immediate, as the average MLB salary nearly doubled in two years, from $44 675 pre-Messersmith/McNally 1975 to $76 066 in 1977. That trend has continued through to today, as players in the four major North American sports have average salaries of $3.0725 million today (Gaines, 2014), making talented agents and financial advisors a necessary part of negotiations.

Similarly, in Europe, when *Union Royale Belge des Sociétés de Football Ass'n ASBL v. Bosman* (1995) opened the door to free agency in European football, it also increased salaries by 235 percent in the big five European leagues (Baker, Heitner, Brocard, & Byon, 2012). The increase in salaries and transfer fees correlated to an increased use of agents and thereby an increase in agent misconduct. One global difference lies in the response to the misconduct as it seems agents are viewed as part of a corrupt system rather than the leaders of the corruption (Baker et al., 2012). In the United States, the agents seem to create the misconduct rather than being one link in the chain of misbehavior.

More Growth in the Agent Industry

Alongside free agency, the growth of television broadcasts also helped the number of agents to spike. The NBA and NFL each have monstrous television deals, but none have topped baseball's earning power. In 2012, MLB signed an eight-year, $5.6 billion contract with ESPN. What sets MLB's television rights and earning power apart, however, is the fact that individual teams also are able to sell their television broadcast rights, unlike their NFL brethren. Currently, six teams have television rights deals or ownership in television networks with total values of more than $1 billion (Brown, 2014). More money in teams' pockets, theoretically, means a greater investment in team payroll, which leads to a greater use of agents.

Unlike European football, where most countries have similar league structures that allow for competition for players, North American sports leagues have remained a virtually competition-free zone for more than three decades (Longley, 2013). However, a watershed moment came via the American Basketball Association's (ABA) nine-season run from 1967 to 1976. Rick Barry, coming off an NBA Finals performance where he averaged 40.8 points per game, felt he had not been paid incentive monies by his NBA club, and Barry signed a three-year, $225 000 contract with the ABA's Oakland Oaks, showcasing what competing leagues do for player salaries. Eventually, the legal issues surrounding Barry's contract paved the way for *Robertson v. NBA* (1975). The case eliminated the NBA's version of the reserve clause and led to free agency in the NBA.

Agents such as IMG's Mark H. McCormack pushed for increases in the number of tournaments in golf and tennis just as the global sports television business matured. The influx of television and sponsorship monies have grown and sustained several tours. For instance, the Professional Golfers' Association (PGA) Tour operates five tours in North America – PGA Tour, Champions Tour, Web.com Tour, PGA Tour Latinoamérica and MacKenzie Tour - Canada – as well as its 2014 startup, PGA Tour China (PGA, 2013). The birth of the Association of Tennis Professionals (ATP) Tour came in 1990 and currently encompasses 61 tournaments in 30 countries, helping to expose its stars to an international audience and multi-national endorsement opportunities (ATP, 2014). These tours provide an opportunity for agents to guide athletes and seek compensation from the tours.

Television has been a part of the sport experience since 1939 when NBC broadcasted the second game of a baseball doubleheader between Princeton University and Columbia University from New York City (Columbia University Athletics, 2009). While professional sports were the torchbearers for the initial expansion of sports television, the earning power of college athletics was not unlocked until 1984. In *NCAA v. Board of Regents of University of Oklahoma* (1984), two college football powerhouse universities banded together to challenge the NCAA's distribution of television rights monies to its member schools. Under its plan, the NCAA mandated that college football teams appear on television no more than six times in two years, and revenues from all appearances would be distributed equally to NCAA member institutions. Suing under restraint of trade, Oklahoma and Georgia emerged victorious, freeing NCAA member schools to negotiate their individual television contracts. The marriage of such agreements and institutions have led to professional level media rights contracts, like the $2.25 billion, 15-year agreement between the Southeastern Conference and ESPN (Ozanian, 2013). With programming needing to fill its 24-hour commitment, ESPN gives exposure to athletes in traditionally non-televised sports, as well as the traditional revenue producing college sports of football and men's basketball. Agents are anxiously awaiting the decision as to whether US collegiate football players at Northwestern University have voted to unionize. Collective bargaining in collegiate football would give rise to business for agents to represent college athletes on their individual bargaining. Agents may step in to negotiate deals with the colleges recruiting the athletes, as well as for their marketing and endorsement opportunities. Some athletes' careers peak while playing the collegiate game and opening this marketing opportunity for athletes will also open business opportunities for agents. Unfortunately, though, it may likely increase the corruption in the agency industry already seen in the professional and a good deal of the collegiate sport industry.

The rise in professional sport industry revenues has placed athletes in much different tax brackets than in past decades. Agents thus are no longer simply contract negotiators, but are often responsible for tax and estate planning, investment advice, and providing other financial management and service options (Mason, 2001). As the NHL saw its percentage of foreign players rise in the 1990s, there became an increased demand for agent services beyond simple contract procedures (Mason, 2001). Dealing with international taxation laws and immigration issues were new challenges presented to NHL agents. The same can be said for MLB, where 26.3 percent of players on the opening-day rosters in 2014 were foreign-born (MLB, 2014), and the NBA, which had a record 92 international players on its 2013–2014 rosters (NBA, 2013). The 92 NBA players represented 39 countries and territories, putting increased expectations on agents who represent such players.

In some cases, it is not uncommon for players to retain the services of an agent and a financial advisor, or often the agent is trying to serve as financial advisor (but frequently without the necessary training). In response to the Tank Black debacle, the National Football League Players Association (NFLPA) added a voluntary registration for financial advisors. An NFLPA registered agent, Black was convicted and served seven years in prison after pleading guilty to charges of money laundering and obstruction of justice and losing a court decision on a charge of stock fraud after running a Ponzi scheme with his athletes' finances (Masteralexis et al., 2013). The NFLPA's program is simply a registration and not a regulatory measure, because under US laws, the union's antitrust exemption only protects it when regulating agents involved in contract negotiations. The reasoning is that if unions regulate which agents are qualified or not, they are restricting the market for those agents not certified. Labor laws protect unions from antitrust scrutiny when they are acting in their own self-interest, such as ensuring only qualified agents negotiate playing contracts involving collectively bargained rights. However, for the NFLPA to restrict those in other aspects of the athletes' business, it would do so with the risk of antitrust litigation from agents either rejected from certification or those not certified. As mentioned above, the MLBPA is one players union that certifies both agents (General Certification) and those who work strictly in a financial setting with no involvement in contract negotiations (Limited Certification) (MLBPA, 2015). In doing so, the MLBPA may also be taking a potential antitrust risk with the limited certification requirements if they reject or disqualify an agent from being certified for areas outside of contract negotiations.

The Modern Sports Agent Industry Landscape

The growth of popularity in professional sport led to a financial windfall for its participants, especially in the final two decades of the twentieth century. As salaries have grown in North America, so has the role of player agents in negotiating contracts, as well as the agents reaping their share of the newly created money market. In Europe, as with North America, agents deal with those sports that are the highest revenue producers (football, athletics, basketball, boxing, rugby, tennis, handball) or have the greatest media and communications exposure (Olympic sports). In both those categories, more financial rewards come to the agent who either serves as intermediary to place the athlete with a team or as an image-management or communications strategist (European Commission, 2009).

With a heavy influx of agents seeking to recruit a static number of clients, competition ensues, driving some agents to commit ethical and legal violations by offering players improper payment (Masteralexis et al., 2013). Without any sense of regulation, the sports agency community threatens to become a modern version of America's Wild West, as underhanded, unethical agents and/or runners endangering college student-athletes' eligibility and offering improper inducements to clients already contracted to another agent. Protection of eligibility for student-athletes has been at the forefront of most legislation aimed at agents who attempt to curry favor with the next wave of professional stars. Regulation of agents would not only protect student-athletes from losing eligibility, it would also protect professional athletes from becoming victims of financial fraud.

With no overarching licensing board for agents, almost anyone can act as an agent, and plenty have tried. In 1999, American rapper Percy "Master P" Miller formed No Limit Sports Management and signed Heisman Trophy winner Ricky Williams from the University of Texas as its first major client. Leland Hardy, Williams' agent at No Limit, negotiated a contract that undervalued Williams' talents and featured little guaranteed money, an out-of-the-ordinary experience for a first-round draft pick (Geisel, 2007).

Even with new regulations in place since Miller's foray into the agency world – the NFLPA now requires that certified agents must have an undergraduate and graduate (Master's or Law) degree from an accredited university (NFLPA, 2012) – there is no lack of lawyers and/or financial advisors attempting to enter the sports industry. Miller's foray has not stopped other entertainers from developing firms to market modern-day athletes. One of the latest is Shawn "Jay-Z" Carter's RocNation Sports, an offshoot of the entertainment company Carter founded in 2008. Carter's agency has enjoyed a much better start than Miller's, having helped Robinson Cano sign a 10-year $240 million contract with MLB's Seattle Mariners in 2013 (Greenburg, 2013).

C. THE REGULATORY FRAMEWORK OF SPORTS AGENTS

Unlike other professions, regulating agents has proven to be a challenge for a number of reasons. No overarching body equivocal to law's American Bar Association or medicine's American Medical Association has been formed to designate a uniform set of qualifications for certification (Masteralexis et al., 2013). While North America's four major sports leagues operate similarly with regard to wrongdoings in the agency world, nuances within each sport make it difficult to effectively devise and apply one set of guidelines across all sports. Despite these challenges, a number of bodies have attempted to regulate the sport agent industry with varying degrees of success. In North America, individual states, as well as the federal government, have drafted legislation in an attempt to regulate agents (Willenbacher, 2004). Internationally, bodies such as FIFA have drafted their set of rules and regulations for agents, while national associations have done the same, at times putting the two at odds (FIFA, 2007). Other international bodies, such as FIBA and IAAF require agents to take tests to be licensed, but they also offer exemptions for lawyers on the grounds that lawyers are regulated by their professional associations.

Union Regulation

The MLBPA under strong leadership turned the modern players union into a force at the negotiating table. As players have relied more on agents, the union has tried to regulate the latter. The birth of free agency and the ensuing proliferation of sports agents led players associations to take steps toward self-regulatory measures. With a seemingly unfettered entry process into the industry, players associations have taken steps to erect greater barriers to entry. Their power arises from their need to protect members from unscrupulous agents and to protect union benefits negotiated through collective bargaining. The union delegates individual negotiations over terms that will impact the collectively bargained ones to agents, so labor law allows for such regulation and protects it from antitrust scrutiny (*Collins v. NBPA*, 1991).

The NFLPA took the lead among the four major North American leagues, gaining exclusive representation rights for its players in 1982. Upon doing so, the NFLPA instituted an agent-certification program that led player agents to effectively act as the union's agents for negotiating players' contracts (Ruschmann, 1986). MLB followed suit soon after, while the NBA and the NHL had certification programs in place for their agents by 1996. Certification, and potential decertification, of agents works at the players' association level because the organizations have expertise in their industry and the ability to pressure members to fall in line for the betterment of the organization (Masteralexis et al., 2013).

The NFLPA's plan to "weed out incompetent agents and to lessen the burden imposed on its regulatory mechanisms" include the "one in three rule," which states an agent must negotiate at least one contract in a three-year period to retain his or her certification; toughening the questions on the NFLPA's certification exam; and capping the maximum commission compensation at 3 percent, the lowest of any of the four major leagues (Karcher, 2006). NFLPA President Eric Winston announced that the NFLPA's Committee on Agent Review and Discipline would soon undertake a review of the regulations governing NFL player agents. Winston's reasoning? "I think when you become an NFLPA-certified agent, that should mean something. And that should mean that a guy who is coming out of college can say, 'OK, you're an NFLPA-certified agent, you are held to a certain standard'" (Mullen, 2014).

In addition to agent certification, the NBPA took major steps toward the regulation of agents with its 2005 collective bargaining agreement. Article VIII, Section 1 of the agreement outlined a rookie pay scale, which, in theory, would make agents less of a necessity and drive more athletes toward agents like Lon Babby, who negotiated Grant Hill's first NBA contract for a flat fee of $100 000 or $1.7 million less than Babby could have earned through a more traditional commission-based system (Karcher, 2006). Should that practice take hold, an agent's commission would be limited, theoretically making the industry susceptible to unscrupulous agents seeking entry into the system. While there has been debate on the relative negotiation strength of the National Hockey League Players Association (NHLPA), the hockey union offered some early lessons in how a union can regulate market competition for agents and their resulting behavior. Alan Eagleson's time as Executive Director of the NHLPA from 1967 to 1991 – during which he also was a player agent – was characterized by secrecy, as Eagleson did not follow the precedent set by other North American sports leagues in publishing player salaries. Despite Eagleson's culture of silence, he laid the groundwork for changes after his tenure ended. Eagleson's replacement, Bob Goodenow, decided to publish player salaries, which eliminated the information asymmetry that favored teams in negotiations and increased transparency by enabling players and agents to ascertain a truer picture of the market for their services (Mason, 2001). Included in the improvements made during Goodenow's succession of Eagleson were higher salaries through salary disclosure and the beginning of the NHLPA's agent-certification program.

League Regulation

While each union took control of its agent certification process, the most recent collective bargaining agreement between the NBA and the NBPA vests in the NBA the power to act as an enforcer of the certification guidelines. As stated in Article XXXVI, Section 2, of the CBA:

> The NBA shall impose a fine of $50 000 upon any Team that negotiates a Player Contract with an agent or representative not certified by the Players Association in accordance with the Players Association's Agent Regulation Program if, at the time of such negotiations, such Team either (a) knows that such agent or representative has not been so certified, or (b) fails to make reasonable inquiry of the NBA as to whether such agent or representative has been so certified. (NBA, 2011, p.451)

In 2014, the Charlotte Hornets drafted P.J. Hairston in the first round. Less than three weeks after the draft, Hairston's agent, Juan Morrow, was determined to not have been certified by the NBPA, meaning he could not negotiate a contract for Hairston (Mattioli, 2014).

NCAA Regulation

At the major college athletic level in the United States, the NCAA is the largest governing body. The NCAA has long sought to maintain a "clear line of demarcation between college athletics and professional sports" (NCAA, 2009, p. 61). By maintaining a stance that college student-athletes do not leverage their athletic ability for pay either directly or indirectly, the NCAA has tried to keep intact its standard of amateurism, clearly separating college sports from the professional level.

Although the NCAA has bylaws prohibiting amateur athletes from retaining their eligibility if they contract with an agent, receive anything of value from an agent, or benefit from an agent's services, the NCAA has no control over the agents themselves, thereby leaving the current NCAA regulations with no distinction between permissible and impermissible conduct on an agent's part. The NCAA, instead, puts the threat of punishment for not following its rules directly on the student-athlete. The NCAA also asks its universities to self-monitor, shifting the responsibility to university compliance departments to determine if a violation has occurred (Masteralexis et al., 2013).

State Regulation

Initially, constituents of American states were able to use common law to take action against agents (Payne, 2011). Prior to 2000, the legal landscape of American athlete-agent law was nebulous and muddy, as power rested with each state. At that time, 28 states had enacted some sort of legal standards for agents, which allowed for civil and/or criminal recourse. In most cases the legislation was enacted in reaction to a scandal involving athletes and agents in those states. In 2000, the National Conference of Commissioners on Uniform State Laws (NCCUSL) attempted to consolidate the differences between the state statutes by approving the UAAA at its annual conference (Sudia & Remis, 2001). In their six-part series, Sudia and Remis determined six key factors the UAAA sought to streamline into one piece of legislation: NCAA regulations; civil and criminal liability of athlete agents and athletes; registration and reporting requirements; loopholes and constitutional defects based on tri-parte classification of athletes; athlete-agent solicitation (gifts and contracts); and agent advertisements and misrepresentations. The UAAA focuses on a combination of a requirement of specific disclosures and warnings by the agent to the athlete and notification to the athletic department. UAAA also requires uniform registration, certification, and background checking of agents seeking to represent student-athletes. Finally, it sets uniform penalties and remedies for violations by agents. Currently, 42 states have adopted UAAA legislation. Just seven states – Alaska, Maine, Massachusetts, Montana, New Jersey, Vermont, and Virginia – have no type of agent-related statutes comprising some combination of UAAA or of individual state law (Elsa, 2011).

In the United States, laws from state to state have proven to face the same issues with parallelism. Almost a decade and a half after the passage of the UAAA, states continue to tweak and expand their own legislation against rogue agents. In 2013, the Oregon House of Representatives passed House Bill 3296, which, among other pieces, adds "runners" to the definition of athlete agents and broadened the pool of athletes affected by agents to the elementary school level. "Oregon is sending a message. Agents must treat our student-athletes with respect. Those who attempt to take advantage of student-athletes in Oregon are not welcome here," said Oregon Senate President Peter Courtney (Schnell, 2013). Oklahoma also recently created a statewide sports agent prosecution team that will investigate charges of agent misconduct (Masteralexis et al., 2013).

Federal Regulation

While the passage of UAAA was meant to codify pieces of state legislation into one doctrine, thereby easing issues such as cross-state registration for agents who had clients in more than one state, the US government felt it necessary to do more. The passing of the UAAA helped to quell some of the fears and issues of non-centralized agent regulation. However, the US federal government felt it needed to fill in the gaps in the UAAA and passed SPARTA in 2004. The law was passed to "protect educational institutions and student-athletes from agent malfeasance in recruitment" (Payne, 2011, pp. 670–671). SPARTA was passed as a complementary piece of legislation, aimed at aiding, not replacing, the UAAA.

Differences in North America and International Frameworks

For the last three decades, North American sport has been marked by a lack of competing leagues at the top levels (Longley, 2013). That lack of competition is markedly different from countries whose sporting associations fall under the umbrella of international organizations such as FIFA and FIBA. From language to issues with who agents can represent, there are fundamental differences in agent regulation between North American and European sport.

In 2014, FIFA took the initiative of streamlining its agent rules and regulations one step further and eliminated the use of the word "agent" altogether (van Maren, 2014). Under the new regulations, which go into effect on 1 April 2015, the term "agent" has been stricken from use, replaced with "intermediary," a term that reflects on FIFA's decision to do away with the agent licensing system it implemented in 1996 (van Maren, 2014). Among the changes introduced in the March 2014 legislation was a more streamlined process of becoming an intermediary. Part of the process included the elimination of a 20-question multiple-choice exam that included questions on both FIFA and national policies. By streamlining their "intermediaries," FIFA's hope is that it has developed a more efficient way of regulating those who do agency-type work on behalf of the world's soccer players.

Unlike FIFA's structure, which allows for dual representation of clubs and players by these intermediaries (FIFA, 2014), FIBA and North American sports leagues do not allow for an agent to represent a team and player. However, there are sources of dual representation in American sports leagues, although those are cases where agents represent coaches and players. These situations raise questions as to whether coaches are members of management and how issues would be handled under the auspices of the National Labor Relations Act (Salvador, 2011).

One similarity that binds the two continents together is a seeming inability to enforce the rules that deter unscrupulous actions by agents. Most of the major legislation aimed at regulating American sports agents has been reactive, rather than proactive. Similarly, many of the penalties levied under SPARTA have been found to be not much of a deterrent. The maximum financial penalty that can be assigned to an agent under SPARTA is $11 000. These monetary fines do little to deter the unscrupulous actions of agents who have the financial capability to absorb such a loss (Willenbacher, 2004).

Similarly, countries whose football associations are aligned with FIFA regulations face nearly the same kinds of problems. Although FIFA has a clearly delineated definition of what constitutes a licensed agent, or an "exempt person," for dealing with transfers, only 25 to 30 percent of international transfers are conducted by licensed agents (Fornalik, 2013). These findings led FIFA to institute changes to its regulations. With such a small percentage of the lucrative international transfer market being handled by licensed agents, FIFA decided to make one of the more sweeping changes to agent regulation in recent memory.

Other International Federations

Federations such as FIBA, IAAF, and World Rugby have adopted regulations for sports agents. Their regulations are geared toward licensing through an exam or through the professional qualification of being a practicing attorney in good standing. In all federations, the agents must have no prior criminal record and must pass an exam evidencing knowledge of the sport and rules for the business of the sport. The regulations also require maintenance of the license through education and attendance at seminars on current issues. Finally, the regulations require agents to use standard contracts and charge standard fees within limits set by the international federations. All the governing bodies have systems by which to sanction agents or strip them of their certification. FIBA uses its Basketball Arbitration Tribunal (BAT) for resolving disputes with agents (FIBA, 2010). Appeals to BAT are final and binding. The other federations would likely end up resolving disputes at the Court for Arbitration for Sport or before an arbitration tribunal in the agent's or athlete's home country.

Challenges for Regulation/Regulators

Unlike the American legal and medical industries, which are regulated by the American Bar Association and American Medical Association, respectively, no such organization has been developed to serve as a true self-regulatory body for sports agents. Additionally, the enactment of laws such as SPARTA and UAAA has not equated to successful enforcement or regulation of an industry. There is a marked difference between having legislation on the books and the active enforcement of such statutes. Since being granted oversight authority by Congress, as of 2010, the Federal Trade Commission (FTC) had not suspended or revoked a single agent's license, nor had it issued any penalties under its new authority. The same rationale held true for more than half of the 42 states with sports agent laws in effect in 2010 (Associated Press, 2010).

While the majority of attention in the United States is paid to agent improper recruitment of college athletes, some of the most well-known agents in the industry have found themselves facing criticism for other unethical actions. Scott Boras, arguably the most powerful active baseball agent, found himself the subject of former MLB Commissioner Bud Selig's contempt. Selig was attempting to clean up the murkiness surrounding a number of issues dealing with baseball in the Dominican Republic. While Selig was pushing for stricter punishments for corrupt employees, Boras was accused of making $70 000 worth of improper loans to Dominican prospect Edward Salcedo (Schmidt, 2011). The MLBPA supported Boras and argued that the loans did not violate its regulations, which led to a war of words between Selig's office and the union. The union's stance backing Boras provides another example of why unions are loathe to punish agents, especially those with a significant client base, such as Boras' stable of All-Stars.

The NCAA has its share of detractors, many of whom decry the organization as hypocritical for becoming a more commercialized enterprise while not compensating its athletes. The NCAA requires universities to self-monitor when many have neither the human resources to invest nor the will to investigate all possible violations, allowing the more nefarious agents to beat the system. The NCAA has no control over agents themselves, thereby leaving current NCAA regulations with no distinction between permissible and impermissible conduct on an agent's part. Former agent Josh Luchs described his method of paying players as giving them small monthly sums of money to remain in contact with him rather than a large one-time payment. Actions like those taken by Luchs make it tougher on university compliance departments and, in turn, the NCAA to determine that a violation has occurred (Mills, 2012).

Financial issues have been a source of worry for the NCAA when pursuing criminal or civil action against agents. During his tenure, the Athletic Director at the University of Southern California stated his support for civil actions against agents by suggesting the NCAA impose a tax on its member institutions with the proceeds funding mandatory civil action against agents who harm schools. In such a proceeding, the NCAA would benefit not only financially, but educationally from the information divulged in court proceedings (Mills, 2012).

Similarly, NCAA bylaw 10.1 states "unethical conduct" by an athlete includes "refusal to furnish information relevant to an investigation of a possible violation of an NCAA regulation when requested to do so by the NCAA or the individual's institution" (NCAA, 2009, p. 47). One example of such information is what the NCAA asks potential MLB draftees to submit through the Prospective Student-Athlete Release. Eighteen questions are included in the release, including several that ask prospective student-athletes to divulge information from conversations with advisors, an ethical breach of the Modern Rules of Professional Conduct 1.6 – confidentiality of information (Karcher, 2012).

Although the NCAA delineates between an "agent" and an "advisor" in its regulations, such regulations essentially prevent baseball student-athletes from having a competent lawyer or agent represent them in contractual negotiations with MLB franchises (Karcher, 2005). Because of the timing of the MLB First-Year Player Draft, college baseball players may still retain their college eligibility after being drafted, something players selected in the NBA and NFL drafts are unable to do (Lockhart, 2010). Additionally, high school seniors and junior college players are eligible for the draft, as well as still having future eligibility at NCAA schools. The same holds true for the NHL draft, which also is open to high-school-age players. The NCAA bylaws attempting to restrict agent involvement with collegiate athletes have a long history of success against legal challenges. One prominent case involved a former Notre Dame football player who initially sought a temporary injunction to allow him to use his final season of eligibility despite having declared for the 1990 draft. Advised he would be selected in the 1990 NFL draft, despite having a year of college eligibility remaining, he declared for the draft and went unselected, which, according to NCAA bylaw 12.2.4.2, caused him to forfeit his remaining eligibility (*Banks v. NCAA*, 1992). In addition, the player agreed to be represented by an agent, therefore enacting NCAA bylaw 12.3.1 – the "No Agent Rule" – which also was grounds for forfeiting his final year of collegiate athletic eligibility. The player's assertion that the NCAA eligibility rules were a restraint of trade was dismissed.

The Banks case was one of the first to challenge the NCAA's no-draft and no-agent rules, and, like many of its peers, it failed to sway the court. However, Oklahoma State pitcher Andy Oliver scored a victory against the NCAA in 2009, securing a temporary injunction when an Ohio judge ruled the bylaws in question were "arbitrary and capricious" (Lockhart, 2010). The decision by Erie County judge Tygh M. Tone "voided" NCAA bylaw 12.3.2.1, which led the NCAA to settle the case for $750 000 and the decision to be vacated. The Oliver decision, however, has been hailed as "strike one" against the no-agent rules. Upon the decision, the MLBPA issued a statement saying that the group "believes that all individuals dealing with professional sports franchises should have access to representation. We hope the Oliver case furthers that goal" (Lockhart, 2010, pp. 197–198).

In Europe, questions abound as to whether sports agent regulation should exist at the EU level. After white papers being produced and policy research being conducted over the years 2007–2011, there is still no accepted decision or plan forward. The questions that remain are whether regulation needs to exist, since agents would be covered by other laws in the European Union, such as those governing job placement, movement of workers (transfers), criminal action, competition restrictions, and the like. Further, questions remain as to whether regulation is best done at the local level through national federations or Member State statutes, or globally through international federations (European Commission, 2009). And while the debate continues, FIFA has deregulated and pushed agent regulation back to its national federations. The question remains as to whether that is the proper form of self-regulation or whether it will create additional mazes of regulations for agents in the global football business.

D.   SUGGESTIONS FOR FUTURE RESEARCH

FIFA's decision to deregulate agents and to push the regulations back is an area ripe for future research. Its decision to streamline its intermediaries came in light of the challenges it faced in attempting to regulate actors over whom the governing body had no control. It will certainly be worthwhile research to determine if this decision by FIFA opens the door for corruption, enables a more local form of control over football agents, or leads to a different, more national or international body to regulate the group.

A second stream of research would be to survey agents on their perceptions of agent regulation as opposed to the current research which relies on anecdotal evidence. One hurdle might be the ability for agents to agree to speak freely, but surveying that group would certainly enable the industry to evaluate the effectiveness of regulation from an important angle.

CONCLUSION

The sports agency industry came to age in the decades following the Mark H. McCormack–Arnold Palmer handshake. As it has evolved into a hyper-competitive business, it has come to be known for its underhanded practices. Regulation has been attempted by governing bodies, governmental entities, and players unions, but none to date have cleaned up the industry. The answer may lie in a national or international self-regulating body.

REFERENCES

Associated Press (2010), 'Report: State agent laws unenforced', accessed 20 May 2015 at http://sports.espn.go.com/ncaa/news/story?id=5470067.
ATP (2014), *2014 ATP World Tour Media Guide*.
Baker, T.A., D.A. Heitner, J.F. Brocard, and K.K. Byon (2012), 'Football v. Football: A comparison of agent regulations in France's Ligue 1 and the National Football League', *Pace Intellectual Property, Sports and Entertainment Forum*, **2**, 1.
Banks v. NCAA, 977 F.2d 1081 (7th Cir. 1992).
Belzer, J. (2013), 'The world's most valuable sports agencies', accessed 20 May 2015 at http://www.forbes.com/sites/jasonbelzer/2013/06/24/the-worlds-most-valuable-sports-agencies-2/.

Brown, M. (2014), 'MLB's billion dollar TV deals, free agency, and why Robinson Cano's deal with the Mariners isn't "crazy"', accessed 20 May 2015 at http://www.forbes.com/sites/maurybrown/2014/01/07/mlbs-billion-dollar-tv-deals-free-agency-and-why-robinson-canos-deal-with-the-mariners-isnt-crazy/.

Collins v. NBPA, 850 F. Supp. 1468 (1991) *aff'd per curium* 976 F.2d 740 (10th Cir. 1992).

Columbia University Athletics (2009), 'Columbia vs. Princeton: First televised sporting event marks 70th anniversary', *GoColumbiaLions.com*, accessed 20 May 2015 at http://www.gocolumbialions.com/ViewArticle.dbml?DB_OEM_ID=9600&ATCLID=3738874.

Deubert, C. (2011), 'What's a "clean" agent to do? The case for a cause of action against a player's association', *Villanova Sports and Entertainment Law Journal*, **18** (1), pp. 1–37.

Edelman, M. (2013), 'Disarming the Trojan horse of the UAAA and SPARTA: How America should reform its sports agent laws to conform with true agency principles', *Harvard Law School Journal of Sports and Entertainment Law*, **4** (2), pp. 145–189.

Edmonds, E. (2010), 'At the brink of free agency: Creating the foundation for the Messersmith–McNally decision – 1968–1975', *Southern Illinois University Law Journal*, **4**, pp. 565–619.

Elsa, D. (2011), 'Athlete agent laws in the United States', *SportsAgentBlog.com*, 2 June, accessed 20 May 2015 at https://docs.google.com/spreadsheet/ccc?key=0AhBoF1Q_EsPhdHFzc1lheUFWRFJNVWxWVkRqSXFPQ1E&authkey=CNPa-8YD&hl=en_US&authkey=CNPa-8YD#gid=0.

European Commission (2009), 'Study on sports agents in the European Union', accessed 20 July 2015 at http://ec.europa.eu/sport/library/studies/study-sports-agents-in-eu.pdf.

European Commission (2011), 'EU Conference on Sports', accessed 20 July 2015 at http://ec.europa.eu/sport/library/studies/final-report-eu-conference-sports-agents.pdf.

FIBA (2010), 'Basketball Arbitration Tribunal (BAT)', accessed 15 July 2015 at http://www.fiba.com/downloads/v3_expe/bat/FIBA%20Book%203%20AG%20-%20chap7.pdf.

FIBA (2016), 'FIBA certified agents', accessed 24 February 2016 at http://www.fiba.com/pages/eng/fc/expe/fibaAgen/agenSear/p/langlc/en/searResu.html.

FIFA (2007), 'Reguations: Players' agents', accessed 20 May 2015 at http://www.fifa.com/mm/document/affederation/administration/51/55/18/players_agents_regulations_2008.pdf.

FIFA (2014), 'Regulations on working with intermediaries', accessed 20 May 2015 at http://www.fifa.com/mm/document/affederation/footballgovernance/02/36/77/63/workingwithintermediariesenweb_neutral.pdf.

Fornalik, J.A. (2013), 'Players agents' role in football transfer market: Evaluating the need of improving FIFA regulations', paper presented at Entertainment Law Seminar, Chicago-Kent College of Law, 14 March.

Fraley, R.E. and F.R. Harwell (1989), 'The sports lawyer's duty to avoid differing interests: A practical guide to responsible representation', *Hastings Communications and Entertainment Law Journal*, **11**, pp. 165–217.

Gaines, C. (2014), 'CHART: NBA tops all sports leagues with highest average salary for players', *Business Insider*, accessed 4 January 2016 at http://www.businessinsider.com/chart-nba-average-salary-2014-4?IR=T.

Geisel, J.J. (2007), 'Disbarring Jerry Maguire: How broadly defining "unauthorized practice of law" could take the "lawyer" out of "lawyer-agent" despite the current state of athlete-agent legislation', *Marquette Sports Law Review*, **18** (1), pp. 225–247.

Greenburg, Z.O. (2013), 'Cano signs $240M deal with Seattle; Jay-Z saves face, sort of', *Forbes.com*, accessed 20 May 2015 at http://www.forbes.com/sites/zackomalleygreenburg/2013/12/06/cano-signs-240m-deal-with-seattle-jay-z-saves-face-sort-of/.

Helyar, John (1995), *The Lords of the Realm*, New York, NY, USA: Ballantine Books.

IAAF (2014), 'IAAF Athletes' Representatives Regulations 2012' (amended April 2014), accessed 18 July 2015 at http://www.iaaf.org/about-iaaf/documents/athlete-representatives#ar-exam.

Karcher, R.T. (2005), 'The NCAA's regulations related to the use of agents in the sport of baseball: Are the rules detrimental to the best interest of the amateur athlete?', *Vanderbilt Journal of Entertainment Law and Practice*, **7**, pp. 215–230.

Karcher, R.T. (2006), 'Solving problems in the player representation business: Unions should be the "exclusive" representatives of the players', *Willamette Law Review*, **42**, pp.737–780.

Karcher, R.T. (2012), 'The NCAA's indirect regulation of lawyer-agents: In direct conflict with the model rules of professional conduct', paper presented at Third Annual Sports Law Symposium, Santa Clara University Institute of Sports Law and Ethics, 6 September.

Lockhart, T.M. (2010), 'Oliver v. NCAA: Throwing a contractual curveball at the NCAA's "Veil of amateurism"', *University of Dayton Law Review*, **35** (2), pp.175–198.

Longley, Neil (2013), *An Absence of Competition: The Sustained Competitive Advantage of the Monopoly Sports Leagues*, New York, NY, USA: Springer Science and Business Media.

Mason, D.S. (2001), 'Industry factors and the changing dynamics of the player–agent relationship in professional ice hockey', *Sport Management Review*, **4** (2), pp.165–191.

Masteralexis, J., L. Masteralexis, and K. Snyder (2013), 'Enough is enough: The case for federal regulation of sports agents', *Jeffrey S. Moorad Sports Law Journal*, **20**, pp.69–105.

Mattioli, K. (2014), 'P.J. Hairston's agent is not certified – and that's a problem', *SportingNews.com*, accessed 20 May 2015 at http://www.sportingnews.com/nba/story/2014-07-10/pj-hairston-agent-juan-morrow-fake-not-real-nba-draft-contract-nbpa.

Mills, M. (2012), 'There is no need to reinvent the wheel: The tools to prevent agent-related NCAA violations may already be in our hands', *Seton Hall Journal of Sports and Entertainment Law*, **22** (2), pp.345–380.

MLB (2014), '2014 opening day rosters feature 224 players born outside the U.S.', *MLB.com*, accessed 20 May 2015 at http://mlb.mlb.com/news/article.jsp?ymd=20140401&content_id=70623418&vkey=pr_mlb&c_id=mlb.

MLBPA (2015), 'MLBPA regulations governing player agents', accessed 20 May 2015 at http://reg.mlbpaagent.org/Documents/AgentForms/Agent%20Regulations.pdf.

Mullen, L. (2014), 'A lot of missteps prompt wholesale NFLPA review', *SportsBusiness Daily.com*, accessed 20 May 2015 at http://www.sportsbusinessdaily.com/Journal/Issues/2014/04/21/Labor-and-Agents/Labor-and-Agents.aspx.

Nahwrold, S.M. (1999), 'Are professional athletes better served by a lawyer-representative than an agent? Ask Grant Hill', *Seton Hall Journal of Sports and Entertainment Law*, **9**, p.431.

NBA (2011), 'NBA collective bargaining agreement', accessed 20 May 2015 at http://www.ipmall.info/hosted_resources/SportsEntLaw_Institute/NBA_CBA(2011)_(newversion_reflectsJeremyLinRuling)May30_2013.pdf.

NBA (2013), 'NBA tips off 2013–14 season with record international player presence', *NBA.com*, accessed 20 May 2015 at http://www.nba.com/global/nba_tips_off_201314_season_with_record_international_presence_2013_10_29.html.

NBPA (1991), 'NBPA regulations governing player agents', accessed 20 May 2015 at http://www.nbpa.org/sites/default/files/users/sean.brandveen/Agent%20Regulations%20PDF.pdf.

NCAA (2009), '2009–10 Division I Manual', accessed 20 May 2015 at www.ncaapublications.com: http://www.ncaapublications.com/productdownloads/D110.pdf.

NCAA v. Board of Regents of University of Oklahoma, 468 U.S. 85 (1984).

NFLPA (2012), 'NFLPA regulations governing contract advisors', accessed 20 May 2015 at https://nflpaweb.blob.core.windows.net/media/Default/PDFs/Agents/2012_NFLPA_Regulations_Governing_Contract_Advisors.pdf.

Ozanian, M. (2013), 'Deal between ESPN and SEC likely the richest ever', *Forbes.com*, accessed 20 May 2015 at http://www.forbes.com/sites/mikeozanian/2013/05/31/deal-between-espn-and-sec-conference-likely-the-richest-ever/.

Payne, R.A. (2011), 'Rebuilding the prevent defense: Why unethical agents continue to score and what can be done to change the game', *Vanderbilt Journal of Entertainment and Technology Law*, **13** (3), pp.657–694.

PGA (2013), *PGA Tour Official 2013–14 Guide*.

Pugh Interview (2014a), Pugh, J. (Interviewer) & Bouris, G., Director of Communications, MLBPA (Interviewee), August 8, 2014.

Pugh Interview (2014b), Pugh, J. (Interviewer) & Francis, C., Director of Communications, NFLPA (Interviewee), August 13, 2014.

Robertson v. NBA, 389 F. Supp. 867 (S.D.N.Y. 1975).

Rudd, A. (2013), 'Agents refuse to accept FIFA deregulation as a done deal', *TheTimes.co.uk*, accessed 20 May 2015 at http://www.thetimes.co.uk/tto/sport/football/article3792517.ece.

Ruschmann, P. (1986), 'Are sports agents facing a regulatory blitz?', *Michigan Bar Journal*, **65** (11), pp. 1124–1127.

Ruxin, Robert H. (2004), *An Athlete's Guide to Agents*, Sudbury, MA, USA: Jones & Bartlett Publishers.

Salvador, A.L. (2011), 'The regulation of dual representation in the NFL', *Texas Review of Entertainment and Sports Law*, **13** (1), pp. 63–83.

Schmidt, M. (2011), 'Selig is said to be unsatisfied with union's stance on Boras', *NYTimes.com*, accessed 20 May 2015 at http://www.nytimes.com/2011/01/05/sports/baseball/05boras.html?_r=0.

Schnell, L. (2013), 'Governor signs measure to increase regulation of sports agents', *OregonLive.com*, accessed 20 May 2015 at http://www.oregonlive.com/ducks/index.ssf/2013/05/governor_signs_measure_to_incr.html.

Shropshire, Kenneth L. and Timothy Davis (2003), *The Business of Sports Agents*, Philadelphia, PA, USA: University of Pennsylvania Press.

Sobel, Lionel (2009), 'The regulation of player agents and lawyers', in G.A. Uberstine (ed.), *The Law of Professional and Amateur Sports*, St. Paul, MN, USA: West Group, pp. 1-2–1-3.

Staudohar, P.D. (2002), 'Baseball negotiations: A new agreement', *Monthly Labor Review*, **125** (12), pp. 15–22.

Steinbreder, John (1996), 'An interview with Mark McCormack', in *Mark McCormack's Guide to Sports Marketing*, Largo, FL, USA: International Sports Marketing Group, pp. 22–41.

Sudia, D. and R. Remis (2001), 'Athlete agent legislation in the new millennium: State statutes and the uniform athlete agent act', *Seton Hall Journal of Sport Law*, **11**, pp. 263–296.

van Maren, O. (2014), 'A short guide to the new FIFA regulations on working with intermediaries', *Asser.nl* Asser International Sports Law blog, 3 July, accessed 20 May 2015 at http://www.asser.nl/SportsLaw/Blog/post/a-short-guide-to-the-new-fifa-regulations-on-working-with-intermediaries.

Willenbacher, E. (2004), 'Regulating sports agents: Why current federal and state efforts do not deter the unscrupulous athlete-agent and how a national licensing system may cure the problem', *St. John's Law Review*, **78** (4), pp. 1225–1256.

PART II

THE EMPLOYMENT
RELATIONS OF
PROFESSIONAL SPORTS

6. The evolution of collective bargaining in sports

James B. Dworkin

INTRODUCTION

In this chapter I will trace the evolution of collective bargaining in the arena of professional sports. The history of collective bargaining in professional sports will be covered through a focus on seven crucial individuals who had an enormous impact on the development of collective bargaining in professional baseball, ranging from John Montgomery Ward in the early days of the sport to one of the modern day Commissioners, Bowie Kuhn. The second section of this chapter updates the state of collective bargaining in the four major sports in the United States: baseball, basketball, football and ice hockey. The chapter concludes with a look into the future and ten trends we are likely to observe.

While I try to focus on the more positive side of professional sports, one does need to realize that there has been much recent attention on issues such as drug usage, gambling, racial prejudice and safety concerns (Pope, Price & Wolfers, 2013). While I do not herein cover these issues in any detail, the interested reader is referred to two excellent recent books covering the Peter Rose gambling controversy (Kennedy, 2014) and the Alex Rodriguez steroid drug usage situation (Elfrink & Garcia-Roberts, 2014). As I note in the final section of this chapter, these issues will continue to haunt all professional sports into the foreseeable future.

One thing that stands out above all else in professional sport today is the extravagant salaries that players receive. While many fans may envy or resent the high salaries paid to professional athletes, it is important to remember that each athlete possesses a very rare set of skills for which he is compensated. Other individuals with such rare skills like actors, actresses, musicians and CEOs of large corporations also receive very high levels of compensation. For example, umpires in professional baseball do receive relatively high salaries but not in comparison to the average player! Why? Because there are many, many more individuals who possess the skills to become umpires than there are those with the rare talents necessary to become professional baseball players. Even first year players are paid upwards of a half a million dollars, depending on the sport. The average player salary in some professional leagues exceeds $3 million per season. The natural question to ask is how did this state of affairs come to be? As most people are aware, for many years athletes were treated as chattels (Ward, 1887) and received paltry wages. They had no alternatives if they wanted to do the thing they loved, play a professional sport. Movement from team to team and from league to league was highly regulated and controlled by the league ownership. Players faced what economists call a monopsonistic labor market (Dworkin, 1981) where their services were owned by one and only one team. In such a labor market environment, an individual player is rather powerless and must accept the contract offer made to him or pursue a different occupation. Players in all professional sports were owned for the life of their short careers by the team for which they played. Individual players did not have agents to represent them in contract negotiations. Rather, the team would make an offer by sending each player a standard contract. The player had two choices. He could sign the contract for the offered wage and continue to pursue the sport he so loved. Or, he could try to bargain for a higher wage, which was seldom successful due to the lack of any bargaining power by the player. No law required the player to sign the contract and so the ultimate action he could take was to sit out the season (go on a one person strike) or retire from the sport. It was theoretically possible that retirement could lead to a successful career in another occupation outside of the sport. But more likely, the player who possessed rare playing skills like speed, extreme coordination and the ability to throw or kick a ball a long distance had no way to transfer these scarce skills to another occupation in the real world. And besides, our ballplayer wants to play the sport he loves, not toil as a miner or in some factory in a laborers job (Dworkin & Posthuma, 2013).

And so, for many years in the early days of professional sports, athletes were underpaid and treated rather poorly by team owners. Players had few options and nobody was advising them on how to improve their lots in life. But this rather grim labor market situation was about to change forever. The change came about in the form of union representation and collective bargaining by these professional athletes.

HISTORY OF COLLECTIVE BARGAINING IN SPORTS

There is a story of how collective bargaining got started in every sport in countries around the world. I do not have the luxury of relating all of these separate exciting stories given space limitations. And so, I will concentrate on one sport in largely one country, professional baseball in the

United States. But even though this is but one example of the history and development of collective bargaining in professional sports, several themes are found in all such developments of collective bargaining for professional athletes. These themes are: (1) the involvement of pioneering and coura-geous individual athletes who wanted to improve their position in life and the position of all of their fellow athletes in the sport; (2) the crucial role of agents and other experts who advised the athletes on their journey; and finally (3) the role of outside forces such as the courts, arbitrators and leg-islation in furthering the cause of these professional athletes.

In baseball there have been so many people who played critical roles in the above three categories. It is unfortunate that many important names must be omitted. Readers interested in a fuller historical treatment should see Dworkin (1981). But it is fair to say that the following seven indi-viduals have had a major impact on developing collective bargaining in professional baseball:

1.   John Montgomery Ward
2.   Curt Flood
3.   Marvin Miller
4.   Andy Messersmith
5.   Dave McNally
6.   Peter Seitz
7.   Bowie Kuhn

Let me briefly explain why in each case.

John Montgomery Ward

While he was a very talented baseball player with a very interesting life story, John Montgomery Ward (Ward, 1887) is perhaps best known for being the President of the first players' union, the National Brotherhood of Professional Baseball Players. The prime mechanism used by the league to keep player salaries low was the reserve rule. Under such a provision, clubs could maintain their players into perpetuity at whatever wage they paid that player. This reserve rule was described by Ward as ". . . a fugitive slave law, which denied the player harbor or a livelihood and carried him back, bound and shackled to the club from which he attempted to escape. Once a player's name is attached to a contract, his professional liberty is gone forever" (Organized Baseball, 1952).

As long as they faced a reserve clause, players could expect careers with one team at low, less than market salaries. It should also be noted that players were at the mercy of the team owners in that they could be traded or sold to a different team in a different city at any time. Rather than trying to eliminate this system, Ward and his fellow players of the day recognized that a modified reservation system was good for baseball. And so, way back in the late 1880s, and before formal collective bargaining, club owners and player representatives negotiated a workable solution to the player reservation system for the time. The owners promised to limit the number of players who could be reserved to 14 per team and to not reduce salaries for any players reserved to a team under this system. The National League owners also promised to repeal the salary limits they had set earlier. However, despite these courageous efforts by early players like Ward, fundamental changes to the player reservation system were still a long way off. It would take almost another century before Ward's dream of player free agency rights would be realized.

Curt Flood

When we fast-forward many years to around 1966, we still see low player salaries and a reservation system intact as it had existed in the days of John Montgomery Ward. The players had a union called the Major League Baseball Players Association (MLBPA), which is still in existence today. Vocal players like Curt Flood were quick to condemn the MLBPA as a company union which did nothing for the membership, the baseball players (Flood & Carter, 1970).

While several other players had attempted to use the courts to nullify the reservation system, Curt Flood's case really turned the tide toward the players. Flood was an outfielder for the St. Louis Cardinals for 12 years prior to being traded to the Philadelphia Phillies club in October of 1969. Rather than accept the trade and join his new team as countless previous players had done, Flood instead asked then baseball Commissioner Bowie Kuhn to negate the trade and declare him to be a free agent. This request was denied and Flood sued organized baseball in January of 1970, claiming baseball's reserve clause violated federal antitrust laws. Flood sat out the entire 1970 season! He was later traded to the Washington Senators but played only about one month before retiring from baseball in April of 1971. Flood's case was ultimately decided by the US Supreme Court in 1972 (*Curtis C. Flood v. Bowie K. Kuhn*, 1972).

The court relied on the principle of *stare decisis* in rendering judgment and dismissing Flood's case. Basically, earlier cases decided in favor of organized baseball would stand (*Federal Baseball Club of Baltimore v. National League*, 1922; *Toolson v. New York Yankees*, 1953).

While Flood did not win his case in 1972, the cause for all baseball players and other professional athletes to win free agency rights was advanced. Two Supreme Court justices (Douglas and Brennan) felt the earlier Federal Baseball Club and Toolson decisions were wrong and that baseball should be held subject to federal antitrust regulation. The key lesson from Flood was that players would not win free agency through the courts. That left two other options, legislation or collective bargaining negotiations. The probability of favorable legislation was not high, so the table was set (the collective bargaining table) for players and clubs to resolve this matter through negotiations. The stage was set for the entrance of Marvin Miller.

Marvin Miller

All successful player unions across all sports need excellent leadership to make progress on the goals discussed above. Professional athletes wanted free agency rights which would help them generate higher, market-oriented salaries. The eventual raising of all player salaries has led to some very interesting modern day problems such as where lower paid National Basketball Association (NBA) players argue that they are victims of the so-called jock tax. It is common today for visiting players to be taxed by the state they visit with their team. However, Tennessee (Pilon, 2013) charges visiting players the flat tax of $2500 a game, which is a much heavier burden for a rookie earning $500 000 per season than for a star player like LeBron James who earns $19 million per season. This problem would not even be spoken of today were it not for the likes of union leaders like Marvin Miller who helped the players achieve their free agency and salary goals.

In the year 1966 professional baseball players thought that their union, the MLBPA, was too passive. Some players like Curt Flood resorted to individual action with little or no success.

Marvin Miller had worked during World War II as a disputes hearing officer at the Wage Stabilization Division of the War Labor Board. After leaving government service Miller worked for three years with the International Association of Machinists and then the United Steelworkers Union. He rose to the position of assistant to President David MacDonald. While working with the steelworkers, Miller made many contacts, one of whom was Professor George Taylor of the Wharton School at the University of Pennsylvania. When the players began their search for a more aggressive executive director, it was association member and veteran pitcher Robin Roberts who asked Professor Taylor if he had any suggestions for a person who could take on the role of full-time executive director of the MLBPA. Professor Taylor suggested Marvin Miller and the players hired him as their executive director in 1966. This hiring signaled the beginning of major changes to come. In Miller the players now had an experienced labor negotiator much more familiar with the ins and outs of collective bargaining than were the owners. Much of the fascinating background to these changes is related in Marvin Miller's own book (Miller, 1991) to which the interested reader is referred.

I will just relate several highlights of Miller's term as executive director of the MLBPA. While there are a myriad of accomplishments that Miller helped the players achieve through the process of collective bargaining, the three key achievements I want to briefly mention are: (1) grievance arbitration; (2) salary arbitration; and (3) free agency. All of these are well covered in Dworkin (1981) and by Miller (1991) himself, so this treatment will not do justice to the importance of these accomplishments.

The players negotiated their first grievance procedure in their first collective bargaining agreement in the year 1968. It was a good start but contained one unusual aspect, in that the final and impartial arbitrator at the last step of the grievance procedure was then baseball Commissioner William Eckert. This situation demonstrates two interesting negotiation principles that cut across the evolution of collective bargaining in all sports. First, progress in negotiations does not come all at once. The MLBPA and Marvin Miller would have preferred a neutral arbitrator as is the standard in almost all collective bargaining contracts. Yet to have success in negotiating a grievance procedure of some type into the first collective bargaining contract proved to be a very important step. The gains achieved in collective bargaining are not typically achieved all at once. A second key principle illustrated is the importance of compromise and that both sides must make concessions. The players would compromise on the grievance arbitration issue at the time and hope to bring back the importance of an impartial neutral in later rounds of negotiations. Fast-forwarding to the year 2014, the baseball grievance procedure is much in the news with the case of Alexander Emmanuel Rodriguez, usually referred to as A-Rod. Arbitrator Frederic R. Horowitz was the neutral panel member who heard the grievance filed by Rodriguez over his long suspension from baseball for his alleged drug usage. Arbitrator Horowitz ruled against Rodriguez and upheld his suspension by Major League Baseball for the entire 2014 season. Rodriguez then filed a Complaint in the United States District Court Southern District of New York (*Rodriguez v. Major League Baseball, Office of the Commissioner of Baseball and Major League Baseball Players Association*, 2013) seeking to vacate the arbitration award, find that the MLBPA breached its duty of fair representation of Rodriguez and find that Major League Baseball breached the collective bargaining agreement. Shortly after this filing Rodriguez dropped his lawsuit, perhaps in acknowledgment that he had little chance to succeed.

Commissioner Eckert heard only two cases before he was fired as club owners hired Bowie Kuhn to be their next Commissioner (Kuhn, 1987). Since Kuhn had been involved in the 1968 collective bargaining negotiations, the parties realized it made no sense for him to be the neutral arbitrator in baseball's grievance procedure. The parties hired David Cole as their first neutral grievance arbitrator and the rest is history. The saga of how Marvin Miller achieved salary arbitration and free agency for baseball players will be told via the grievance cases filed by Andy Messersmith and Dave McNally, and ultimately resolved in favor of the players by neutral arbitrator Peter Seitz. But before advancing to those interesting gains made by the players, more on Marvin Miller. His example of union leadership has been proven to hold many lessons for unions in other sports in other countries, and even for management. One lasting legacy of Miller's was his hiring of great deputies and his preparation for succession. In his case, the first deputy was attorney Donald Fehr, who later became the executive director of the MLBPA. But this lesson of good leadership and preparing for the next leader has not been lost on the management side of other professional sports (Boudway, 2014a). NBA Commissioner David Stern, who has held that position since February 1, 1984, stepped down 30 years to the day after his first day on the job. His protégé is Adam Silver, who joined the NBA in 1992 as Stern's special assistant and has been Deputy Commissioner since 2006. Silver is widely regarded as being very capable and prepared to run the NBA and should prove both a formidable and worthy opponent in future rounds of negotiations with the NBA players union. Just as Miller mentored and prepared his successor Donald Fehr for duty as executive director of the MLBPA, Stern did a wonderful job in doing the same so that Adam Silver was ready on day one to be the NBA Commissioner.

Andy Messersmith and Dave McNally

The table was now set for the MLBPA and Marvin Miller to challenge baseball, and one of all professional sport's most restrictive labor market practices, the reservation system. Negotiating a grievance procedure with a neutral arbitrator as the final step gave the players the opportunity they had anticipated since the days of John Montgomery Ward. All that was needed was the right situation to arise to enable player free agency rights (Gilbert, 2013).

That opportunity came along in the form of baseball players Andy Messersmith and Dave McNally. Messersmith had a one-year contract in 1974 with the Los Angeles Dodgers for $90000. A dispute between him and the Dodgers over a no-trade clause enabled Messersmith to play the entire 1975 season (for $115000) without a signed contract. The Dodgers utilized paragraph 10(a) of the Uniform Player's Contract to reserve Messersmith to their team for the 1975 season.

With pitcher Dave McNally of the then Montreal Expos, the situation was similar. He had played in 1974 with a signed contract but, unable to agree to terms for the 1975 season, had been reserved to the Expos under the same paragraph 10(a) of the Uniform Player's Contract. He only played for a portion of the 1975 season before retiring from the game.

When the 1975 season concluded both declared they were free agents and eligible to negotiate with any club of their choosing. The MLBPA argued that since each player had already been reserved to his respective team for one season under paragraph 10(a), each now had the right to be a free agent. The baseball establishment had a very different take on this situation. The owners argued that instead of the one year of reservation maintained by the MLBPA, the reservation rights established in paragraph 10(a) of the Uniform Player's Contract were perpetual. This issue reached a boiling point in October of 1975 when the MLBPA filed a grievance on behalf of both pitchers seeking to have a neutral arbitrator declare them to be free agents. The stage was set for baseball's most famous grievance arbitration case of all time. It was time for arbitrator Peter Seitz to step up to the plate.

Peter Seitz

Before delving into this case, free agency in all professional sports has spawned a plethora of research over the ensuing years. Sports economists have written on a fascinating variety of topics ranging from price discrimination, tournament incentives, the reserve clause and labor mobility, salary caps and luxury taxes (Kahane & Shmanske, 2012).

Professional journals have also been established such as the *Journal of Sports Economics*, which regularly publishes research articles focusing on the evolution of collective bargaining in professional sports. Two recent examples are papers by Poplawski and O'Hara (2014) on the feasibility of new National Hockey League (NHL) cities given the recently negotiated collective bargaining agreement; and Nichols (2014), who discusses the impact of visiting team travel on game outcomes and National Football League (NFL) wagering markets. These are but a few examples of the research being performed on the evolution of collective bargaining in professional sports. Without Peter Seitz's arbitration on free agency, much of this recent research would not have occurred!

Prior to the actual arbitration hearing on the Messersmith/McNally grievances, baseball owners went to unprecedented lengths to avoid arbitration and preserve the reservation system. An attempt to prevent these grievances from going to arbitration failed in court. The actual arbitration hearing on this crucial issue lasted only three days – November 21, 24 and December 1, 1975. Contrast that with the 11-day arbitration hearing in the most recent Alex Rodriguez case, dealing with one player's alleged drug abuse. The Seitz arbitration affected all players in all sports for generations to come.

At the hearing the owners made two familiar arguments often heard in labor arbitration cases. Argument number one was these cases were not arbitrable, or not properly before the arbitrator. And argument number two was that even if found to be properly before Arbitrator Seitz, these grievances should be denied based on the merits of the cases. The baseball owners lost on both counts. An interesting account of the hearing and the events after Seitz's decision is given by former Baseball Commissioner Bowie Kuhn (Kuhn, 1987).

The Seitz ruling confirmed that the reservation clause in a player's contract was valid for one year only and not into perpetuity as the owners had argued. Shortly after the grievance decision was made public on December 23, 1975, Major League Baseball took two actions. First, they fired Arbitrator Seitz to demonstrate the magnitude of their displeasure with this decision. As Kuhn puts it in his book, ". . . in American arbitration practice, it is commonplace to dismiss an arbitrator who has slain one of the parties' sacred cows. Seitz had done just that" (Kuhn, 1987, p. 160). Arbitrator Peter Seitz was a well-respected neutral who was a long-standing member of the National Academy of Arbitrators. The harsh criticism Seitz received way back in 1975 from Kuhn and others is rather reminiscent of the same treatment given to arbitrator Frederic R. Horowitz in 2014 after the rendering of Rodriguez (Dickey, 2014). In the latter case, the criticism came from the grievant and his agent. The lesson from all of this is that well-respected arbitrators like Seitz and Horowitz, both of whom either were or are members of the prestigious National Academy of Arbitrators, face a lot of public scrutiny for the decisions they make, whether the decisions favor the owners or the players.

Seitz himself was rather dismayed by his dismissal, and a few years after his award wrote to Kuhn, saying:

Normally, a hapless pitcher, being removed from the mound in the course of an inning will get a few kind words from the manager for his efforts, perhaps a reassuring pat on the back and even an opportunity to doff his cap in deference to the applause of the more sensitive and appreciative audience. This is part of what makes baseball a sport rather than a cockfight. I am afraid that too many of the franchise owners, your clients, are unaware of this. (Kuhn, 1987, p. 160)

We will have to wait and see how Arbitrator Horowitz responds to similar criticism over his recent decision.

The second action baseball owners took challenged Seitz's decision in a federal court in Kansas City before Judge Oliver. Baseball argued that Arbitrator Seitz had no jurisdiction over the reservation system issue and, even if he had such jurisdiction, his decision on the merits was wrong. Here again we have a strikingly similar parallel between what the baseball owners tried to do in 1975 and what Alex Rodriguez was trying to do in 2014. Both situations involve the attempt to overturn or nullify an arbitration award. While Rodriguez dropped his case before a final decision could be made, we know for certain that Major League Baseball was unsuccessful in having the Peter Seitz decision overturned in court. The significance of this situation should not be underestimated. A system of player reservation which had existed in baseball for close to a century and which had survived previous unionization efforts and three Supreme Court cases was now rendered inoperative by a single individual, Peter Seitz, acting as the neutral arbitrator under the grievance procedure both parties had agreed to insert into their collective bargaining agreement. This single decision was perhaps Marvin Miller's biggest accomplishment as it led to a system of free agency in baseball and eventually in many other professional sports across the globe. For the first time professional athletes had their salaries determined more by market forces than by ownership rules and regulations such as the reservation system. What happened next in baseball was the negotiation of a new Basic Agreement which included free agency (Gilbert, 2013).

Bowie Kuhn

Famous basketball player agent David Falk, when speaking on consummating Patrick Ewing's $5 million dollar contract with the New York Knicks on August 20, 1985, noted that "The entire process taught me more about business and negotiation than I had learned to that point. It validated my approach to negotiations and it confirmed the value of preparation combined with creativity" (Falk, 2009, p. 31).

While Falk's statement relates to his negotiations for one player with one club, combining preparation with creativity also applies to collective negotiations over an entire Basic Agreement. To maintain some sort of labor market equilibrium in baseball, both owners and players must come to the table prepared to compromise. Both sides realized that even though the players had won free agency rights through the Seitz decision, a negotiated compromise to preserve certain aspects of the player reservation clause would have to be reached for the good of the game. Bowie Kuhn was heavily involved in these negotiations. Here is what happened.

Commissioner Bowie Kuhn was up against MLBPA Executive Director Marvin Miller in this round of negotiations. Miller had previously achieved many things for his baseball players, including grievance arbitration, higher minimum salaries, pensions, and travel and meal money per diems. The recently announced Peter Seitz arbitration decision now set the stage for another big achievement, free agency.

Commissioner Bowie Kuhn was a Princeton undergraduate and a graduate from the University of Virginia Law School. He was the Commissioner of Baseball from February 4, 1969 until September 30, 1984, a 15-year period in which the game underwent major changes. His predecessor was the little remembered William Eckert and his successor was Peter Ueberroth, who was much better known for his work in the Olympics arena. All of the major changes which came about through collective bargaining in professional baseball occurred during the Bowie Kuhn era. These changes had vast implications not only in baseball but in professional sports around the globe.

Kuhn served as legal counsel for Major League Baseball for almost 20 years prior to becoming Commissioner, so he was not a newcomer to the game like both his predecessor and his successor in the Commissioner's job. To be fair about his impact, one must look at both the gains made by the players through collective bargaining and the gains made by the game itself during his time in office. In the labor relations area his 15 years were marked by several strikes (the most important one in 1981), the beginning of the end of baseball's reservation system due to the Peter Seitz arbitration award. Yet it is not fair to conclude that Commissioner Kuhn did not improve the status of the game. His tenure was also marked by unprecedented fan interest in the game and the generation of huge television revenues for the teams which continues to this date.

While people sometimes remember Kuhn for smaller incidents, like early in his tenure when he was very critical of pitcher Jim Bouton's book on baseball (Bouton, 1970), he is also credited with expanding the fan base by holding World Series games at night. That first night game on October 13, 1971 was viewed by 61 million fans, a far greater number than a typical afternoon game would have received. Kuhn was right! Many fans know that former Commissioner Bud Selig was very tough on players like Alex Rodriguez who abused drugs. Far less widely known is the fact that Commissioner Bowie Kuhn was also tough on players who abused drugs. More will be said later about drug usage in all professional sports and how that subject has been prominently featured in collective bargaining contracts.

But for now, let's return to free agency and the ensuing collective bargaining contract in baseball. Remember that until Seitz, every player on every club was controlled for his entire career through the reservation system. The Seitz decision, if not modified through collective bargaining, would enable every player to become a free agent after a one-year option renewal of his existing major league contract. We had gone from one extreme to another in the stroke of an arbitrator's pen. There must be a compromise that would be workable for all parties. And there was such an agreement worked out through collective bargaining.

It was not an easy process, but after much wrangling, threatened lockouts and an order to the owners by Kuhn to open their spring training campus, a settlement was finally reached on July 12, 1976, on the eve of the 1976 All-Star Game in Philadelphia (McKelvey, 2001).

While the system agreed to in 1976 has undergone several tweakings over the ensuing almost 40 years, the basic labor market structure agreed to in 1976 established a new era for player freedom in the labor market. Then and today, a baseball player faces the following three career stages. First, in the first three years of a player's career (some exceptions exist), the club retains monopsonistic control over a player's services similar to the early days of the game. One big difference is that the parties have negotiated minimum salaries for players early in their careers. So a good player in his rookie season probably will not earn $10 million, but he will earn at least the minimum salary, which is around $500 000. One interesting point to mention here is that unlike most other areas where unions negotiate wages for all workers through the process of collective bargaining, in professional sports, unions negotiate minimum salaries only, and after each player individually negotiates his salary with his club utilizing a player agent.

In the second phase of a baseball player's career, he becomes eligible for salary arbitration, another product of collective bargaining. Players eligible for salary arbitration cannot change teams for a higher salary, but they can exchange final offers with their club. An example is in order. The Cincinnati Reds have a Cuban-born pitcher by the name of Aroldis Chapman who pretty regularly can throw a baseball 100 miles per hour. In his previous season (2013), he earned $2 million. Chapman is 25 years old and the salary demand he filed for the 2014 season was $5.4 million, while the Cincinnati Reds offered him $4.6 million, a difference of $800 000. Each season over 100 arbitration eligible players file such offers with their teams, and each year most can reach a negotiated solution without going to arbitration. A few players each season have their salaries for the ensuing year finalized by an arbitrator, who is limited to selecting either the owner's last offer or the player's last demand as the actual salary to be paid in the ensuing season. This process is called final offer arbitration, which is interesting because of its built in self-destruct mechanism which encourages the parties to settle their differences bilaterally (Feuille, 1975).

Note two highly significant aspects of this system. First, it preserves the right of teams to maintain control of all players during their first six major league seasons. There is no threat of a younger career player jumping to another team, although trades are possible. Second, players can generate higher salaries. Because of salary arbitration, a player never really loses. Had Aroldis Chapman gone to arbitration, he either would have been awarded the club's offer ($4.6 million) or his demand ($5.4 million) – in either case a hefty increase from a previous salary in 2013 of $2 million. Chapman and the Reds eventually agreed on his salary for 2014 at $5.0 million (the midpoint between the two positions) and therefore avoided salary arbitration. Salary arbitration for mid-career players is an example of how collective bargaining has preserved something each side wanted, player control by the clubs and higher salaries by the players.

The 1976 Major League Baseball collective bargaining agreement established for the first time a third category for a baseball player's labor market status, actual free agency. After a player has completed six full seasons and run through all of his salary arbitration eligibility years, he can move to the team which will make him the highest offer. While the rules have changed over time, the basic thrust of free agency in professional baseball and other sports remains intact, the ability of a player to sell his services to that professional club willing to pay him the highest salary. The monopsonistic player reservation system labor market of earlier years has changed into a competitive labor market for a rather large portion of a player's career. This free agency system has produced astounding salary settlements such as the one recently announced for Los Angeles Dodgers pitcher Clayton Kershaw, who signed a seven-year contract worth $215 million. Not that long ago players could not even imagine earning $1 million over an entire career, much less over $30 million for a single season. While labor unions regularly are criticized today for no longer being powerful or relevant (Rosenfeld, 2014), in professional sports we have seen quite a different story unfold. The business of baseball and other professional sports (Miller, 1990) has been changed forever by the process of collective bargaining. As Burk (1994) has aptly stated, baseball was never just a game, but men at work (Will, 1990).

The next section will bring us up to the present day with some discussion of the current status of collective bargaining in sports.

CURRENT STATUS OF COLLECTIVE BARGAINING IN SPORTS

While some make the argument that baseball might be over (Mahler, 2013), the popularity of many sports has never been greater. Part of the reason for that is television, but also fans love fast-moving, action-packed sports like football, ice hockey, rugby and basketball. Baseball is slow moving when compared to some of its competitors for the fan dollar.

Another reason for the familiarity and hence the popularity of many sports today is due to collective bargaining and all the associated notoriety that coverage of strikes, lockouts and player contract negotiations bring daily. Just to cite one example of how far these games have come because of collective bargaining, consider the case of the recently deceased baseball legend and Hall of Fame member Ralph Kiner. The answer to the baseball trivia question "Which three Pittsburgh Pirates players hit the most career home runs?" finds Wille Stargell in first place with 475, Ralph Kiner in second place with 301 and Roberto Clemente in third place with 240 home runs. Kiner had a wonderful 10-year baseball career (Weber, 2014) eclipsed by his long run as a broadcaster almost until his recent death at age 91. Kiner played well before collective bargaining, yet even so he was among the highest paid baseball players of his era. Kiner played for a rather hapless team throughout his career (Pittsburgh Pirates) and never appeared in a World Series. After a dreadful season for his team in 1952 (42 wins and 112 losses), and despite his own stellar performance in leading the league in home runs, Kiner's salary was reduced for the ensuing season. According to the legend of the time, the Pirates General Manager (Branch Rickey) cut Kiner's pay and told him, "Son, we can finish last without you."

That scenario could never happen today in any professional sport due to the gains the players have made through collective bargaining described earlier in this chapter. While recent books have been written about the demise of unions and how the process of collective bargaining is under duress in many industries (Rosenfeld, 2014; Stranger, Clark & Frost, 2013), professional sports collective bargaining presents a very different scenario of success. Very recently a group of college football players in the United States announced their intention to form a labor union to represent their interests against Northwestern University and the National Collegiate Athletic Association (NCAA) (Wolverton, 2014). These college athletes posted a letter online which stated, in part, that they "recognize the need to eliminate unjust NCAA rules that create physical, academic, and financial hardships for college athletes" and that "to remain silent while players are denied justice is to be complicit in inflicting injustice on future generations of college athletes" (Wolverton, 2014).

While it remains to be seen how much success these college athletes will have with this endeavor, it is instructive to view their efforts in light of what we have seen at the professional level. One could argue about whether college athletes are employees or students, or perhaps a bit of both. However, their quest for justice is very similar to the situation Curt Flood talked about in his book (Flood & Carter, 1970) and a big reason he risked his own career to affect the future of so many other athletes. These collegiate athletes have seen that collective bargaining and unionization have worked to improve the lives of so many professional athletes in a variety of sports across the globe. Why shouldn't they also see if this process might work for them or perhaps many other future collegiate athletes.

The process of collective bargaining has evolved and come a long way since the days of John Montgomery Ward. Today, players enjoy high salaries and many other benefits they could only dream of in earlier years. In the United States, the four major sports of baseball, basketball, football and hockey recently went through the latest round of collective bargaining negotiations. Here is what happened.

If there ever was the opportunity for collective bargaining to sputter and phase out in professional sports it occurred recently in the United States with all four of the major Basic Agreements due to expire in a short time span. Given all of the duress unions and collective bargaining have been under in other settings, would a similar fate befall the players in the professional sports arena (Dworkin & Posthuma, 2013)?

The National Football League Basic Agreement expired on March 3, 2011. The National Basketball Association Basic Agreement expired shortly thereafter on June 30, 2011. Major League Baseball was next with an expiration date for its Basic Agreement on December 11, 2011. And finally, the National Hockey League Basic Agreement expired on September 15, 2012. What happened in each of these major negotiations is related in some detail by Dworkin and Posthuma (2013), so I will just provide a summary.

In Major League Baseball the parties agreed to a five-year contract without resorting to a strike or lockout. This new agreement will guarantee labor peace in baseball for an uninterrupted 21 seasons. A major issue addressed in these negotiations was drug testing and player safety, both of which will be covered in the last segment of this chapter.

Professional football negotiations featured an off-season lockout of the players which lasted from March 11, 2011 through July 25, 2011. The eventual outcome was a historic ten-year deal on a new Basic Agreement which meant losing only one exhibition game. As in the other sports, key issues at the table were the division of revenues between the owners and the players, and the safety and welfare of the athletes.

Negotiations in the NBA followed a similar path of adversarial relations between the parties as in previous rounds of negotiations. The players decertified their union, federal antitrust suits were filed and the regular season was shortened due to a lockout of the players by the clubs. The typical 82-game season was shortened to 66 games with the season beginning on Christmas Day of 2011. Note that even with all of this strife, the parties eventually agreed to a new ten-year Basic Agreement. Similar to what happened in the NFL, one of the most contentious issues was revenue sharing between the parties.

In the NHL the negotiations were also very contentious, in a sport that is no stranger to losing an entire season (2004–2005) due to a labor dispute. This time around things were not as bad as in 2004–2005. In the most recent round of negotiations the owners locked out the players on September 16, 2012. Weeks dragged on with little contact between the parties nor hope of resurrecting the season. After 113 days of the lockout, forcing the cancellation of 625 games, a deal was finally reached on January 6, 2013 which shortened the regular season to 48 games. This new Basic Agreement runs for ten years with either side able to opt out after eight years. The division of revenues was the major issue separating the parties in these tough negotiations.

These four very prominent negotiations featured three lockouts and one settlement without incident (baseball). All four deals are for multiple years in length, which is very positive for the stability of these sports. Prominent issues were very similar in all cases, featuring money (revenue sharing and salary caps) and player safety and health concerns. Despite some bumps and bruises, the process of collective bargaining stood up well. It is a process predicated on compromises between the parties and that is exactly what occurred in these four major sports. Neither side got everything they wanted, but each party got enough of what they wanted to be satisfied with signing extraordinarily long Basic Agreements. Both parties seem at least temporarily satisfied with what they could negotiate both in terms of financial and non-financial issues. This leads to the question of what the future will hold in this area of collective bargaining in professional sports. Several trends which emerged in this most recent round of negotiations bear watching.

WHAT THE FUTURE HOLDS/CONCLUSIONS

Based on all of my research, writing and reading on the evolution of collective bargaining in sports, the future, while uncertain, most probably will feature the following ten trends.

1. Expansion. Since collective bargaining has been proven to succeed for professional athletes, it can be expected that we will see other groups associated with sports attempt to unionize and utilize collective bargaining. A good example is the recent 2012 lockout of NFL referees (Jessop, 2012). The usage by the NFL of substitute referees during the lockout period produced such an outcry among fans that once the integrity of the game was questioned, a settlement quickly ensued (Gregory, 2012).

It is interesting to watch other groups like collegiate football players turn to unionization, although it has been argued that their chances in the United States would be better served if they pursue internship instead (Boudway, 2014b). Other fringe groups will attempt to unionize, which will provide ample opportunities for future research (Frick, 2012).

2. Research Proliferation. The unionization of athletes brings about the possibility of much fruitful empirical, theoretical and descriptive research. Journals have started up to cover sports economics issues and many researchers have become interested in a field rich with data and fascinating topics. To get a flavor for the variety of excellent work in this arena, the reader is referred to the two-volume *Oxford Handbook of Sports Economics* (Kahane & Shmanske, 2012) cited earlier. Much interesting research remains to be done.

3. Adaptability. Part of the reason for the success of collective bargaining in sports is due to its flexibility and adaptability. This has been discussed earlier, but a key factor has been the ability to negotiate master contracts which both set minimum salary levels for players early in their careers (sometimes for all career stages) and allow for individual salary negotiation between more senior players and clubs. Using player agents has been and will continue to be a feature of bargaining in professional sports. Better, more senior athletes can thus secure higher compensation levels. Just think how different things would be if professional athletes were paid like other unionized workers, perhaps meaning that every single player occupying a certain position (goalie, catcher, guard and quarterback) would earn exactly the same salary. That scenario would be certain to cause some huge problems. Expect to continue to see the flexibility and adaptability of collective bargaining in differing situations to work to the advantage of both owners and players in professional sports.

4. Safety Concerns. While much attention is focused on large player salaries and other economic issues, a major theme running through-

out all collective bargaining in professional sports in recent years has been the focus on player safety. This theme is certain to continue into the future (Barrett, 2013).

Probably more important than any other reason for this interest in player safety is the large number of young boys and girls involved in contact sports. Young athletes idolize professional stars and try to emulate their behaviors, sometimes with little concern for their own safety. The seriousness of concussions and other brain injuries will continue to be studied and will be a key feature in future bargaining sessions, as it has been recently in football, basketball, hockey and baseball (Belson, 2012).

5. Retired Players. Both because of the safety issues mentioned above, but also due to many older former professional athletes playing prior to the higher salaries brought on through free agency, much attention has been and will be focused on aid to retired and former athletes. This will be an interesting trend to watch as normally the highest priority for union negotiators will be the welfare of current employees. Watch for this trend of more focus on retired athletes to continue. Many stories of former players down on their luck due to playing day injuries or for failing to manage finances wisely are in the news. Homeless former athletes do nothing for the image of their professional sport. That is why owners and players in professional leagues like the NFL have created through collective bargaining so-called Legacy Funds to enhance pensions for players who retired nearly two decades earlier (NFL and NFLPA, 2011).

These trends toward more attention being paid to both player safety and post-career welfare are positive developments expected to continue across all professional sports into the future.

6. Drug Usage. Recent bargaining in almost all professional sports has featured a heavy dose (no pun intended) of attention toward drug usage by athletes. Collective bargaining contracts contain many pages of language dealing with drug prevention. Baseball's Basic Agreement contains a 55-page Joint Drug Prevention and Treatment Program. The bottom line is that the fans want to be assured that the stars they watch are performing at high levels due to hard work and their natural talents, and not due to some performance enhancing drugs. Several star players found guilty of such drug abuse find themselves left out forever of prestigious Hall of Fame balloting and

election. Because all parties seek fairness in the outcome of athletic contests, the parties will continue to focus on ways to insure drug-free participation in professional sports. The fans will accept nothing less.

7. Fan Interest. And speaking of the fans in professional sports, another key area to watch is the rising cost of attending games. This may not seem an issue for collective bargaining, but without fan interest and their ability to attend games at a somewhat reasonable cost, professional sports will be in some jeopardy. It is predicted that future collective bargaining contracts will feature more fan-friendly issues to make it possible for a family of four to attend a contest. As things stand as measured by the Fan Cost Index (FCI), in professional football it cost on average $427.42 in the 2011 season to take a family of four to one game (Fan Cost Experience, www.fan-costexperience.com; Team Marketing Report, www.teammarketing.com).

The bottom line is that professional teams, leagues and players must devise creative ways to bring the average fan back to the games. Otherwise, only the wealthy can afford attendance at professional games, while the average fan will either watch their favorite sport on television or attend minor league contests. Making the games affordable to the average fan is a rather large challenge faced by collective bargaining.

8. Internationalization. It is also predicted that a major focus of future bargaining will be to internationalize professional sports, much like is the case with professional ice hockey. We will see an increasing number of franchises in foreign countries and most likely future leagues will have quite an international flavor. We already witness games being played in foreign lands to test certain markets. Just consider the marketing and merchandise sales possibilities on an international scale. Collective bargaining will be put to the test as teams in different countries face different labor laws, customs and regulations. I expect that several of the US sports covered in this chapter will feature teams in foreign countries other than Canada soon.

9. Recognition. I argued earlier for the importance of non-players to the success of collective bargaining in the realm of professional sports. Examples from professional baseball were MLBPA Executive Director Marvin Miller and Baseball Commissioner Bowie Kuhn, both of whom presided in an era of changes brought forth through collective bargaining. After several years have passed and many people have had the chance to weigh in on the significance of these

changes, due recognition will finally be given to these pioneers of the field through their election or selection to the Hall of Fame in the particular sport in which they had a major impact. Such recognition is already overdue.

10.   It's All About the Money. Former baseball catcher and worldly philosopher Yogi Berra reputedly once said that "Prediction is difficult – especially about the future." While Yogi may be correct about prediction, one thing we know for certain is that the preeminent issue that will continue to dominate collective bargaining in professional sports is the division of revenues produced through the games between the owners and the players. This has never been nor never will be an easy issue to resolve. But fortunately for all involved parties, they have used the process of collective bargaining to resolve their differences over the money issue. Nobody gets everything they want, but everybody gets some part of what they want. And that compromise is the true essence of collective bargaining. It has worked well in professional sports for over 50 years and will continue to do so into the foreseeable future. Out of conflict between the owners and players has come accord. This accord is largely due to the successful usage of the process of collective bargaining. This success is expected to continue into the future.

REFERENCES

Barrett, Paul M. (2013), 'Pain point: Will brain injury lawsuits doom or save the NFL?', *Bloomberg Businessweek*, January 31, 2013.
Belson, Ken (2012), 'Study bolsters link between routine hits and brain disease', *New York Times*, December 3, 2012.
Boudway, Ira (2014a), 'He's got next: David Stern passes the NBA to Adam Silver', *Bloomberg Businessweek*, January 16, 2014, pp. 48–53.
Boudway, Ira (2014b), 'College athletes should drop unionization and declare themselves interns', *Bloomberg Businessweek*, February 6, 2014.
Bouton, Jim (1970), *Ball Four*, New York, NY, USA: Dell.
Burk, Robert F. (1994), *Never Just a Game: Players, Owners and American Baseball to 1920*, Chapel Hill, NC, USA: University of North Carolina Press.
Curtis C. Flood v. Bowie K. Kuhn, 407 U.S. 258 (1972).
Dickey, Jack (2014), 'The persecution of Alex Rodriguez', *Time*, January 27, 2014, p. 23.
Dworkin, James B. (1981), *Owners versus Players: Baseball and Collective Bargaining*, Boston, MA, USA: Auburn House.
Dworkin, James B. and Richard Posthuma (2013), 'Professional sports: A tale of conflict and accord', in Howard R. Stranger, Paul F. Clark and Ann C. Frost (eds), *Collective Bargaining Under Duress: Case Studies of Major North American Industries*, Labor and Employment Association Research (LERA) Series, Ithaca, NY, USA: Cornell University Press.
Elfrink, Tim and Gus Garcia-Roberts (2014), *Blood Sport: Alex Rodriguez, Biogenesis and the Quest to End Baseball's Steroid Era*, New York, NY, USA: Dutton.

Falk, David (2009), *The Bald Truth*, New York, NY, USA: Pocket Books.
Federal Baseball Club of Baltimore v. National League, 259 U.S. 200 (1922).
Feuille, Peter (1975), *Final Offer Arbitration: Concepts, Developments, Techniques*, International Personnel Management Association.
Flood, Curtis and Richard Carter (1970), *The Way It Is*, New York, NY, USA: Trident Press.
Frick, Bernd (2012), 'Career duration in professional football: The case of German soccer referees', in Leo H. Kahane and Stephen Shmanske (eds), *The Oxford Handbook of Sports Economics*, Vol. I, New York, NY, USA: Oxford University Press.
Gilbert, Daniel A. (2013), *Expanding the Strike Zone: Baseball in the Age of Free Agency*, Amherst, MA, USA: University of Massachusetts Press.
Gregory, Sean (2012), 'Flag on the play: Rent-a-refs have butchered the NFL's brand', *Time Magazine*, October 8, 2012.
Jessop, Alicia (2012), 'Evaluating the terms of the new deal between the NFL and referees', *Forbes Magazine*, September 27, 2012.
Kahane, Leo H. and Stephen Shmanske (eds) (2012), *The Oxford Handbook of Sports Economics, Volumes 1 and 2*, New York, NY, USA: Oxford University Press.
Kennedy, Kostya (2014), *Pete Rose: An American Dilemma*, New York, NY, USA: Sports Illustrated Books.
Kuhn, Bowie (1987), *Hardball: The Education of a Baseball Commissioner*, New York, NY, USA: Times Books.
Mahler, Jonathan (2013), 'Is the game over?: How baseball lost its place in American culture', *New York Times*, September 28, 2013.
McKelvey, G. Richard (2001), *For It's One, Two, Three, Four Strikes You're Out at the Owners' Ball Game: Players versus Management in Baseball*, Jefferson, NC, USA: McFarland & Company.
Miller, James Edward (1990), *The Baseball Business: Pursuing Pennants and Profits in Baltimore*, Chapel Hill, NC, USA: University of North Carolina Press.
Miller, Marvin (1991), *A Whole Different Ball Game: The Sport and Business of Baseball*, New York, NY, USA: Birch Lane Press.
NFL and NFLPA (2011), *Collective Bargaining Agreement between the NFL and NFLPA*, August 4, 2011.
Nichols, Mark W. (2014), 'The impact of visiting team travel on game outcome and biases in NFL betting markets', *Journal of Sports Economics*, **15** (1), pp. 78–96.
Organized Baseball (1952), *Report of the Subcommittee on the Study of Monopoly Power of the Committee on the Judiciary*, House of Representatives, HR 2002, 82d Cong., 2d sess. (1952), p. 16.
Pilon, Mary (2013), 'For some players, tax ensures a loss even after a win', *New York Times*, December 12, 2013.
Pope, Devin G., Joseph Price and Justin Wolfers (2013), 'Awareness reduces racial bias', National Bureau of Economic Research (NBER), Working Paper No. 19765.
Poplawski, Wade and Michael O'Hara (2014), 'The feasibility of potential NHL markets under the new collective bargaining agreement', *Journal of Sports Economics*, **15** (1), pp. 64–77.
Rodriguez v. Major League Baseball, Office of the Commissioner of Baseball and Major League Baseball Players Association (2013). Filed with the New York Supreme Court, Index No. 653436/2013, October 3, 2013; Withdrawn, February 8, 2014.
Rosenfeld, Jake (2014), *What Unions No Longer Do*, Boston, MA, USA: Harvard University Press.
Stranger, Howard, Paul F. Clark and Ann C. Frost (2013), *Collective Bargaining Under Duress: Case Studies of Major North American Industries*, Labor and Employee Relations Association (LERA) Series, Ithaca, NY, USA: Cornell University Press.
Toolson v. New York Yankees, 346 U.S. 356 (1953).
Ward, John Montgomery (1887), 'Is the base-ball player a chattel?', *Lippincott's Magazine*.

Weber, Bruce (2014), 'A legend at bat and in the booth dies at 91', *New York Times*, February 7, 2014.
Will, George F. (1990), *Men at Work: The Craft of Baseball*, New York, NY, USA: Macmillan.
Wolverton, Brad (2014), 'College football players seek to form a labor union', *Chronicle of Higher Education*, January 29, 2014.

7. Arbitration, negotiation and contracts in sport

Jack Anderson

INTRODUCTION

This chapter examines the contractual relations between individual sports participants and their employing club. There are four points of note. First, using the case study of the professional footballer working in England, this chapter outlines the contractual web of employment relations surrounding such participants, including the role of agents. Second, the chapter then moves to a discussion of fundamental issues of contract law, namely the sports participant's capacity to contract, which is of particular interest where the participant is of a young age. Third, the chapter assesses the content of a hypothetical standard sports contract. In illustration of these points, the contract used will be the standard Football Association of England Premier League (FAPL) contract. Finally, the chapter will finish on issues relating to the termination of contracts (and particularly where a player seeks to end a contract prematurely in order to facilitate a transfer to another club) and thus conclude on the debate between the desire, on the one hand, to promote contractual stability in a sport and the need, on the other hand, to respect players' legal rights to employment mobility.[1]

CONTRACTUAL AND SPORTING WEB

In the first decade of the twentieth century, the English Court of Appeal in *Walker v Crystal Palace FC* (1910)[2] allowed the plaintiff to avail of compensation under the Workmen's Compensation Act 1906 for an accident sustained during a football game. Farwell LJ dismissed the club's appeal noting that: "It may be sport to the amateur, but to the man who is paid for it and makes his living thereby it is his work."[3] A century later it appears very odd that a judge would have to clarify the legal rights of the "worker-footballer" and their legal relations with their "employer-club" in such a manner. That being said, the contractual relations entered into by Mr Walker and his club Crystal Palace FC in the early 1900s would be equally unrecognizable to the professional footballer employed today by

Crystal Palace in the English Premier League, and that modern contract of employment relationship is the principal concern of this chapter. That relationship is examined in both its legal context (general principles of contract and employment law in the UK)[4] and its sporting context, for instance, as informed by the relevant regulations of football's international governing body (FIFA – Fédération Internationale de Football Association), namely FIFA's Regulations on the Status and Transfer of Players (FIFA, 2009).[5] In practice it must be admitted that the key to understanding the contractual web through which a modern professional football must operate begins not with that player's employing club, but with that player's agent.

Role of Agents

In November 2013, the FAPL published figures regarding payments to agents for the period from October 2012 to the end of September 2013. The headline figure was that the 20 Premier League clubs at the highest level of football in England paid a record £96 million in fees to agents within that year. This was an increase of £19 million since the previous year. Chelsea FC spent the most (£13 721 721) and the aforementioned Crystal Palace spent the least (£869 531). Clubs in the FAPL agreed in June 2008 that from season 2009–10 onwards each club would publish, on 30 November of each season, the total amount they paid to authorized agents during the period from 1 October of the previous year to 30 September of that year. The underlying idea of the initiative had been to bring greater transparency to the football transfer market amid concerns among supporters and managers that large sums were being wasted on agents' fees. The first set of figures released in 2009 revealed that £71 million had been paid in agents' fees. The year on year rise in agents' fees (up 35 per cent from 2009 to 2013) suggests that the policy is having little impact in curbing club spending on agents.[6]

The significant amounts paid out in agents' fees prompts the following questions: what do football agents do to justify such fees and how closely and by whom are they regulated?

The answer relating to the role of football player agents is straightforward, epitomizing the standard definition of agency at common law. That agency relationship, which is fiduciary in nature, exists where an express or implied agreement between the principal (the player) and agent permits that agent to act on the principal's behalf such that the legal effect of such acts is that the principal is bound by them and through them may incur legal obligations to third parties who have dealt with the agent. In general terms, therefore, a football agent brokers a player's employment contract with, or transfer to, a club by way of giving advice and representation in connection with that transaction and, in the performance of such a role, acts in the player's best interests by seeking, for instance, to augment the player's income through personal sponsorship and endorsement deals and the provision of legal, financial planning and tax advice. More specifically, the main duties and responsibilities of football agents at common law (which can be modified somewhat by contract, are subject to some indirect statute-based provisions, and must be abided by applicable sporting regulations) are sixfold.[7]

First, and principally, the agent should carry out, generally in person and with reasonable dispatch, the business they have agreed to undertake with reference to their terms of appointment and the instructions of the principal. Where no definite instructions have been given to the agent, or where the agent has discretion, the general rule is that the professional sports agent should follow the ordinary, normal course or customs of such a business.

Second, every agent has a duty to exercise proper care, skill or diligence in the carrying out of their undertaking.

Third, it is the duty of an agent to keep accurate accounts of all of their transactions and to avoid both the improper mixing of the principal's property with their own and to avoid payments made to the agent on the principal's behalf. Failure to keep proper accounts and the failure to be prepared to produce them to the principal at any time can give rise, in the case of a dispute, to a presumption in favour of the principal's grievance.

Fourth, a long-established duty of an agent at common law is to use the materials and information obtained through their capacity as an agent solely for the purposes of the agency and not to use that information in any manner inconsistent with good faith towards the principal such as, for instance, by divulging it to third parties. Where an agent is found to have breached any of these common law duties, the principal's remedy is in effect to claim in damages for breach of contract for the loss (and no more) that is the natural and probable consequence of the breach of duty.

Fifth, an agent should not enter into any transaction likely to risk putting their duty towards their principal in conflict with their own interests. This is subject to a situation where the agent has first made the fullest disclosure of the exact nature of their interest known to the principal. Where non-disclosure occurs, the integrity of any non-disclosed transaction is immaterial and voidable at the principal's option.

Finally, an agent must not acquire any secret profit or benefit from his agency other than that in the principal's reasonable contemplation at the creation of the agency relationship. Put simply, any profit or benefit accruing to the agent over and above that contemplated by the agreement between the agent and principal should be revealed to the principal. Again, the integrity of any secret profit transaction is immaterial and breach of the rule can result in all related profits and the value of all related benefits being paid over to the principal.

The definition of a secret profit or benefit includes any bribe or secret commission – known in English football parlance as a "bung" – received by the agent from a third party with whom the agent is dealing on their principal's behalf and without the knowledge or consent of the principal (or otherwise not in the principal's reasonable contemplation at the creation of the agency). The scenarios that might be envisaged in football is where a club, or someone acting on their behalf, pays a player's agent a secret commission in order to secure the services of a player or where the manager of a football club is paid a secret commission by the player's agent in order to secure a contract for the agent's player at that club.

Given the fiduciary nature of the agency relationship, as built on the high level of trust and confidence between the parties, the common law has taken a direct and strict line on the receipt of secret commissions, whether by gift or consideration, by agents. Where it can be shown that a bribe has been paid to an agent by a club to facilitate a contract between that player and the club, the presumption at common law is that the contract is invalid. On discovery of the receipt of the secret commission/bribe/side deal, the general position at common law is that the principal may immediately dismiss the agent and the principal is entitled to treat the transaction entered into as void *ab initio*. More recently, the common law approach, which has been strengthened in the UK by the enactment of both the Fraud Act 2006 and the Bribery Act 2010, was discussed by the Court of Appeal in *Imageview Management Ltd v Kelvin Jack* (Imageview, 2009),[8] which concerned an incident where a football agent in negotiating for his client makes a secret deal with the club for himself on the side.

The facts of *Imageview* (2009) are of interest in what they reveal about the work and operation of player agents in football. Briefly, in July 2004 the defendant, Trinidad and Tobago's international goalkeeper, sought to conclude a deal with Dundee United (a football club in Scotland) in order to play professional football. Jack entered into a two-year contract with the claimants (and specifically with a Mr Mike Berry who conducted a sports agency business through Imageview Ltd) in which he agreed to pay them 10 per cent of his monthly salary if Imageview successfully made arrangements for him to sign with a British club. Berry negotiated a two-year contract for Jack with Dundee United. At the same time, Berry agreed that Dundee United would pay Imageview Ltd a fee of £3000 for getting Mr Jack, a non-EU citizen, a work permit. Imageview duly obtained a work permit for Jack and the football club paid the £3000 fee, though it was uncontested that the actual value of the work done in terms of obtaining the permit was no more than £750.

Problematically, Berry did not tell Jack about the work permit arrangement. A year or so into the deal Jack found out about the side deal and stopped paying his agency fees to Imageview. The proceedings in question related to Imageview's claims for unpaid agency fees and counterclaims by Jack arguing that the monies relating to the secret side deal should be paid to him and that he was entitled to claim back any agency fees already paid to Imageview. At the heart of the substantive issue – an agent's duty of fidelity where there is a realistic possibility of a conflict of interest – was Imageview's contention that the undisclosed side deal was not a conflict of interest in the sense that the side deal was, bluntly, "none of Mr Jack's business" and moreover that it was a private and separate arrangement and as such was collateral to the fiduciary duty to the principal. Jacob LJ held that Imageview's negotiation of a side deal had given rise to a clear conflict of interest:

> Put shortly, it is possible that the more it got itself, the less there would or could be for Mr Jack. Moreover, it gave Imageview an interest in Mr Jack signing for Dundee as opposed to some other club where no side deal for Imageview was possible . . . The law imposes on agents high standards . . . Footballers' agents are not exempt from these. An agent's own personal interests come entirely second to the interests of his client . . . An undisclosed but realistic possibility of a conflict of interest is a breach of your duty of good faith to your client.[9]

Moreover, the English Court of Appeal noted that this duty should not cause an agent a problem because all that the agent had to do to avoid being in breach of duty was to make a full disclosure. In this, the Court approved of defence counsel's use of former US Supreme Court Justice Louis Brandeis' celebrated maxim that "sunlight, is after all, the best of disinfectants."[10] In application to the facts at hand, the Court noted that if Berry had told his client that when he was going to negotiate with Dundee United, he was also going to make a deal with the club for himself, then, if Jack had had no objection, there would have been no problem, but instead of doing that Mr Berry made a secret deal and breached his duty of fidelity towards his client.[11] The depth and reality of this conflict of interest meant that, although "there can be cases of harmless collaterality and cases where there is just an honest breach of contract" that was not the case here:[12] the secret profit was not only greater than the work done, it related to, and conflicted with, the very contract that was being negotiated for the principal and thus the agent must forfeit any right to remuneration.[13]

In light of the above, the Court of Appeal held that Jack need pay no more fees to Imageview; was further entitled to repayment of the fees paid by him; and could recover all of the £3000 work permit fee received by Imageview. In sum, the Court of Appeal concluded that what had occurred in the case in question was "surreptitious dealing" driven by a secret commission rather than the player's interest. More generally, the Court found it regrettable that it was still necessary in the twenty-first century to remind agents about conflicts of duty and interest and the necessity for transparency in the dealings of agents if confidence in them is to continue:

> In our age it is more important than it ever was for the courts to hold the precise and firm line drawn between payments openly, and therefore honestly, received by agents, and undeclared payments received by agents secretly, and therefore justly liable to *all* the legal consequences flowing from breaches of an agent's fiduciary obligations.[14]

How Does Football Regulate Agents?

In light of *Imageview* (2009), and given that England is one of the largest football markets in world sport, the question of how football agents are regulated in that jurisdiction is of wider interest. The succinct answer is that regulation has been left largely to the private competency of the Football Association. The Football Association's Agents Regulations (FA, 2009) have a colourful past and have on occasion been challenged in the courts.[15] That colourful past is related to allegations in 2006 suggesting that offers of illegal payments or bungs were not uncommon in football transfers. The source of those allegations, which expressly criticized the role of agents, were twofold – claims made by the then Luton Town FC manager Mike Newell and a special investigation by the BBC current affairs television programme *Panorama* broadcast on 19 September 2006.

Those allegations resulted in the so-called Stevens or Quest inquiry into the payment of bungs, wherein Lord Stevens, the former Metropolitan Police Commissioner, led a team of forensic accountants in their examination of 362 transfers, which took place in the Premier League between January 2004 and January 2006. The Lord Stevens' inquiry, which issued its final, extended report in June 2007, prompted a probe – called Operation Apprentice – into corruption in football by the City of London Police's Economic Crime Department and Her Majesty's Revenue and Customs (HMRC). This investigation in turn led to a number of leading figures in football being arrested on suspicion of conspiracy to defraud and false accounting.[16] More relevantly, the Stevens' inquiry recommended a series of regulatory and compliance-based reforms designed to promote greater transparency in, and more thorough auditing of, player transfers, including the operation and role of agents in such transactions.[17]

That history aside, the key underlying objective of the Football Association's Agents Regulations (FA, 2009) is the implementation of a robust and durable licensing regime in order to promote transparency and equality of bargaining power both within the agency relationship and externally in terms of the sporting public's interest and confidence in the dealings of agents. The practical manifestation of this objective is the promotion of standard representation contracts. Under the FA's regulatory scheme for agents it is a requirement that a player, acting on independent legal advice, or a club, must have entered into a validly executed written "representation contract" prior to that agent carrying out any agency activity on his or its behalf. Standard player–agent/club–agent representation contracts, which contain certain obligatory terms, are provided by the FA.

FUNDAMENTALS OF CONTRACT LAW AND SPORT: CAPACITY TO CONTRACT

Identification of young talented sports participants and signing them to contract (either a contract to play for a club or for agency representation or for endorsement or sponsorship purposes) has led to a number of high-profile court cases, principally involving the young sports person's "capacity" to contract. The general rule at English common law is that a minor's (under 18's) contract is voidable at the minor's option: it is not binding on the minor, but is binding on the other party.

The underlying policy of the general rule at English common law towards a minor's capacity to contract is not to restrict that minor's freedom of contract, but to protect them from exploitation of their inexperience in such matters, such that their naivety might result in them being manipulated into an unnecessarily lengthy or otherwise objectively unfair contract.

Nevertheless, it has long been established that contracts for "necessaries" (typically, goods and services supplied to them for their maintenance) are binding on a minor. The word "necessaries" has been interpreted to extend to contracts made for the minor's benefit such as contracts of apprenticeship, education and service. In *Roberts v Gray* (1913),[18] for example, a minor had attempted to escape his contractual obligations to go on tour as a professional billiard player. The English Court of Appeal held that the contract was one for necessaries and for his benefit in terms of teaching, instruction and employment opportunity, and thus was binding on the minor as a whole. An even broader perspective on contracts of service, apprenticeship and education made to the binding benefit of minors can be found in *Doyle v White City Stadium* (1935).[19]

In that case, the claimant-minor applied in 1932 to the British Boxing Board of Control (BBBC) for a licence to fight as a professional boxer. Under the terms of the licence agreement, the claimant, Jack Doyle, agreed, as was standard practice, to adhere strictly to the governing rules and regulations of the BBBC. The fundamental regulation at issue was the then provision that, where during the course of a fight a boxer was disqualified for misconduct in the ring, that boxer had to forfeit their fee or purse and would only receive "bare travelling expenses". In the summer of 1933, Doyle agreed to fight Jack Petersen for the British heavyweight title in a deal that was to see Doyle paid £3000 win, lose or draw. At the fight, held in White City Stadium on 12 July 1933, Doyle was disqualified in the second round of the bout for repeatedly punching his opponent below the belt, and the organizers of the event withheld his purse.

Subsequently, Doyle argued that, for lack of capacity, he should not be bound by governing BBBC regulations. The Court of Appeal held that, by looking at the contract as a whole, Doyle should be held bound by it, with the Court of Appeal noting in particular that the disqualification/ forfeiture clause was designed principally to encourage clean fighting and was therefore as much in the interests of the claimant himself (a young, inexperienced fighter) as any other contestant that there should be rules to safeguard him "as a contestant from any improper conduct on the part of those with whom he may engage in fighting".[20]

It must be remembered that, notwithstanding *Doyle v White City Stadium* (1935), there is no general principle to the effect that any contract of employment, apprenticeship or education which might be considered beneficial to a minor, is automatically binding on that minor. The courts have stressed that the contract must be read as a whole, as in *Shears v Mendeloff* (1914)[21] where a minor who was a professional boxer had appointed the claimant as his sole manager on commission and agreed not to take any engagements under any other management without the claimant's consent for three years. In that instance, the court held that the contract was unenforceable against the minor, on the grounds that it was fundamentally a "trading" contract, and contained oppressive terms and thus could not be construed as being of benefit to the minor.

A more modern expression of that principle can be found in *Proform Sports Management Ltd v Proactive Sports Management Ltd and Another* (2006).[22] That litigation surrounded the signing in December 2000 of a player representation agreement between a then 15-year-old Wayne Rooney and the claimants. Under the terms of the agreement, which Rooney and his father signed without any independent legal advice, the claimants were appointed to act as Rooney's "executive agents" and to carry out all the functions in respect of personal representation on behalf of Rooney's work as a professional footballer for a period of two years.[23] The claimants alleged that, during the course of the stated agency agreement, the defendants, and notably the second defendant, Paul Stretford, a director of the defendant company, also entered into a player representation agreement with Rooney. In that light, the claimants brought an action for damages for the tort of unlawful interference with and/or procuring a breach of contract against Proactive Sports Management and Stretford.

In the proceedings at hand, the defendants applied for a summary dismissal of the claim on the grounds that no liability for breach could be made out in circumstances where said contract was voidable. In other words, where the person who is alleged to have been induced to breach a contract in any event enjoys the right to rescind that contract, it follows logically that there could be no cause of action in tort for procuring breach of that contract. Further, the defendants argued, it would not matter in such circumstances whether the contract had already been avoided, because if the contract was one that the minor was entitled to avoid, then liability for the tort of wrongful interference with, or of inducing the breach of, the contract could not arise.

Reviewing the principles and case law surrounding the capacity of minors to contract, the High Court noted that if the agreement with Proform Sports Management could be deemed analogous to a beneficial contract of apprenticeship, education or service it would be enforceable against Rooney and therefore the tortious-based action could follow. Nevertheless, on reading the contract as a whole, and taking into account the fact that Rooney was already with a football club (Everton) and was prevented by FA rules from becoming a professional footballer until he reached 17, the agreement could not be seen as one that enabled Rooney to earn a living or to advance his skills. Consequently, the general rule that a minor's contract was voidable at his option applied to the stated agreement. In sum, the High Court granted the defendant's application for dismissal of the claim, holding that the Proform Sports Management agreement was more analogous to the relatively oppressive "trading" contract consider in *Shears v Mendeloff* (1914) and could not be reconciled with the binding, enforceable class of contract considered by the Court of Appeal in *Doyle v White City Stadium* (1935).

Reference to *Proform Sports Management Ltd v Proactive Sports Management Ltd and Another* (2006) was made in the initial court applications in a dispute between leading professional golfer Rory McIlroy and his former sports management representatives, Horizon Sports Management. A preliminary hearing on this matter took place in the Commercial Court in Dublin on 14 October 2013. In October 2014, the Irish High Court was informed that the parties had agreed a confidential settlement. The core of the dispute as revealed at the preliminary hearing appeared to be that McIlroy, who has since established his own sports management company, was unhappy with the amount of commission that Horizon earned in their original deal (estimated at over £4.25 million because of McIlroy's £85 million five-year deal with Nike).

McIlroy was also claiming that, although he was not a minor at the time, he had no independent legal advice on hand when he signed the original deal with Horizon in December 2011, seemingly signed as a Heads of Agreement only in "circumstances of great informality" on the day of Horizon's Christmas party. Under that "unconscionable and restrictive" deal, McIlroy, in a claim that included negligence, breach of contract and breach of fiduciary duty, further alleged that the fees paid to Horizon were improvident in nature, namely a 5 per cent cut on on-course winnings and a 20 per cent off-course cut of pre-tax sums for sponsorship and appearance fees. (It must be noted that the arrangement was amended in March 2012 with Horizon losing its right to the on-course sums and a reduction in the off-course commission rate to 15 per cent.)

Horizon counter-claimed for breach of contract of the five-year management deal (for £1.65 million). As stated, the matter was settled confidentially. If argued in open court the proceedings would have provided an interesting contemporary insight into the constituent and lucrative elements of an allegedly "unconscionable" sports agency contract.[24]

THE CONTENTS OF A SPORTS-RELATED CONTRACT

Form 26 of the FAPL Rules (2013–14) provides a good working model of a standard contract for a Premier League footballer. That standard contract will provide the template for the remainder of this chapter, although it must be admitted that the terms of such a contract can vary greatly depending on the age, talent and even the playing position of a player. Two introductory points need to be made on Form 26.

First, and in an overall sense, and with reference to clause 18 (in respect of the "specificity of football" clause), Form 26 seeks to ensure that contracts in the English Premier League (and all parties to it) have due regard to the "special relationship and characteristics involved in the employment of football players". In practical, albeit implied terms, this means that the contract is integrated or incorporated firmly within the governance structure of world football and ultimately to the world governing body's (FIFA's) regulations on the registration, contractual status and transfer of players (FIFA, 2009). In parallel, it means that, where grievances arise under such contracts, all parties are bound both to submit all matters of dispute, including those relating to breach or termination of contract, to football-specific tribunals, and to accept the ultimate jurisdiction of the Court of Arbitration for Sport (CAS).

Second, and more specifically, the substantive nature of a standard Premier League contract is now characterized by three fundamental, express terms: the duties and obligations of the players; the duties and obligations of clubs; and breach and termination of contract by the club or by the player.

Duties and Obligations of Players

Under clause 3 of Form 26, a Premier League player typically agrees, when directed by an authorized officer of his employing club, to a dozen duties and obligations (many of which are typical of that demanded of all professional sports participants):

1. to attend matches in which the club is engaged;
2. to participate in any matches in which he is selected to play for the club; to attend at any reasonable place for the purposes of training and match preparation;
3. to play to the best of his skill and ability at all times;
4. except to the extent prevented by injury or illness to maintain a high standard of physical fitness at all times and not to indulge in any activity which might both endanger such fitness or inhibit his mental or physical ability to play, practise or train and might invoke any exclusion of the player's injury cover pursuant to any policy of insurance maintained for the benefit of the club on the player;
5. to submit properly to such medical examinations the club may reasonably require and undergo any subsequent treatment recommended by said medical advisers;
6. to comply with and act in accordance with all lawful instructions of any authorized official of the club;
7. to play football solely for the employing club or as otherwise authorized by that club;
8. to observe the laws of the game when playing football and to play the sport safely by not wearing anything (such as jewelry) which could be dangerous to the player or any other person;
9. to observe the FAPL Rules and internal club rules but in the case of the latter to the extent only that they do not conflict or seek to vary the express terms of the player's contract;
10. on termination of contract for any cause to return to the club in

a reasonable condition any property (e.g., a car) which has been provided by the club to the player in connection with that player's employment;

11.   except as agreed otherwise between the parties to use as his regular place of residence a place that can be deemed reasonably suitable (i.e., nearby) for the performance by the player of his duties and particularly his training duties;

12.   not to knowingly or recklessly do, write or say anything or omit to do anything which is likely to bring the club or the game of football "into disrepute" by causing the player or club to be in breach of FAPL rules.

Duties and Obligations of Clubs

The primary duty of the club is to pay the player the remuneration agreed for the duration of the contractual engagement between the parties (clause 5 of Form 26). Outside of that fundamental obligation, clause 6 of Form 26 outlines seven standard contractual obligations of a Premier League club towards one of its player-employees; similar to the duties and obligations of players, these express terms, which can be varied by agreement between the parties, are paramount to the interpretation of the contract unless overridden by the general law. In this, football clubs in England are aware that players, as with any employee, can avail, where appropriate, of the equal treatment protections of the various anti-discrimination in the workplace legislative provisions of English law such as the Sex Discrimination Act 1975; the Race Relations Act 1976; the Disability Discrimination Act 1995; and the Equality Act 2010. The seven key duties expected of clubs are:

1.   to observe all FAPL rules and its own club rules;
2.   to provide the player each year with copies of said rules especially those which affect the terms and conditions of the player's employment and with which he is expected to comply;
3.   promptly to arrange appropriate medical examination and treatment at the club's expense for the player in respect of any injury or illness suffered by the player in the course of employment and not to use or reveal the contents of any medical reports arising therefrom for any purpose other than the assessment of the player's health and fitness;
4.   to comply with all relevant statutory provisions relating to industrial injury and health and safety in the workplace, including the adoption of policies for the security, safety and physical well-being of the player when carrying out his contractual duties;

5. in any case where the club would otherwise be (vicariously) liable as the employer for any acts or omission of the player in the lawful and proper performance of his playing or training duties, the club is contractually obliged to defend the player against any proceedings brought against him and to indemnify the player from any damages awarded;
6. to give the player every opportunity to follow any course of further education or vocational training;
7. to release the player as required for representative international duty pursuant to FIFA regulations.

To reiterate, the primary duty of the club is to pay the player the remuneration and expenses agreed under contract. A player's remuneration beyond their basic wage can include all reasonable hotel and other expenses wholly and exclusively incurred by the player in the performance of his contractual duties and, more importantly, any related bonuses and incentives (as related to, for example, goals scored, appearances made and league points accumulated). Apart from basic wages paid as a salary or a certain amount per match and associated travelling expenses, payments to footballers that are normally chargeable to tax as employment income include signing-on fees, share of a transfer fee, net monies from any benefit or testimonial matches, loyalty bonuses and termination payments.[25]

Image Rights

Apart from the above, other kinds of payments to professional footballers might also be taxable, and the tax authorities in the UK (HMRC) have occasionally had reason to investigate a number of professional football (and cricket and rugby) clubs in an apparent attempt to assess the manner in which such clubs might be using payments for image rights in lieu of salary and thus avoiding income and other taxes, including national insurance contributions. The legal and commercial issues surrounding the image rights of athletes (that is the athlete's right to prevent unauthorized use of their name, likeness or particular characteristics or even idiosyncrasies, such as a nickname, associated with their personality) and the merchandising and promotional activities associated with the exploitation of such rights (by the individual themselves and/or by their club) is a huge area in itself and is beyond the brief of this chapter. Suffice to say that, although there is no specific right to protect one's image under English law (in contrast Canadian, French, Italian, Spanish and several states in the US recognize "personality rights"), the evident commercial value in the "image" of modern sports personalities has often been commercially exploited and has led to disputes in the UK courts relating to issues of copyright, trademark, defamation, data protection and torts such as breach of confidence and passing-off.[26]

The specific, tax-related concern here is with a current HMRC investigation into a practice whereby sports image rights are used to disguise the true (taxable) character of payments made by a club to a player with the underlying idea being to reduce the tax burden on a player and thus make it more attractive for non-UK nationals, who might be put off by UK tax rates, to sign for Premier League clubs.[27] A brief background to this area of concern is that when a footballer (and the focus here is on a Premier League player) signs for a club he traditionally has two options regarding image rights: either he seeks to profit from selling his own reserved image rights or he permits the club to use his image (on merchandising for photographic and promotional purposes etc.) for an annual payment.[28]

A practice has developed, however, where the player, in advance of his contract of employment, and presumably on the advice of his agent or advisers, forms a company registered and located offshore or in a known tax haven jurisdiction. The player effectively transfers the rights to exploit his image exclusively (and/or on a worldwide basis) to that company in return for shares in the company and also agrees to undertake any promotional activities as may be directed by that company. The company then contracts on behalf of the player with third parties, and notably the player's employing club, in regard to the exploitation of the player's image rights. Any consideration made in respect of such contracts (and some estimates are that such payments can equate to anything from 10 to 20 per cent of the player's salary) are directed towards that offshore company and thus reduce the tax burden on the player and club.

In *Sports Club, Evelyn and Jocelyn v Inspector of Taxes* (2000),[29] it was held that there was nothing necessarily illegitimate with a tax avoidance scheme that detaches the payments structure of the player's image-rights-related services away from that player's core playing services such that any monies received from the former cannot be regarded as income from that player's employment. Nevertheless, the judgment in that case contained the general caveat that such image rights arrangements would not be vulnerable to the usual rates of tax, and would not be seen as a smokescreen for additional remuneration, only where they could be viewed as having a genuine, independent commercial value to third parties over and above the standard playing services provided by such players for such clubs.[30] Bluntly, the HMRC's recent, revised interest in such arrangements is that while in exceptional cases (e.g., David Beckham) the image rights of a player may be worth more to a club than his contribution on the field, for the vast majority of players, even at the elite level, their individual image rights and associated promotional services may be of little commercially exploitable value.[31]

CONTRACTS IN SPORT: TERMINATION

What happens if a club or player attempts to end contractual relations with the other party prematurely and before the natural expiry period of the contract?

Club-Led Termination of Contract

In the Premier League, and pursuant to clause 10 of Form 26, a club is entitled to terminate the employment of a player by providing 14 days' written notice to the player if the player "shall be" guilty of gross misconduct or fails to heed any final written warning given under standard, internal disciplinary procedures or is convicted of any criminal offences where the punishment consists of a sentence of imprisonment of three months or more (which is not suspended). Clause 10 then goes on to sketch the due notice, rights of appeal and, pending such an appeal hearing, any provisional suspensions that might surround the termination procedure. In reality, club-led terminations are rare, and it is often the case that clubs seek to avoid the implication of a material breach of contract and, in effect, affirm the player's repudiatory breach.

There are a number of reasons for club-led terminations being so rare at the elite professional level of football – two are noteworthy. First, and pragmatically, players are expensively acquired commodities and thus because it is a costly exercise to purchase players, it is unsurprising that clubs are most reluctant to end contractual relations prematurely. Moreover, termination under clause 10 applies only in circumstances of "gross" misconduct, for instance, a conviction resulting in a custodial sentence. Consequently, it can be argued that the subliminal message to clause 10 is that where a dispute can be resolved short of termination, it should be so resolved, and done so through the relatively sophisticated grievance and disciplinary procedures provided under contract.

Second, where an employer dismisses an employee, that employer subjects themselves to the requirement and vagaries of the relevant provisions of employment law, and notably to the case law and principles surrounding unfair dismissal. An illustration of the "vagaries" of this process as applying to football can be shown in *Wise v Filbert Realisations* (2004),[32] which was a successful appeal by a footballer in England to the Employment Appeal Tribunal (EAT) concerning his complaint of unfair dismissal by his then employer, Leicester FC, and emanating from a club suspension imposed on the player for fighting with a teammate.

Ultimately, the EAT decided that, although Wise most likely committed an assault equivalent to the criminal offence of occasioning actual bodily harm, and even though the subsequent internal appeals process thoroughly reviewed the incident, the first instance hearing of the matter (by the club chairman) was so defective, and had infected all subsequent dealings with the incident to such an extent, that Wise's appeal should be allowed and a finding of unfair dismissal substituted. The EAT's decision in the stated case was a very rare instance of that tribunal hearing an elite-level, sports-related dispute. Given the maximum compensatory award for unfair dismissal in England is, as of July 2013, set at £74 200, it is likely that an elite footballer would not venture to the EAT (the average *weekly* earnings of Premier League footballer is estimated to be around £30 000) but bring any unfair dismissal claim to the High Court.[33] The costs, delay, adversarial nature and adverse publicity associated with the litigation process is yet another reason for employing clubs to avoid the "nuclear" option of termination of contractual relations.

Player-Led Termination of Contract

Under clause 11 of Form 26, a player is entitled to terminate his contract by providing 14 days' notice in writing if his employing club can be shown to have been guilty of serious or persistent breaches of the terms and conditions of the contract or has failed to pay any remuneration or other payments or bonuses or benefits due to the player as they fall due or within 14 days thereafter. The issue of what constitutes a serious or persistent breach of contract by a club towards a player will very much depend on the facts of the case and the specifics of the contract, though it must also be placed in its overall context. That context has two elements to it: one narrow and specific to players' interests; one broader and applicable to many sports outside football.

At its narrowest, a player's view of a material breach of contract by their employing club is, in reality, often motivated by a number of aggravating personal factors (including the player's agent). These include: the player who is not getting regular first team football; or the player who after a good run of form with his club or a series of high-profile international appearances feels that he is now undervalued by his club; or the player who is of the opinion that better offers await from other clubs. In practical commercial terms, and with respect to the relevant legal and regulatory framework in which player transactions occur in football, there are a number of ways in which the parties can mutually agree to deal with these problems: the unhappy player can be sent out on loan to another club; contracts can be renegotiated to reflect the player's good form; or the parties may simply agree that at the next available transfer window, and usually the end of that playing season, the player can transfer to another club and may, if he wishes, sign a pre-contract arrangement with another club of his choice. Moreover, clubs' and players' legal representatives are aware that, in terms of ordinary contract of employment law on personal services in the UK, where an employee seeks, because of a breakdown in the necessary level of fidelity that must exist between such parties, to move to another employer, attempting to maintain or enforce existing contractual relations, by way of injunctive relief, will likely be refused by the courts on the grounds that it would be futile to compel the parties to do so and, in any event, would be impossible to supervise.

More broadly, the context surrounding a player seeking to bring a premature end to their contract in order to move to another club reveals issues that go to the very heart of the operation and administration of modern football, namely the tension that arises between players' demands for rights of employment mobility similar to those generally available to all paid workers (i.e., the right to take up paid employment with another at any time on serving due notice) as against the efforts of clubs and governing bodies to ensure that the specific sporting nature of the professional football industry is not undermined by contractual instability (i.e., such that the specific seasonal, financial and league structure of football can be preserved and that for competitive balance purposes the better resourced teams cannot gratuitously cherry pick the best players from less well-resourced teams).

In legal terms, the epicentre of this tension can, in terms of professional football, be located in the Court of Justice of the European Union's (EU's) decision in *Bosman* (1995).[34] The full extent of that decision with regard to the free movement of professional sports persons in the EU and the impact it has had on the transfer and registration of football players globally is, again, beyond the brief of this chapter. Suffice to say that the key repercussion from *Bosman* was that, in consultation with the European Commission and player representative bodies, it led to football's world governing authority producing its player status regulations (FIFA, 2009). Part IV thereof (articles 13–18 FIFA) concerns the general regulatory guidelines on the termination of a professional player's contract of employment with a club.

In establishing its position on the maintenance of contractual stability between professional players and clubs, article 13 FIFA sets out FIFA's absolutist, and somewhat utopian, *pacta sunt servanda* position: a contract between a professional and a club may only be terminated upon expiry of the term of the contract or by mutual agreement. The remaining provisions on contractual stability are, however, more rooted in the commercial and contractual reality of the professional football industry, and, although a contract cannot be unilaterally terminated during the course of a season (article 16 FIFA), a contract may be terminated by either party where there is "just cause" (article 14 FIFA). Moreover, an established player who has, in the course of the season, appeared in fewer than 10 per cent of the official matches in which his club has been involved may terminate his contract prematurely on the ground of "sporting just cause" in the 15 days following the last official match of the season of the club with which he is registered (article 15 FIFA). An article 14 FIFA termination is without consequences of any kind – either payment of compensation or imposition of sporting sanction. An article 15 FIFA termination, which is established on a case by case base with due reference to the player's individual circumstances, will not attract the imposition of sporting sanctions, though compensation may be payable to the affected club.

At first instance, the basic framework surrounding these provisions appears quite straightforward. In general terms, article 15 FIFA can be said to equate to the old common law and implied duty on an employer to provide work for a skilled employee or, more properly, not to unreasonably withhold work from the employee to the detriment of that employee's specialized skills. Self-evidently this is not to say that player has a "right to play" or a "right to be selected" for the first team, more that if the player, and particularly a more experienced player whose career may be drawing to a close, is, in effect, surplus to requirements at a club (and is losing fitness and sharpness as a result of not playing at the highest level), that player may have sporting just cause to move on (and thus the opportunity to obtain one final lucrative transfer move). Accordingly, under some circumstances, it could be argued that article 15 FIFA covers a situation where the player argues that they have, to all intents and purposes, been constructively dismissed by their employer, but rather than contest that "dismissal" (and the word is used advisedly), the player seeks to settle the matter with his employing club through article 15 FIFA, and move on.

Although the criteria surrounding "sporting just cause" are relatively vague and remain to be evaluated on a case by case basis, at least article 15 FIFA provides some reference point (e.g., the less than 10 per cent game rule) as to when such a situation might arise. Article 14 FIFA is shorn of any guidance as to what the meaning and scope of the phrase "just cause" might entail and thus the provision might be seen to be vulnerable to being used as a basis for vexatious, disruptive challenges by opportunistic claimants. The more positive perspective, and the one favoured here, is that the phrase is necessarily and deliberately broadly drawn and, moreover, that its inherent ambiguity allows authorities to adopt a flexible and creative approach to individual cases and thus aids the principle of contractual stability. In this, a working definition of the phrase, as drawn from a series of CAS awards, might be that a "just cause" equating to a valid reason for prematurely terminating a contract can be based on a contention that the party (employee or employer) could not reasonably have been expected in the circumstances to have continued with the extant contract given that the necessary level of trust, confidence and fidelity between the contracting parties has been shown to have broken down irretrievably.

The definition of just cause becomes important when considering the application of article 17 FIFA, which sets out the monetary and sports-specific consequences for players and clubs who, it is alleged, have terminated a contract without just cause. Unsurprisingly, the manner in which the amount of compensation due is calculated pursuant to article 17(1) FIFA compensation has prompted much debate and has resulted in a number of CAS awards. The CAS award of most interest is that involving *FC Shakhtar Donetsk (Ukraine) v Matuzalem Fancelion da Silva (Brazil) and Real Zaragoza SAD (Spain) v FC Shakhtar Donetsk (Ukraine) & FIFA (Matuzalem*, 2008).[35] This dispute summarizes most of the contentious issues and it also provides a good, concluding insight into the international transfer of modern elite footballers and the contractual machinations that can surround such transactions.

Matuzalem

In June 2004, the then 24-year-old Matuzalem (the player) signed an employment contract with Shakhtar Donetsk (the club). It was of a fixed term (and relatively standard) nature for five years, effective from 1 July 2004 until 1 July 2009. Under the terms of the agreement, the player could be transferred to another club only with the consent of the club and payment of compensation to the club (relative to all the associated costs of the transaction such as the cost of the player's rights and search for a substitute). Where, however, a club received a transfer offer in amount of €25 million or above, the club agreed to release the player. On 2 July 2007 (on completion of the protected period) the player notified the club of the fact that he was unilaterally terminating their contractual relationship with immediate effect. On 19 July 2007, the player signed a new contract with Real Zaragoza and was then loaned to Lazio in Italy. In July 2007, the club reacted in three ways: it wrote to the player reminding him that he could transfer within the duration of his contract only with the prior agreement of the club and given that that was not forthcoming only on payment of the €25 million; it wrote to Real Zaragoza informing them that they were jointly and severally liable for the payment of the buyout pursuant to article 17(2) FIFA; and finally it initiated proceedings with FIFA.

FIFA held that the €25 million "buyout" clause should not be interpreted as a penal or liquidated damages clause applicable in case of a breach of contract by the player. Nevertheless, there was no doubt that given the unilateral and premature termination of the contract of employment by the player, the player had committed a breach of contract and was therefore liable to pay compensation to the club and, moreover, FIFA found, Real Zaragoza should be held jointly and severally responsible for the payment of such compensation. FIFA calculated the amount of compensation at €6.8 million as based on the remuneration-related, residual value of the player's employment contract with the club; the unamortized fees and expenses paid by the club for the acquisition of the player; and a certain amount of aggravated damages linked to the bad faith of the player, who had accepted an increase in his financial entitlements shortly before leaving the club. The club were unhappy with the amount of compensation awarded by FIFA and appealed the decision to CAS, inter alia, on the grounds that FIFA did not properly or fully apply all the objective criteria contained in article 17(1) FIFA.

At CAS, and throughout the proceedings, it was uncontested by the player that he had unilaterally and prematurely terminated the contract without just cause or sporting just cause. However, relying on a previous CAS award – the so-called *Webster* award (*Webster*, 2007)[36] – the player argued that once *outside* the protected period a player should be entitled to move to another club simply on the paying off of the residual value of their contract and that there is no economic, moral, regulatory or legal justification for a club to be able to claim the "market value" of the player as a lost profit. The essence of *Webster* (2007) was that Andy Webster, a Scotland international, terminated his contract unilaterally with Hearts for Wigan in May 2006, having spent three years of a four-year contract with the Edinburgh club. The Scottish club sought what they considered to be the player's market value at the time of his premature departure (about £4.6 million). CAS awarded compensation of about £150 000 equating to the residual remuneration value in the remaining one year of the contract.

In *Matuzalem* (2008) the player sought to apply *Webster* (2007) by acknowledging that the termination of his contract before its expiry was contrary to FIFA regulations and by further acknowledging that he would have to compensate his club for his move to Zaragoza, but what he contested vehemently was the manner in which that compensation was calculated under article 17 FIFA. The player further argued, qua *Webster*, that the payable compensation should take into account the fact that he had moved after the protected period and thus damages should be limited to the residual, remuneration-related monies left on the (now dead) contract. In contrast, the club argued that the compensation should be based more generally on all the losses associated with the commercial value of the contract rather than its basic employment value and that this approach was consistent with the "mischief" (unilateral termination or breach of contract without cause before expiry) which the regulations were intended and designed to deal with.

Much to the dismay of professional football players' representative body FIFPro (in favour of a *Webster*-inspired enhanced employment mobility principle for its members) and much to the delight of FIFA (in favour of any reiteration of the need for respect for the contractual stability rationale of its regulations) the CAS Panel in *Matuzalem* (2008) found for Shakhtar Donetsk and ordered that they be paid nearly €12 million in compensation plus interest at 5 per cent per annum from July 2007. A review of the *Matuzalem* award prompts four points of interest. Two of these points are specific to the award itself; and the remaining two are of wider significance. The first is that both *Webster* (2007) and *Matuzalem* (2008) must be distinguished a little as to their facts in that both awards featured players who had admitted that they had unilaterally and prematurely breached their contract, albeit outside the protected period. For breaches within the protected period, the usual and strict interpretation of article 17 FIFA continues as determined by its role as a punitive measure for breaches of the core principle of contractual stability. A practical repercussion of this may well be that the effective maximum length of contract given to modern footballers will from now on be aligned closely with the protected period and thus be either of a two- or three- year length as appropriate to the age of the player concerned.

The second point of note that can be gleaned from *Webster* (2007) and *Matuzalem* (2008) is that in both instances the player admitted liability and thus what was in contention was the amount of compensation payable to the affected club. The amount of compensation can lie anywhere on the spectrum between, on the one hand, an effective buyout by the player of the remainder of his contract to, on the other hand, damages for the full commercial value loss of the player including losses sustained in acquiring the player, the loss of chance to exploit the player's marketability and even some aggravating damages for any bad sporting faith shown by the player. In this, however, the devil is also very much in the detail in the sense that the amount of compensation remains dependent on the manner in which a CAS Panel applies, at its discretion, the various compensation criteria outlined in article 17 FIFA to the individual circumstances at hand. In *Matuzalem* (2008) the CAS Panel was extremely thorough in this regard, and the heads of damages through which it addressed article 17 FIFA-related compensation have, rightly or wrongly, provided a template for future awards.

There are two brief and final points of interest in *Matuzalem* (2008). First, it is of interest because to a large extent it was acknowledged that the player's motivation for moving was driven more for personal reasons than economic gain. The player's wife had not settled in Ukraine and the player's contract with Real Zaragoza was, initially at least, broadly similar to what he had been paid by his previous club. Whether that motivation is credible or not, the general point is that where the very fabric or fidelity of the relationship in a contract of employment for personal services has, for whatever reason, been torn, there is rarely any point in trying to compel the parties to repair it. As stated earlier, in many instances, clubs accept this reality and facilitate a transfer; in others, the matter is brought to a tribunal and even to CAS.

Second, there has been an elongated legal postscript to *Matuzalem* (2008). To recap, in 2009, Matuzalem and Real Zaragoza were ordered by CAS to pay Shakhtar Donetsk almost €12 million for breach of contract, following the player's move from Shakhtar to Zaragoza in 2007. In August 2010, FIFA ruled that Shakhtar could request a ban for Matuzalem if he failed to pay on time, and this was confirmed by CAS in June 2011. That CAS ruling was appealed to the Swiss Federal Tribunal where it was struck down on public policy grounds, namely that the ban was wholly disproportionate, excessive and arbitrary in the manner in which it limited the player's economic freedom and existence. The Swiss Federal Tribunal further noted (in a comment that puts much of the debate around sport-related contracts in its rightful perspective) that "the abstract goal of enforcing the contractual obligation of football players to their clubs has clearly less weight than the consequences of a de facto lifelong ban on any football-related activity" (Levy, 2012).[37]

CONCLUSION

This chapter attempted to look at the application of the ordinary (English) law of contract of employment for personal services to the hiring of professional footballers. This chapter has further attempted to portray the various legal and arbitral dramas that can be played out within the dry, technical clauses of a professional footballer's contract of employment. Such contracts do not exist in a vacuum and can be better seen in three dimensions. First, the elite footballer's contractual relationship with their employing club is often one strand in a complex web of contractual agreements involving agents, advisers, sponsors and, indirectly, the administrative demands of national, regional and international federations. Second, though paid handsomely, it should also be borne in mind that elite athletes, and particularly those in contact sports, have an abridged, precarious and at times unpredictable career path and one that can be ended prematurely by injury. Finally, the key aspect of a professional footballer's contract of employment is that of remuneration. Recent studies of the financial models in English and European football have revealed that current wage/revenue ratios in elite European football leagues are unsustainable (e.g., in the English Premier League the ratio was at 70 per cent in 2013 (Deloitte, 2013)). Enhanced financial regulations mandated by European football's governing body (UEFA – Union of European Football Associations) came into effect in 2013/2014 (so-called financial fair play), and a repercussion here has seen clubs seeking to exploit the loan system in football where they look to "contract but immediately lease out" a player to another club. Accordingly, the rather pithy conclusion to this chapter is that the most influential factor on the nature of a player's contract with his employer is not law but, as it ever was, finance.

NOTES

1. The "web" of contractual relationships that surround modern professional players is dealt with succinctly by Lewis, A. and Taylor, J. (eds) (2008) *Sport: Law and Practice*. 2nd Ed. London: Tottel Publishing, chap. D1. This chapter has also benefitted from Gardiner, S. et al. (2013) *Sports Law*. 4th Ed. London: Routledge, chaps. 12–14 and James, M. (2013) *Sports Law*. 2nd Ed. Basingstoke: Palgrave MacMillan, chap. 11. See also the previous work of this author, Anderson, J. (2010) *Modern Sports Law*. Oxford: Hart, chap. 7.
2. *Walker v Crystal Palace FC* [1910] 1 K.B. 87.
3. *Walker v Crystal Palace FC* [1910] 1 K.B. 87, p.93.
4. This chapter is generally informed by McKendrick, E. (2012) *Contract Law: Text, Cases and Materials*. 5th Ed. Oxford: OUP and Emir, A. (2012) *Selwyn's Law of Employment*. 17th Ed. Oxford: OUP.
5. FIFA (2009) *Regulations on the Status and Transfer of Players*. [Online] Available from: www.fifa.com/mm/document/affederation/administration/regulations_on_the_status_ and_transfer_of_players_en_33410.pdf (accessed: 7 March 2014).
6. Premier League (2013) *Premier League Releases Agents' Fees*. [Online] Available from: www.premierleague.com/en-gb/news/news/2013-14/nov/premier-league-release-agents-fees-nov-2013.html (accessed: 7 March 2014).
7. This chapter is generally informed by Munday, R. (2013) *Agency: Law and Principles*. 2nd Ed. Oxford: OUP.
8. *Imageview Management Ltd v Kelvin Jack* [2009] E.W.C.A. Civ. 63.
9. *Imageview Management Ltd v Kelvin Jack* [2009] E.W.C.A. Civ. 63, paras 5–6.
10. *Imageview Management Ltd v Kelvin Jack* [2009] E.W.C.A. Civ. 63, para 7.
11. *Imageview Management Ltd v Kelvin Jack* [2009] E.W.C.A. Civ. 63, para 1.

12. *Imageview Management Ltd v Kelvin Jack* [2009] E.W.C.A. Civ. 63, paras [29]–[46] for an analysis of the "collateral" issue.
13. *Imageview Management Ltd v Kelvin Jack* [2009] E.W.C.A. Civ. 63, para 44.
14. *Imageview Management Ltd v Kelvin Jack* [2009] E.W.C.A. Civ. 63, para 65.
15. Football Association (2009) *FA Agents Regulations.* [Online] Available from: www.thefa. com/football-rules-governance/more/agents/agent-regulations (accessed: 10 March 2014). The most significant challenge has been *Stretford v The FA* [2007] E.W.C.A. Civ. 238.
16. See Kelso, P. (2010) Inquiry's Last Chapter Will Leave Business of Football Clear for All to See. *Daily Telegraph.* London: 15 January.
17. See, for example, FAPL Rule T9 in FAPL Rules (2013–14) *Premier League Handbook* 2013–14. [Online] Available from: www.premierleague.com/content/dam/premier-league/site-content/News/publications/handbooks/premier-league-handbook-2013-14. pdf (accessed: 10 March 2014).
18. *Roberts v Gray* [1913] 1 K.B. 520.
19. *Doyle v White City Stadium* [1935] 1 K.B. 110.
20. *Doyle v White City Stadium* [1935] 1 K.B. 110, p.126.
21. *Shears v Mendeloff* (1914) 30 T.L.R. 342.
22. *Proform Sports Management Ltd v Proactive Sports Management Ltd and Another* [2006] E.W.H.C. 2903 (Ch).
23. The key clauses in the agreement are noted at *Proform Sports Management Ltd v Proactive Sports Management Ltd and Another* [2006] E.W.H.C. 2903, para 5.
24. See the coverage by McDonald, D. and MacGinty, K. (2013) Rory McIlroy's Former Agent in Counter Suit. *Irish Independent.* Dublin: 15 October.
25. The tax treatment of footballers by HMRC gives a good insight into the types of payment typically made to footballers as earnings. See HMRC (2014) *EIM64100 – Tax Treatment of Association Footballers: General: Arrangement of Guidance.* [Online] Available from: www.hmrc.gov.uk/MANUALS/eimanual/EIM64100.htm (accessed: 10 March 2014).
26. For a recent dispute that has close analogies to sports-related "image rights" actions, see *Robyn Rihanna Fenty & Ors v Arcadia Group Brands Limited and Top Shop/Top Man Limited* [2013] E.W.H.C. 2130 (Ch.), where the pop star, Rihanna, brought a passing-off claim against a high-street retailer in relation to T-shirts which carried a photograph of her on their front.
27. See generally Rees, P. (2009) Clubs Fear Impact of Tax Probe. *The Observer.* London: 27 September.
28. See sub clauses 4.4–4.6 of Form 26 of FAPL Rules (2013–14), which, except to the extent specifically agreed otherwise by the parties, obliges the player not to exploit their image in a club context in any manner and/or in any media nor grant the right to do so to any third party.
29. *Sports Club, Evelyn and Jocelyn v Inspector of Taxes* [2000] S.T.C. (S.C.D.) 443. The case concerned image rights payments to Dennis Bergkamp and David Platt by Arsenal Football Club.
30. The reasons for the decision can be found at *Sports Club, Evelyn and Jocelyn v Inspector of Taxes* [2000] S.T.C. (S.C.D.) 443, paras [70]–[101].
31. See Russell, J. (2012) Newcastle United Settles Image Rights Tax Dispute with HMRC. *Daily Telegraph.* London: 6 March.
32. *Wise v Filbert Realisations* [2004] U.K.E.A.T. 0600 03 0902, 9 February.
33. Deloitte (2013) *Annual Review of Football Finance.* [Online] Available from: http:// www.deloitte.com/view/en_GB/uk/industries/sportsbusinessgroup/sports/football/ annual-review-of-football-finance/index.htm (accessed: 10 March 2014).
34. Case C 415/93 *Union Royal Belge des Société de Football Association ASBL v Bosman* [1995] ECR I-4921.
35. CAS 2008/A/1519-1520 *FC Shakhtar Donetsk (Ukraine) v Matuzalem Fancelion da Silva (Brazil) and Real Zaragoza SAD (Śpain) v FC Shakhtar Donetsk (Ukraine) & FIFA.*

36. CAS 2007/A/1298, 1299 & 1300 *Wigan Athletic FC v Heart of Midlothian; Heart of Midlothian v Webster & Wigan Athletic FC; and Webster v Heart of Midlothian.*
37. See decision of the Swiss Federal Tribunal: 4A_558/2011 of 27 March 2012 and discussion by Levy, R. (2012) *Swiss Federal Tribunal Overrules CAS Award in Landmark Decision.* Lawinsport.com [Online] Available from http://www.lawinsport.com/articles/regulation-a-governance/item/swiss-federal-tribunal-overrules-cas-award-in-a-landmark-decision (accessed: 10 March 2014).

8. Industrial action in professional sport: strikes and lockouts
Craig A. Depken II

INTRODUCTION

Strikes and lockouts occur in imperfectly competitive labor markets where workers and owners argue over the distribution of economic rents generated by labor. While the number of strikes in the United States has been falling over the past several decades, several high-profile work stoppages in North American professional sports provide an opportunity to discuss the history of the mechanics of the sports labor market in North America and why work stoppages appear to be more common in the late twentieth and early twenty-first century than in the decades of the late nineteenth and first three quarters of the twentieth century.

On the surface, strikes and lockouts seem to be rather crude instruments of negotiation. When negotiations between labor and ownership about the distribution of rents generated in an industry or by a business reach a deadlock, workers might strike, thereby reducing the supply of labor to zero, in essence removing the ability for owners to generate revenues and profits. The aspiration by labor is to raise the cost of the impasse to such an extent that a negotiated compromise is preferred by ownership. On the other hand, owners might lockout labor thereby reducing the demand for labor to zero, in essence removing the ability of the workers to earn a wage. The aspiration of owners is to raise the cost of the impasse to such an extent that a negotiated compromise is preferred by labor. In each instance, one side feels they (a) have a natural economic advantage over the other side such that they can outlast the other or (b) that they have more complete information about the actual amount of rents available to be split between labor and owners and are therefore willing to press their advantage (Kennan, 2008).

In a historical context labor strikes were most often associated with abusive monopsonists who faced little outside pressure to increase wages, improve working conditions, offer fringe benefits, or otherwise increase the distribution of rents to workers. In these situations, public sympathy understandably often sided with workers as they were the more obvious underdog in the negotiations. Whether workers were always the underdogs as claimed is not clear. However, over time the one-mill towns and the standard monopsony model have fallen to internal and external competitive pressures and regulatory and legislative interventions in labor markets. Coincidently, the number of work stoppages in the United States has declined precipitously during the post-World War II period. In the United States in 1952, there were 470 strikes involving some 2.74 million workers who were idle for approximately 48.8 million work days, or the equivalent of 38 percent of the estimated total work year of the US labor force. By 2013, there were 15 such strikes, involving 55000 workers who were idle for approximately 290 thousand work days or less than 0.005 percent of the estimated work year of the US labor force (Bureau of Labor Statistics, 2014).

Perhaps workers and owners have reached an equilibrium in which both sides recognize the extreme costs involved with work stoppages and therefore avoid the so-called Hicks (1932) paradox that both sides bear otherwise avoidable high costs to reach a negotiated settlement. Perhaps the previous battles between labor and owners, especially in the form of non-wage issues such as fringe benefits, pension plans, working conditions, vacation time, paternity and maternity leave, have been codified both in the agreements between labor and owners but also in state and federal legislation, and have reduced the incentive for workers to strike. Perhaps the increased mobility of much of the US workforce has coupled with a reduction in overall union participation so there are not as many opportunities for workers to strike en masse as in the past. Finally, product markets might have become more competitive over the past sixty years and therefore the available rents to distribute between owners and workers might have sufficiently declined such that work stoppages are less appealing to both sides.

While industrial action seems to be on the decline in the overall economy, in professional sports the trend is moving in the opposite direction. After several decades with few, if any, overt work stoppages, the past forty years in North American professional sports have been characterized by a sharp rise in work stoppages.

There are several possible explanations for the increased number of work stoppages since the 1970s. One is the dramatic increase in total revenues earned by the various leagues in North America, driven mostly by increased revenue from television contracts. The greater a league's revenue the greater the debate about how the revenues will be distributed between players and owners; this can lead to increased odds of a strike or lockout, especially when a new Collective Bargaining Agreement (CBA) is being negotiated. Second, the use of CBAs has arguably increased the number of margins over which players (as a group) and owners (as a group) must negotiate, thereby increasing the risks that the negotiation will reach stalemate. Finally, team owners might find themselves in a stronger negotiating position than players and move to lockout the players before a strike can be called so to push players (as a group) into a situation where the negotiated settlement is preferred to the imposed work stoppage; evidence from the National Hockey League (NHL), National Football League (NFL), and the National Basketball Association (NBA) suggest that team owners are winning the negotiated CBAs.

THE RESERVE CLAUSE: THE CASE OF MAJOR LEAGUE BASEBALL

The contention between team owners and players has a long history and is not unique to one particular sport in North America. All four sports, baseball, football, hockey, and basketball, have had and continue to have labor–ownership tension most often centered on player salaries but also, as in the case of the NFL, on player safety and health.

Consider the labor market for professional baseball players. Professional baseball in the 1870s and 1880s was still in its infancy. Attendance was relatively low and uncertain, revenue streams such as television and radio were decades into the future, and the number of viable teams was uncertain from year to year. Standard contracts in baseball were for a single year after which, at the end of each season, players became unrestricted free agents and could sign with whichever team they wished. Because the market for baseball labor was competitive among teams, player salaries were pushed higher as a limited number of teams competed for a limited supply of the best players. Indeed, from what limited salary data that are available from this period, this was indeed the case – among 29 high-quality professional baseball players, average salary in 1881 was $1242 ($29 200 in 2013 dollars) and in 1886 was $2521 ($64 400 in 2013 dollars), a 20.59 percent average annual increase during that period (Dunbar, 1914). By 1889 the average salary was $3223 ($84 200 in 2013 dollars), which represented a 9.28 percent average annual increase between 1887 and 1890 (Ashcraft & Depken, 2009).

What can explain the decline in the annual increase in average player salaries after 1886? The decrease might have been a delayed reaction to the recession of 1882–1885. The recession might have sufficiently reduced disposable income such that consumers stopped attending baseball games, thereby reducing team revenues and leading to a reduction in player salaries. Unfortunately, reliable attendance data are not available until the 1890s and therefore it is not possible to ascertain to what extent the recession played a role in the significant decline in player salary increases after 1886. However, another important event occurred in that year. In 1887, the owners of professional baseball teams agreed to add the so-called reserve clause to contracts they signed with individual players. The reserve clause, quite literally the last clause in a player's annual contract, tied the player's services to the team indefinitely. The reserve clause represented the end of free agency in professional baseball until 1976, when restricted free agency was reintroduced.

Imagine you are one of the best players in the league and from one year to the next you lose your ability to negotiate with whichever team you like and instead are forced to deal with only one team owner who holds ultimate rights over your baseball career. The team owner can offer you a lower wage and there is no ability to counter with an offer from another team, in which case you might ultimately take a substantially lower salary. The team owner might offer incentives in a contract for reaching certain production milestones but can then order the manager to not play you when you approach these milestones. The team owner might decide to trade you or sell your contract to another team without you having a say in the matter. All of these possibilities seem to tilt the negotiating table toward owners and away from players. Understandably baseball players were very concerned about the reserve clause and yet it took almost a full century before the players could erode it significantly.

The reserve clause was the final attempt by team owners to cooperatively maintain a cap on increasing player salaries. Team owners understood early on that competing for players would continue to bid up salaries to the point where team profitability would be reduced and, perhaps, team viability brought into question. In an attempt to mitigate this competition, the team owners originally reached a gentleman's agreement in which owners agreed to avoid recruiting a list of reserved players designated by each team at the end of the season. Unfortunately, this reserve list was not binding and team owners continued to recruit players from other teams. At the same time a competing league came into being which was not privy to the gentleman's agreement. Thus, team owners' recourse to the reserve clause, while perhaps callous from the point of view of fans and players, was espoused by owners as the only way to put a limit on player salaries.

Regardless of the reserve clause's impact on competitive balance and the monopolization of talent, it had an immediate negative impact on salary levels for various players and for overall salary growth in the years immediately after the reserve clause was instituted. The reserve clause represented a shift in rents from players to team owners and was implemented without consulting the players or their representatives, something that understandably upset players.

Perhaps because they truly believed their rhetoric or because they realized that the reserve clause represented a large shift in negotiating power from players to team owners, during the period of the reserve clause team owners constantly warned of dire consequences if the reserve system was removed. There were concerns that a small number of teams, likely large-city teams, would seek to monopolize talent at exorbitant costs. As a result there was concern that large-city teams would become too good and would dominate the league over time, thereby permanently distorting competitive balance. Team owners warned that this could contribute to the financial instability of the individual teams and of the league itself, thereby placing in jeopardy the very existence of the sport.

While player salaries were increasing during the 1870s and 1880s, there is no evidence that team owners were caught in a so-called winner's curse in which the team that wins a bidding war for a player pays more than the player is actually worth to the team (Ashcraft & Depken, 2009). The implication is that there is no reason to assume that player salaries would increase to arbitrarily high levels that would put the league in financial distress. It is possible, however, that competition for a limited number of high-quality baseball players might have increased the proportion of revenue dedicated to player salaries.

Another reason the owners of National Association teams and later National League teams were paying more for players was outside competition for baseball talent. During the 1880s two additional leagues competed for baseball players. In 1884, the United Association formed and employed 268 players on twelve teams; in that year the National League employed 157 players on eight teams. Furthermore, the National League faced more substantial competition from the American Association which fielded teams from 1882 through 1892 and hired an average of 176 players per year. While both of these leagues eventually disbanded, they represented an increase in the demand for baseball talent, putting upward pressure on player salaries.

Because the reserve clause tied a player to his team indefinitely it had two immediate impacts. First, the reserve clause starved competing leagues of baseball talent because players who were under contract with a reserve clause were off the market, unless the team owner was willing to sell/trade the player's contract to another team. Such selling/trading might be expected to happen within a league on a more regular basis than between leagues, especially in the early days of professional baseball when the landscape was much less solidified than it is in the modern era.

The second impact of the reserve clause was that it starved players of alternative outlets to which to sell their baseball services. This served to considerably weaken the negotiating strength of players and to push their salaries down or dramatically reduce the increases they might have otherwise earned.

After the American Association disbanded in 1892, the next league to enter the market was the American League, which formed in 1901. In 1903, the National and American Leagues merged to create Major League Baseball (MLB). While both leagues remained ostensibly independent in many ways, they shared one important element: they both incorporated the reserve clause in their standard contract.

In 1914 the Federal League was formed to compete with MLB. Although the league only lasted for two years, in 1914 the league employed 212 players and in 1915 employed 224 players on eight teams. However, the Federal League faced substantial challenges, not the least of which was the reserve clause, which limited the availability of high-quality baseball talent to the Federal League. In 1915, the Federal League sued MLB claiming that it violated antitrust legislation by cornering the baseball labor market. Both leagues came to a settlement that promised to compensate the owners of the teams in the Federal League, but the owners of the Federal League's Baltimore Terrapins pursued their own antitrust case against the National League of MLB; the case eventually was heard and decided upon by the US Supreme Court in 1922.

The Supreme Court's decision leveled a strong blow against the baseball players by exempting professional baseball from antitrust litigation because, as Justice Oliver Wendell Holmes wrote, "personal effort, not related to production, is not a subject of commerce." This interpretation of sport, that it is a game and not a source of commerce, seems rather naive given that baseball had been surviving quite nicely as a profit-making venture for over forty years by this time.

This *de jure* antitrust exemption was used to reinforce the reserve clause throughout the rest of the twentieth century, and the other major North American sports were granted *de facto* exemption, especially on the structure of the reserve system for players.

During the twentieth century there was a long-simmering resentment on the part of the players against the reserve clause as well as overall working conditions. Resentment against low salaries and bait-and-switches concerning bonuses arguably contributed to the 1919 Black Sox Scandal in which several players on the Chicago White Sox agreed to throw the World Series to the benefit of gamblers.

In 1953, George Toolson sued the New York Yankees, which had reassigned him from its AAA minor league affiliate in Newark to the Binghamton Triplets, a team at the bottom of the minor league hierarchy, claiming that the reserve clause violated antitrust statutes. The US Supreme Court stood by its original 1922 decision and stated that if the reserve clause was thought to violate the spirit of antitrust legislation then Congress should address this issue legislatively.

In 1969, Curt Flood of the St. Louis Cardinals was notified that he had been traded to the Philadelphia Phillies. Flood did not want to relocate to Philadelphia and argued that he should not be forced to be traded. The team and league ignored his appeal, and, in response, he retired from professional baseball and sued MLB under antitrust legislation and for 14th amendment violations. His case was ultimately dismissed by the Supreme Court in 1972.

One possible reason that Curt Flood felt empowered to sue MLB in the way that he did was that in 1968 the Major League Baseball Players Association (MLBPA) had successfully negotiated the first CBA with the owners. The major advancement for the players in the CBA was that the minimum wage was increased for the first time in two decades, from $6000 to $10000 per year. In 1970, the players successfully negotiated for arbitration to solve disputes between players and owners, which set the ground for many gains by players in the future.

Thus, by the late 1960s and the early 1970s the pendulum of negotiating power was swinging away from owners toward players. While players still faced the reserve system, they were making large gains toward increasing their individual power to negotiate over salary.

In 1973, the MLBPA successfully pushed for final offer arbitration for those players who had three years of experience and were not under contract. The idea was to provide younger players who had established their credentials an opportunity to renegotiate their salary from that which they had signed while under a strict reserve clause, the assumption being that the strict reserve clause would naturally lower the player's salary because of the monopsony power the reserve clause provides the owner.

Arbitration was soon followed by restricted free agency, introduced in 1976 in response to a threatened lawsuit by Dave McNally and Andy Messersmith. Both players argued that their contract had expired and that they were therefore under no obligation to sign with their previous teams. Team owners put up a rather timid defense of the reserve clause and offered the MLBPA a compromise to avoid the lawsuit going forward. Starting in 1977, all players with six years of MLB experience and who were no longer under contract had the freedom to negotiate and sign with whatever team they wished. Thus the owners recognized that the Curt Flood lawsuit and arbitration had inflicted serious damage on the reserve clause as an institution.

After the removal of the reserve clause, salaries among the best players started to increase, but the vast majority of players did not experience an immediate increase in salaries. However, over time, free agency, arbitration, and the dramatic increase in league revenues combined such that average salaries in the league surpassed $3 million per year and minimum salaries were approximately $500 000 per year by 2014.

THE RESERVE CLAUSE IN OTHER NORTH AMERICAN SPORTS

The other major professional sports in North America have experienced similar paths over their histories. Early efforts to constrain player salaries and maximize franchise values led to each sport having some form of reserve clause tying athletes to their respective teams indefinitely. Over time, in no small part because of the success of the MLBPA, other players unions have successfully attained limited free agency rights which have also correlated with increasing salaries. The NHL introduced free agency in 1973, the NFL in 1993, and the NBA in 1996.

Each of these other leagues came to free agency through different means and when facing different pressures. For instance, the NHL, comprised of teams in Canada and the United States, remained a dominant league for approximately sixty years before it faced considerable competition by rival leagues in North America and in other countries (Santa, 1992). By the late 1960s there were a large number of non-NHL opportunities for players to entertain, which had the dual consequence of increasing player salaries overall but increasing the opportunity cost of signing with an NHL team because of the league's restrictions on future negotiations. The NHL thus found itself forced by outside competition rather than threats from the players association directly to introduce free agency.

The NFL had a reserve system similar to that seen in other sports until 1989, when it introduced so-called Plan B free agency. Under Plan B each team could retain limited rights to 37 players of their choosing each season. No protected player was able to sign with another team without the original team having the chance to sign him or the original team would be compensated by the other team. As teams were reluctant to pay each other for the right to sign Plan B players, those players protected under the system were essentially retained by their original teams for the majority of their careers.

In 1992, eight players sued the NFL arguing that Plan B free agency violated antitrust laws. Unlike professional baseball, the NFL does not have a *de jure* antitrust exemption, although it often appears to have a *de facto* exemption. In this case the NFL lost their argument and Plan B was ended after the 1992 season; full free agency was introduced in 1993

(Freeman, 1992). As with other sports, player salaries increased with free agency and increasing league revenues.

The NBA had long put restrictions on player movement and player salaries, starting with the inaugural season in 1947. However, over the first forty years of the league there was an uneasy partnership between players and owners, especially given the relatively fragile financial position of the league vis-à-vis the other leagues in North America. This tenuous partnership was dramatically altered when the NBA Players Association (NBAPA) discovered in 1991 that team owners had dramatically under-reported league revenues, which, in turn, reduced the total amount of money available for player salaries and pensions. The NBAPA sued the owners and, after a protracted fight, won an award of $92.7 million in additional player salaries and pension funding. This now damaged relationship came to a head after the 1995 season when owners imposed a lockout on the union until a new CBA could be agreed upon. After an unsuccessful move to decertify the union, which would have allowed players to sue the league under antitrust violations, the league and owners ratified a new CBA which granted unrestricted free agency to all players who were not under contract.

The repeated lesson from all four sports is that when players associations effectively push back on the reserve system, owners have eventually acquiesced. While in baseball the reserve system was maintained for almost one hundred years, in the other three sports the reserve system did not last as long in absolute terms. What happened in the four sports after free agency? Was the outcome as dire as predicted by team owners?

FREE AGENCY IN NORTH AMERICAN SPORTS

While the average salaries in all sports increased dramatically after free agency was instituted, very rarely were individual franchises placed in financial distress to the point of bankruptcy or forced sales. On the contrary, almost every sport enjoyed a period of increased revenues, increased attendance, increased franchise values, and increased league profits even as player salaries increased. One explanation is that higher salaries provided incentive for higher quality of play which, in turn, increased fan interest and willingness to pay to watch or attend games.

To those who appreciate free markets, the movement toward free agency was a welcomed development. However, there were many concerns that a true free-agent market would strongly empower players to negotiate ever higher salaries at the expense of owner profits. How could owners push back against the increased negotiating power of baseball players? One approach used in MLB was for owners to collude to not pursue free agents during the 1985, 1986, and 1987 seasons. However, the collusion backfired and the owners ultimately paid $280 million in damages for their actions.

Moreover, even as free agency seemed to improve the finances of the franchises in various leagues, there was little evidence that free agency caused the distortions in competitive balance that owners had feared during the pre-free-agency period. In professional baseball, football, and hockey, competitive balance improved after free agency. Only in professional basketball did free agency not seem to have a dramatic impact on competitive balance, but this might have more to do with the way the game is played and teams are constructed than with the particular right to free agency.

Over the past forty years, the free agency rights that players secured in the four major North American sports have provided an opportunity to empirically test the predictions of team owners that salaries would escalate beyond feasibility, that competitive balance would be permanently altered, and that players would become journeymen who lacked loyalty to any particular team.

Study after study has shown that free agency correlates with an increase in player salaries, as would be expected after monopsony power is reduced, but that competitive balance and player mobility do not dramatically change after free agency is introduced. The reasons for these empirical regularities were enumerated by Simon Rottenberg (1956) long before free agency was introduced to any of the major North American sports. In his seminal paper, Rottenberg posited that teams organized around the profit motive discover decreasing (net) returns when hiring high-quality talent and therefore fears that one or a few teams would monopolize all of the high-quality talent in a league are misguided. Furthermore, because teams play in markets differentiated by size, disposable income, and preferences, the natural equilibrium is for a league to have some disparity in quality across teams.

Free agency seems to have correlated with an increase in work stoppages. In almost every professional sport in North America the number of work stoppages has increased after free agency has been granted. However, as can be seen in Table 8.1 the majority of work stoppages have been lockouts rather than strikes, suggesting that ownership is the underlying cause of the work stoppages rather than players. The general working population has free agency in that individuals are very rarely tied to their employer for any meaningful length of time, and yet the general population is experiencing a decrease in the number of work stoppages. This suggests that it is not free agency per se that is the underlying cause of work stoppages.

Even while experienced players secured the right to negotiate with any team over wages and other compensation, team owners aimed to restrict professional sports labor markets. However, many of the limitations, such as minimum ages on incoming players, would be considered illegal under US antitrust laws unless they are included in a CBA with a certified union. Therefore, while it appears somewhat counterintuitive that team owners would want the players to be unionized, dealing with unions provides ownership, and to some extent players, much wider latitude in placing restrictions on their respective sport's labor markets.

THE CBA: SAVIOR AND BANE

From the point of view of both the players and owners, the CBA is both a blessing and a curse. For owners, the CBA permits limitations on player mobility, on minimum and maximum salaries based on experience or age, and the CBA stipulates what team owners are expected to cover in terms of travel costs, uniforms, and health care. These stipulations provide a level of certainty concerning costs that owners naturally appreciate.

On the other hand, players also enjoy a level of certainty as the CBA mandates specific benefits, minimum salaries, workplace conditions, and, most importantly for incumbent players, limits on the entry of amateur talent, all of which likewise provides some level of certainty for players.

Placing explicit limits on how amateur talent is distributed across the league's teams, for example, by reverse-order draft, on how long young players are reserved to their assigned teams, and on how salaries for both young and veteran players will change over time are examples of rules that are often embedded in the CBA which would arguably be illegal if they were imposed outside of the CBA.

On the other hand, it is not uncommon for the CBA of a particular sport to fail to cover all contingencies. For example, in 2014 the NFL discovered that its CBA did not have a specific protocol concerning punishment and rehabilitation for players accused or found guilty of domestic violence. Another example was the explicit omission of any protocol concerning performance enhancing drugs in MLB CBAs negotiated during the 1990s and early 2000s. While CBAs evolve over time as a sport, its ownership, and player behaviors change, they are often a point of contention as owners seek to alter certain portions of the CBA to their favor and players try to do the same.

Indeed, the increasing importance of the CBA seems highly correlated with the advent of free agency. Perhaps owners, having ceded ground on free agency, push back through the CBAs, thereby attempting to offset some of the gains made by the players. Therefore, while free agency itself might not be the direct cause of work stoppages, especially lockouts, free agency might be an indirect cause as owners seek ever more limits on the labor market through the CBA. Thus, the increase in work stoppages over the past forty years across the four major North American sports is highly correlated with the renegotiations of existing CBAs (see Table 8.1).

The purported reasons for the work stoppages are almost always centered on salary growth, how much of a league's total revenue will be dedicated to player salaries, and the minimum wages paid to incoming players. It is understandable that team owners would want to limit salary growth, perhaps in the form of a hard salary cap, as in the case of the NHL and the NFL, or through a soft salary cap, as in the case of the NBA. Owners might also agree to luxury taxes that seek to penalize teams who spend more than a specific amount on player salaries, as in the MLB and the NBA.

In leagues with salary caps the CBAs generally specify the percentage of league revenue that is dedicated to player salaries. The lockout in the NHL in 2012 centered on this issue. Team owners often seek to protect revenue streams, say from luxury box sales in the team's venue, from being included in the player salary pool. On the other hand, players often push for a more liberal definition of league revenues.

In a somewhat counterintuitive result, veteran players might actually push for higher minimum wages, not to provide a better standard of living for young players but to increase the costs of possible replacements for veterans, thereby ensuring that some of the veteran players will have a longer career than they otherwise would have.

Thus, the CBA provides benefits to both players and owners in certain areas but introduces costs in the form of market restrictions for both parties. Which party wins the negotiation of a new CBA is difficult to ascertain, but the evidence from work stoppages in all North American sports other than MLB suggests that team owners are in a stronger position than players, notwithstanding the temptation to bluff in negotiations (Carson et al., 1982).

FREE AGENCY, CBAs, AND THE RISE OF LABOR DISPUTES

After free agency is instituted in any particular sport, labor disputes seem more likely to lead to a work stoppage of some kind, either a strike by the players or a lockout by the owners. It is tempting to blame free agency for this, but upon closer inspection what seem to be more strongly correlated with work stoppages are negotiations over a new CBA.

As listed in Table 8.1, the occurrence of work stoppages has increased, and the overwhelming reason in most recent years is the lockout. Why are so many work stoppages clustered in the last forty years?

For example, in professional baseball, there were eight work stoppages between 1972 and 1995, and each corresponded with renegotiating the CBA. For instance, in 1990, after the third decision against owner collusion, the owners locked out the players for 32 days. In 1994, the players went on strike, cancelling the post-season to the dismay of many fans. It seemed at the time that the players might have gone too far in protecting the salary increases they had enjoyed over the previous twenty years. Team owners lobbied for a salary cap, and fans were noticeably upset about the fact that multimillionaire ballplayers were striking for ever more money. However, the union's solidarity proved too much for the owners, who compromised with players, abandoned the salary cap, and instead implemented so-called luxury taxes on teams that spend above a certain threshold in annual player salaries.

In 2004, the owners of the 30 NHL teams decided to abandon negotiations with the NHL Players Association and locked out the players. This was not the first time that owners in one of the major team sports in North America had resorted to this tactic, but it was the first time that the owners signaled they were willing to sacrifice an entire season to force the players to compromise in favor of the owners. Indeed, the 2004–05 season was entirely lost and the new CBA was agreed in July 2005.

The new CBA in the NHL dramatically altered the market for hockey talent and represented a substantial victory for owners, at least in the short run. The CBA introduced a new team salary cap, caps on individual player salaries as a proportion of total team salary, and strict limits on the amount of total league revenues dedicated to player salaries. In what seemed like a victory for players, the minimum wage in the NHL was increased from $180 000 to $430 000 in 2005, with steady increases in the league minimum wage every two years in the future. Nevertheless, the cap on team and individual wages caused a dramatic decrease in the average salary after the CBA. In the year before the lockout, average salary was $1.83 million; in the year after the lockout average salary was $1.46 million (Depken & Lureman, 2013). This revaluation of hockey talent caused an estimated $300 million to be transferred from players to owners.

At the end of the 2009 NFL season the then current CBA expired and negotiations began almost immediately. However, players and owners could not agree on the distribution of league revenues between players and owners, nor on what, exactly, league revenues were. For many years, NFL

Table 8.1   Work stoppages in major North American sports

Sport	Type	Years	Days	Games missed	Reason
MLB	Strike	1972	13	86	Pension, salary arbitration
	Lockout	1973	17	None	CBA
	Lockout	1976	17	None	CBA
	Strike*	1980	8	92 pre-season games	CBA
	Strike*	1981	50	712	Team compensation
	Strike*	1985	2	None	CBA/arbitration
	Threatened lockout*	1990	32	None	CBA
	Strike	1994–95	234	1994: 669 & World Series 1995: 252	Salary cap
NHL	Strike*	1992	30	30 games rescheduled	CBA
	Lockout*	1994–95	103	468 & Allstar game	New CBA
	Lockout*	2004–05	310	2004–05 season	New CBA
	Lockout*	2012	120	628 & Allstar game	New CBA
NFL	Strike & lockout	1968	13	None	First CBA
	Threatened strike	1970	22	None	New CBA
	Strike	1974	41	None	New CBA
	Strike	1982	57	98	Revenue distribution
	Strike	1987	24	14	Free agency
	Lockout*	2011	146	Training camp & Hall of Fame game	Revenue distribution
NBA	Lockout	1995	80	None	New CBA
	Lockout*	1996	1	None	Television revenue distribution
	Lockout*	1998	191	464 & Allstar game	New CBA
	Lockout*	2011	161	256	New CBA

Note: * Indicates work stoppage occurred after the league had free agency.

owners had excluded luxury suite revenues from overall league revenues, arguing that the revenues were very much stadium and franchise specific and not revenue generated by league efforts, such as the national television contract. The 2010 season was played without a CBA and therefore there was no team salary cap. However, player salaries did not increase dramatically in that year. The 2011 season was jeopardized by a lockout of the players because of the continued disagreement between the players association and the owners. However, perhaps after witnessing what happened in the aftermath of the lost NHL season, the lockout was lifted when players and owners ratified a new CBA after only the Hall of Fame game and two weeks of pre-season games were cancelled.

The NBA has also experienced work stoppages centered on the negotiation of CBAs. In 1998, the players were locked out for 204 days at the expense of approximately 40 percent of the season. Players mitigated the costs of the lockout by playing charity events and creating short-term loans among themselves.

STRIKES VS. LOCKOUTS: WHO HAS THE UPPER HAND IN THEORY?

Industrial action, be it a strike or a lockout, seems contrary to economic reasoning. Both forms of action seem to create a lose-lose situation in which both workers and owners lose wages and profits that might ultimately be greater than whatever compromise position might be obtained through continued negotiation.

A lockout is more likely to occur when owners feel they have the upper hand in the negotiations; a strike is more likely to occur when labor feels they have the upper hand in the negotiations. It might seem that players have the upper hand in negotiations; after all, the highest salaries have been secured during the free agency period. However, one reason that the salaries for superstar players have increased after free agency is because the players are pitting the various team owners against each other in a bidding war. A CBA, by its very nature, pits all of the players, in the form of their union, against all of the owners as a group. In this case, owners might feel that they have the upper hand for several reasons. First, in most North American sports there are very few viable alternative leagues in the world that can offer the same fame and fortune. Therefore, while individual players no longer face monopsony for their entire career, the players as a group essentially still face a monopsony that can take a very strong negotiating stance on any number of aspects of the CBA.

As can be seen from Table 8.1, in every sport other than baseball work stoppages have been lockouts after free agency was introduced. This suggests that over time owners have become stronger negotiators, perhaps because there is more revenue at stake for the owners; the CBAs have become more complicated; and shorter average careers have made players unions less effective in negotiating elements of the CBA that have long-term consequences.

In other cases, ownership might have outside revenues that might allow them to better survive an extended work stoppage. For example, there was a possibility that the NFL lockout of 2011 would lead to the entire season being cancelled. If this had happened, arguably the league would have suffered a setback in terms of popularity. However, team owners had a special clause in their national television contract that they would be paid the full amount of the contract even if there were no games played that season. Therefore, if the lockout had ended the season each team owner would have received approximately $150 million in revenues while having essentially zero costs for the season (outside of front-office and coaching salaries, stadium maintenance, and any debt service they might have had). Armed with this deep pool of reserves, team owners were likely confident that they could outlast the players as a group and that the CBA would be negotiated more to their liking than to that of the players.

MOVING FORWARD

What do we expect in the future? It seems that MLB has reached an equilibrium that has kept it from entering a work stoppage since 1994. This twenty-plus year reign of relative labor peace might serve as an example for the other leagues to follow to also avoid future work stoppages. On the other hand, in hockey, football, and basketball it seems that work stoppages have become a default condition when a new CBA is being negotiated. This might be a signal of ownership strength in these leagues or could indicate that the elements of the CBA have not been negotiated to an equilibrium status.

One interesting development is that the salaries for superstar players have increased sufficiently such that career earnings, endorsements, and other investments can provide former players with enough wealth to become minority owners of professional franchises. Nolan Ryan is part of the ownership team of the Texas Rangers, Magic Johnson is part of the ownership team of the Los Angeles Dodgers, and Shaquille O'Neal is a minority owner of the Sacramento Kings. Michael Jordan was a minority owner of the Charlotte Bobcats and in 2010 became the first modern professional athlete to become a majority owner of a franchise in one of the four major North American sports. Wayne Gretzky was a part-owner of the Phoenix Coyotes and Warrick Dunn is a minority owner in the Atlanta Falcons. As more players become minority and majority owners it is possible that labor strife in North American sports could attenuate as ownership might be less aggressive in their pursuit of particular aspects of the CBAs.

In the early twenty-first century, many North American sports franchises regularly earn positive profits, almost all enjoy increasing value over time amid the increasing popularity of their sport (even if some sports are relatively more popular than others), and all are discovering ever more revenue streams that suggest increasing revenues in the future. To the extent that these new revenue streams reduce financial disparity across teams within a league, they might help discourage work stoppages that might arise from stalemate negotiations caused by inter-team disputes. Therefore, if owners and players can avoid lost seasons such as that suffered by the NHL in 2004, they will likely be dividing an ever growing pie. While outside competition might be the best antidote for labor strife, it is possible that an increased melding of (former) players and owners might serve a similar function, thereby reducing the likelihood and duration of future work stoppages.

REFERENCES

Ashcraft, Jennifer and Craig Depken (2009), 'The introduction of the reserve clause in Major League Baseball: Evidence of its impact on select player salaries during the 1880s', mimeo, Department of Economics, UNC Charlotte.
Bureau of Labor Statistics (2014), 'Major work stoppages in 2013', USDL-14-0217, released February 12, 2014.
Carson, Thomas, Richard Wokutch, and Kent Murrmann (1982), 'Bluffing in labor negotiations: Legal and ethical issues', *Journal of Business Ethics*, **1** (1), pp. 13–22.
Depken, Craig and Jeff Lureman (2013), 'Wage disparity and the 2005 NHL collective bargaining agreement: An empirical analysis', mimeo, Department of Economics, UNC Charlotte.
Dunbar, William (1914), 'Baseball salaries thirty years ago', *Baseball Magazine*, July, pp. 291–292.
Freeman, Mike (1992), 'NFL is in violation of antitrust laws, jury decides', *Washington Post*, September 11, 1992.
Hicks, John (1932), *The Theory of Wages*, New York, NY, USA: Macmillan Publishing.
Kennan, John (2008), 'Strikes', in Steven N. Durlauf and Lawrence E. Blume (eds), *The New Palgrave Dictionary of Economics*, Second Edition, Basingstoke, Hampshire, UK: Palgrave Macmillan.
Rottenberg, Simon (1956), 'The baseball players' labor market', *Journal of Political Economy*, **64** (3), pp. 242–258.
Santa, Sue (1992), 'Skating on thin ice: NHL owners and players clash over free agency', *Washington University Law Review*, **70** (3), pp. 915–934.

9. Power games: understanding the true nature of season-ending labor disputes in Major League Baseball and the National Hockey League

Peter Bouris and Rafael Gomez

INTRODUCTION

Ten and twenty years respectively separate most fans from the twin labor disputes that cancelled the entire 2004–05 National Hockey League (NHL) season and the 1994 Major League Baseball (MLB) World Series. Despite their lack of temporal currency both events still cause much consternation, especially amongst those fans whose teams were poised to enjoy serious playoff runs. In baseball, Canada's two franchises (the Montreal Expos and Toronto Blue Jays) never fully recovered, and in one case (the Expos) the team actually relocated to another city.[1] The NHL and MLB therefore hold the ignominious distinction of being the only professional sports leagues to have ever cancelled their respective championships due to labor disputes.

Why did these season-ending work stoppages occur? What were the motives involved? And perhaps more importantly, who benefited the most from such high-stakes bargaining? We feel these questions deserve a serious second look and indeed a second asking largely because the existing sports literature has failed to account for these events in a meaningful way and because popular perceptions of both work stoppages are, we feel, woefully off the mark. Indeed, a number of myths surrounding both the 1994 baseball and the 2004–05 hockey work stoppages need to be dispelled right at the outset.

The first is that rather than reflecting disagreements over money or misperceived information, the season-ending nature of these disputes was a symptom of a broader systemic conflict, one that arose over the need to control and shape the structures by which each of the game's revenues were being generated and distributed. Rather than disagreements over the "share of the pie," they were struggles over which party – owners or players – had the power to decide "how the pie would be baked". It was this fundamental quality that contributed to the season-ending nature of the two disputes.

The question at the time of each lockout/strike was the same: should the game continue to expand as it had in preceding rounds of legitimate bargaining[2] (30 years in the case of baseball and 12 years in the case of hockey), with players in de facto fashion dictating the terms by which the game would evolve? Or should ownership sacrifice some measure of short-term financial gain so as to temper the ever growing demands of respective player unions? After all, viewed from the perspective of the time, ownership was not quite sure how far player demands would go. One minute players might be asking for unrestricted free agency, but fairly soon they could be demanding that players have a hand in managing the league's finances. Interestingly, a confirmation of just such an attitude developing amongst members of the Major League Baseball Players Association (MLBPA) in the run up to the 1994 strike can be found in Andrew Zimbalist's book *Baseball and Billions*.[3] In the final chapter, entitled "The Future," Zimbalist gives the following account of an interview he had with Donald Fehr:

> Don Fehr, [then] director of the [baseball] Players' Association, told the author that he would be willing to consider a salary cap/profit sharing plan provided that the association was given veto power over important structural decisions. In fact, Eddie Einhorn asked rhetorically during a recent public address: "What do we need owners for anymore?" Don Fehr wonders why they were ever needed. (Zimbalist, 1992, p. 170)

Notably, the struggle for power over important structural decisions was occurring not only between the obvious combatants, players (labor) and owners (capital), but also amongst the owners themselves. The free spending reckless owners in large markets like New York and Los Angeles had to be reined in by the tight-fisted authoritarian ones like Chicago's Jerry Reinsdorf in baseball and Bill Wirtz in hockey.

In this chapter, we want to replace the accepted narrative of why these disputes occurred with a behavioral employment relations model of decision making. In delineating this model we borrow heavily from some elementary but pervasive concepts in the study of strategic bargaining. The first concept recognizes that collective bargaining is best viewed as a repeated game, one in which players can react to other players' past actions. Equilibria not possible in a one-shot setting are therefore possible in a repeated game built on sequential offers (Cabral, 2000, p. 58). For example, binding oneself to a course of action (such as eliminating or penalizing certain available options) prior to a negotiation makes no sense in standard economic terms; but from a strategic standpoint such behavior can change another's expectation of what one will do, thereby changing that other party's decision of what to do, to one's own benefit.

In the context of labor negotiations, a credible pre-commitment that is *ex-post* suboptimal can therefore have *ex-ante* strategic value (Dixit & Nalebuff, 1993).

In baseball and hockey, ownership negotiated extremely poor television deals prior to their respective season-ending labor disputes. Why would the NHL and MLB do this? Such decisions only make sense when viewed from the perspective of a credible pre-commitment in which owners wanted to successfully bargain on a lack of ability to pay basis with players (Haber, Malin-Adams & Khamalah, 2008), something they were unable to do in the past when lucrative television deals were sitting on the table.[4]

The application of these rather well-known game-theoretic concepts to the 2004–05 NHL and 1994 MLB labor disputes exposes a more complex set of motivations behind much of management's public posturing and respective decisions to abrogate their season finals. Indeed, it is the central contention of this chapter that owners, in both cases, were fully prepared to forfeit the end of their seasons irrespective of what concessions (short of full capitulation) players would have made. This interpretation is consistent with the idea that only credible pre-commitments (that is, those with real visible costs) have payoff value by successfully altering subsequent counterparty behavior.

This chapter is divided into three major parts. Part one summarizes the history of labor relations in both hockey and baseball since the formation of player unions in the mid-to-late 1960s, which is to say during the so-called "modern era" of play. This section does not provide a detailed chronological account of each round of bargaining; rather it extracts only those relevant historical features that exerted the greatest impact on the season-ending nature of the two labor disputes. Part two is concerned with uncovering the underlying causes of the two season-ending work stoppages. Part three ends with a discussion of who ultimately won, ownership or players, both in the immediate aftermath of the disputes and with ten and twenty years of historical distance by which to judge the outcomes.

THE STRUCTURE OF LABOR RELATIONS IN BASEBALL'S AND HOCKEY'S MODERN ERA

Union Formation in Baseball and Hockey

Both baseball and hockey established official trade unions in the mid-1960s after unsuccessful (earlier) attempts.[5] In baseball the MLBPA was formed in 1965, with former United Steelworkers veteran Marvin Miller taking over as its leader on 12 April 1966. Initially, things looked pretty bleak. Apart from ownership's concerted efforts to sabotage Miller's early organizing work, the union was, to put it mildly, under severe financial strain.[6] And yet, amidst this desperate situation, there were certain inherent advantages to taking over such a newly established organization. One advantage lay in the union's relatively small membership base. With approximately 500 players the union's manageable size provided the fertile ground from which Miller's conscious raising approach would prove immensely successful. Miller was also sensitive to the criticisms made about unions and their bosses and therefore made a point of seeing every player at least once a year during spring training meetings with teams. Not only did he urge players to attend those meetings, but he also made a point of urging players to stop by the union's head office in New York. One can only imagine the logistical problems Miller would have encountered had he made such an offer to all the members in the Steelworkers' union. At the time of Miller's departure it had 1.25 million members. In Miller's words, "If you wanted to meet every member, it would have taken until the year 2000" (Helyar, 1994, p. 26).

Miller also realized that before the players could be mobilized they needed to be informed. In the words of John Helyar (1994, p. 26), "Miller set about making this a demonstration project: a union as democracy." Furthermore, he understood that the players were at a decided disadvantage when it came to understanding the nature of negotiating. So he set out to guide them, continually pointing out the inequities of the existing collective bargaining system. These early efforts, combined with the owners' belligerence, made Miller look like the Great Emancipator.[7] It also set the foundation for the players' growing militancy. Commenting on the owners' "hardball" tactics and their effect on Miller's popularity, a pitcher named Jim Boutin made the following comment,

> If they'd (owners) have just said, "We'll raise the minimum salary to $10,000, then raise it $1,000 a year for the next twenty years. Then we'll throw in an annual cost-of-living increase on the meal money." If they'd have just done something like that, nobody would have looked to Marvin Miller. But with everything they did, they helped Marvin. (Helyar, 1994, p. 27)[8]

In hockey, the earliest signs of player collective action occurred in 1947 when the players (prior to officially forming a union) were able to extract a modest pension plan from the NHL. In January 1957, the National Hockey League Players Association (NHLPA) was first formed, with legendary Detroit Red Wing Ted Lindsay as union president. A minimum salary for players of $6,500 was successfully bargained for largely on the back of a large 1956 CBS television contract. The nascent union, however, did not last out the year as a result of ownership threats and interference.

In 1967, around the time Marvin Miller took over the MLBPA, the NHLPA was reborn, and Alan Eagleson[9] became its new head. He was a Toronto lawyer who also represented some of the players in the union as their agent. Two years after Eagleson took over, the union was able to gain salary arbitration, although it was limited to the option year provided for in the then Standard Players' Contract (SPC).[10]

Outwardly, at least, it seemed that Eagleson's tenure as head of the NHLPA was a positive one. He led the NHLPA throughout the 1970s and 1980s without the rough patches or drama of Marvin Miller's experience in baseball. This was partially due to the fact that the NHL, at the time, was different than other major North American sports leagues in that labor agreements were reached with much less formality, contention and fanfare. Often, the collective agreements were simply transcripts of informal verbal meetings between the league commissioner and Alan Eagleson.

This state of affairs changed dramatically in 1989 when Ed Garvey, then head of the National Football League Players Association (NFLPA), convinced over 200 NHL players to fund a study of Eagleson's performance. Around the same time a reporter named Russ Conway began his own investigation of Eagleson after hearing rumors that something was seriously amiss about the inner workings of the NHLPA. In September 1991, he published the first of many installments in a series called *Cracking the Ice: Intrigue and Conflict in the World of Big-Time Hockey*, which was intended to last six months in the Boston area *Eagle-Tribune*, but ran for most of the early 1990s, earning Conway a Pulitzer nomination. The exposé revealed that Eagleson had engaged in a staggering litany of unethical and criminal conduct over many years (Conway, 1995). The result sent shockwaves through the NHL and the sports world generally. Eagleson was told he would have to discontinue serving as a player agent, leave his law firm and personally guarantee $2 million in loans that he had illegally made with union funds to friends and law associates in order to keep his job. Eagleson officially stepped down in 1992 and two years later was indicted on 32 counts of racketeering, embezzlement and fraud following a multi-year Federal Bureau of Investigation inquiry.

A Short History of Negotiations in Baseball: 1970–90

In 1972, after successfully negotiating a grievance arbitration system in order to resolve disputes between players and owners, baseball players initiated the first ever strike in the history of North American professional sports. It lasted for 13 days and occurred shortly after MLB had signed a lucrative $70 million ($400 million in current dollars) television deal with NBC. After ownership refused to agree to any TV revenue sharing or to increase their contributions to players' healthcare costs and pension plans, the players voted unanimously to strike. It became clear in the 1972 dispute that the players were more unified than the owners, many of whom felt pressure from their new television contract with NBC to ensure that baseball would in fact be played. The owners ultimately agreed to increased healthcare benefits and inflation adjusted pension contributions.

In 1975, MLBPA members were granted free-agency rights after an arbitrator struck down the reserve clause – the ability for owners to hold a player's rights in perpetuity.[11] This happened as a result of players Andy Messersmith and Dave McNally, with support from the MLBPA, successfully challenging MLB in a private court.

The next labor dispute in baseball occurred in 1976 when, in an effort to roll back these new found free-agency rights, the owners locked out the players for a total of 17 days. The negotiations continued after the owners lifted the lockout, and the result was another win for the players. The principle of free agency was guaranteed and eligibility was agreed to after six years, with players having the right to demand a trade after five years. Additionally, at Miller's insistence, the collective agreement again improved the player pension program.

The 1980–81 bargaining session was much more difficult for the union. Miller began by filing an unfair labor charge with the National Labor Relations Board (NLRB) asserting that owners had violated the "good faith" bargaining provision in American labor law after rejecting all of the union's offers regarding free-agent compensation. Adding insult to injury, the owners refused to bargain with Miller directly, who had become somewhat of a bogeyman for them. Miller stepped aside as a result and allowed Donald Fehr to take his place as head of the union bargaining committee. As was the case in 1976, however, the owners showed a lack of unity; with some owners expressing a desire to just reach the best deal possible while others remaining steadfast in the hope of achieving the best-of-all possible deals. After a drawn-out off-season dispute that delayed the start of the 1981 season and cancelled a total of 713 games, the owners again capitulated and agreed to raise the minimum player salary and further improve their contribution to the players' pension fund.

The 1985 lockout was shorter than the 1980–81 work stoppage, but it ended with the first ever shortfall between union demands and the actual bargained outcomes. Though Miller served as an advisor to the union during the bargaining process, Donald Fehr was now fully in charge of negotiations. This time, however, the union seemed to lack the solidarity it had gained over the past 15 years. Part of the problem was that the MLBPA had become a partial victim of its own success. Player compensation had grown considerably since the formation of the union in 1967

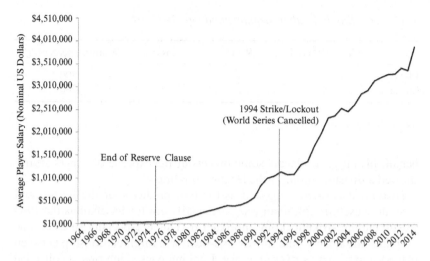

Source: Author's calculations with salary data from sportslistoftheday.com and stevetheump.com.

Figure 9.1   Average Major League Baseball player salaries, 1964–2014

(see Figure 9.1) and, as a result, players were less concerned with preserving something that had once united them: the pension plan. Prior to free agency, baseball players were not earning enough money to set themselves up for life, which meant they had strong concerns about their pension the same way regular industrial workers would. However, the high levels of base player compensation, which were arguably a result of the free-agency gains fought for by the MLBPA, seemed to be splitting the players apart. The result was that for the first time since 1965, the union agreed to accept less than one-third of the league's national television and radio revenues in order to fund the pension plan.

The 1990 lockout saw the union return to form. This time, with Marvin Miller completely out of the picture and Don Fehr fully in charge, the union fought off an ownership proposal to peg player compensation to a fixed percentage of league revenues. Fehr would not accept this without the union having a significant voice in league-wide decision making. Naturally, the owners balked (pun intended) at this and so the proposal was dropped – yet another victory for the players and another showcasing of union solidarity versus divided ownership. The union did not waver during this bargaining session, even when the league commissioner tried to reach a private agreement with some key players and owners. Since the commissioner is ultimately employed by the teams to bargain on *their*

Table 9.1   Baseball labor dispute standings, 1972–94*

	Games played*	Wins	Losses	Winning percentage
Players	5	4	1	.800
Owners	5	1	4	.200

Note: *6th game about to begin.

behalf, his move to placate some owners at the expense of others clearly showed a division amongst the league's top brass.

History, it is often suggested, is the best predictor of the future, and in some sense this aphorism was particularly apt for baseball as the 1994 season-ending strike/lockout approached. This is especially so when one examines the stormy (and mostly one-sided winning) relationship between players and owners surveyed above. Looking back, each time a collective bargaining agreement came up for renewal, a lockout or a strike ensued. Because the basic agreements each lasted three to five years, this meant that five industry wide work stoppages occurred between 1972 and 1990. If these labor battles were transposed into their respective win/loss box columns prior to the 1994 strike/lockout, they would probably have read as shown in Table 9.1.

Given the storm clouds that preceded the 1994 round of bargaining, it was perhaps obvious that a lockout or strike was imminent. However, before we begin our evaluation of what actually occurred in 1994 and whether the MLBPA was able to pull off yet another win, we need to describe the history of hockey labor relations over the same period. In this way we can understand the bargaining dynamics common to both leagues as well as what distinguishes them as strategic bargaining cases.

A Short History of Agreements in Hockey: 1975–2003

In 1975, the NHL faced stiff competition in attracting top talent from the World Hockey Association (WHA), a rival league that was in existence from 1971 to 1979. Many NHL caliber players were attracted to the new league because of the WHA's willingness to abolish any draft/reserve clauses in its contracts. The competition for talent strengthened the bargaining position of the NHLPA and, as a result, owners in principle accepted free agency in the NHL without the costly strikes or court challenges present in baseball.[12] However, free agency in the NHL was contingent on the concept of "equalization" – the notion that the team acquiring a free agent would have to compensate the team losing that player with another player of roughly equal talent. This process made many teams reluctant to exercise their ability to sign free agents, in practice neutralizing much of free agency's potential to raise salaries.

As was mentioned earlier in the context of the NHLPA's formation, nothing dramatic, at least when compared to the Miller years in baseball, occurred in hockey until revelations of Eagleson's malfeasance surfaced in the early 1990s. As a result, no legitimate collective bargaining occurred in hockey until 1992, when Bob Goodenow, then a deputy within the NHLPA, took Eagleson's place. Goodenow initially borrowed a page from the Marvin Miller handbook and spent much of his time educating the players about inequalities in the existing collective agreement and the extent of Eagleson's collusion with ownership. In short order, Goodenow led a ten-day strike after the league refused to negotiate a replacement deal following Eagleson's resignation and the expiration of the 1991 collective agreement. The 1992 strike was the first ever player work stoppage in NHL history.

The main issues in that bargaining session were the number of rounds in the draft (more rounds meant that owners controlled more players' rights and could use this to dampen salaries) and the amount of compensation required for "equalization" in free agency. The players, by all accounts, won in the sense that they retained 68 percent of league revenues available for compensation, created an allotment of choice for arbitrators in "equalization" disputes and reduced the eligibility age for free agency. Additionally, free agency was liberalized by reducing the required compensation for when a team signed a free agent. The owners, sensing they were losing control with Bob Goodenow now at the helm of the NHLPA, ultimately forced John Ziegler (president of the NHL since 1977) out of office in 1992. They eventually hired Gary Bettman, a reputedly savvy negotiator and someone schooled, given his time at the National Basketball Association (NBA), on how to negotiate[13] and implement a player salary cap (LaPointe, 1992).

The evidence of player "bargaining dominance" in the post-Eagleson era can be seen in the numbers. Between 1990 and 1994 NHL player salaries doubled (see Figure 9.2) even though the 1993–94 season was played without a collective agreement. This effectively led to the next work stoppage in NHL history, the 1994 lockout. At the time, the league claimed that small-market teams were struggling to keep up with the costs of rising player compensation. League commissioner Gary Bettman insisted on a payroll tax (effectively a salary cap), with Goodenow adamant that the union would not accept such a proposal. The owners' contention of a lack of ability to pay was undermined, however, by one of Bettman's first acts as president – the signing of a five-year, $155 million deal with

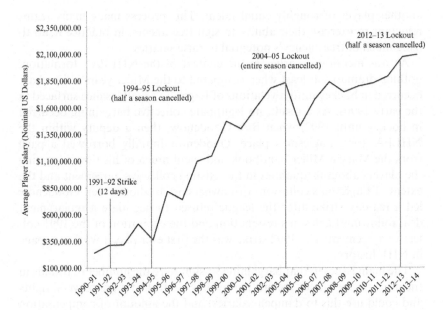

Source: Author's calculations from data obtained at www.capgeek.com and hockeyzoneplus.com.

Figure 9.2   Average National Hockey League player salaries, 1990–2014

the Fox Media Company. The deal, a money flow to the league, was slated to start during the 1994–95 season. The deal was significant, not only because of the money involved, but because a network television contract in the United States was long thought of as unattainable during the Ziegler era.

In a major sign of how much ownership valued the Fox deal, the salary cap proposal was dropped by the league. In return the players agreed to increase restrictions on salary arbitration and to cap rookie salaries for players under the age of 25. Although the deal was initially hailed as a victory for the owners, a quick look at Figure 9.2 again shows that average salary growth of NHL players post-1994, if anything, outpaced the growth prior to the 1994 lockout. Also of note, the 1992 strike and 1994 lockout were the first times in NHL history that both sides truly engaged in adversarial bargaining, with Ziegler/Bettman representing the owners and Goodenow representing the players. The ten-day strike at the start of the 1992 playoffs and the 1994 lockout that resulted in a shortened season were also, in retrospect, clear harbingers of things to come.

Table 9.2   Hockey labor dispute standings, 1992–94

	Games played*	Wins	Losses	Tie	Winning percentage
Players	2	2	0	0	1.00
Owners	2	0	2	0	.000

Note: *Previous games played under unfair and informal rules.

Transposing hockey's two legitimate labor battles into their respective win/loss/tie columns, they would probably have read as shown in Table 9.2.

In short, the NHLPA looked poised after the 1994 lockout to join the MLBPA as one of the most successful player unions in sports history. The fact that a nine-year deal was signed between players and owners meant that the next round of bargaining would begin at some point during the 2003–04 off-season.

A TALE OF TWO SEASON-ENDING DISPUTES

The Case of Baseball in 1994–95

The 1994–95 MLB labor dispute was (at the time) the mother of all sports labor stoppages. With Miller completely out of the picture, the owners were looking to reverse union gains that had accumulated since the 1960s. They viewed the previous 30-year period as being severely dictated by the players, a trend they intended to reverse. No longer would a nervous commissioner step into the middle of a labor dispute and give in to union demands. To ensure that this would never happen again, the owners fired Fay Vincent in 1993 (technically forcing him to resign). Bud Selig was elected in his place. Selig was the new acting commissioner and a big time "hawk." The owners also implemented a different decision-making formula. No longer would a simple one vote majority be enough to settle an impasse. What was required going into the 1994 labor negotiations was a 21 vote majority. With only seven holdouts, the owners as a collective unit had in fact "bound" themselves to further the interests of only the most hawkish of owners. In the parlance of game theory, this was an effort by the owners to eliminate the possibility of breaking ranks through a telegraphed pre-commitment device made apparent to their counterparty, the MLBPA.

Due to this, there was a great deal of speculation entering the 1994

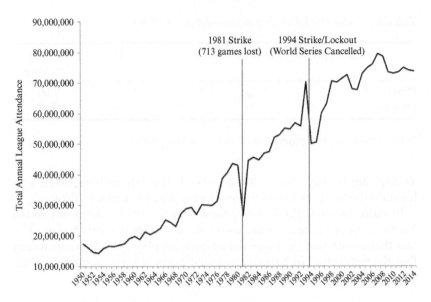

Note: League expansion periods are 1961–77, 1993–98.

Source: Author's calculations based on figures compiled from www.baseball-reference.com.

Figure 9.3   Total Major League Baseball attendance, 1950–2013

season about what would happen. Ultimately, many fans and pundits knew something big was in the works, yet league attendance had never been greater, peaking at over 70 million attendees the year prior, a figure that was only bettered in the following decade (see Figure 9.3).

The 1994 season lasted until August, at which point the players went on strike. This was done intentionally prior to the playoffs, potentially depriving the owners of their greatest source of revenue.[14] However, the players' strike was not random, nor was it done to achieve a clear bargaining objective. It was a reaction to the owners' unilateral imposition of a salary cap that would have inherently reduced players' salaries across the board. The owners' used the league's exemption under the Sherman Act (US antitrust law) to impose a collective agreement without the players' consent, thus prompting the strike. Though this exemption no longer applies,[15] at the time the only variable the players really controlled was the timing of the strike, and they rationally picked a time that would cost the owners the most money, which was right before the playoffs.

The owners claimed that 19 of the league's 28 clubs were losing money, which is why they imposed the salary cap. Along with this, the owners proposed the elimination of salary arbitration and the imposition of a 50/50 split of league revenues (a provision the union successfully fought off in 1990). This was a clear power-play by the owners, trying to reverse much of what the union had fought for and won in the previous decades under Miller and Fehr.

As the players remained on strike, federal mediators attempted to help broker a settlement; but the strike carried forward. As a result, the World Series was cancelled for the first time since 1904.[16] The NLRB soon threatened to issue a complaint over the owner-imposed salary cap, leading the MLB to back off a salary cap and instead propose a so-called luxury tax. The union tentatively accepted the owners' revenue sharing formula but made its own luxury tax proposal of 25 percent on team payrolls of $54 million or more. However, the owners were calling for a more stringent revenue sharing structure and rejected the union offer.

Early in 1995, even President Bill Clinton became involved by inviting the two sides to the executive mansion to try to broker a deal. In an effort to increase pressure on both sides, Clinton set 7 February 1995 as a deadline for an agreement. Despite the president's efforts, the deadline came and went, and there was still no end to the dispute in sight.

In March 1995 Donald Fehr stated that he would end the strike if the NLRB, after its own investigation, issued an injunction on the owners calling on them to restore salary arbitration and open markets for free agents. The NLRB did eventually rule that ownership's imposed settlement was not a product of good faith bargaining and the union, as promised, ended its strike. The owners promptly responded by locking-out the players and threatening to use replacement players to start the 1995 season.

However, by the time April arrived, with players remaining steadfast behind their union and their president Donald Fehr, the owners abandoned their call for a salary cap and instead created their own system of league-wide revenue sharing. The lockout was lifted and the 1995 season was only shortened by a few weeks.

One of the most notable aspects of the 1994–95 strike/lockout was what it revealed about the union and new league commissioner Bud Selig. For the union, the 1994 strike/lockout demonstrated that it had not succumbed to the "paradox of success" – that is not allowing its past track record of bargaining wins to cloud its judgment in successive bargaining periods (see Appendix A). Almost uniquely amongst professional sport unions, the MLBPA managed to maintain a remarkably high degree of unity during one of the bitterest disputes in sports history.

On the league side, the 1994–95 strike/lockout revealed for the first time in many decades an ownership group more resolute than ever before. Owners that had seemed divided and splintered in almost every bargaining session, finally, under a new commissioner (he himself a small-market team owner), appeared ready to submit to a committed and long-term bargaining posture. Though not observable at the time, the owner-resolve exhibited in the 1994–95 strike/lockout may have been one reason why baseball subsequently completed three rounds of bargaining without a serious threat of a work stoppage from either side (ESPN, 2006).

The Case of Hockey in 2004–05

In the annals of North American sports labor disputes, the 2004–05 NHL lockout has since supplanted the 1994–95 baseball strike/lockout as the messiest and most adversarial. In many ways, especially from a fan and local economic standpoint, it was a social and economic disaster.[17]

What prompted the season-ending lockout of 2004–05? According to the owners and much of the popular press, it was all down to team and league finances. At the end of the 2003–04 season, players' salaries encompassed 75 percent of league revenues, while attendance (see Figure 9.4) and television ratings for the league were allegedly on a steady decline.

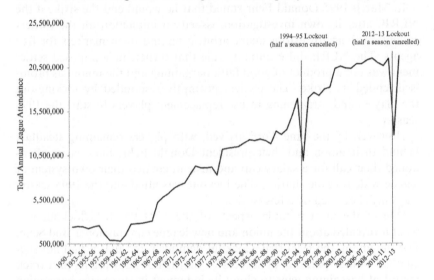

Note: League expansion periods are 1967–74, 1979, 1991–94, and 1998–2000.

Source: Author's calculations based on data from www.hockeydb.com.

Figure 9.4   Total National Hockey League attendance, 1950–2013

According to some, hockey's popularity in the United States was danger-ously moving towards fringe sport levels.[18] The owners were adamant that any new collective agreement would have to address the imbalance in the proportion of revenues that players were receiving as well as improve the financial situation of many struggling clubs. Given that Goodenow was adamant from the beginning that he would not accept any kind of salary cap, it seemed inevitable that the labor dispute would be long and protracted.

Despite these expectations, the union started bargaining with a con-cession. It initially offered a 5 percent rollback of salaries. The league countered by proposing what would be another concession for the union: a salary cap. This initial salary cap offer would have placed a ceiling of $31 million on each team's player compensation level.

The commissioner was consistently asserting the league's need for "cost certainty," hence his rationale for a cap on player compensation. There was a great deal of dispute over the degree to which the league was facing financial problems. Between the NHL's "independent" Levitt Report stating that it had lost, on aggregate, $224 million in the previous season and the business publication *Forbes* magazine calculating that the league had lost only roughly half that amount ($123 million), there was no clarity on the extent of the league's net revenue position. The one thing most outside observers did agree on, however, was that the league was losing money, though the question of how much was still up for grabs.

On 9 December 2004, the union offered another concession in the form of a 24 percent rollback of player salaries. Sensing the union's weakness, the league returned with a proposal that included the 24 percent rollback the union had offered, along with a salary cap and, for good measure, the abolition of player salary arbitration. Later, the league increased its salary cap proposal but, on the whole, this did not do much to bring the owners and players closer to an agreement. Finally, on 16 February 2005, with well over half the season gone, Bettman officially cancelled the season. The Stanley Cup final would not be played for the first time since 1919.[19]

A final agreement was of course reached, signed in the off-season months, and it included the 24 percent salary rollback the union had originally proposed *in lieu* of a salary cap, a rookie pay scale, player com-pensation pegged to 57 percent of league revenues and the salary cap Bob Goodenow had vowed he would never accept. The agreement was signed on 13 July 2005 and Bob Goodenow resigned two weeks later, perhaps acknowledging that he had lost most of his credibility with the NHLPA members and that, crucially, the NHLPA had given up all the previous gains he had achieved in his first rounds of negotiations with Zeigler and Bettman.

UNDERLYING CAUSE(S) OF THE 2004–05 NHL AND 1994–95 MLB SEASON-ENDING LABOR DISPUTES

The Fallacy of the "Salary Cap" as a Remedy for Small-Market Teams

Before we make any definitive statements as to what the true causes of the two season-ending disputes were, it is useful to engage in a short thought experiment. Assume for the moment that a salary cap was indeed needed in order to save small-market teams. Furthermore, assume that the player associations in both cases (not just one) agreed to a salary cap and that the salary cap was set low enough so as to perform the task of dragging down overall salaries. The question would then be "In what financial state would the MLB and NHL's small-market teams be in several years later, assuming that such a salary cap proposal had been imposed?" The answer, as we know from the experience in hockey, is "Exactly in the same situation both leagues were in prior to the strike/lockouts."

The reason for this is that the disparity between large-market teams and small-market teams is not based on a team's cost structure; the often quoted refrain used by Bettman to explain the need for a salary cap was "cost certainty." Nor is it based on how competitive a team is on the field/ice as evidenced by the underperformance of the most valued and profitable franchise in hockey, the Toronto Maple Leafs. Rather, the disparity between large- and small-market teams is based on three other factors:

1. the competitiveness of the local television market (the more competitive, the higher the bidding for local television rights);
2. the number of potential television viewers in the local market;
3. the total number of gate receipts, which is based on ticket price and average home game attendance.

The imposition of a salary cap has therefore done nothing to alleviate these disparities in any sport, including hockey.

Proponents of the salary cap would probably come to a different conclusion. The salary cap, according to supporters, has done a considerable amount to help small-market teams in the NBA and National Football League (NFL) (Saccucci, 2012). Yet, if the true source of the disparity lies with inequitable local television contracts, then it would make sense that the NHL and MLB devise a system whereby local television revenues could be redistributed fairly, akin to what the NFL does. The only time owners have ever proposed such a system in either sport was in baseball, and it occurred in conjunction with ownership's 1994 salary cap proposal. One suspects, however, that if an agreement with the players on a salary cap had ever been reached, that the revenue sharing provision would have quickly been disposed.

Finally, there is still a deep suspicion amongst players about the profit statements of ownership. Indeed, even if true, the claim that small-market teams lose money simply misses the point, given that the "value" of a franchise upon resale has never been lower than when first purchased by a team owner (Ozanian, 1994). On a personal level, who claims that they lose money on a house purchase simply because, as a home owner, one has to pay bills and property tax every year? Money is ultimately lost (or gained) upon resale. Furthermore, the accounting practices of sport owners are notorious for the imaginative way in which they can turn operating profits into losses. On this precise point, Paul Beeston, past general manager and current president of the Toronto Blue Jays, was once quoted as saying that, "Anyone who quotes profits of a baseball club is missing the point. Under generally accepted accounting principles, I can turn a $4 million profit into a $2 million loss and I can get every national accounting firm to agree with me" (Zimbalist, 1992, p. 620).

Ultimately, we are left with no alternative but to reject the premise made by both ownership groups in 1994–95 and in 2004–05 respectively that the salary cap was necessary to control escalating salaries which, in turn, threatened the financial lifeblood of small-market teams. Consequently, by rejecting this assertion, we are left with the central question: "What, then, were the *true* causes of such disastrous labor relations outcomes?"

Ownership Induced Work Stoppage as a Signalling Device

In addressing this question we need to first recognize that both labor disputes were provoked by the owners. Although technically it was the MLBPA that made the decision in August 1994 to go on strike, the union in effect had no choice. Because of baseball's antitrust exemption, the owners were ready to implement a salary cap with or without the players' agreement. Moreover, the players decided to strike at a time in the season when the owners stood to gain the most financially. In the past, the owners had always capitulated in time to save the season. This time, however, they did not.

What became increasingly clear in both work stoppages – though hardly mentioned in the press at the time – was that NHL and MLB owners were sending a signal to players and also to themselves. The signal was one which conveyed several messages.

The first message was designed to alter player expectations regarding owner capitulation. No longer would large-market teams who were profit-able regardless of the nature of collectively bargained deals with players be able to pressure a league commissioner into ending a labor dispute early and give in to the demands of the union. In baseball, the owners elected Bud Selig to prevent this while in hockey a remarkably similar strategy was pursued when the owners fired John Zeigler and hired hard-nosed negotiator Gary Bettman in 1993. The owners in baseball also implemented a less flexible internal decision-making formula. No longer would a simple one vote majority amongst owners be enough to settle an impasse. What was required going into the labor negotiations in 1994–95 and 2004–05 was a clear voting majority. With only seven holdouts (in baseball's case), the league, as a collective unit, had in fact bound itself to further the interests of only the most hawkish owners. As in a game of chicken, the player who chains his hands to the steering wheel usually wins.

The second message for the players was one which concerned their public perception. The contemporary view of players as being pampered and overly paid is one which works to the owner's advantage. By provoking a strike in baseball and convincing fans of the need for a salary cap system to save small-market teams, NHL and MLB owners were confident that fans (who, for the most part, had seen their own incomes stagnate) would come to resent the astronomical salaries of professional hockey and baseball players. The attitude often expressed at the time of the impasses was, "How can people making so much money and playing a kids' game go on strike?" The feeling that "money" had ruined the game was everywhere.[20] The owners were hoping that this public pressure would force certain players to waiver over their commitment to the union. This pressure would then trickle up to Don Fehr and Bob Goodenow in the form of growing discontent amongst the rank and file, forcing a deal with management at the risk of seeing the union implode. This is essentially what happened in hockey when a group of players mused publicly about starting their own negotiations with the league, circumventing the NHLPA's stated policies of union solidarity (Liebman, 2009). This never occurred in baseball for reasons owing to the nature of player representatives and the long tradition of player involvement; but certain members of the MLBPA felt compelled to issue threats to any player who crossed the picket line and would consider playing alongside replacement players. It seems that even in the strongest sports union of all, there are always players less committed to losing an entire season out of their limited careers.

Finally, the owners wanted to use the 1994–95 strike/lockout and 2004–05 lockout as a means of sending a message to themselves. In effect, they were telling the recalcitrant owners of the day – the Steinbreners, the Turners, the Dolans and the Illichs – that the free spending days were over and that they must now enter into an era of cost containment and owner cooperation.

Season-Ending Lockouts as a Means of Guaranteeing Future Labor Peace

Apart from these rather disparate messages, the "forced strike/lockouts" and the resulting owner resolve to sacrifice lucrative post-season and TV revenues had another purpose. The owners hoped that by making this stand they could begin to alter the nature of the player associations, from being unions which aggressively fought for the interests of their members, to ones which successfully protected owners from themselves. In other words, the union would in fact become a labor contractor, whose purpose would be to provide an orderly workforce which could guarantee industrial relations cooperation over the long term. This is a crucial point that deserves more elaboration.

The owner desire for long-term labor stability stems primarily from the need to placate the television industry and its (current) billion dollar revenue streams. In the words of Gerald Scully (1989, pp. 193–194), "Part of the value of the network TV contract arises from the assumption that the games will be reliably supplied. This requirement puts pressure on the owners to resolve disputes through collective bargaining rather than precipitate players' 'strikes'." This statement appears to undermine our earlier contention that the owners had in fact been willing to sacrifice an entire season from the outset. The question arises: "Why would the owners provoke the players into striking at a time in the season when they would be hurt the most financially?"

One answer may be that the owners simply made a colossal mistake and unknowingly misjudged player resolve. This, however, seems very unlikely. For one thing, the NHL and MLB owners had taken various steps prior to the beginning of their respective seasons which demonstrated that they were in fact preparing for a long-drawn-out strike/lockout. The forced retirement of commissioner Fay Vincent and his replacement with Bud Selig was self-explanatory in baseball, likewise was the ouster of John Ziegler and his replacement with Gary Bettman in hockey. The changing of the rules governing owner majority voting was another indication that the leagues had begun to burn their bridges in preparation for the coming labor relations battle. We can therefore be fairly certain that the owners knew all along that the players were committed to avoiding the imposition of a salary cap and, in the case of baseball, were willing to go on strike at a time when they could inflict the greatest damage.

Stemming from this last statement, we might be inclined to think that the owners were simply not rational – that is, that they consciously decided to choose the worst means by which to achieve their ends, the means being the provocation of a strike and the imposition of a lockout at a time when they [the owners] would lose the most financially, and the end being the imposition of a salary cap. But an explanation which is based on an actor's irrationality is too easy a crutch to fall back on and is not particularly appealing.

An alternative explanation, however, can be crafted that incorporates owner actions within the framework of rational decision making. By rational we mean that the owners in both baseball and hockey consciously chose the most desirable strategy (given player union resolve and solidarity up that point) with which to achieve their end. In order to make this claim, however, we must first alter our assumption of what the ultimate goal of ownership was in provoking these disputes. Perhaps owners had another agenda all along, and that instead of imposing a salary cap per se, the owners were in fact intending the season-ending nature of the dispute to alter a number of player expectations, the key one being the expectation that owners would eventually capitulate every time there was a labor dispute. This was an assumption that both player associations (albeit for a much longer time in baseball) had come to accept. And, indeed, both baseball's (long) and hockey's (more recent) history had proved the players right. This belief, however, was particularly bad for the "Lords of the Game" because it meant that anytime the owners ever made a threat, that threat was no longer seen as credible. This lack of fear on the part of the NHLPA and MLBPA actually came with a quantifiable price tag.

Ending Player Militancy and Undoing the Television Revenue Conundrum

With little or no fear of losing most labor battles, players had become less risk averse with regard to entering into a strike or waiting out a potential lockout. Constant labor disruptions, as mentioned earlier, hurt the owners not only through forgone gate receipts but also when it came to the more lucrative business of negotiating long-term television contracts. We saw that there was a clear catch-22 every time an individual team or the league signed a lucrative television deal in that in order for the deal to be on the best terms possible for the team and league, owners had to ensure that the games would be played without disruption and on schedule. But in order to keep the games running smoothly owners were always forced, at the risk of losing those TV contracts, to do everything possible to placate the players.

One way for the owners to get out of this vicious cycle was to negotiate smaller television contracts prior to bargaining or to allow previously agreed-upon deals to expire in the run-up to collective bargaining rounds. In this way, they would have less to lose by not giving in to union demands. Likewise, by ownership not capitulating as quickly, players would begin to alter their readiness to strike.

The poor TV deals in the run-up to the 1994–95 and 2004–05 work stoppages have typically been seen as having been "forced" upon owners when CBS decided not to renew their baseball contract in 1993 (Crupi, 2012) and when Fox decided not to renew its hockey contract in 2001 (Campbell, 2009). But if bad TV deals are recast as a long-term strategy designed to bind owners to a course of action and alter player expectations of what owners would do, and in turn alter player behavior to owners' own benefit, then inking less lucrative TV deals becomes rather effective in maintaining an owner bargaining advantage.

Naturally, the preferred option for owners would be to maintain lucrative television contracts while at the same time stemming the frequency with which employment disruptions arise, or possibly eliminating them altogether. But how could this be done?

The only viable way to do this back in 1994–95 and 2004–05, in the context of strongly mobilized unions, was to pursue a strategy of extended strike/lockout. In baseball, because of the owners' power to impose a settlement under the Sherman Act exemption, a de facto lockout was achieved by forcing a strike. A prolonged work stoppage is always better for owners because the onus falls on the players to continually justify their position to the increasingly reactionary fan base. But most importantly, by binding themselves in the way they did prior to negotiations, the owners committed themselves to *not* negotiate, or at the very least to negotiate in less than "good" faith. Though such a strategy carried with it some very big risks, the potential gains, if successful, would be even larger.

Many still believe that the MLB strike and NHL lockout could theoretically have ended in one day, provided that the players had given in just a little. However, if, as we argue, the ultimate goal of ownership was to fundamentally alter the expectations of players (both from the standpoint of their perception of the owners as being weak and divided and also to end the players' expectation of ever increasing gains from labor strife), then even if players had met most of the owners' financial demands, it would still not have been enough to end the impasse. The owners realized that the pattern of relatively quick agreements following previous work stoppages, even if it favored them in the short run, was merely setting the stage for yet another battle down the road. What owners truly wanted out of the 1994–95 and 2004–05 disputes was an extended period of labor peace in order to manage growth in league revenue on their terms.

Summary: Short-Run Pain for Long-Term Gain

So, returning to our key question of why NHL and MLB ownership provoked season-ending labor disputes, it was precisely because the owners were desperately trying to ensure that revenues accruing from future (more lucrative) television contracts flowed to them instead of the players. The owners realized, perhaps through the tutelage of a new MLB commissioner and NHL league president, that the pressure to achieve a resolution through collective bargaining did not favor ownership's cause, even if it preserved a single season worth of revenue. So, they finally decided in 1994–95 and 2004–05 to not only alter the perception of them as being divided and weak, but to also begin to alter the function of their respective unions. The unions should not protect the interests of their members; rather, they should protect owners from their own misguided efforts to acquire scarce player talent. Indeed, this "revised" role for the respective players associations was really a hallmark of how sports unions were evolving in the post-Fordist era, something Marvin Miller himself had questioned as early as 1981 when he mused about whether baseball owners had been influenced by Ronald Reagan's firing of striking air traffic controllers (Miller, 1991, p. 121).

What is certain, though, is that NHL and MLB top management had been emboldened prior to each of the season-ending disputes in a manner which was uncharacteristic of their past rounds of bargaining. Indeed, one might ask why it took the owners so long to adopt a position which had become common industrial relations policy in much of the Anglo-American world. Capital had significantly reasserted its control over labor, with give backs by unions, even during times of relative prosperity, becoming the norm. Perhaps, from this perspective, we should not be surprised by ownership's reactionary mood in 1994–95 and 2004–05. Instead, we should perhaps be asking the question, "Why did it take so long to develop?"

Ultimately, the causes of the 1994–95 baseball and 2004–05 hockey work stoppages were decidedly more complicated and more subtle than the ones still often circulated by the popular press. The issue of "who gets what share of the revenue pie" was not the chief reason for a season to be lost and a World Series not to be played. The phrase, "who has the power to decide what share everyone should get" is perhaps a more accurate depiction of the true cause of the 1994–95 and 2004–05 labor disputes.

Having dealt with the critical issues facing both players and owners at the time, we are finally ready to conclude this chapter by outlining who ultimately won and lost as a result of the 1994–95 and 2004–05 labor negotiations.

THE *ULTIMATE* WINNERS AND LOSERS

Our argument up to now has been that both season-ending disputes were instigated by one party (ownership) and with bargaining positions that were strengthened by mutual strategies of: (i) credible pre-commitment (for example, deliberately negotiating substandard television revenue deals) and (ii) punishment/retaliation (in the form of playoff/season abrogation) for perceived past wins by the union. Subsequent labor peace and tempered player demands (in baseball) and the acceptance of a salary cap (in hockey) were the most obvious long-term owner payoffs. The fact that most popular observers fail to recognize these features of the negotiated settlements and instead blame both parties as needlessly greedy suggests that ownership pulled-off a *double whammy*, effectively constraining public sympathy towards players while dictating the terms upon which bargaining has been conducted in the NHL and MLB ever since.

There are many who would disagree with our assessment and claim that the 2004–05 hockey lockout and 1994–95 baseball strike/lockout were both won by the players. Such a determination is made by examining two clearly measured variables: in one case (baseball) a salary cap was never imposed and in both cases average player salaries rose quite dramatically. But what many fail to realize is that player compensation soared in a fairly unique way. The expansion in pay happened, in the case of hockey, through player–agent and complicit-ownership exploitation of loopholes in the 2004–05 collective bargaining agreement (Mirtle, 2011). These loopholes allowed free agents to sign unusually long contracts with front loaded compensation. In baseball, as has long been the case, the explosive growth in pay occurred mainly at the expense of rookie and early career players (Rosenheck, 2012). As in many other spheres, the rise of MLB and NHL player salaries occurred for players managing to reach free-agency status (those with more than six years in the league). For players whose careers ended prior to free-agency eligibility – which is to say a majority of all players and for professional minor leaguers – the conditions were not as pretty. As Josh Rosenheck noted in the *Economist*:

> ... athletes whose stars burned brightly and briefly, such as Marcus Giles or Joe Magrane, never received a fraction of the wealth they generated for their employers. The union's rank and file would be far better off if [the union] had dedicated more of [its] bargaining chips to pursuing sharp increases in the league's minimum salary, or to challenging the amateur draft.

To illustrate our point, despite having the longest careers in professional sports, baseball and hockey players still do not complete on average six seasons of play (see Figure 9.5). Yet collectively bargained free-agency

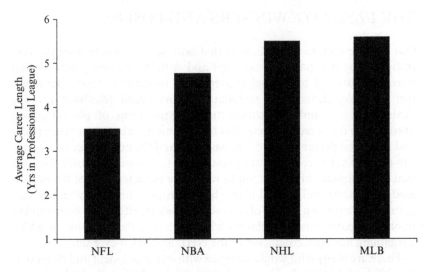

Source: RAM Financial Group. Accessed 30 November 2014 at http://www.ramfg.com/
RAM-Financial-Group-Solutions-Professional-Athletes-Athletes-Services.

Figure 9.5   Average career length across four professional sport leagues

status in baseball only kicks in after year six, and in hockey it arrives even
later (year seven). This is much like the first pensionable age of 65 instituted in late nineteenth-century Germany, when average life expectancy
was only 45.

What is more, even in baseball, where players successfully staved off a
salary cap – the only major professional sport in North America without
such a clause in the collective bargaining agreement – player demands and
militancy since 1994 have been noticeably dampened. In the post-1994–95
labor dispute era, as compared to the era preceding it, baseball players
have seemed content to allow the overall baseball pie to continue to grow
without many musings about having a say in how this occurs, recognizing perhaps that the biggest driver of athletes' salaries is not how they
split revenue with the owners but the growth of the sport as a whole.
And whereas collectively bargained agreements were rather standard in
length (three to five years) prior to 1994, afterward they have been much
longer. This has favored management because it is on the backs of these
long-term collective bargaining agreements – with their work-stoppage-
free guarantee – that the NHL and MLB have been able to sign such
lucrative television (and other media rights) deals in the post-internet era.
Moreover, the deals are now almost always set to expire just after the

next round of bargaining. With much less to lose, owners have been much more successful in maintaining the status quo and then signing even more lucrative deals on the back of long-term stability in the league's labor relations. In the end, it appears elite NHL and MLB players and owners are not interested in prolonged work stoppages and are rather more interested in maintaining the monopoly privileges of the major professional leagues. Players have perhaps determined that receiving relatively *less* of an *overall larger* sport market pie is better than fighting for a more equitable share of revenue.

This was not, as seen in our historical review, the attitude of the MLBPA and NHLPA prior to the respective season-ending strike/lockouts. Viewed from the vantage point of *ex-ante* strategic value, an outcome that is only revealed optimal once second and third period choices by counterparties are factored into the overall payoffs, it is clear that the winners in both disputes were the owners. And more precisely, small and medium sized owners were the greatest winners of all. They were the ones with more interest in fostering an end to the preceding era of large-market-owner defection and of chasing television deals to keep up with ever spiralling player salaries.

CONCLUSION

Absent an irrational need to punish another party, a costly strike that is eventually settled serves no rational economic purpose. So why did owners and professional athletes abrogate an entire season and forfeit the most lucrative period of playoff operations, especially given, in the end, they eventually reached a deal? If one relaxes assumptions of perfect information we can perhaps arrive at an explanation that makes prolonged strike duration a by-product of misperceptions and lack of information. But information asymmetries alone are not enough to explain decisions which clearly have some *ex-ante* strategic value lurking beneath the surface.

At the beginning of this chapter we presented a brief overview of the nature of work stoppages in MLB and the NHL up to and including the season-ending disputes of 1994–95 and 2004–05. While we did not deny that lack of trust and bottom line monetary issues were obviously present in the baseball and hockey strike/lockouts, we argued that a proper explanation had to go deeper and explain why the two parties had consistently been at loggerheads for so long.

The answer to that question was twofold. In the case of MLB the owners provoked the players into striking in 1994 by imposing a clearly one-sided collective agreement that established the first ever salary cap in baseball, which was their right under baseball's exemption from American antitrust law. They did this in the hope of turning public opinion against the players. Moreover, the strike had to be provoked to occur when it did – at a time in the season when owners were prepared to gain the most financially – because in this way players would finally begin to alter their perception of owners as being not only greedy but divided and weak.

A similar rationale for owner instigation was present in the NHL dispute – for example, the establishment of a salary cap by management – despite a differing labor relations history and financial model. Without the special antitrust exemption enjoyed by the MLB at the time (since curtailed in the Curt Flood Act of 1998), hockey ownership could not impose their desired agreement and therefore locked out the players at the beginning of the 2004 season. This is despite the fact that the NHLPA was willing to reduce player salaries with an across-the-board cut of 5 percent and to continue negotiating while playing under the terms of the expired contract. But hockey owners, as was the case in baseball, allowed the lockout to happen on their terms, and only after laying the public relations groundwork throughout the off-season – commissioning the Levitt Report suggesting that players were overpaid and thus ruining competitive balance in the game. But it was clear, given the nature of NHL demands, that owners were fully prepared (and indeed expecting) for the eventuality that players would not accede over the terms of a salary cap.

Producing a fundamental and permanent shift in the balance of power towards management was the ultimate goal in both disputes. Whether ownership eventually imposed or abandoned their salary cap proposals was less important than if in the process they weakened the public perception of players and their respective unions, extracted some other major concessions, altered player expectations of owner resolve and, perhaps most crucially, tempered future player demands thereby reshaping the pattern of subsequent bargaining.

The overarching similarity between both the baseball and hockey disputes was that in each case the owners believed the union and its players had taken control of the bargaining process and were *implicitly* (if not *overtly*) affecting fundamental business decisions. The need to find ever greater television deals and the use of league expansion fees to cover operating losses was no longer a sustainable strategy for ownership in both cases. A confirmation of this interpretation was the fact that owners, prior to both disputes, actively committed to future actions which were *ex-post* suboptimal. In the case of the NHL and MLB, the leagues inked some of the least lucrative television deals in their respective histories – something most commentators have misconstrued as an exogenous *constraint* rather than a manipulated *cause* (Staudohar, 2005, p. 28). Viewed as strategic moves, these decisions reduced the opportunity cost of a work stoppage and allowed the MLB and NHL commissioners to credibly claim an inability to pay during bargaining. Owners were in reality not so focused on what percentage of "the pie" they would keep (that would come later), but were instead concerned with who ultimately got to shape "the pie." Moreover, the MLBPA's consistent wins, and the NHLPA's string of wins since Eagleson's resignation, meant that owners were ready to inflict a retaliatory cost on the union, especially if in the process it could lead to future acquiescence and reduced union militancy.

Such were the "high stakes" that led to such contentious bargaining periods for both players and owners in 1994–95 and 2004–05. At the time, each party was bargaining to retain future control of revenue generation in the game, but it was ownership's fixation on *ex-ante* strategic value that is ultimately the criteria by which success should be judged. Viewed over a long-run time horizon – and in the context of two formerly combative player unions that are now less willing to entertain lengthy work stoppages – the owners clearly scored an impressive victory. The durability of this win depends on the future nature of NHLPA and MLBPA leadership (see Appendix A) and ownership behavior (see Appendix B).

NOTES

1. Conspiracy theorists (in Canada at least) allege that MLB provoked the players into striking in order to avoid an all-Canadian city final which would have been even more disruptive to major television contract negotiations that were scheduled to occur that off-season. The Montreal Expos, after falling attendance and an owner who had no intention of keeping the team in Montreal, moved to Washington, DC in 2004 and are now called the Washington Nationals. Toronto's attendance, after posting consecutive league record attendances (they were the first franchise to surpass the 4 million attendance mark), dropped to just over 2 million for the following twenty years.
2. By *legitimate bargaining* we are referring here to the beginning of true collective bargaining between a union and management, something which began in baseball with the arrival of Marvin Miller in 1966 and in hockey – despite having formed a union around the same time – with the ouster of its first corrupt leader Alan Eagleson and the arrival of Bob Goodenow in 1992.
3. In hockey, the element of emboldened union leadership was more nascent but clearly growing once the NHLPA appointed Bob Goodenow as the head of the NHLPA in 1992 upon Alan Eagleson's resignation. In Goodenow's first few months on the job, he led the players out on a successful (from a player bargaining standpoint) 12-day strike on the eve of the Stanley Cup playoffs.
4. In addition, because in repeated games one party can react to a counterparty's past actions, the practice of "retaliation," or the imposition of a penalty that is also costly to the retaliator, should not be viewed as merely punitive, but seen as a tactic that can confer strategic value. Punishments that make no sense in standard economic terms therefore have strategic value in a repeated bargaining situation.
5. In the early days of America's pastime, the players unsuccessfully attempted to form some kind of collective representation multiple times. The Players' Protective

Association collapsed in 1900 because of team contraction in the National League. The Baseball Players Fraternity fell apart in 1912 after Ty Cobb was suspended for beating up a heckler in the stands. A few decades later, the American Baseball Guild folded in 1946 because of how little the players were getting paid. The low pay caused some players to defect to the Mexican league. In hockey Ted Lindsay (Detroit Red Wings) and Doug Harvey (Montreal Canadians) attempted to form the first NHL players union in the late 1950s after the league had refused to provide adequate pensions and refused to release financial information to the players. The owners broke the union by trading players involved with the organization or sending them to the minor leagues. After an out-of-court settlement over several players' issues, the players disbanded the organization.

6. When Miller started the job, the association had $5,400 in a checking account and a battered filing cabinet in Frank Scott's office in Biltmore Hotel. See, Miller (1991, p. 143).

7. Miller is not without his critics, however, and not just from those siding with management. In a piece written in the *Economist* at the time of his death in 2012, *New York Times* journalist Dan Rosenheck (2012) argues that while Miller may have negotiated a system of free agency that maximized total wages, it also created a grossly unfair dichotomy amongst the players. In Rosenheck's words, "Reduced competition amongst free agents is great for veterans. But it's not great at all for young players, who are effectively still bound by the old reserve clause. Making it through six full seasons in the major leagues is no small feat, particularly for pitchers, who are highly prone to injury in their early-to-mid 20s."

8. Miller's early organizing attempts were also aided by some of baseball's inherent advantages. One advantage lay in the fact that baseball players had relatively long careers. This meant that players were less susceptible to "short run" offers to improve their collective bargaining agreements. The determination to ensure that the long-term interests of players were looked after was already in evidence by the time Marvin Miller was elected president. Baseball players, for example, had a pension plan before any other sport. In addition, they had an equitable manner of distributing the retirement benefits according to years played rather than career earnings. This egalitarian spirit is one which is still in evidence today.

9. One of Eagleson's broader contributions to the league and players was masterminding the Canada Cup, which prior to professional athletes being allowed to compete in the Olympics, was the only tournament designed to create a true national world champion in hockey. In its early incarnations, the Canada Cup generated significant revenues for both players and the league.

10. Most SPCs are relatively similar. They begin by stipulating that the prospective employee is a skilled hockey player. The SPC is a contract of adhesion in the sense that because it is drawn up by the team, it is then interpreted by courts against the team in case of ambiguities. The SPC as it stands now is a product of collective bargaining and shows give-and-take between the players and management.

11. This occurred despite the ruling of the infamous *Flood v. Kuhn* case in 1972 when player Curt Flood lost his battle in a public court trying to end baseball's "reserve clause," which guaranteed the rights of a player to the team that drafted him in perpetuity. Three years after the Flood case the players launched a private suit and won.

12. Though there were notable individual NHL player court challenges, the most successful court challenge to NHL's reserve clause actually came from the WHA. In an effort to eliminate the NHL's version of the reserve clause the WHA filed a suit in 1972 against the NHL seeking to bar the NHL from obtaining injunctions for more than sixty NHL players who had signed WHA contracts. See Liebman (2009, pp. 85–86).

13. Bettman's abilities as a negotiator were also due in some measure to his education. He was a graduate of Cornell's Industrial and Labor Relations program in 1974, where at the time Robert McKersie was the leading exponent of strategic choice theory. It is likely Bettman would have applied his ideas to collective bargaining issues.

14. Players are not "paid" salaries, neither during the off-season nor during the playoff rounds. They can receive playoff bonuses from their respective clubs, however.
15. The Supreme Court first granted antitrust exemption to professional baseball in *Federal Base Ball Club of Baltimore Inc v. National League of Professional Base Ball Clubs*, 259 U.S. (1922). In *Federal Base Ball Club*, the Court held that professional baseball was not interstate commerce for purposes of the Sherman Act and therefore must be exempt from Sherman Act liability. Professional baseball is therefore still the only sport that enjoys an exemption from antitrust liability (Liebman, 2009). However, the Curt Flood Act of 1998 has applied antitrust restrictions on baseball, as well as extended the Clayton Act (1914) labor exemption to protect the players union from antitrust law. Its passage stemmed from the 1994–95 strike/lockout when a federal judge ended the lockout with an injunction and claimed that labor issues did not fall under baseball's antitrust exemption. This lead the owners and players to cooperate in lobbying for a federal law to codify this notion. The Curt Flood Act also extended some antitrust exemptions (carved out from the new full application of antitrust) for baseball on matters concerning merchandise and television contracts from which other professional sports benefit.
16. In 1904, owing to a business dispute between two rival owners, there was no World Series played between the champions of the American and the National Leagues (then under separate ownership).
17. As reported in Staudohar (2005), Canada's gross domestic product diminished by $170 million Canadian dollars as a result of the cancelled season.
18. Arthur Levitt, the former chairman of the Securities and Exchange Commission in the United States, who was hired by NHL owners to conduct an internal audit of league health, declared that the league was on "a treadmill to obscurity" (Buteau, 2004).
19. The Stanley Cup was not played in 1919 because of the Spanish Influenza epidemic.
20. An example taken from a contemporary (1994) sport page will suffice. Writing in the 5 December 1994 issue of the *Toronto Star*, Garth Woolsey began his column on the baseball and hockey lockouts with the following often trotted statement, "Money. Some people say it makes the world go 'round. Some of us have noticed it's what makes the world of sports grind to a stop, too."
21. In football, for example, management has successfully alienated the star players from the rank and file. The 1987 NFL strike failed because the owners successfully cut "sweet" deals with quarterbacks and running backs, compelling them to cross the picket lines.

REFERENCES

Buteau, Michael (2004), 'NHL lost $273 million last season, Arthur Levitt says', *Bloomberg. com*, Bloomberg, 12 June, accessed 23 October 2014 at http://www.bloomberg.com/apps/news?pid=newsarchive&sid=alou9Zj5lOfk&refer=canada.

Cabral, L. (ed.) (2000), *Introduction to Industrial Organization*, Cambridge, MA, USA: MIT Press.

Campbell, K. (2009), 'Campbell's cuts: Making new friends', accessed 9 December 2014 at http://www.thehockeynews.com/articles/22727-Campbells-Cuts-Making-new-friends. html.

Conway, R. (ed.) (1995), *Game Misconduct: Alan Eagleson and the Corruption of Hockey*, Toronto, Canada: Macfarlane Walter & Ross.

Crupi, A. (2012), 'Play Ball! Fox, Turner to re-up with MLB multibillion-dollar deals wrap up baseball rights through 2021', accessed 1 December 2014 at http://www.adweek.com/news/television/play-ball-fox-turner-re-mlb-143856.

Curt Flood Act of 1998, Pub. L. No. 105-297, § 3, 112 Stat. 2824 (1998).

Dixit, A.K. and B.J. Nalebuff (eds) (1993), *Thinking Strategically: The Competitive Edge in Business, Politics, and Everyday Life*, New York, NY, USA: W.W. Norton.

ESPN (2006), 'Timeline of baseball's labor troubles', accessed 28 November 2014 at http://
sports.espn.go.com/mlb/news/story?id=2635604.

Haber, L.J., N. Malin-Adams and J.N. Khamalah (2008), 'Labor negotiations, misperceptions, and repeated prisoner's dilemma: A simulation', *Journal of Collective Negotiations
in the Public Sector*, **32** (4), 329–341.

Helyar, J. (ed.) (1994), *Lords of the Realm: The Real History of Baseball*, New York, NY,
USA: Villard Books.

LaPointe, J. (1992), 'The N.H.L. employs a head for business', accessed 29 November
2014 at http://www.nytimes.com/1992/12/13/sports/hockey-the-nhl-employs-a-head-for-
business.html.

Liebman, J.M. (2009), 'Tip your cap to the players: 2007–2008 off-season reveals NHL's
salary cap benefits on players', *Sport Lawyers Journal*, **16** (1), 91–109.

Miller, M.J. (ed.) (1991), *A Whole Different Ball Game: The Sport and Business of Baseball*,
New York, NY, USA: Carol Publishing Group.

Mirtle, J. (2011), 'Burke: Richards deal amounts to cap circumvention', accessed 1
November 2014 at http://www.theglobeandmail.com/sports/hockey/leafs-beat/burke-
richards-deal-amounts-to-cap-circumvention/article615788/.

Ozanian, M.K. (1994), 'The 11 billion pastime: Why sports franchise values are soaring even
as team profits fall', *Financial World*, (May 10), 50–59.

Rosenheck, D. (2012), 'Labour relations in baseball: Not so fast', *The Economist*,
accessed 30 November 2014 at http://www.economist.com/blogs/gametheory/2012/12/
labour-relations-baseball.

Saccucci, E.P. (2012), 'Revisiting the NHL collective bargaining agreement: Undermining
the spirit of the cap, implications to the agent, and prospective remedies for the league's
consideration', *Sports Lawyers Journal*, **19** (1), 145–172.

Scully, G.W. (ed.) (1989), *The Business of Major League Baseball*, Chicago, IL, USA:
University of Chicago Press.

Staudohar, P.D. (2005), 'The hockey lockout of 2004–05', *Monthly Labor Review*, **128** (12),
23–29.

Zimbalist, A. (ed.) (1992), *Baseball and Billions: A Probing Look Inside the Big Business of
Our National Pastime*, New York, NY, USA: Basic Books.

APPENDIX A: MODELLING THE MLB AND NHL SEASON-ENDING DISPUTES

It is fair to say that unlike most other labor disputes that occur in industry, professional sports disputes are insulated from the typical threats used by management such as permanent plant closure, outsourcing/off-shoring and/or labor-displacement through the use of technology. These are unlikely, if not impossible, options in a sport owner's toolkit. There is the 1987 NFL precedent of replacement players being used, to be sure, but the laughable play and the empty stands in many cities would not bode well for any league intent on following the NFL route. It is therefore almost always the case that what determines the eventual outcome of a labor dispute in professional sports is chiefly dependent on one variable: *union solidarity*.

Accounting for Sport Union Solidarity

If union solidarity is high, as evidenced in the history of baseball labor relations, then even the most committed and *ex-post* costly course of action by management can, at best, achieve only an *ex-ante* strategic advantage in a subsequent round of play. If union solidarity wavers, however, as was seen in hockey, a credible pre-committed managerial course of action (for example, signing a poor television deal and cancelling an entire season) can yield substantial dividends. The point is, because of the scarce supply of elite talent and fan attachment to the stars of the game, if a pro-sport union manages to stay cohesive it will typically win out over management in the long run. So the question becomes what determines such cohesion and player solidarity?

Union solidarity (US) and strength can be represented by the following model:

$$US = f(-S, +PI, -/+OB, -/+CL, -TR)$$

S = union size
PI = player involvement in the union
OB = owner belligerence
CL = average career length
TR = threat of reprisal for being actively involved in the union

The variables are derived from our earlier discussion of the history of the MLBPA and NHLPA. We begin with the baseball players union given that it has been the most effective sports union in furthering the

222 Research handbook of employment relations in sport

goals of its members. In our summary of MLB bargaining since the mid-1960s, we identified various reasons for why the union has historically had such a high degree of success. The dependent variable, union solidarity (US), was found to be inversely correlated with the size of the union (S), hence the negative sign. The small size of the MLBPA, as recognized early on by Marvin Miller, allowed for easier communication and less alienation. Player participation in the union's affairs was encouraged from the outset by Miller. He knew that the more players participated, the more of ownership's tactics they would understand and, consequently, the less skeptical and more committed they would become to the union. Of course, baseball has its share of stratification and, as in any other sport, there are stars and there are plumbers. What is interesting, however, is that in baseball the stars of their respective teams also function as player representatives. There are several advantages to such a system. The first is that younger players tend to respect the fact that the marquee players are working to ensure the common good of all members. This is not the case in other sports, most notably in the NFL.[1] A second reason why the system of star player representatives has been so effective is that it has made the position of player representative "less susceptible to retribution" from management. In the early days, player reps who were not of marquee quality were either traded from team to team or sent down to the minors. Indeed, the importance of having a respected player representative on every team was not lost on Marvin Miller (Helyar, 1994, p. 25): "To the extent the player rep job was always pushed on to a rookie or a relief pitcher, the union wasn't going to work." This therefore explains the positive sign for variable PI. Owners have never tried to accommodate the union. Instead, they have traditionally been hostile to the players association's meddling in league affairs. These "hardball" tactics actually were counterproductive in the case of baseball, because they fermented player militancy. Hence, OB has a positive sign. Professional athletes have short career lengths. Thus, the shorter the length of employment, the less long-term commitment there is to a union. In baseball, however, careers tend to be longer than most other sports. The correlation is, therefore, positive for CL. Finally, the more intimidated a worker is, the less likely it is that he or she will be strongly committed to the union. The sign for TR is therefore negative. In baseball we have seen how the veteran and star system of player representatives eliminated the threat of owner reprisals and therefore reduced the influence of TR.

In applying the same model of union solidarity to the NHLPA prior to 2004–05 lockout, it is fair to assume that the S variable is about the same as for MLBPA. Both have members involved with leagues that have about an equal number of teams with roughly similar sized rosters. Therefore, the NHLPA is small in size for a union and this therefore enhances union solidarity. For the PI factor, while it was not the case that the NHLPA members were not involved with the union, the level of commitment was not as high as in the MLBPA. The NHLPA under Eagleson did not have the same tradition of involvement that Miller cultivated amongst players in baseball, and though this changed somewhat when Goodenow entered the picture in 1992, of relevance here is that between 1994 and 2004 the league expanded by six teams thereby adding another 120 players to the NHLPA. Some claim that during this long hiatus in between bargaining rounds and amidst expansion, union leadership lost touch with an expanded league and a new generation of player members. Regarding owner belligerence (OB), in the hockey dispute, the owners employed an extremely high degree of militancy as evidenced by the unprecedented opening round concessions they tried to extract from players. OB, as a factor, should have enhanced the solidarity of the hockey union; but unlike baseball, hockey players were not as schooled in the tactics used by management during a round of bargaining. Therefore, if we assume that OB is mediated by PI, we can see that a high degree of owner belligerence in hockey actually worked against the union. The CL variable is a significant factor in hockey. Hockey players, on average, have notably shorter careers than the average worker and earn considerably less than baseball players despite having similar average career lengths, meaning they would be less willing to sit out a long-drawn-out labor dispute, assuming all else is equal. This then means that the CL variable weakens the union's solidarity in hockey when compared to baseball, and especially to the average salaried worker. Finally, the TR factor of reprisal for union activity, though historically relevant, was not really a factor in hockey at the time.

In sum, when comparing the two unions per the model, baseball players had greater solidarity in 1994–95 than hockey players in 2004–05 due to greater PI, a positive effect from OB fostering player militancy, and having a positive versus negative effect due to the CL variable. Marvin Miller's legacy was still measurable in the MLBPA given how knowledgeable and active the players were in the 1994–95 bargaining process. The NHLPA, because of its history of paternalism during the Eagleson and Ziegler years (1967–92), never truly developed a strong culture of involvement and unity, even under Goodenow.

NOTE

1. In football, for example, management has successfully alienated the star players from the rank and file. The 1987 NFL strike failed because the owners successfully cut "sweet" deals with quarterbacks and running backs, compelling them to cross the picket lines.

APPENDIX B: ACCOUNTING FOR WORK-STOPPAGE DURATION

While a significant difference between the two disputes was the greater strength of the baseball union relative to the hockey union, the other main difference between these two disputes was the extent to which the owners in hockey were obdurate in 2004–05 and appeared to have won while in baseball the owners seemed to have caved in and lost in 1994–95. This is important to note if we wish to account for the unprecedented duration of the two disputes (232 days in baseball and 306 days in hockey).

The following model can be used to predict work-stoppage length (LS) in professional sports:

$$LS = f (+FC, +US, +OS, +SC, -TV)$$

US= union solidarity
FC= fan commitment
OS= owner solidarity
SC= success of union in previous strikes
TV= size of television contract

The above model shows work-stoppage length as a function of union solidarity (just surveyed), fan commitment, owner solidarity, the success of the union in previous strikes, and the size of the given league's television contract. Beginning with hockey's dispute, fan commitment was dangerously low in the United States as a whole. However, the NHL still had very high fan commitment in Canada, as well as in traditional markets in the United States such as Boston, Philadelphia, New York, Chicago, Detroit, and Buffalo. So we still see high fan commitment contributing to the length of the stoppage. The OS factor was extremely high in the hockey lockout. All the owners were united on what they wanted, and they had a strong leader in Bettman. Therefore, we can conclude that OS was very significant in effecting the length of the lockout in hockey. The success of the union in previous work stoppages (SC) appears to have had a neutral impact in hockey's case. The union only had two true adversarial bargaining periods in its history (in 1992 and 1994–95). In those cases, the NHLPA was successful in bargaining away a salary cap and payroll tax; but compared to baseball under Miller, it had not had any real track record of exhibiting true union solidarity given how informal hockey's bargaining process was before Bettman became the league commissioner. The TV variable was significant in the way the OS variable was. After the 2003–04 season, the NHL did not pursue a major network deal (as it had with Fox in 1994), and ESPN did not renew its contract with the NHL. As a result, the league was operating through the lockout without any television contract on the table and hence there was almost no real opportunity cost to the lockout. Seeing that the length of the stoppage is inversely related to the size of the television contract, it is no surprise that the lockout lasted for such a significant period considering that the television contract the league had in place was not just small, but actually non-existent.

For baseball, as already discussed, US was stronger in baseball than in any other professional sports league, creating conditions for a longer work stoppage. FC was ultimately higher than in hockey, although as the dispute dragged on there were increasing concerns about fan disengagement. Indeed, as seen in Figure 9.3, the effect of the World Series cancellation showed up in depressed league attendance records that lasted almost a decade. At the time of the strike/lockout, however, fan loyalty to America's national pastime did cause the dispute to last longer than it may have otherwise. Owner solidarity (OS) was not quite as strong in baseball as in the hockey dispute. Some of the larger-market owners were not in favor of the league's proposal for a payroll tax, and some were just simply interested in ending the dispute all together regardless of the outcome. This factor lowered the duration of the dispute relative to hockey, but relative to past disputes in baseball, the ownership had never been more unified. This helps explain why the dispute lasted more than ten times longer than any previous dispute. The SC factor was very high in baseball. The union had several victories in previous bargaining sessions which prepared and motivated union members during the 1994–95 bargaining session. This success also caused the owners to "dig in their heels" and to retaliate by cancelling the World Series, knowing the union had historically been successful in fending off concessions and gaining its own provisions in previous collective agreements. As a result, this factor also enhanced the length of the work stoppage. The TV factor was also very significant in the baseball dispute. Though the owners were under pressure from major networks to ensure that baseball would be played, the end of the extremely lucrative 1988–89 CBS–ESPN deals meant that owners, for the first time, were negotiating with no existing TV deal in place and hence no opportunity cost over and above gate receipts (which they claimed were not enough to cover costs). This factor, as in hockey, served to increase the length of the stoppage.

Both disputes were unprecedented in the annals of professional sports history. According to the model above, however, hockey's labor dispute did not have as many factors as baseball did working in favor of such a long work stoppage. Given that the major difference centered on US and OS factors, the reason for the longer work stoppage in hockey we feel centers on the solidarity differences in union and ownership ranks. Perhaps, with attendance and television ratings on steady declines, hockey ownership had less to lose going into the 2004–05 bargaining session. This gave them, under the principle of least interest, the greater bargaining power. Hockey owners felt they were in such a tenuous financial position going into negotiations that they were willing to maintain their lockout until the union completely capitulated.

PART III

THE MANAGEMENT OF PROFESSIONAL SPORTS AND SPORTING CAREERS

10. The game of (your) life: professional sports careers
Christine Coupland

INTRODUCTION

So much has been written about sport and people's engagement with it that it makes it difficult to know where to begin to draw together some strands for future potential researchers. The study of sports careers has attracted scholars from anthropology, philosophy, sociology, psychology, and medicine who are keen to explore and explicate the workings of sport from almost as many perspectives as there are people interested in it. With this plethora of possible avenues for research, in order to achieve any depth, some decisions have had to be made on the focus for this chapter. As the title suggests, I have decided to discuss the careers of sports professionals, such as those athletes who have for a period of time made a living from their sports craft; in particular, I will discuss the early and often abrupt end of the sports career and the need for transition. This firmly locates our interest in the notion of sport as work. Taking this focus enables us to apply and discuss career theories that have emanated from studies of the intersection of the individual and the institution of work and apply them to professional sports careers. There are strong arguments that support the notion that professional sport is more like work and less like play or leisure. Simply demonstrated, performance is publically measured, penalties occur if ability fades, routines and practices are determined by others, and contracts of employment depend on performance (Coupland, 2015).

Although there is no agreement on a common definition of career, a recent review of the literature provided the following comprehensive description: "an individual's work-related and other relevant experiences, both inside and outside of organizations that form a unique pattern over the individual's life span" (Sullivan & Baruch, 2009, p. 1543). Physical movement across and within real or imagined boundaries and contexts and the individual's interpretation thereof are recognized by this definition.

Having a career as a professional sports person has a large degree of uncertainty about it. However, there is one certainty to this career, that is, it will end rather prematurely in comparison to other careers (in terms of life span) and will therefore require individuals to recraft a new career and reconstruct a version of themselves in order to move forward with their working lives. One role of career theorists is to explore and explain how we make sense of life transitions. Some scholars, seeking certainty, endeavor to craft normative models in an attempt to predict and control these processes. Normative models are valuable principally because they enable better conceived attempts at intervention to render the process a more positive, or at least less negative, experience for the sports professional who is working through this. That said, the standard career is an abstraction, a set of expectations. Linear career paths have given way to non-linear, discontinuous careers (Sullivan, 1999) causing the non-traditional career (however defined) to be increasingly the focus of empirical research. People's actual careers are different; career performance varies. It is this variation in performance and how an individual makes sense of their progress through life that makes the understanding of careers important for understanding social life. Basic principles around work careers apply to professional sports careers in several ways: they are socially differentiating, differences in career performances lead to differing rewards, rewards are not necessarily material, and the ultimate reward is prestige or a satisfactory sense of self (Goldschmidt, 1990, p. 109).

In this chapter I will briefly outline how professional sports careers have been studied traditionally. In contrast, career theory as applied to work, features differing levels of attention being paid to contexts, structure and agency, boundaries, dynamics, and methodologies (Chudzikowski & Mayrhofer, 2011). In the main, in contemporary work contexts, the most influential current career theories have largely assumed positions of choice for the individual around career change.[1] I propose that by looking at professional sports contexts as necessarily bounded through body-work and thus body-decline, the notion of choice is constrained, but that these theories offer some explanation of boundaries as understood by the boundary crosser. Further, some career theorists have focused on stages within a career; this relates to the notion of dynamics, that is, change over time. Although it has been contested how fixed or universal these may be, there is an assumption of increasing skill and knowledge mastery in life followed by gradual decline. I argue that it would be worthwhile to consider some kind of stage theory applied to the professional sports person that may be crafted around patterns of increasing body mastery (perhaps precluding alternative and potentially oppositional skill/knowledge mastery) with a sudden decline requiring a new start in a new career. Furthermore, scholars who have considered the sports person as relatively unique in honing the body for their work have drawn upon Bourdieu's notion of bodily capital where the individual and the trainers are engaged in an entrepreneurial project – turning the sports person into a lucrative project. According to studies of social and career capital within work careers, again, this is expected to accrue over experience. For the professional sports person this is by no means a predictable outcome and merits further consideration; thus, some evaluation of the usefulness of theories of embodied, social, and career capital will be presented.

A REVIEW OF SPORTS CAREER ORIENTED SCHOLARS' INTERESTS

Research on career transitions in sport has grown over the last 30 years, and themes around (1) predictors of transition (choice/agency), (2) the quality of the transition (positive or negative and interventions possible), (3) consequences of transitions (i.e. what happened next), (4) types of transitions (e.g. drop out/injury), and (5) models of transitions, have emerged as foci of interest for scholars (Park et al., 2013). Reviews have been carried out on sport-career-transition research from host disciplines of social gerontology, thanatology, and life transition, which, while providing some insight, require further integrative conceptual development and research (Gordon & Lavallee, 2011; Taylor & Lavallee, 2010; Wylleman et al., 2004).

Park et al. (2013) summarized some key findings from a recent extensive review of sport career research. First, just under 50 percent were empirical studies of the physical, psychological, emotional, and social consequences of athletes' retirement from playing sport at a high level. Furthermore, a number of studies considered the impact of a sports person's agency (or lack of) in their retirement decision. Ideas around social death or dying were drawn on to describe and explicate the process (Blinde & Stratta, 1992; Zaichkowsky et al., 2000). Loss of identity (Butt & Molnar, 2009; Lynch, 2006) as the playing career ends was also a focus of some research. A sense of social exclusion (McKenna & Thomas, 2007), or betrayal and rejection (Butt & Molnar, 2009) featured from the findings of the research in differing contexts. With regard to physical concerns, injuries, pain, and other health issues were found to be a source of career transition difficulties (Muscat, 2010). Perhaps, predictably, active professional and Olympic athletes experience higher physical self-worth than former active sports people, and the transition time is an acute period of distress caused through perceived negative body image (Kerr & Dacyshyn, 2000; Lavallee & Robinson, 2007). Some research focused on the degree of preparedness of the professional and high-performing athletes for career transitions from playing at a high level to either a lower standard or not at all.

Research indicated that pre-retirement planning did result in better vocational adjustment (Coakley, 2004). However, Lavallee (2005) found that many athletes did not take advantage of career transition intervention programs, even if they were available. There was a perception that by focusing on the end of their playing career, even if planning the inevitable, it would somehow provide a distraction from their sport performance. Finally, there can be no doubt that the professional sports person, for varying reasons, may encounter difficulties in moving from a high-level playing career to something else. From Park et al.'s (2013) review, studies noted a range of concerning maladaptive coping strategies during this phase of a sports career, including alcohol dependence, increased smoking, drug use, and suicide (Douglas & Carless, 2009; Wippert & Wippert, 2008).

Over time researchers' foci on providing effective interventions for more successful sports career transitions has moved from a traditional therapeutic approach, where the athlete is treated as coping with possible trauma, to providing life and social skill support programs pre-transition, thus the attention is drawn away from remedy towards prevention. Today's researchers, in the main, see transition as a process rather than an event (Wylleman et al., 2004), where the career is viewed from a holistic, life-span perspective, which encompasses playing at a professional level, lower levels and beyond to a post-play career, and includes all domains of athletes' lives. Some authors argue that the transition from playing to not playing sport at a high level is unlike retirement from work occupations for three main reasons: it occurs at an earlier age; it will progress into an occupational career of some kind; and that the termination of a work career need not always be a negative event requiring adjustment (Wylleman et al., 2004). I argue, contrarily, that the athletes' experience is actually similar but more acute, and thus this transition actually demonstrates a more intensified career transition, hyper real in some sense, condensed into shorter periods allowing little time for adjustment. The professional sports person does retire from playing at an early age but still with a requirement, an expectation, to get another job in order to be financially secure. This means that they are under similar pressures to those who are retiring from work (more so if there has been insufficient time to accrue a retirement pension of some kind). Furthermore, a successful professional sports person will already have experienced other transitions from amateur, youth, and pre-professional to a more elite level which requires greater and increasing dedication to sports activities, resulting in, one could argue, less time to spend on other life activities (Baker et al., 2003). A drive to excel at sport may engender a lack of skill in dealing with non-sport activities (simply due to intensive focus elsewhere) and a less developed understanding around life choices (Stronach & Adair, 2010).

Research has illustrated that former athletes showed difficulties dealing with non-sport situations. Arguably, delayed identity shifts may be predicted to occur at the end of a playing career due to a lack of non-sporting life experiences during sport careers (Muscat, 2010). Thus, I propose that immersion in the field of professional sports is so strong that it will be difficult to imagine or prepare for exit. So, it is more intense, with different pressures to move on with a working sense of self. On a more positive note, it can be argued, utilizing a holistic, life story perspective, that a professional playing career termination could be regarded as an opportunity for social rebirth (Coakley, 1983), a transition process effecting a re-engagement with non-sporting life experiences, an adjustment which is mediated by a degree of voluntariness with regard to at what time and in what manner the process is instigated. Therefore, it is suggested that career theorists have a relevant and practical contribution to make to the field that will benefit from the application of non-traditional, or multiple, theoretical perspectives.

BOUNDARIES AND CHOICE

In keeping with a professional sports context, contemporary work careers too are characterized by fragmentation and a need to transition, which leads individuals to have to manage their careers by being prepared to be flexible. Hall's (1996a; 1996b; 2004) protean career theory describes a career as managed by the individual according to their own values. It describes a career orientation that is driven by the individual's decisions based on their own core values and is measured by subjective success criteria (Hall, 2004). Its conception came about during a time of a de-stabilization of organizationally controlled careers. Contexts of de-layering, downsizing, and decentralization precluded opportunities to effectively plan ahead in terms of recognizing, developing, and rewarding talent with an organizationally defined successful career path. When it was first conceived it was positioned as different from a traditional career where control was firmly located in the individual who saw success in psychological terms rather than through principally objective signs such as salary, position, and status. See Table 10.1 for a comparison to prevailing thought.

What may be of interest to sports careers scholars is that research based on successful midlife career changers (whose goal was to make more authentic definitions of self and success utilizing both subjective and external evaluators of success) found that in addition to measuring high on a protean orientation scale, the biggest difference compared to population means is on the "openness to new experiences dimension" (Hall, 2004).

Table 10.1   The view from 1976, cited in Hall (2004, p. 4)

Issue	Protean career	Traditional career
Who's in charge?	Person	Organization
Core values	Freedom growth	Advancement
Degree of mobility	High	Lower
Success criteria	Psychological success	Position level salary
Key attitudes	Work satisfaction, professional commitment	Organizational commitment

This has some explanatory value for the professional sports person who is so immersed in current playing activities that this kind of thinking is rare. The protean careerist views the career as a series of learning cycles (Hall, 1996c) brought about by considering and trying out new possibilities. The emphasis is not, perhaps surprisingly, on developing competencies (i.e. vocational training for some other profession) but rather on developing meta-competencies around adaptability and self-awareness (or identity) so the individual learns from their experiences and is able to identify and develop appropriate competencies as required (Briscoe & Hall, 1999).

Although there are evident boundaries within the playing professional's career, the one most researched appears to be the transition from professional playing status to something else. Some research indicates that pre-retirement planning, including psychological preparation before the end of the playing career and a clear goal outside sport, facilitates adjustment (Warriner & Lavallee, 2008). However, Lavallee (2005) found many athletes did not use career transition intervention programs even if they were available due to a perception that it would be a distraction from their sport performance. That said, for sports people who appeared to have a balanced attitude to life while competing, Kerr and Dacyshyn (2000) found that this was retained once the playing career was over. This suggests that Hall's idea of protean attitudes to career may be relevant throughout a sports career. That is, the person's values and ability to psychologically adapt, evidenced through self-directed career management and the pursuit of personal goals and values (Hall, 2004), can surface whether immersed in a sport or not. Sargent and Domberger (2007) combined image theory with the development of a protean career orientation in their study of graduates transitioning into work. The shock of transition was compared with self-images (of values, goals, and plans) and occasionally resulted in image violation which precipitated a change of career. Although the quality and quantity of these shocks represented a new avenue of research for researchers who are interested in turnover and retention (Sargent &

Domberger, 2007), I argue that post-professional sports careers could benefit from research attention from a similar perspective.

Boundaryless careers were, initially, broadly described as the opposite of organizational careers and indicated a progressive approach to the study of careers. In the large amount of research generated since the evolution of "boundaryless careers" as an explanatory concept,[2] the notion of what a boundary is has expanded. When Arthur and Rousseau (1996b) reformulated the following two concepts it was in the light of increasing understanding of a future of uncertainty around work careers.

- **"Career"** – *Old meaning*: a course of professional advancement; usage restricted to occupations with formal hierarchical progression, such as managers and professionals. *New meaning*: "the unfolding sequence of any person's work experiences over time."
- **"Boundary"** – *Old meaning*: a limit; the division between familiar and hostile territory. *New meaning*: "something to be crossed in career behavior or in taking on complexity" (Arthur & Rousseau, 1996b, pp. 29–30).

According to career theorists, there are two types of mobility: a physical movement, the transition across boundaries, and the psychological, which is the perception of the capacity to make transitions. Most research in this area has focused on physical crossings, thus there remains much that can be done to demonstrate the usefulness of paying attention to movement and meanings simultaneously (Coupland et al., 2012). I argue that any movement in terms of career progression requires both psychological readiness and physical opportunity.

The boundaryless career has evolved in its meaning from one that describes a changing relationship with the employing organization in the early days of its use to an evocation of potential freedom (Cohen & Mallon, 1999), which has generated much debate. In order to develop the debate, and in keeping with Pringle and Mallon's (2003) call to attend to individuals' changing perceptions of boundaries, our interest, as sports scholars, lies in how perceived boundaries are negotiated in order for people to make sense of "one's place in the world" (Gunz et al., 2000, p. 50).

A REVIEW OF STAGE THEORIES – SPORT AND LIFE CYCLE

Career theories of work and sports contexts are embedded in their own cultural environments. According to a recent critical evaluation of developmental theories and their impact on work-career research by Sullivan and Crocitto (2007), early theories presumed the worker was a man who would work for one or two organizations until retirement while his wife stayed at home caring for the children. These assumptions led to the development of linear stage models of career development such as Super (1957) and Levinson (1978) and were based on psychological perspectives such as those of Erikson (1963). These theories, which were based on a system of structured hierarchies during a period of economic growth, are less applicable now in a time of instability and unpredictability in the area of work. Super's theory developed from an understanding that at different stages in life we attend to different priorities; his 1957 five stage model reflects the presumed contextual stability for individuals:

- *Growth*: becomes concerned/aware about the future and starts to take control.
- *Exploration*: of both self and world of work, moving from general to specific choices.
- *Establishment*: settling into occupation and adopting a lifestyle.
- *Maintenance*: holding position, keeping abreast of developments.
- *Disengagement:* slowing down, ideas for retirement, establishing alternatives to work.

Despite criticisms around contextual relevance in unstable work conditions, the stage theory still emerges in empirical studies of careers (Chen, 2011; Hom et al., 2010; Lyons et al., 2012). Super's work has progressed to consider life span and life space, while relating work decisions to other life decisions for a more rounded theory (Super, 1980). More recently, Savickas (2006) has integrated the stage theory approach, much criticized for ignoring the social contexts of career enactment, to include environmental and social variables. In his development of the theory of career construction (Savickas, 2006; 2012), which acknowledges that as individuals and circumstances are constantly moving so the individual/work institution interface evolves, he extends Super's stage theory to include the external environment. The theory seeks to retain the most useful theoretical elements, while concentrating on how individuals use their skills and opportunities. For example, instead of measuring personality traits, personality scores can be replaced with a focus on accounts or stories of career experiences and how individuals use vocational identities to adapt to a sequence of job changes while remaining coherent to themselves and recognizable as plausible by others (Savickas, 2006). The argument is made that in contemporary times an individual can expect to occupy and transition from ten or more jobs in a working life – thus how an individual makes sense of these transitions is relevant for understanding what matters and gives meaning to work.

In other than work contexts, early research looked at how talented individuals in the fields of art, science, and sport developed in terms of the stages they appeared to progress through: (1) initiation; (2) development; and (3) mastery (Bloom, 1985). Stambulova (1994, 2000) further developed a stage theory and applied it specifically to elite sporting careers. The stages thus identified were: (1) the beginning of a sport specialization; (2) the transition to intensive training; (3) the transition to high-achieving adult sports; (4) the transition from amateur to professional; (5) the transition from culmination to the end of a playing sports career; and (6) the end of a sports career.

Thus, career transition in sport includes a view from "the stage in the lifecycle" research where researchers consider how things such as age or pressure from others influence whether an athlete decides to carry on in sport or retire. Wylleman et al. (2004) developed a life-span model around a series of predictable transitions through athletes' careers. These are regarded as normative transitions as part of a universal sequence of age related to biological, social, and emotional events which occur across a life span. Normative transitions involve sports people exiting one stage and entering another so they are predictable and anticipated. Non-normative transitions result from important events that take place which require a response from the athlete, thus are unpredicted, unanticipated, and involuntary – for example, the loss of a personal coach, deselection from a team, or the threat of injury. Some transitions for athletes are not negative, moving from one level to a more elite level of the sport which involves greater dedication and time spent on sport activities. However, other life activities decrease (Baker et al., 2003) and the focus of athletes narrows from other life activities to focus more on sport, arguably promoting an obsessive drive to excel.

A more holistic view was argued to be pertinent by Wylleman et al. (2004) as it needs to incorporate a beginning to end perspective and include other domains of life, for example, academic, psychosocial, and professional influences at particular stages in a person's life. One contrast with vocational stage theories is that the sports scholar's attention ceases at the age of 35, as in Stambulova's model, for example. This suggests a lack of scholarly interest in how the professional sports person develops later in life, which may well mirror the professional sports person's own perspective, but nonetheless implies that they are no longer of interest.

Many athletes begin competitive sport at an early age, thus involvement in sport is reinforced by significant others. When associated with personal success this leads to a strong self-identification of the self-as-athlete

(Baillie, 1993 p.400). As previously suggested, the level of dedication and commitment required thereafter may result in a premature narrowing of focus, with academic and social goals being subordinated to athletic achievement, and hence a potential lack of consideration of alternative career options (Blann, 1985). Drawing upon theories of career development, Gati (1986) has argued that the career development decision-making model works on the understanding that the individual sequentially eliminates occupational alternatives to arrive at career decisions at different stages of their career. It may be argued, therefore, that athletes' focus on the promise of a professional sporting career has resulted in a premature elimination of other alternatives. The subsequent and ongoing investment in the self-as-athlete reinforces a lack of consideration of alternatives beyond the playing career. This explains to some extent a lack of take up of post-playing career planning (Lavallee, 2005) by some professional sports people.

In professional sport there is an inevitable end to playing; whether it occurs suddenly through injury or slowly through deterioration in skills over time, it is a transition which cannot be avoided. Scholars have argued that these are difficult transitions due to the intense identification of an athlete with their sport: "who am I if I can no longer compete" (Day et al., 2012, p.420). Further, these authors argue that similarities may be drawn between elite sport people and high-potential managers. They are selected for special scrutiny, given developmental opportunities, and performance expectations are high. Fractured, fragmented, and multiple career paths have become more usual for working individuals due to changing work contexts. Thus, there is evidently room for potential integration around the study of difficult career transitions and their identity implications in work and sports contexts.

SOCIAL, CAREER, AND BODILY CAPITAL – EXPLANATORY POTENTIAL FOR SPORTS CAREERS

Social capital as a concept has been a popular export from social theory into everyday language that describes relationships between people and groups. It directs attention to those non-monetary forms of capital as important sources of power and influence (Portes, 1998). One definition describes social capital as any aspect of social structure that creates value and facilitates actions of individuals within the social structure (Coleman, 1990). The first systematic contemporary analysis of social capital was made by Bourdieu (1985, p.248), who defined it as "the aggregate of actual or potential resources which are linked to the possession of a durable network of more or less institutionalized relationships of mutual acquaintances or recognition." The acquisition of social capital requires deliberate investment (in terms of time, etc.), constructed and maintained through investment strategies oriented to the institutionalization of group relations. Because of an athlete's immersion in sport and often lack of social interactions outside sporting circles, their social capital may be low. Processes of social capital are characterized by uncertainty, unspecified obligations, uncertain time horizons, and possible violation of reciprocity expectations – so they are not typical market exchanges (Portes, 1998).

Chudzikowski and Mayrhofer (2011) argue that Bourdieu's (1977) work may be used as a framework for theoretically organizing career studies. It can be drawn upon to describe and explain the overall functioning and dynamics of a given social order. Other career theorists have attempted to conceptualize social capital with regard to career success and have identified some useful arguments around weak tie theory and structural hole theory (Seibert et al., 2001). I will elaborate on these arguments further and demonstrate their potential to aid the understanding of sports career progression.

Weak tie theory (Granovetter, 1973) considers the strength of a social tie (relationship) used by a person when trying to find (typically) a job. If the ties are with a close social group they are thought to be strong. Information possessed by any one member tends to be shared quickly. Ties outside one's own social clique are likely to be weak. Weak ties tend to bridge densely interconnected social cliques and thus provide a source of unique information and resources, for example, information about new job openings or promotion possibilities or new projects (Seibert et al., 2001). We could apply this argument to sports people transitioning within their playing careers and exiting from them. It clearly has explanatory potential with regard to lack of resource or alternative understanding from outside the close social group of professional sports people. Furthermore, it explains an initial reluctance to leave the sphere of sport even when the playing career has ended.

Structural holes are about the pattern of relationships among people in a network. A structural hole exists when two people are not connected to each other, for example, your ex-school friend does not know your co-worker. It is suggested that it is an advantage to have many unconnected relationships – that is, many structural holes – as they provide more unique access to information and greater visibility to more people, thus increased career opportunities (Burt, 1992). Park et al. (2013), in their review of studies of sport career transitions, found a number of cases of former professional athletes who had difficulties in dealing with non-sport situations. They were found to have delayed identity shifts due to a lack of non-sport life experiences during their sports careers (Muscat, 2010). It can be argued that this is an example of strong ties and possibly a description of relationships with few structural holes. In other words, the sports person has operated professionally, mainly closely connected to a small clique, a social group which is emotionally intense, has frequent contact, and is connected in multiple ways (e.g. friends as well as co-workers). Information which is possessed by any one member is shared quickly; however, the range of information is limited.

This kind of thinking has been applied to how people move from job to job, become knowledgeable about other spheres of work, are psychologically prepared for change, and subsequently make career moves. It is clear that applying this kind of thinking to professional sports people and their careers may provide new perspectives on the process. Studies have found that athletes have attributed limited life choices post-professional sport to a lack of opportunities for personal development (Chow, 2001; Stronach & Adair, 2010; Swain, 1991). Professional sports people, it is argued, regard post-play planning when actively competing as a distraction from their sport performance (Petitpas et al., 1992). It is thus suggested that this may, with hindsight, be recognized as lost opportunities for the development of career and social capital which would better enable a future transitional process.

Social relationships create habitus which is expressed in everyday contexts; however, specifically with regard to sport, beliefs which order our behavior are not just states of mind but states of body (Coupland, 2015) where the body is a living memory pad operating through practical metaphors (Bourdieu, 1990). Bourdieu's concepts of habitus and cultural capital have explanatory potential here as theoretical schema in terms of explaining broader relationships between the embodied self and the organized individual. Behavior is not determined by this system but it provides a practical sense that inclines us towards one way of being rather than another. The concepts are linked together in a formula "(habitus) (capital) + field = practice" (Bourdieu, 1984), where practice is the result of various habitual schemas and dispositions combined with resources (capital) being activated by social conditions (field) which they in turn reproduce and modify (Crossley, 2001).

Using an example from professional sport, Wacquant (1995) found in his ethnographic study of boxers in Chicago that objective structures of the social world of boxing became embodied in the boxers' habitus. A particular habitus makes it more likely that an individual acts, perceives, and thinks according to the rules of the field and the moves appear as natural (Chudzikowski & Mayrhofer, 2011). In other words, an individual acts "intentionally without intention" (Bourdieu, 1990, p. 12) and according to one's sense of possible options.

Bourdieu's thinking included attention to the body, which can be called "bodily capital" and is relevant to a study of professional sports people's careers. He proposed that "The way people treat their bodies reveals the deepest dispositions of the habitus" (Bourdieu, 1984, p. 190). It follows therefore that sport training produces a particular type of body with mastery over particular kinds of movement which is socially produced through diet, exercise, and etiquette. Furthermore, if we compare the creation of physical capital through changes in materials to facilitate production, human, or bodily, capital involves changes in individuals' skills and capabilities. We can apply this to the professional sports person. It can be argued that traces of physical capital are converted into economic capital through sport or training for sport, or other physical endeavors, called bodily capital (Wacquant, 1995). Those who are engaged in crafting this bodily capital into optimum playing capital (both those instigating training and those who carry it out) may be regarded as entrepreneurs in bodily capital as it is possible to produce value in terms of income and recognition for the benefit of the individual and the industry more broadly. As a means of production, therefore, the sports person's body is worked upon to accentuate talent and body shape for the requirement of the sport. However, one certainty of this process is its temporality – despite all best efforts the body will succumb to injury, wear and tear, and an ageing process that renders the sports person unable to compete with younger, faster, stronger bodies. The body will erode under physical pressures thus rendering the opportunity to take entrepreneurial advantage from it short and likely to be curtailed rapidly in the event of severe injury.

If we apply this to professional sports people intensely engaged in their playing careers, it is evident that alternatives for the post-playing career are rarely considered, and, even if they are, they may be regarded as inappropriate or undesirable for their current attention.

DISCUSSION

In the chapter I have briefly appraised traditional sports career transition research in order to identify key themes, patterns, and foci which have been the concern of sports scholars. Furthermore, I have identified and described some of the vocational career theories which have been more normally applied to the individual who is in intersection with the institution of work. Although there are important differences in the perspectives which guide the research, I argue that there is much that can be useful for sports scholars who are interested in understanding more fully how professional sports people come to terms with moving on from the active, playing part of their lives.

Sports scholars' interests have clearly developed from simply evaluating the process of retirement from playing professionally to also considering how best to provide interventions prior to retirement, so the individual is better equipped for this transitional phase of their life. In contemporary work contexts readiness for transition is the basis of all career counseling. With an expectation of changing jobs (not always voluntarily) on average ten times in a working life span, effective research has been demanded to understand and enable this process from an organizational and an individual perspective. Empirical research has enabled important theories to be developed to attend more closely to context and to demonstrate the importance of utilizing a range of theoretical perspectives in order to address different questions of the work/individual relationship.

One example of this process has occurred around Super's stage theory of life span (1957; 1980). It was originally based on traditional questionnaire research measuring personality traits and has remained very influential. It was primarily applied in the field of vocational counseling, where it became apparent over time that a major criticism included a lack of attention to individuals' particular accounts of what was important at certain times in their lives. Further, in such an unpredictable work environment a sense of progression through stages was difficult to ascertain. Put simply, the context of work has changed so it is less predictable and less organized; it is a space in which the individual makes sense of opportunities and challenges presented to them over time. This has caused a shift in career theorists' concerns, and an increasing number are looking at how people make sense of this readiness for transition. Thus, I argue that the developed versions of these theories (Savickas, 2006; 2012) may be useful for sports scholars in order to better understand how professional sports people may be encouraged to develop a meta-competency around adaptability but without a loss of focus on their playing career.

Some studies of sports professionals have already identified that there are individuals who exhibit an element of balance throughout their playing careers (Kerr & Dacyshyn, 2000) and thus are balanced in their approach to moving on to something else. I suggest this may be recognizable as a similar set of competencies outlined by Hall (2004) as "protean," where the individual draws upon a set of personal values that sustain movement across and between work organizations and career moves. This is not to suggest that the protean individual is any more agentic – the structures of work that they experience are just as real and difficult to navigate around; rather they appear to have a set of skills that enables them to temporarily psychologically disengage from the path they are currently taking and imagine another path as quite possible. This individual is able to create coherence for their selves even though the paths may be perceived to be quite divergent externally. This meta-competency would be valuable to professional and other elite sports people and suggests some potential for the application of this work-career theory to sports careers in future research.

Ideas around embodied capital have already been utilized effectively to explain the total immersion of sports people in their playing world.[3] What I have attempted to contribute in this chapter is some developed ideas around how this immersion affects sports people's ability to build social capital to go beyond playing sport. The career capital theories that are based around weak and strong ties (Seibert et al., 2001) have potential to explain some people's ability to move from job to job. Future research could apply this kind of thinking to sports people at different points in their playing careers to identify whether it has any explanatory potential in their field.

One element which is apparent from the sports scholars' studies of transitions is the required increasing engagement of sports people as they progress in terms of performance. The elite athlete is expected to spend more time honing performance as a result of their success. It is evident that this precludes paying attention to very much else, and it is perhaps not surprising that even if transitional programs are offered to professional sports people, their take up is low (Lavallee, 2005). This is perhaps explainable utilizing Bourdieu's notion of habitus, where a particular habitus makes it more likely that an individual thinks according to the rules of the field (Chudzikowski & Mayrhofer, 2011).

Below are some examples of responses from professional sports people who are currently playing at a high level when asked about their craft:

> It was always part of my life, kept growing up and that's probably the only thing I was really born to do (Player)
> It is all I know (Player)
> It's in my blood (Player)
> (adapted from Coupland's (2015) study of professional rugby league players)
> It's a kind of possession
> (adapted from Wacquant's (1995) study of professional boxers)

The extracts quite simply demonstrate the powerful hold that being a professional sports person has on their ability to imagine themselves as anything else.

As entrepreneurs in developing (and selling) others' bodily capital, professional sports organizations have some remit to provide conditions that may engender the development of meta-competencies around adaptability. These would not only enable the survival of the athlete beyond playing but encourage the holistic development of the individual. Therefore, it may be that it is more clearly the responsibility of sports organizations to manufacture changes in the field (and thus the habitus, where habitus is regarded as an organized way of asking questions of the social world) (Wacquant, 2011, p. 91). These would be required to render discussions around the currently active sports professional, which demonstrate balanced thinking about working and contributing beyond playing as quite normal and to be encouraged and expected. Thus, the rules of the field can be seen to increasingly incorporate legitimate plans for disengagement, and the post-playing career may be seen as a progression to something equally valuable rather than an end to a useful contribution.

CONCLUDING COMMENTS

This chapter has discussed the careers of sports professionals, that is, those athletes who have for a period of time made a living from their sports craft. This firmly locates our interest in the notion of sport as work. Taking this focus has enabled us to apply and discuss career theories that have emanated from studies of the intersection of the individual and the institution of work and apply them to professional sports careers. It is clear that new understandings may be gained by applying interdisciplinary perspectives to differing social contexts and that opportunity exists for future empirical research in the sports field that develops the utility of theories of work careers.

NOTES

1. See, for example, Boundaryless and Protean career theories (Arthur & Rousseau, 1996a; 1996b; DeFillipi & Arthur, 1996; Hall, 1996a; 1996b).
2. See Sullivan and Arthur (2006) and Inkson et al. (2012), for a re-examination of the concept.
3. See, for example, Wacquant (1995; 2011).

REFERENCES

Arthur, M. and D.M. Rousseau (eds) (1996a), *The boundaryless career: A new employment principle for a new organizational era*. New York, NY, USA: Oxford University Press.

Arthur, M.B. and D.M. Rousseau (1996b), 'A career lexicon for the 21st century', *Academy of Management Executive*, **10** (4), 28–39.

Baillie, P.H.F. (1993), 'Understanding retirement from sports', *Counselling Psychologist*, **21** (3), 399–410.

Baker, J., J. Cote, and B. Abernethy (2003), 'Sport-specific practice and the development of expert decision making in team ball sports', *Journal of Applied Sport Psychology*, **15**, 12–25.

Blann, F.W. (1985), 'Intercollegiate athletic competition and students' educational and career plans', *Journal of College Student Personnel*, **26**, 115–116.

Blinde, E. and T. Stratta (1992), 'The "sport career death" of college athletes: Involuntary and unanticipated sports exits', *Journal of Sport Behaviour*, **15**, 3–20.

Bloom, B.S. (1985), *Developing talent in young people*. New York, NY, USA: Ballantine.

Bourdieu, P. (1977), *Outline of a theory of practice*. Cambridge, UK: Cambridge University Press.

Bourdieu, P. (1984), *Distinction: A social critique of the judgement of taste*. London, UK: Routledge.

Bourdieu, P. (1985), 'The forms of capital', in J.G. Richardson (eds), *Handbook of theory and research for the sociology of education*. New York, NY, USA: Greenwood, pp. 241–258.

Bourdieu, P. (1990), *The logic of practice* (trans. Nice). Cambridge, UK: Polity Press.

Briscoe, J.P. and D.T. Hall (1999), 'Grooming and picking leaders: Using competency frameworks: Do they work? An alternative approach and new guidelines for practice', *Organizational Dynamics*, **28** (2), Autumn, 37–51.

Burt, R.S. (1992), *Structural holes: The social structure of competition*. Cambridge, MA, USA: Harvard University Press.

Butt, J. and G. Molnar (2009), 'Involuntary career termination in sport: A case study of the process of structurally induced failure', *Sport in Society*, **12**, 240–257.

Chen, C.P. (2011), 'Life-career re-engagement: A new conceptual framework for counselling people in retirement transition', *Australian Journal of Career Development*, **20** (2), 25–31.

Chow, B.C. (2001), 'Moving on? Elite Hong Kong female athletes and retirement from competitive sport', *Women in Sport and Physical Activity Journal*, **1**, 47–81.

Chudzikowski, K. and W. Mayrhofer (2011), 'In search of the blue flower? Grand social theories and career research: The case of Bourdieu's theory of practice', *Human Relations*, **64** (1), 19–36.

Coakley, J.J. (1983), 'Leaving competitive sport: Retirement or rebirth?', *Quest*, **35**, 1–11.

Coakley, J.J. (2004), *Sports in society: Issues and controversies*. 8th Edition. London, UK: McGraw-Hill.

Cohen, L. and M. Mallon (1999), 'The transition from organizational employment to portfolio working: Perceptions of "boundarylessness"', *Work Employment and Society*, **13** (2), 329–352.

Coleman, J.S. (1990), *Foundations of social theory*. Cambridge, MA, USA: Harvard University Press.

Coupland, C. (2015), 'Organizing masculine bodies in rugby league football: Groomed to fail', *Organization*, **22** (6), 793–809.

Coupland, C., B. Allan, and C.J. Elliott (2012), 'Women acting up: Temporary boundary crossings', Paper presented at the *Gender Work and Organization Conference*.

Crossley, N. (2001), *The social body: Habit, identity and desire*. London, UK: Sage.

Day, D.V., S. Gordon, and C. Fink (2012), 'The sporting life: Exploring organizations through the lens of sport', *Academy of Management Annals*, **6** (1), 397–433.

DeFillipi, R.J. and M.B. Arthur (1996), 'Boundaryless careers and contexts: A competency based perspective', in M.B. Arthur and D.M. Rousseau (eds), *The boundaryless career*. New York, NY, USA: Oxford University Press, pp. 116–131.

Douglas, K. and D. Carless (2009), 'Abandoning the performance narrative: Two women's stories of transition from professional sport', *Journal of Applied Psychology*, **21**, 213–230.

Erikson, E.H. (1963), *Childhood and society*. New York, NY, USA: Norton.

Gati, I. (1986), 'Making career decisions – a sequential elimination approach', *Journal of Counseling Psychology*, **33**, 408–417.

Goldschmidt, W. (1990), *The human career: The self in the symbolic world*. Cambridge, MA, USA: Blackwell.

Gordon, S. and D. Lavallee (2011), 'Career transitions in competitive sport', in T. Morris and P. Terry (eds), *The new sport and exercise companion*. Morgantown, WV, USA: Fitness Information Technology, pp. 567–581.

Granovetter, M.S. (1973), 'The strength of weak ties', *American Journal of Sociology*, **6**, 1360–1380.

Gunz, H., M. Evans, and M. Jalland (2000), 'Career boundaries in a boundaryless world', in M. Peiperl, M.B. Arthur, R. Goffee, and T. Morris (eds), *Career frontiers: New conceptions of working lives*. Oxford, UK: Oxford University Press.

Hall, D.T. (1996a), 'Long live the career', in D.T. Hall (ed.), *The career is dead – long live the career*. San Francisco, CA, USA: Jossey Bass, pp. 1–12.

Hall, D.T. (1996b), 'Protean careers of the 21st century', *Academy of Management Executive*, **10**, 8–16.

Hall, D.T. (1996c), 'The new protean career', in D.T. Hall (ed.), *The career is dead – long live the career*. San Francisco, CA, USA: Jossey Bass, pp. 15–45.

Hall, D.T. (2004), 'The protean career: A quarter century journey', *Journal of Vocational Behaviour*, **65**, 1–13.

Hom, P.W., F.T. Leong, and J. Golubovich (2010), 'Insights from vocational and career developmental theories: Their potential contributions for advancing the understanding of employee turnover', in J.J. Hui Liao and A.J. Martocchio (eds), *Research in personnel and human resources management (Volume 29)*. Bingley, UK: Emerald, pp. 115–165.

Inkson, K., H. Gunz, S. Ganesh, and J. Roper (2012), 'Boundaryless careers: Bringing back boundaries', *Organization Studies*, **33** (3), 323–340.

Kerr, G. and A. Dacyshyn (2000), 'The retirement experiences of elite female gymnasts', *Journal of Applied Sport Psychology*, **12**, 115–133.

Lavallee, D. (2005), 'The effect of a life development intervention on sports career transition adjustment', *Sport Psychologist*, **19**, 193–202.

Lavallee, D. and H.K. Robinson (2007), 'In pursuit of an identity: A qualitative exploration of retirement from women's artistic gymnastics', *Psychology of Sport and Exercise*, **8**, 119–141.

Levinson, D.J. (1978), *The seasons of a man's life*. New York, NY, USA: Knopf.

Lynch, D. (2006), *Adjustment to retirement of horse racing jockeys*. (Unpublished Master's thesis). Victoria University, Melbourne, Australia.

Lyons, S.T., L. Schweitzer, E. Ng, and L. Kuron (2012), 'Comparing apples to apples: A qualitative investigation of career mobility patterns across four generations', *Career Development International*, **17** (4), 333–357.

McKenna, J. and H. Thomas (2007), 'Enduring injustice: A case study of retirement from professional rugby union', *Sport, Education and Society*, **12**, 19–35.

Muscat, A.C. (2010), *Elite athletes' experience of identity changes during a career-ending injury: An interpretative description*. (Unpublished doctoral thesis). University of British Columbia, Vancouver, Canada.

Park, S., D. Lavallee, and D. Tod (2013), 'Athletes' career transition out of sport: A systematic review', *International Review of Sport and Exercise Psychology*, **6** (1), 22–53.

Petitpas, A.L., S. Danish, R. McKelvain, and S. Murphy (1992), 'A career assistance programme for elite athletes', *Journal of Counselling and Development*, **70** (3), 383–386.

Portes, A. (1998), 'Social capital: Its origins and applications in modern sociology', *Annual Review of Sociology*, **24**, 1–24.

Pringle, J.K. and M. Mallon (2003), 'Challenges for the boundaryless career odyssey', *International Journal of Human Resource Management*, **14** (5), 839–853.

Sargent, L.D. and S.R. Domberger (2007), 'Exploring the development of a protean career orientation: Values and image violations', *Career Development International*, **12** (6), 545–564.

Savickas, M.L. (2006), 'Career construction theory', in J.H. Greenhaus and G.A. Callaghan (eds), *Encyclopaedia of career development*. Thousand Oaks, CA, USA: Sage, pp. 85–89.

Savickas, M.L. (2012), 'Life design: A new paradigm for career intervention in the 21st century', *Journal of Counseling and Development*, **90**, 13–19.

Seibert, S.E., M.L. Kraimer, and R.C. Liden (2001), 'A social capital theory of career success', *Academy of Management Journal*, **44** (2), 219–237.

Stambulova, N.B. (1994), 'Developmental sport career investigations in Russia: A post perestroika analysis', *Sport Psychologist*, **8**, 221–237.

Stambulova, N.B. (2000), 'Athletes' crises: A developmental perspective', *International Journal of Sport Psychology*, **31**, 584–601.

Stronach, M. and D. Adair (2010), 'Lords of the square ring: Future capital and career transition issues for elite indigenous Australian boxers', *Cosmopolitan Civil Societies Journal*, **2** (2), 46–70.

Sullivan, S.E. (1999), 'The changing nature of careers: A review and research agenda', *Journal of Management*, **25**, 457–484.

Sullivan, S.E. and M. Arthur (2006), 'The evolution of the boundaryless career concept: Examining physical and psychological mobility', *Journal of Vocational Behaviour*, **69**, 19–29.

Sullivan, S.E. and Y. Baruch (2009), 'Advances in career theory and research: A critical review and agenda for further exploration', *Journal of Management*, **35** (6), 1542–1571.

Sullivan, S.E. and M.M. Crocitto (2007), 'The developmental theories: A critical examination of their continuing impact on careers research', in H. Gunz and M. Peiperl (eds), *Handbook of career studies*. Thousand Oaks, CA, USA: Sage, pp. 283–309.

Super, D.E. (1957), *Psychology of careers*. New York, NY, USA: Harper.

Super, D.E. (1980), 'A life span, life space approach to careers', *Journal of Vocational Behaviour*, **16**, 282–298.

Swain, D.A. (1991), 'Withdrawal from sport and Schlossberg's model of transitions', *Sociology of Sport Journal*, **8**, 152–160.

Taylor, J. and D. Lavallee (2010), 'Career transition among athletes: Is there life after sports?', in J.M. Williams (ed.), *Applied sport psychology: Personal growth to peak performance*. 6th Edition. Columbus, OH, USA: McGraw-Hill, pp. 542–562.

Wacquant, L. (1995), 'Pugs at work: Bodily capital and bodily labour among professional boxers', *Body and Society*, **1** (1), 65–93.

Wacquant, L. (2011), 'Habitus as topic and tool: Reflections on becoming a prize fighter', *Qualitative Research in Psychology*, **8**, 81–92.

Warriner, K. and D. Lavallee (2008), 'The retirement experiences of elite gymnasts: Self identity and the physical self', *Journal of Applied Sport Psychology*, **20**, 301–317.

Wippert, P. and J. Wippert (2008), 'Perceived stress and prevalence of traumatic stress symptoms following athletic career termination', *Journal of Clinical Sport Psychology*, **2**, 1–16.

Wylleman, P., D. Alfermann, and D. Lavallee (2004), 'Career transitions in sport: European perspectives', *Psychology of Sport and Exercise*, **5**, 7–20.

Zaichkowsky, L., E. King, and J. McCarthy (2000), 'The end of an era: The case of forced transition involving Boston University football', in D. Lavallee and P. Wylleman (eds), *Career transitions in sport*. Morgantown, WV, USA: Fitness Information Technology, pp. 195–205.

11. If you want to play sport professionally, which sport should you choose?
Greg Maynes, Heather Mitchell,
Peter Schuwalow and Mark Stewart

INTRODUCTION

In this study we consider professional sports people; that is, those who make a living solely from their participation in sports. In the past professional sports people could play one sport in summer and another in winter, and be successful in both. For example, Eddie Eagan, representing the United States, won a gold medal for boxing in the 1920 Olympics and one for the bobsled in the 1932 Winter Olympics, and Deion Sanders played both baseball and National Football League (NFL) professionally. With the increasing demands on professional sports players they must now devote themselves exclusively to one sport. The choice of sport needs to be made at a relatively young age, usually around the end of high school. This study examines the choice from an economic supply and demand perspective.

To play professional sport requires a great deal of natural talent, much hard work, good coaching and usually a fair amount of luck. However, the opportunity to earn a living from sport also depends on the sport chosen. An assessment of the world's only two truly global sports of football (soccer) and athletics (track and field) illustrates this point. These two sports, as they are both contested by virtually every nation, are extremely competitive. This is because there is a large supply of players and competitors chasing limited places on teams (football) and/or prize money (track and field).

However, if the question of sporting success is re-phrased to 'which sport should you choose if you would like to become a professional?', the inferences may be quite different. To address this issue, we looked at both the demand for, as well as the supply of, potential professional sportsmen and women. This study posits the theory that the number of participants making a living from their sport is indicative of the demand for their services. If both demand and supply are considered, athletics is still likely to remain one of the world's most competitive sports as so few could be considered to be professional track and field athletes, while it is still contested by almost every nation. On the other hand, the number of opportunities to play football (soccer) professionally throughout the world is likely to make this sport a better choice if your aim is to become a pro.

The comparison between the demand and supply of sportsmen and women can also be used to address other issues such as does golf offer more opportunities than tennis? What about a talented young sportsman trying to decide whether to concentrate on rugby league or rugby union, or Australian football or cricket? Obviously the decision regarding which sport is chosen will largely depend on a person's predisposition towards that sport. However, there are many examples of brilliant teenage sportsmen and sportswomen needing to choose which sport they should pursue. In 2014 Nick Kyrgios reached the quarter finals at Wimbledon but he was also a promising basketball player before deciding to focus on tennis. Renaldo Nehemiah gave up NFL to focus on hurdles while Marion Jones gave up professional basketball for track and field.

This study marries some previous research regarding the competitiveness of different sports (a measure of the supply of sportsmen and women) with the number of opportunities there are to play sport professionally (representing the demand for their services), and then tries to assess which sport a gifted young sportsman or woman should choose if they are trying to maximize their chances of becoming a professional. The study will proceed as follows. In the second section some of the previous work in the area is reviewed; in particular the 2007 paper by Mitchell and Stewart titled 'A competitive index for international sport' in *Applied Economics*. This paper constructs an index of competitiveness for different international sports, thereby allowing judgements to be made regarding how difficult it is to be successful in these sports. That is, this previous research is used to rank sports in terms of their competitiveness. The third section looks at the team sports of Australian football, baseball, cricket, football (soccer), rugby league and rugby union and tries to assess the number of job opportunities available in each. That is, we endeavour to count the number of sportsmen in the world who are making a living from playing these different professional team sports. The next section does the same as the previous section, except it focuses on the individual sports of athletics (track and field), golf and tennis. Then the fifth section marries all of this information (the competitiveness of the different sports and the number of job opportunities for professional sportsmen and sportswomen) so that judgements can be made regarding which sports give the best opportunities to earn a living. In the final section some conclusions are drawn.

PREVIOUS LITERATURE

There is a large literature on the national characteristics associated with sporting success. Some of the more important papers include Ball (1972), Levine (1972), Grimes, Kelly and Rubin (1974), Hogan and Norton (2000), Johnson and Ali (2000; 2002), Bernard and Busse (2001), Hoffmann, Lee and Ramasamy (2002), Sterken and Kuper (2003) and Moosa and Smith (2004). These papers focus almost exclusively on Olympic success and generally find that large (in terms of both aggregate GDP and population) wealthy countries, as well as communist (or formerly communist) countries perform best.

The paper by Mitchell and Stewart (2007) conducts a thorough review of this literature and uses these papers as a guide to select variables that are then tested for their ability to explain the number of medals won by each nation at the Athens Olympic Games. This was done by using an econometric Poisson model that eventually includes GDP, Population, Birth Rate, Fertility and Life Expectancy, as well as dummy variables to take account of whether the nation was an Aid Donor and whether it currently is or was formerly Communist. The model's forecasts were quite accurate. For example, it predicted that the United States would win 100.04 medals at the Athens Olympic Games and it actually won 103, while it predicted that China would win 69.14 and it won 63.

Using the Poisson model's medal predictions the Competitiveness Index (CI) for each individual Olympic sport *i* was calculated to be:

$$CI_i = \frac{\sum \text{the Poisson predicted medals of participating nations in sport } i}{\sum \text{the Poisson predicted medals of all nations}}$$

If a single sport at the Athens games were contested by every nation that was a member of the International Olympic Committee (IOC) it would have an index of 1.00. The CIs calculated using this formula for the individual sports contested at the Athens games clearly showed track and field athletics (with a CI of 0.97) to be the most competitive of all Olympic sports. Swimming was the second most competitive, while the sports of synchronized swimming, modern pentathlon, trampoline and canoe kayak slalom were the least competitive with CIs in the range of 0.56 to 0.40.

The advantage of using these CIs is that the relative sporting strength of each country is considered. A simplistic approach would be to count the number of nations involved in the different sports and then use this to construct the index. This calculation, however, would take no account of a nation's propensity to produce sporting champions. For example, such an index would deem two sports to be equally competitive if one was contested by the United States, Russia and Japan, and the other was contested by Chad, Mali and Niger.[1]

The paper then went on to use this same technique to assess the competitiveness of various non-Olympic sports and competitions. Included here were, American sports (any sport played exclusively in the United States), Australian football, baseball, the Commonwealth Games, cricket, football (soccer), golf, rugby league, rugby union and tennis (men's and women's). When selecting which nations to include as being involved in these different sports, a country was only listed if it had a professional involvement. That is, although most sports are played to some extent in many places around the world, a country was only included as participating in that sport if it is either played professionally in that country, or if that nation contributes a significant number of professional players to that sport when it is played professionally elsewhere in the world.

Table 11.1 (team sports) and Table 11.2 (individual sports) show the updated CIs from Mitchell and Stewart's (2007) paper.[2] The sports in these tables are arranged in descending order from the most to the least competitive.

The indices in Tables 11.1 and 11.2 depend on how widely the sports are played throughout the world, as well as the propensity of the nations that are involved in these sports to produce successful sportsmen and sportswomen and sporting teams.

Therefore, the closer the index is to 1.00 the greater is the supply of players and competitors trying to reach the top. That is, the larger the index the more competitive is the sport as there are likely to be more (and better) sportsmen and sportswomen around the world trying to win. In this sense these indices are indicative of the supply of worldwide sporting talent across these sports.

Table 11.1   Team sports

	Number of nations	Average GDP per capita (US$)	Competitive index
Football (Soccer)	205	7,900	1.00
Baseball	8	18,288	0.24
Rugby Union	11	16,982	0.09
Cricket	20	9,240	0.07
Rugby League	5	20,120	0.04
Australian Football	1	26,900	0.01

Table 11.2   Individual sports

	Number of nations	Average GDP per capita (US$)	Competitive index
Athletics	179	9,564	0.97
Athletics (men)	178	9,612	0.97
Athletics (women)	155	8,797	0.92
Tennis	59	14,978	0.78
Tennis (men)	52	15,706	0.68
Tennis (women)	44	16,789	0.71
Golf	38	17,905	0.54
Golf (men)	37	18,243	0.54
Golf (women)	25	16,732	0.43

Note: The athletics indices are based on the number of nations that took part in the track and field competitions at the Athens Olympic Games.

An examination of these CIs shows that football (soccer) is the most competitive of any single sport as it is played throughout the world. The implication is that it would be very difficult for either an individual or a team to reach the top in this sport. Baseball is the next most competitive sport, mainly because it is played in Japan and the United States, the nations with the world's largest and second largest economies. The model rates rugby union as being more competitive than cricket. This occurs because rugby union is played in France (a large wealthy nation). France has a greater effect on the index than does the combined effects of the cricket playing nations from the Caribbean and South Asia. Tennis is more competitive than golf. The reason for this is that golf is not commonly played in the former communist countries,[3] unlike tennis. The model shows women's tennis to be more competitive than men's tennis. This is an interesting conclusion given the current debate regarding equal prize money for men's and women's tennis. The reason why the model places women's tennis ahead of men's is that at the time of this analysis there were no male professional players from China, but there were female Chinese professionals.

The current study has set itself the task of answering the question: 'if you would like to be a professional sportsman or woman, which sport should you choose?' If only the CIs from Tables 11.1 and 11.2 were used to answer this question the conclusion would be: 'don't try to become a professional footballer (soccer player), it is just too competitive!' This, however, would be the equivalent of trying to understand what determines prices by only looking at supply. That is, just as prices are determined by the balance between demand and supply, which sport should be chosen will depend on both the number of available jobs (the demand for professional players) as well as the competition for these jobs (the supply of players competing for places on teams or prize money in the individual sports).

Clearly, when endeavouring to answer the question posed in this study, 'if you would like to be a professional sportsman or woman, which sport should you choose?', we need to consider the demand side as well as the supply side of the equation. That is, although the unadjusted indices are indicative of labour supply, if you would like a job as a professional sportsman or woman then there also must be a demand for your services. Therefore, the next step in this analysis is to assess how many job opportunities there are across these different sports.

In the next two sections of the study an attempt is made to tally the number of jobs available for professional sportsmen and sportswomen around the world in the various team and individual sports. Then in the section that follows these figures are married with the competitive indices that were shown in Tables 11.1 and 11.2 to address the central question of the study, 'which sport should you choose if you want to be a pro?'

TEAM SPORTS[4]

This section aims to count the number of sportsmen in the world that earn a living from the team sports of Australian football, baseball, cricket, football (soccer), rugby league and rugby union. It should be noted that this is a difficult task and many judgements and estimates have been made. That is, we have often made broad assumptions that may or may not be completely correct. We have, however, tried to explain exactly what we have done and the reasons for the decisions in each case. Nevertheless, we believe that the final figures for each sport are sufficiently accurate for our purpose.

Evidently the earnings of professional sportsmen and sportswomen are very unevenly distributed, with a few making large amounts of money, while most make very little. The distribution of sporting income is not assessed in this study. The test that is applied is whether a sportsperson could earn a full time living from their sport.

Australian Football

As the name suggests, Australian Football is only played professionally in Australia. Although there are a number of professional and

Table 11.3   Australian football

	$AUD	$US
Total player payments per team	6,300,000	4,725,000
Average player payment	165,789	124,342
Minimum player payment	50,200	37,650
Number of teams	16	
Players per team	38	
Total number of players	**608**	

Sources: Please refer to Appendix (Australian Football Data Sources).

semi-professional leagues around the country, we have decided to only include players from the nationwide Australian Football League (AFL) as being full time professionals. Table 11.3 summarizes the arrangements in the AFL for the 2006 season. As the minimum player payment of $37,000US ($50,200AUD) is well above Australia's GDP per capita, clearly these players would have no need to earn income from other sources, and as such should be considered full time professionals.[5]

Baseball

Professional baseball is primarily played in six countries: the United States, Canada, Japan, South Korea, Taiwan and Venezuela. The world's premier competition is the 30 team Major League Baseball (MLB) based in the United States and Canada. Each of these teams has a maximum roster of 40 players. For the 2005 season the average salary for all MLB players was $2,479,125US, while the minimum salary was $316,000US. Clearly, all of these players are full time professionals. In addition to the 30 MLB teams, there are 246 clubs operating in the US Minor Leagues. Each of these teams is affiliated to a MLB club and as such their players are well paid. The rosters for the Minor League teams vary from 25 to 35 players. Therefore, we estimate the potential professional baseball player population in the United States and Canada to be 8,580 (1,200 in the majors and 7,380 in the minors).[6]

Considering Japan and South Korea, there are 12 teams in Japan divided into two leagues, and South Korea has eight teams. Each Japanese team has a roster of 66 players, while the South Korean teams have approximately 55 players. Although salary information is difficult to access for these leagues, we believe these players are professional as US players are often enticed to play in Japan and South Korea. Therefore, we estimate

Table 11.4   World baseball

League name	Location	No. of teams	Average no. of players per team	Total no. of players
CPBL	Taiwan	6	40	240
Jball	Japan	12	66	792
KBO	Korea	8	55	440
LVBP	Venezuela	5	˙44	219
Major Leagues	USA and Canada	30	40	1,200
Minor Leagues	USA	246	30	7,380
Totals		**307**		**10,271**

Note: CPBL = Chinese Professional Baseball League; Jball = Japanese Baseball League (now known as the NPB or Nippon Professional Baseball); KBO = Korean Baseball Organization; LVBP = Liga Venezolana de Beisbol Professional (or the Venezuelan Professional Baseball League).

Sources: Please refer to Appendix (Baseball Data Sources).

that these two nations have 792 and 440 professional baseball players respectively. Taiwan has eight professional teams and Venezuela five.[7]

Table 11.4 gives a total figure of 10,271 professional baseball players across these six nations.

Cricket

The major competitions in professional cricket are international test matches, international one-day cricket, domestic first-class, one-day and now twenty-twenty games. These games are played in all the world's test cricket playing nations. As we are trying to count the number of professional cricketers in the world, we concentrate on the domestic competitions, as it is assumed that any player on a national team will be a full time professional and will be playing at least some of the time in a domestic competition.

The domestic competitions in Australia include the Pura and Ford Ranger Cups; in England and Wales there are the County Championship, the National League and the C & G Trophy; India has the Duleep Trophy and Ranji Trophy; while in New Zealand there are the State Championship and State Shield; Pakistan has the Quaid-e-Azam Trophy and ABN-Ambro Trophy; in South Africa there are the Super-Sport Series and Standard Bank Cup; Sri Lanka has a Provincial Tournament and a Premier League; while in the West Indies there are the Caribbean Beer Series and KFC Cup. Although Zimbabwe and Bangladesh also

Table 11.5   World cricket

Countries	No. of teams	No. of players
Australia	6	186
Bangladesh	6	84
England and Wales	18	387
India	26	364
New Zealand	6	84
Pakistan	11	154
South Africa	5	124
Sri Lanka	4	56
West Indies	6	115
Zimbabwe	4	56
Totals	**92**	**1,610**

Sources: Please refer to Appendix (Cricket Data Sources).

play test cricket, their domestic competitions are relatively small and under-developed.

With the popularity of cricket in many of these countries (especially in South Asia), and the high profile of many of the players, we expect that these players are earning a living from their sport.

Although we have settled on a figure of 1,610 professional crick-eters worldwide, we recognize that there may be an issue of double counting, with some cricketers playing in more than one domestic competition in a year. However, given that we have not included any players from the minor counties in England or District sides in Australia (many of whom are also professional), we believe our estimate to be reasonable.

Football (Soccer)

World football (soccer) is organized by the Fédération Internationale de Football Association (FIFA). FIFA is made up of six confederations that broadly represent the continents. The confederations and their regions are:

1.   the Asian Football Confederation (AFC), which represents Asia plus Australia;
2.   the Confédération Africaine de Football (CAF), for Africa;
3.   the Confederation of North, Central American Caribbean Association Football (CONCACAF), which represents all of the Americas other than South America;

4. the Confederación Sudamericana de Fútbol (CSF), for South America;
5. the Oceania Football Confederation (OFC), which represents Oceania other than Australia;
6. the Union des Associations Européennes de Football (UEFA), in Europe.

FIFA has a membership of more than 200 national football federations, which are all assigned to one of these confederations. Each country's national federation enters its national teams in the various FIFA competitions (the most famous of which is the World Cup), and they also usually run their own domestic competitions. FIFA lists the number of first division clubs within each confederation (see Table 11.6), and we have assumed that each of these clubs employs 25 full time professional players. For some countries' teams this may be an over-estimate in terms of the number of players making a full time living from their sport, but in most cases we think it is an under-estimate. That is, the premier football competition in each country will almost always be professional and most clubs will employ more than 25 players each.

The other issue is that most countries have many divisions in their football leagues that are also professional. In recognition of this we have researched the second divisions of the major European leagues and added these players to Table 11.6. The second divisions we have included are: the Coca-Cola Championship in England, the Bundesliga 2 in Germany, the Ligue 2 in France, the Serie B in Italy, the Erste Divisie in the Netherlands, the Liga De Honra in Portugal and Segunda Division in Spain.

Table 11.6 World football (soccer)

Confederation	Region	No. of teams	Estimated no. of players
AFC	Asia	123	3,075
CAF	Africa	76	1,900
CONCACAF	North and Central America	139	3,475
CSF	South America	143	3,575
OFC	Oceania	8	200
UEFA	Europe – First Divisions	693	17,325
UEFA	Europe – Second Divisions	142	3,550
Totals		**1,324**	**33,100**

Note: *Assumes 25 players per team.

Sources: Please refer to Appendix (Football, Soccer, Data Sources).

Table 11.7   World rugby league

League	Location	No. of teams	Average no. of players per team	Total player payments per team (US$)	Average player payments (US$)	Total no. of players
NRL	Aust and NZ	15	27	2,524,500	93,041	407
Super League	UK and France	12	27	3,207,547	120,283	320
Totals		**27**				**727**

Sources: Please refer to Appendix (Rugby League Data Sources).

Therefore, we estimate there to be 33,100 professional footballers (soccer) players) in the world. Clearly football (soccer) is the largest employer of professional sportsmen in the world and as such should provide the best opportunity to make a living from playing sport. The difficulty, however, is that as the whole world also plays football, the competition for these team positions are intense.

Rugby League

Rugby league is played primarily in five countries: Australia, France, New Zealand, Papua New Guinea and the United Kingdom. However, there are really only two full time professional leagues in the world, the Australian National Rugby League (NRL) and the English Super League. The NRL has 14 teams in Australia and one in New Zealand. The Super League has 11 teams in England and one in France. The player payment data in Table 11.7 shows that these players should all be considered to be full time professionals.

Rugby Union

Rugby union is played to some extent in many countries around the world; however, from the viewpoint of professional sport, there are only a few competitions in Europe and in the Southern Hemisphere that can be regarded as fully professional. These include the English Guinness League; the French Ligue de Football Professionnel; and the Celtic League (recently re-named the Magners League for the 2006/07 season). Also there is the annual Heineken Cup, which involves teams from England, France, Italy, Ireland, Wales and Scotland. In the Southern Hemisphere there is the Super 14 competition that involves 14 provincial/state teams

Table 11.8   World rugby union

League	Location	No. of teams	Average no. of players per team	Total no. of players per team
French Ligue	France	14	33	468
Guinness	UK	12	41	492
Heineken Cup	Europe	24	36	864
Magners League	UK and France	11	36	400
Super 14s	Aust, NZ and SA	14	31	436
Total		**75**		**2,660**

Sources: Please refer to Appendix (Rugby Union Data Sources).

from Australia, South Africa and New Zealand. These competitions are now effectively all professional.

Table 11.8 shows our estimates of the number of professional rugby union players in all of these competitions, with the total being 2,660. Although it is possible that there will be some double counting as some clubs and players participate in both their local competition as well as the European wide Heineken Cup, we believe our figure to be realistic, as we have under-estimated in other areas. For example, we know there is professional rugby played in Argentina and Italy, as well as the various rugby 7s competitions played around the world. Also, the domestic competitions played in Australia, New Zealand and South Africa will be associated with some degree of professionalism, that is, at least some sportsmen will be able to make a living from them.

INDIVIDUAL SPORTS[8]

This section aims to count the number of sportsmen and sportswomen in the world that earn a living from the individual sports of athletics (track and field), golf and tennis. As already stated, sporting income is very unevenly distributed; however, again, the test that is applied is whether a sportsperson could earn a full time living from their sport, and the number of these opportunities that exist in the world is estimated. Also, the same qualifying remarks that were made at the start of the previous section need to be reiterated. That is, tallying the number of professional sportsmen and women is not an easy task and some broad judgements have been made.

Athletics (Track and Field)

To assess how many track and field athletes are making a full time living from their sport we needed to get some measure of the prize money and income from other sources that is available, and how many athletes are in a position to obtain some of this money.

The major competitions in athletics are the Olympic Games (once every four years) and the World Championships (once every two years). Other important championships include the World Indoor Championships, World Cup, European Championships and Commonwealth Games. There are also more specialist major championships including the World Cross Country Championships, World Road Running Championships, World Marathon Championships, World Race Walking Cup, World Junior Championships and World Youth Championships, and these are all held at regular intervals. Some of these competitions have prize money, but many do not.

To assess the amount of prize money in track and field we only look at competitions that are sanctioned by the world governing body, the International Association of Athletics Federations (IAAF). The IAAF runs the World Athletics Tour (WAT), which is a series of professional athletics competitions held throughout the world, where athletes compete for the right to take part in the World Athletics Tour Final that is held in September each year.

Table 11.9 summaries this prize money and shows that in 2006 it adds to just over $15 million US. This, however, would be far short of the total amount of prize money available as these are the minimum amounts of prize money needed for the IAAF to sanction the meetings as part of the WAT. For example, the IAAF states that the Zurich Golden League meeting must have at least $500,000US prize money to retain its Golden

Table 11.9   World Athletics Tour minimum prize money 2006

	Minimum prize money (US$)	No. of meetings	Total prize money (US$)
Golden League and Super Gr Prix	500,000	12	6,000,000
Gr Prix	230,000	12	2,760,000
World Athletics Final	3,020,000	1	3,020,000
World Cup in Athletics	3,260,000	1	3,260,000
Total Prize Money			**15,040,000**

Sources: Please refer to Appendix (Athletics, Track and Field, Data Sources).

League status, but in 2005 there was $932,537US available. In addition to this there are another 86 indoor and outdoor meetings authorized by the IAAF that would all offer some prize money.[9] Other than these competitions, there are numerous marathons and road races that also offer various degrees of financial reward. The most lucrative of these races are the major city marathons such as Boston, London, Berlin, Chicago and New York, where the total prize money is also in the millions of dollars.[10]

There are two major sources of non-prize-money income available to international athletes: personal sponsors and national athletics federations. As track and field is a truly global sport, many firms looking for worldwide exposure offer lucrative sponsorship deals to the top track and field athletes. Although personal sponsorship income often only goes to the most elite, funding from national athletics federations usually goes far deeper. With the competition among nations for medals at major international championships now being so intense, virtually every country allocates some funding to their best athletes. For example, the United Kingdom paid their best 40 track and field athletes £7,200,000 between 2005 and 2009. This amounted to £45,000 per annum each.[11] Although this is at the high end of direct athlete support, even the poorest nations usually give their best athletes something to help with their preparation for major championships.

Taking all of these things into account we estimated there to be 430 track and field athletes in the world that make a full time living from their sport. This number was chosen as it represents the best ten athletes in all 43 individual Olympic events (22 events for men and 21 for women). Any athlete that is in the world top ten in their individual event would be competing in the IAAF WAT meetings and as such would be in the running for prize money. Also, if they were in the top ten they would have some chance at a medal at the next major championship (either Olympics or World Championships). This being the case their national athletic federation would be supporting them to some degree, and they may also have additional income from personal sponsors.

Golf

The PGA Tour website shows prize money won by each player across their three tours (PGA Tour, PGA Nationwide and Seniors Tour).[12] By summing across these three lists we were able to show that in 2006 there were 909 professional players representing 37 different nations with prize money of more than $25,000US. The Ladies Professional Golf Association (LPGA) website shows there were 141 women from 25 different countries with 2006 prize money of $25,000US or more.

Table 11.10   Team sports index numbers

	Unadjusted CI from Table 11.1	No. of teams	Average no. of professional players per team	Total no. of professional players	CI adjusted for the number of professionals
Rugby League	0.04	27	27	727	0.023
Cricket	0.07	92	18	1,610	0.018
Rugby Union	0.09	75	35	2,660	0.016
Football (Soccer)	1.00	1,324	25	33,100	0.013
Baseball	0.24	301	34	10,271	0.010
Australian Football	0.01	16	38	608	0.005

Tennis

The Association of Tennis Professionals (ATP) website shows prize money won by each male player across singles, doubles and mixed doubles. In 2006 there were 369 professional players representing 52 different nations with prize money of more than $25,000US. The Women's Tennis Association (WTA) website only shows aggregate prize money for the current (2007) year. Therefore, we needed to extrapolate from these figures, but were able to estimate there to be 197 women from 44 different countries with prize money of $25,000US or more.[13]

Which Sport Should You Select to Become a Pro?

Table 11.10 shows our best estimates of the total number of job opportunities in the various team sports. Clearly, football (soccer) is the largest employer of professional sportsmen in the world. Table 11.11 shows our assessment of the total number of sportsmen and sportswomen making a living from the individual sports. For men, golf is the biggest employer, followed by tennis then athletics, whereas for women the order is athletics, tennis then golf.

As we know, the number of jobs is only one side of the equation. That is, when deciding which sport offers the best opportunities to earn a living, the competition for these places also needs to be considered. Tables 11.10 and 11.11 also show the CI for each sport from Tables 11.1 and 11.2; as well as this CI adjusted for the number of job opportunities that exist in these sports is shown (final column). The adjustment is done by first dividing the unadjusted CI (shown in the first columns of Tables 11.10

Table 11.11   Individual sports index numbers

	Unadjusted CI from Table 11.2	Total no. of professional players	CI adjusted for the number of professionals
Athletics	0.97	430	1.00
Athletics (men)	0.97	220	
Athletics (women)	0.92	210	
Tennis	0.78	566	0.62
Tennis (men)	0.68	369	
Tennis (women)	0.71	197	
Golf	0.54	1,049	0.23
Golf (men)	0.54	909	
Golf (women)	0.43	140	

Note: There was no easy way of calculating the adjusted CIs for the men's and women's individual sports.

and 11.11) by the number of professionals in each sport. To express these figures as index numbers we divide by the value for track and field athletics, which is the most competitive of all sports. This gives athletics an index of 1.00, and all of the other indices in both Tables 11.10 and 11.11 are expressed relative to this. The higher the adjusted CI (the closer to 1.00) the more competitive, implying that it is more difficult to earn a living from that sport. Again, the sports in these tables are arranged in descending order, from the most to the least competitive.

These tables show that the individual sports considered in this study are all far more competitive than the team sports. For example, the least competitive of our individual sports, golf, with an adjusted CI of 0.23, is ten times more competitive than the most competitive team sport of rugby league with an adjusted CI of 0.023. This is because although many countries are involved in these individual sports, their professional opportunities are limited. The relatively small number of professionals in individual sports is related to the fact that most cities around the world host professional team sports games each week, but with individual sports events these are usually once a year affairs in a particular city.

Our results also clearly show there to be fewer opportunities for women to make a living from sport than for men. This is related to our first point, as there are not many female professional team sports (none are assessed in this study); therefore sportswomen are confined to individual sports, where life is very tough.

As stated previously, according to our analysis, track and field athletics is by far the most competitive sport in the world. This is because it is contested by virtually every nation, but employment opportunities are small with only 430 professional athletes worldwide. There is an interesting point of comparison between athletics and football (soccer). Both are similarly competitive in terms of their unadjusted CI, but the number of job opportunities in football (soccer) (more than thirty thousand across the globe) make it a much better option in terms of becoming a professional. That is, although the unadjusted CI shows football (soccer) to be the most competitive sport in the world, when job opportunities are considered it ranks as being less competitive than rugby league, cricket and rugby union. Only baseball and Australian football are classified as being less competitive than football (soccer). Baseball is deemed less competitive mainly due to the large number of job opportunities in North America, while Australian football's low rank is function of it only being played in one country, therefore the supply of people trying to become professional Australian footballers is limited.

Note that the order of competitiveness (according to our adjusted CIs) runs from rugby league, then cricket followed by rugby union. This appears to be largely driven by the number of professional opportunities available across these sports. Rugby league is the most competitive (only 727 professional players), cricket is next with 1,610 professional players, while rugby union is the least competitive with its 2,660 professional players worldwide.

Among the individual sports golf is the least competitive of the sports considered here. This is because golf has a lower unadjusted CI and there are a large number of professional golfers (over one thousand) in the world.

CONCLUSION

This study has used statistical techniques to compare the competitiveness of the different sports with the number of opportunities there are to become sports professionals, then ranks the various team and individual sports in terms of the prospects they offer to sportsmen and sportswomen to become professionals. The conclusions (embodied in Tables 11.10 and 11.11) can be used to make comparisons between these sports.

The absolute differences between some of the adjusted CIs are quite small. For example, that between cricket and rugby union is only 0.002, but this represents a relative difference of more than 10 per cent. So even though our figures on the number of professionals in each sport may not be accurate, the errors are unlikely to be large enough to affect the relative competiveness of the sports.

The study has not considered every sport played professionally, but it should not be difficult for someone to calculate the CI for their sports of interest. The predicted medals for almost every country are available in the appendix of Mitchell and Stewart (2007). Using these, together with information on the number of professionals and sports playing nations, a comparison of competiveness can easily be made using the methodology in this chapter.

In the introduction we mentioned Kyrgios, Nehemiah and Jones, who had all succeeded in their chosen sports, but what of the ones who failed? Perhaps their chances of success would have been improved had they considered demand and supply when choosing their sport. Although ability and passion are essential in sporting success, when a person has these in near equal measure in more than one sport, economic considerations can help make a more informed decision.

NOTES

1. The paper by Mitchell and Stewart shows Japan, Russia and the United States to be the nations with the social, demographic and economic characteristics that are most likely to produce international sporting success, while Chad, Mali and Niger are the three countries least likely to be successful at sport.
2. The differences between the indices presented here and those in the 2007 paper are: for golf and tennis a nation is now only included if they have a single professional player with annual prize money in excess of $25,000US; there are now separate indices for men's and women's golf; France is now considered a rugby league playing nation, since the establishment of the Catalan Dragons that now play in the English Super League competition; Venezuela and Taiwan have been added to the baseball playing nations (see the next section for details).
3. China is the only former communist country with professional golfers.
4. The sports are assessed in alphabetical order.
5. All of this data comes from www.afl.com.au, accessed August 2006.
6. The references for the data relating to each sport can be found in the Appendix. This is the case for all of the sports discussed in this chapter.
7. Table 11.1 lists eight baseball playing nations. Adding Cuba and the Dominican Republic gives this figure, as although they do not have lucrative professional leagues, they do provide many professional players to the leagues listed in Table 11.4.
8. The individual sports are also assessed in alphabetical order.
9. This data has come from the IAAF website (www.iaaf.org) accessed August 2006.
10. http://worldmarathonmajors.com/.
11. This information is from www.uksport.gov.uk, accessed August 2006.
12. These golf tours are now known as the PGA Tour, Web.com Tour and Champions Tour. There are other professional golf tours around the world where players can win prize money.
13. The extrapolation was done by noting that the data was taken on in March 2007 (one quarter of the way through the year), therefore the prize money cut-off point was set at $6,250US, which is equivalent to a quarter of $25,000US.

REFERENCES

Note: Much of the data for the individual and team sports are taken from websites that are listed in the Appendix. Therefore these websites are not listed under references.

Ball, D. (1972), 'Olympic Games competition: structural correlates of national success', *International Journal of Comparative Sociology*, **12**, 186–200.

Bernard, A. and M. Busse (2001), 'Who wins the Olympic Games: economic resources and medal totals', Tuck School of Business, Dartmouth National Bureau of Economic Research, Yale School of Management, April 2001.

Grimes, R., W. Kelly and P. Rubin (1974), 'A socio-economic model of national Olympic performance', *Social Science Quarterly*, **55**, 777–782.

Hoffmann, R., C. G. Lee and B. Ramasamy (2002), 'Public policy Olympic success', *Applied Economics Letters*, **9** (8), 545–548.

Hogan, K. and K. Norton (2000), 'The "price" of Olympic gold', *Journal of Science Medicine in Sport*, **3** (2), June, 203–218.

Johnson, D. and A. Ali (2000), 'Coming to play or coming to win: participation success at the Olympic Games', Working Paper, September 2000 Department of Economics, Wellesley College, Massachusetts, USA.

Johnson, D. and A. Ali (2002), 'A tale of two seasons: participation medal counts at the Summer and Winter Olympic Games', Working Paper, January 2002 Department of Economics, Wellesley College, Massachusetts, USA.

Levine, N. (1972), 'Why do countries win Olympic medals? Some structural correlates of Olympic Games success: 1972', *Sociology Social Research*, **58**, 353–360.

Mitchell, H. and M. F. Stewart (2007), 'A competitive index for international sport', *Applied Economics*, **39** (5), 587–603.

Moosa, I. A. and L. Smith (2004), 'Economic development indicators as determinants of medal winning at the Sydney Olympics: an extreme bounds analysis', *Australian Economic Papers*, **43** (3), 288–301.

Sterken, E. and G. Kuper (2003), 'Participation performance at the Olympic Summer Games', *Economy Sport*, **3**, 13–20.

APPENDIX: DATA SOURCES

Note: These websites were accessed during 2006 and 2007.

Athletics, Track and Field, Data Sources

http://worldmarathonmajors.com
http://www.iaaf.org
www.uksport.gov.uk

Australian Football Data Sources

http://www.afl.com.au

Baseball Data Sources

http://asp.usatoday.com/sports/baseball/salaries/default.aspx
http://baseballguru.com/rewwong/koreanbaseballprimer.html
http://en.wikipedia.org/wiki/Korean_Baseball_Organization
http://en.wikipedia.org/wiki/Major_League_Baseball
http://ww1.baywell.ne.jp/fpweb/drlatham/players/players.htm
http://www.cpbl.com.tw/
http://www.doosanbears.com/
http://www.hanwhaeagles.co.kr/
http://www.hd-unicorns.co.kr/
http://www.lgtwins.co.kr/
http://www.lotte-giants.co.kr/
http://www.lvbp.com/
http://www.mlb.com/NASApp/mlb/mlb/homepage/narrowb.jsp
http://www.mlb4u.com/pcontracts.php
http://www.samsunglions.com/english/index/index.asp
http://www.skwyverns.com/
http://www.tigers.co.kr/

Cricket Data Sources

http://en.wikipedia.org/wiki/Carib_Beer_Cup
http://en.wikipedia.org/wiki/KFC_Cup
http://en.wikipedia.org/wiki/List_of_current_first-class_cricket_teams
http://worldsoccer.about.com/od/englishpremierleague/a/playmoney.htm
http://www.auscricket.com.au/
http://www.cricinfo.com
http://www.cricket.com.au
http://www.ecb.co.uk/

http://www.highveldstrikers.co.za/players.html
http://www.nzcricket.co.nz/
http://www.southafrica.info/ess_info/sa_glance/sports/cricket.htm
www.independent.co.uk

Football (Soccer) Data Sources

http://en.wikipedia.org/wiki/List_of_football_(soccer)_competitions
http://worldsoccer.about.com
http://www.bundesliga.de/en
http://www.fifa.com/en/WorldLeagues/index.html
http://www.fpf.pt/
http://www.lfp.es/
http://www.lfp.fr/
http://www.rsssf.com/nersssf.html
http://www.soccer-corner.com/Clubs.Netherls.Eerste-Divisie.htm

Golf Data Sources

http://www.asiantour.com/aboutus.htm
http://www.ausgolf.com.au/australasiantour.htl
http://espn.go.com/golf/schedule/_/year/2006
http://www.europeantour.com
http://www.golfweb.com/tournaments/schedules
http://www.lpga.com/
http://www.officialworldgolfranking.com
http://www.pgatour.com/champions/stats/stat.109.2006.html
http://www.pgatour.com/r/stats/2006/109.html
http://www.pgatour.com/story/9797138/
http://www.pgatour.com/webcom/stats/stat.109.2006.html
https://en.wikipedia.org/wiki/2006_Champions_Tour
https://en.wikipedia.org/wiki/2006_Nationwide_Tour_graduates
https://en.wikipedia.org/wiki/2006_PGA_Tour

Rugby League Data Sources

http://stats.leagueunlimited.com/history.asp
http://www.superleague.co.uk/
www.nrl.com
www.playtheball.com
www.therfl.co.uk

Rugby Union Data Sources

http://en.wikipedia.org/wiki/Guinness_Premiership
http://www.avironbayonnaisrugby.fr/
http://www.bathrugby.com/
http://www.bo-pb.com/#
http://www.borderreivers.org/
http://www.bristolrugby.co.uk/2787_3090.php
http://www.cardiffblues.com/index.cfm
http://www.connachtrugby.ie/
http://www.gloucesterrugbyclub.com/
http://www.leicestertigers.com/3_8.php
http://www.leinsterrugby.ie/members/index.asp?locID=37anddocID=-1
http://www.london-irish-amateur.co.uk/
http://www.munsterrugby.ie/playerprofilelistpage/33.html
http://www.newcastle-falcons.co.uk/3_6.php
http://www.newportgwentdragons.com/squad.aspx
http://www.northamptonsaints.co.uk/
http://www.ospreysrugby.com/team_squad.php
http://www.quins.co.uk/default.ink?refid=
http://www.salesharks.com/
http://www.saracens.com/
http://www.scarlets.co.uk/
http://www.scottishrugby.org/pro-rugby/edinburgh-gunners/
http://www.scottishrugby.org/pro-rugby/glasgow-warriors/
http://www.sua-rugby.com/
http://www.tigers.co.uk/3_8.php
http://www.ulsterrugby.com/6_9.php
http://www.worcesterrugby.co.uk/
www.bettingzone.oddscheacker.com
www.erugby.com
www.rugbyheaven.smh.com.a

Tennis Data Sources

http://en.wikipedia.org/wiki/Association_of_Tennis_Professionals
http://en.wikipedia.org/wiki/Women's_Tennis_Association
http://www.atptennis.com
http://www.wtatour.com

12. Discrimination issues and related law
Klaus Vieweg and James A.R. Nafziger

INTRODUCTION

The great South African leader and amateur heavyweight boxer, Nelson Mandela, took sports seriously. He did so both for its own sake and as an instrument to achieve social justice in the era of apartheid. After he became President, he sought to employ sports as a means for unifying the races and projecting a progressive image of South Africa. But serious as he was about the role of sports, he famously observed that sport "laughs in the face of all types of discrimination."[1]

Discrimination in the sports arena is, of course, no laughing matter. It is one of the most serious issues of sports law. In recent years measures to combat discrimination in sports have been fundamental as the law has tried to keep pace with new issues and developments.[2]

Today, anti-discrimination laws govern sports universally but haphazardly. Gaps exist in the applicable laws and regulations as well as in their enforcement at both international and national levels. Although issues of unlawful discrimination against athletes arise largely in culturally bound contexts of national statutes, broader human rights law is clearly applicable. Indeed, an emerging theme of international sport law involves responses to acts of national, racial, and gender discrimination in particular. Thus, uniform prohibitions against unwarranted discrimination in sports competition, generated at the international level, are gradually replacing arguments protecting such discrimination on the basis of national natural cultural traditions.

In an era of open competition the anti-discriminatory regime of the Olympic Movement increasingly applies directly and indirectly to all athletes in major international competition. The regime's specific rules have also shaped anti-discriminatory measures by sports associations, organizations, and other stakeholders in sports at all levels of competition. The Olympic Charter, as the paramount authority in the Olympic Movement, provides that "[a]ny form of discrimination with regard to a country or a person on grounds of race, religion, politics, gender or otherwise is incompatible with belonging to the Olympic Movement."[3] Other provisions in the Charter commit the International Olympic Committee (IOC), in staging the Summer and Winter Games, "to encourage and support the promotion of women in sport at all levels and in all structures with a view to implementing the principle of equality of men and women."[4] Moreover, "[t]here may be no age limit for competitors in the Olympic Games other than as prescribed in the competition rules of an IF [International Federation] as approved by the IOC Executive Board."[5] Generally, the IOC's role is "to act against any form of discrimination affecting the Olympic Movement."[6]

This chapter surveys critical and emerging legal issues involving discrimination against athletes, with an emphasis on the applicable law. We draw primarily on examples from the United States, Germany, and the European Union.

The task of combating discrimination in the sports arena is problematic. For example, requests for special accommodations or a change in the rules of the game to compensate for the physical shortcomings of individual athletes present a tension between equality and the competitive ethos of sport.[7] One might argue that the very idea of special accommodations is inappropriate for sports competitions because these competitions, by their very nature, are intended to identify and reward the very best, rather than accommodate inequalities due to individual handicaps.

Biological disparities between men and women, whether anatomical or physiological, are a fundamental problem in the organization of sports and sports competition. Equality of opportunity is essential, but what form should it take? Three basic approaches are possible: (1) a special treatment approach, with a concomitant preference for the establishment of separate but equal athletic opportunities for women because of a concern that women will be crowded out by men if denied exclusive participation rights; (2) a formal equal treatment or integrating model whereby the only criterion for participation is an individual's ability, leading, inexorably, to mixed-gender teams and competitions; or (3) a combination of these two approaches.

Fixing a minimum age to protect the health of both young and aging athletes is also problematic. For example, a minimum age of 16 for female athletes to participate in international gymnastics competition seems to be in their best interest, but it is obviously just an arbitrary point on a sliding scale of age, given that calendar age and biological age are rarely identical. Thus, age limits may discriminate against athletes who have matured biologically before they are 16. Similarly, aging athletes may be biologically fit beyond the calendar age that precludes their continuing eligibility for competition.

SPECIFIC EXAMPLES

Disabilities

Traditionally, the principle of equal opportunity in sports distinguished between able-bodied and handicapped persons. In time, the concept of competition for disabled persons gained acceptance, thereby generating new types of competition – for example, wheelchair basketball – as well as the definition of disability categories. At the international level, certain competitions are pointing the way to the future – in particular, the Paralympics, which originated in 1960. Today, salient issues involve (1) the participation of handicapped persons using technological aids in able-bodied competitions; (2) the exclusion of athletes because of a risk of self-injury; (3) the participation of able-bodied athletes in contests for the disabled; and (4) the classification of disabled sports by type and degree of disability.

One of the key principles for protecting disabled athletes is the concept of mainstreaming so that individuals with disabilities can participate in the least restrictive environment. Thus, for example, the main statute in the United States to combat disability-related discrimination – the Americans with Disabilities Act (ADA) of 1990[8] – requires that "reasonable modifications" be made for qualified persons with disabilities. Under Title I of the ADA, the employment qualification standards may include "a requirement that an individual shall not pose a direct threat to the health and safety of other individuals in the workplace," while Title III declares that public accommodations are not obliged "to permit an individual to participate . . . where such individual poses a direct threat to the health and safety of others . . . that cannot be eliminated by a modification of policies, practices, or procedures or by the provision of auxiliary aids or services."

In England and Wales the Disability Discrimination Act (DDA) of 1995, as amended in 2005,[9] required reasonable adjustments to accommodate disabled individuals. Thereafter, the Disability Discrimination Act 2010 consolidated all earlier legislation. Similarly, EU law imposes a positive duty to make reasonable accommodation for disabled persons. Article 5 of Council Directive 2000/78, which is binding on Member States as to the objective to be achieved, provides that in order "to guarantee . . . equal treatment in relation to persons with disabilities, reasonable accommodation shall be provided . . . unless such measures would impose a disproportionate burden on the employer."[10]

Casey Martin

PGA Tour, Inc. v. Martin[11] is a highly publicized case concerning a disabled athlete, Casey Martin, who is a professional golfer from the state of Oregon in the United States. He is afflicted with Klippel-Trenaunay-Weber Syndrome, a degenerative circulatory disorder that obstructs the flow of blood from his right leg to his heart. Martin argued that he was entitled to use a golf cart in professional golf tournaments as a reasonable accommodation for his disability. The *Martin* case, which continues to govern legal issues surrounding disability and mainstreaming in sports both within and beyond the United States, marked the first stage in a growing controversy surrounding the integration of disabled athletes into mainstream competitive athletics.

The PGA Tour did not actually dispute that Martin had a disability for which the use of a golf cart was both a reasonable and a necessary accommodation. Rather, it defended its actions based on the ADA, which provides an exemption from the modification requirement if "the entity can demonstrate that making such modifications would fundamentally alter the nature of such goods, services, facilities ... or accommodations."[12] The case was then argued on the basis of whether waiving the PGA Tour rule requiring golfers to walk the course without the use of a cart would fundamentally alter the nature of the PGA Tour event.

The US Supreme Court held that there are two ways in which a rule change may fundamentally alter the activity in question: by changing "such an essential aspect of the game of golf that it would be unacceptable even if it affected all competitors equally," or by giving the disabled person not only equal access but "an advantage" over other competitors.[13] As regards the first part of the inquiry, the Court concluded that allowing the use of a cart would not change an essential aspect of the game of golf because "the essence of the game has been shot-making."[14]

The Supreme Court then inquired whether the modification in question – the use of a cart – would give Martin an unacceptable competitive advantage. The Court held that the ADA required the PGA to make an individualized assessment of Martin's claim. Relying on the trial court's finding that Martin "easily endures greater fatigue even with a cart than his able-bodied competitors do by walking,"[15] the Court found that using a cart did not give Martin an advantage and that it was the PGA's duty under the ADA to allow him to use one.

A forceful, thought-provoking dissent argued that

> the very *nature* of competitive sport is the measurement, by uniform rules, of unevenly distributed excellence. This unequal distribution is precisely what

determines the winners and losers – and artificially to "even out" that distribution, by giving one or another player exemption from a rule that emphasizes his particular weakness, is to destroy the game.[16]

Oscar Pistorius

South African sprinter Oscar Pistorius, having been born without fibula bones, had both legs amputated below the knee before his first birthday.[17] He nevertheless aspired to be a star athlete. He trained hard and competed impressively, using a series of prosthetic devices as he advanced in age and stature. Eventually, he reached the point of eligibility for major international competition, including the Olympics. The question then became whether he should be allowed to do so using a pair of J-shaped carbon fibre blades known as "Cheetahs" attached to his legs.[18]

Pistorius' bid for the 2008 Summer Olympic Games presented a possible conflict with a March 2007 amendment to the competition rules of the International Association of Athletics Federations (IAAF).[19] It banned the "use of any technical device that incorporates springs, wheels or any other element that provides the user with an advantage over another athlete not using such a device."[20] Undoubtedly, the artificial limbs used by Pistorius were technical devices and afforded him a performance advantage over and above anything he could have achieved without such limbs. The crucial question, however, was whether the artificial limbs overshot their permissible aim of compensating for his lack of lower legs by constituting an impermissible enhancement – what some have called "techno-doping."[21] A 2007 study conducted by German professor Gert-Peter Brüggemann for the IAAF found that Pistorius' limbs used 25 percent less energy than able-bodied runners needed to run at the same speed and that they led to less vertical motion combined with 30 percent less mechanical work for lifting the body.[22] Brüggemann concluded that Pistorius had considerable advantages over athletes without prosthetic limbs.[23] Based on these findings, the IAAF ruled against Pistorius' use of the Cheetahs in competitions conducted under the IAAF rules, including the 2008 Summer Olympics.[24]

In May 2008, however, the Court of Arbitration for Sport (CAS) reversed the ban, clearing the way for Pistorius to pursue his dream, although he ultimately failed to qualify for the Olympics. The Court concluded that there was insufficient evidence that the prosthetics device provided an overall advantage to Pistorius when concomitant disadvantages were taken into account.[25] What mattered, instead, was the whole package of benefit and detriment over the entire course of the race – the net status of performance, in other words – rather than the impact of the prosthetic limbs in isolation.[26] For instance, while Pistorius' prosthetics may return more impact energy than the human foot, as the Brüggemann study found,[27] this benefit might be offset by slower starts,[28] a handicap in rainy and windy conditions, and difficulty in navigating bends in the track. Similarly, just as Pistorius has the advantage of suffering no fatigue in his legs below his knees, so also is he subject to the disadvantage that only the muscles above his knees produce propulsive effects.[29]

Of course, the net effect of technical aids on a disabled athlete's overall performance is difficult if not impossible to quantify accurately, and any attempt to do so is bound to have significant resource implications.[30] Perhaps one reason why Martin has not set off a barrage of suits by disabled athletes seeking an accommodation to participate in mainstream sports is that, because of the ethos of competition, most disabled athletes do not want or accept any actual or perceived favors. To receive or to be suspected of receiving special aid devalues the athletic achievement. A related issue is whether disabled athletes should be allowed to participate in competitions for both able-bodied and disabled athletes.

Stephen Kuketz

In *Kuketz v. Petronelli*,[31] Stephen Kuketz, a wheelchair racquetball player, brought an action against a fitness club employee, alleging that the latter's refusal to permit him to compete, with substantial rule modifications, against able-bodied opponents in a competitive racquetball league violated federal and state anti-discrimination laws. The trial court entered summary judgment in favor of the employee. Kuketz appealed the decision. The appellate court held that allowing a wheelchair user two bounces, but his able-bodied opponents only one bounce, fundamentally altered the nature of the game of racquetball. Thus, no accommodation of Kuketz was required under Title III of the ADA. The essence of the game of racquetball is hitting a moving ball with a racquet before the second bounce. The modifications Mr. Kuketz sought created a new game with new strategies and rules. Thus, the fitness club was not required to modify its racquetball competitions to accommodate Kuketz.

To summarize: Under the ADA in the United States, the plaintiff bears the burden of proving that a requested modification is reasonable; once this burden is met, the defendant must make the modification unless it proves either that doing so would alter the fundamental nature of its business or that the requested modification poses a direct threat to the health or safety of others.

Age

The growing prowess of older athletes – for example, boxer Henry Maske's victorious return to the ring at age 43[32] – has prompted an important debate about age discrimination in sports, given a lack of applicable law in national legal systems. In the United States, the most comprehensive applicable federal statute dealing with age discrimination is the Age Discrimination in Employment Act of 1967 (ADEA),[33] which covers only employers of at least 20 persons over the age of 40. Its reach is further limited to team sports. In addition, both maximum and minimum age limits set by professional sports leagues and governing bodies as part of their eligibility requirements have been held to fall within the non-statutory labor exemption and thus to be immune from antitrust scrutiny, so long as they are the products of lawful collective bargaining processes between a sports organization and a players union. Moreover, the breadth of the defenses available would likely shield the employing sports organization from liability. For example, age differentiation is not unlawful per se, for example, where it is based on reasonable factors other than age, such as an aging athlete's diminishing speed, strength, and stamina, or where age is a bona fide occupational qualification reasonably necessary to the sport in question. Not surprisingly, given these limitations, most ADEA cases involve claims by coaches, support staff, and administrators rather than by professional athletes.

The situation is similar in Europe, where the right to equal treatment is fundamental. In its controversial *Mangold* decision,[34] the European Court of Justice (CJEU) interpreted the "general framework for equal treatment" established by Council Directive 2000/78 to prohibit age discrimination, which allegedly existed irrespective of the Directive as a principle of EU law. In Germany, the transposition of the Directive into national law through the General Equal Treatment Act[35] made clear that the traditional division of sports competition into classes according to age might be legal. As there is no special legislation for sports and, as yet, no case law, the following remarks are confined to the presentation of the problem that would have to be resolved according to the principles of proportionality and balancing of interests.

There have been repeated calls to introduce a maximum age limit for boxers as a health measure. Comparable restrictions have already been put in place for football/soccer referees. Likewise, minimum ages seek to protect the health and safety of young athletes, as in professional North American-style football in the United States and Canada. Ensuring an athlete's or official's fitness to carry out assigned duties could sufficiently justify this unequal treatment, given the difficulty of setting the "correct" age limit and the frequent divergence between an athlete's calendar and biological age.

Thus, both maximum and minimum age limits have become common in sports, as is the merging of several age groups into one peer group. Minimum age limits are particularly noteworthy. The physical and psychological impact of a competitive sport upon an underage competitor is regarded as unacceptable.[36] Such regulations, though they may appear enlightened, raise many questions, however. Is the minimum age scientifically grounded or is it based primarily upon tradition? Is it not contradictory that there is no minimum age for participation in training regimes, although these are frequently more punishing than the competitions themselves? And how does the minimum age in the sports setting compare with general labor protections for children and young people in the workplace?

Enforcement problems are serious insofar as the principle of equal treatment calls for strict and precise enforcement. Whether official documents should be regarded as more reliable than journalistic research – the controversy surrounding several extremely young looking Chinese gymnasts at the 2008 Olympic Games in Beijing come to mind – remains to be seen.

Udo Steiner,[37] formerly a judge of the German Constitutional Court, has addressed the duty of the state to protect the life and bodily integrity of children in competitive sports. His commendable conclusion is as follows:

> For the time being, children's high-level sports are constitutionally permissible. Under Article 2, para. 2 of the German Basic Law (*Grundgesetz*), the state should concentrate its efforts on promoting the physical and mental development of our children, particularly in the area of school sports. This active duty to protect the health of future generations takes precedence over the frequently desired watchdog role of the state in children's high-level sports which are not central to society.[38]

GENDER AND GENDER IDENTITY

Introduction

Sexism can occur in almost every aspect of sports. Restrictions on women's athletic opportunities run the gamut from rules excluding women from participation in certain sports events or teams to any failure to provide equal funding, prize money, locker rooms, practice times, competitive facilities, and sports equipment for female athletes. Specific examples include the longstanding absence of 5,000 meter and 10,000 meter running events for women in the Olympic Games[39] and of women's boxing before 2009, as well as the application of different game rules to women's sports contests, for example, a half-court rule in high school girls' basketball when a full-court rule operated for boys.[40]

Similarly, entire sports in international competition are limited to female athletes, thereby discriminating against male athletes. These sports include rhythmic gymnastics and synchronized swimming.

Constitutional guarantees provide a basic means of protecting athletes against discrimination on the basis of gender. For example, the Fourteenth Amendment to the United States Constitution provides that "no State shall make or enforce any law which shall ... deny to any person ... the equal protection of the laws." Once again, the predominant Equal Protection claim in the sports context involves women who challenge their exclusion from all-male teams. An action founded on the Equal Protection clause of the Fourteenth Amendment requires some "state action." The appropriate standard of review must then be determined. Courts apply different standards depending on the class of individuals alleging a violation and the interest affected by the classification.

In German law, eligibility claims are assessed on an individual basis. Such claims may derive from section 20, subsection 1 of the Act against Restraints of Competition or from sections 826 and 249 of the German Civil Code in conjunction with section 19, subsection 4 of the Act against Restraints of Competition. Its basis in the Constitution is the doctrine of the third-party effect of constitutional rights. According to this doctrine, conflicting constitutional rights – in this instance, freedom of association (Article 9, section 1 of the German Basic Law) and the right to equal treatment irrespective of gender (Article 3, section 1, subsection 1, para. 3 subsection para. 1) – must be taken account of, even in horizontal relationships between private parties and not just in vertical relationships between a private individual and the state. Any conflict must be resolved according to the principle of proportionality, with both rights being given maximum effect by balancing the interests involved.

The current situation in the European Union is similar. Article 19 of the 1992 Treaty on the Functioning of the European Union (TFEU) (formerly Article 13, EC) authorizes the Council to take measures to fight discrimination, and the CJEU has declared that the principles of equality of opportunity and non-discrimination are grounded in the common constitutional principles of the EU Member States (Article 6, section 2, TFEU). But the CJEU also regards freedom of association as a fundamental right arising from Article 11 of the European Convention on Human Rights and Fundamental Freedoms (ECHR) as well as the common constitutional principles of Member States. Therefore, the principle of proportionality must be considered in balancing freedom of association against contending freedoms and non-discrimination rules.

Pursuant to the CJEU's Meca-Medina ruling,[41] professionalized and commercialized sport activities are subject to the TFEU, especially its assurance of fundamental freedoms and the non-discrimination rule, as well as the prohibition of restraints on competition and misuse of a monopoly. It follows that a process of fair balancing that considers all affected interests and the specific conventions of sport, especially the central principle of equal competitive opportunities and fairness, is characteristic of the European as well as of the German approach. Questions such as whether a sport is considerably affected by gender-related differences and whether there is an inequality in performance between males and females due to their different and incommensurable physiques, techniques, or style are of the utmost importance. After balancing these interests, the court typically decides in favor of the sport associations, relying on arguments such as the monopolistic structure; the health of athletes; the number of athletes; the interest in limiting a particular program or competition; marketing opportunities; and the public interest in a gender-defined sport – for example, rhythmic gymnastics and synchronized swimming as exclusive sports for women. The reason there have been few court rulings on gender discrimination in sports in Germany may reside in the power of the associations. Attempts at achieving inclusion are more likely to succeed at the lower, association level of organization – for example, to provide for pre-adolescent, mixed-gender teams in football.

Caster Semenya

The gender confusion involving heavily muscled women athletes from Eastern Europe and the Soviet Union during the Cold War is now history, but issues remain regarding the testing and participation of mixed-gender or intersexual athletes, particularly those with hyperandrogenism.[42] The issue of gender-testing of women athletes, based on sampling of chromosomal material, dates back to the 1968 Olympic Games in Mexico City, when the testing was introduced in response to claims that some Eastern European athletes were either men disguised as women or women transformed by testosterone and steroids. Once barred from women's events, transsexuals are now eligible for gender reclassification when they produce evidence of sex-reassignment surgery and post-operative hormone replacement therapy.

South Africa's Caster Semenya, the world champion in the women's 800 meter run at the 2009 World Athletics Championships in Berlin,[43] generated enormous publicity when laboratory testing revealed an unusually high level of male hormones in her system.[44] Semenya's unusual appearance and a significantly improved performance of over eight seconds within one year, however, led to questions about her gender. As a result, the IAAF ordered a medical examination during the World Championships in order to clarify her gender. Although similar cases had already arisen, the athletes concerned had been given the opportunity to end their careers out of the public eye. In Semenya's case, though, her gender was questioned by the General Secretary of the IAAF at a press conference after the final of the 800-meters race.

In order to clarify gender, a laborious series of examinations is necessary. In South Africa, in particular, the gender test ordered by the IAAF, which was apparently performed unbeknownst to Semenya, was heavily criticized amid accusations of discrimination, racism, and neocolonial behavior by the IAAF. After the World Championships, it emerged that Athletics South Africa (ASA) had already cast doubt upon Semenya's gender and had already carried out a gender test.

The case of Caster Semenya prompted efforts to establish guidelines for gender classification. As a result, new IAAF rules on hyperandrogenism provide both a process for expert review of such cases and rules governing acceptable levels of androgen and countermanding androgen resistance.[45] During the same period of time WADA, the World Anti-Doping Agency, developed provisions for therapeutic-use exemptions applicable to testosterone-deficient males.[46] A contending view has argued against any tests to verify gender.[47]

Women Ski Jumpers

Several world-class women ski jumpers brought a civil action in the courts of British Columbia, Canada, claiming that the Vancouver Organizing Committee of the 2010 Winter Games had violated Canada's Charter of Rights and Freedoms. Their claim was based on the Committee's routine implementation of a decision by the IOC to bar women ski jumpers from the Winter Games. In reaching a final judgment, the British Columbia Court of Appeal[48] first upheld findings of the provincial Supreme Court[49] that the gender-based bar to participation was, indeed, discriminatory; that the organizing committee's planning, organizing, financing, and staging of the 2010 Games was tantamount to a governmental activity under a Canadian constitutional test of an ascribed activity; and that the organizing committee was therefore subject to the anti-discrimination provisions of Canada's Human Rights Charter in making all local arrangements within its control for the Winter Games.

The courts held, however, that the organizing committee, in its contractual relationship with the IOC, could not control the selection of sports or sports events in the program; it therefore had no discretion to allow women's ski jumping. The critical decision-maker was a non-party to the action, namely the IOC, to which the Charter did not apply. The class action brought by the women ski jumpers therefore failed. Although the decision seems technically reasonable in the context of a conflict between national and international authority and fully in conformity with the authority vested in the IOC under international sports law, it seems reasonable to ask whether the outcome was fair. Eventually, the IOC agreed to include women's ski jumping, beginning with the 2014 Winter Games in Sochi.

Sexual Orientation and Transsexuality

Discriminatory measures include those involving not only gender per se and gender identity, but also sexual orientation. Gay, lesbian, and transgender athletes often face significant targeting, baiting, and discrimination. If no specific legal provisions outlaw discrimination on the basis of sexual orientation, a question may arise whether protection can be afforded by laws prohibiting discrimination on the basis of gender. Anti-discrimination protection for gay, lesbian, and transsexual athletes remains the exception, rather than the rule.[50] In the European Union and Germany, the situation is the same as for sex discrimination. The ECHR, for instance, explicitly prohibits sexual-orientation-based discrimination. In addition, Article 3 § 1 of the German Constitution requires that like things be treated alike. This problem might arise, for example, if a same-sex couple wishes to participate in competitions which are traditionally mixed, such as pairs skating or ice dancing, or if a couple insisted on having separate same-sex competitions. Under the balancing of interests approach discussed above, these claims would likely fail.[51]

In the United States, no federal laws expressly protect athletes from discrimination or harassment on the basis of sexual orientation,[52] although a proposed federal statute, the Employment Non-Discrimination Act, would have prohibited discrimination on that basis in employment relationships. Protection at the state level is patchy. Some states have chosen to extend their sex-based civil rights protections to sexual orientation and gender identity, but many have not.[53] The existing case law has tended to focus on the Equal Protection clause, Title VII of the Civil Rights Act, and Title IX of the Education Amendments as possible bases for protecting homosexual athletes against at least some kinds of discrimination based on sexual orientation.

Transgender athletes pose a dilemma in some contexts. In gender-affected sports, where sex-related differences in strength, oxygen transport in the blood, and power-to-weight ratio can affect performance, the two sexes usually compete separately to ensure fair play. To enforce this separation and to prevent men from passing themselves off as women, the IOC once required a mandatory gender verification test, using various strategies ranging from visual inspection of genitalia to chromosomal analysis for all females competing in the Olympics.[54]

The existence of separate men's and women's divisions in sports competition poses a dilemma for post-operative male-to-female and female-to-male transsexuals who wish to participate. In the case of male-to-female transsexuals, especially those whose reassignment surgery took place after puberty, there is concern about a potential competitive advantage as these athletes have been influenced by performance-enhancing hormones during their pre-operative life. The popular belief is that male-to-female transsexuals retain the athletically advantageous male physical characteristics. To the contrary, castration, involving removal of the gonadal source of testosterone, and estrogen therapy, cause a reduction in skeletal muscle mass and in blood hemoglobin. While the larger male skeletal bone mass remains, it is now being powered by a smaller skeletal muscle mass, which decreases the power-to-weight ratio. Female-to-male transsexuals undergoing testosterone therapy risk exclusion by the prevailing anti-doping rules, although some sports may permit the athlete to obtain a medical waiver.

In addressing the issue of classifying transgender athletes for competition, the generally unappealing options include total exclusion, rigid assignment to birth sex, and the establishment of separate transsexual divisions and competitions. A more meaningful route might be to use body-based classification schemes, such as weight, height, and body mass, of the sort required in boxing.[55] The policy preference, in recent years, has been to permit transgender athletes to compete as their "corrected" rather than their birth gender. In 2004, for instance, the IOC announced that it would permit transsexual athletes to compete in their acquired gender if the athlete's reassignment surgery took place before puberty or, if after puberty, whenever hormone therapy has been given long enough to minimize any gender-related advantages.[56] The same year, the British Parliament passed the Gender Recognition Act,[57] which prohibits discrimination based on transsexual status but allows prohibitions and restrictions in gender-affected sports where these are necessary to secure fair competition or the safety of competitors.[58]

Race

Past discrimination in Germany and the United States
In the past, discrimination due to race and ethnic origin in sports was a serious threat to organized sports and the rights of athletes. The fate of

Jewish sports in Germany after Hitler's *Machtübernahme* in 1933 mirrored the fate of the Jewish people in the Third Reich.[59] Two Jewish sports umbrella associations with their affiliated sports clubs and associations served as a rallying point for 20,000 athletes who were excluded from other clubs and associations or were forced to leave them (*"Arier-Paragraph"*). Jewish sports clubs and associations were subject to fluctuating political interference. They were discriminated against in their use of sports arenas, being forced to register sports events at the local police station 48 hours before they began.

In 1936, the USOC threatened to boycott the Berlin Olympics if Jewish athletes were not included in the German pool of participants. The imminent boycott by the United States[60] played a positive, though minor, role. For example, the Jewish high jumper Gretel Bergmann was invited to take part in the German training camp but not in the Games themselves, and the National Socialist sports body refused to recognize her high jump record. After 73 years, the case of Gretel Bergmann resurfaced, and her story became the subject of a feature film.[61] Later, due to emigration, the number of Jewish sports club members declined and, unfortunately, with the so-called *Reichspogromnacht* of 1938, sports open to Jews in Germany ceased.

In the United States, minority athletes also experienced discrimination and exclusion. During the early years of professional and collegiate sports, a period extending from the Civil War to the early 1900s, blacks were allowed to participate, but they were subject to taunts and physical attacks flowing from racial discrimination. These early years of inclusion were followed by a period of segregation during which formal and informal rules excluded blacks from participating in sports alongside whites at both amateur and professional levels. It was not until the 1950s and 1960s that professional leagues and college sports were finally desegregated, although other forms of race discrimination persisted. Protests and boycotts were used to draw attention to this type of discrimination and to provoke political action. For example, at the 200-meters presentation ceremony during the 1968 Olympics in Mexico City, Tommie Smith and John Carlos, their clenched fists encased in black gloves, publicized the Black Power Movement that was directed against racial discrimination in the United States. In the aftermath of their protest, the USOC excluded them from the Olympic Games for violating the cardinal rule against political protests at the Games.

A robust anti-race-discrimination framework has been put in place composed, inter alia, of strict scrutiny review under the Fourteenth Amendment as well as federal statutes outlawing race discrimination in employment, federally funded programs, and, in general, contracting.[62] In the European context, Article 19 of the Treaty on European Union (TEU) (ex: Article 13 EC) – as implemented through Council Directive 2000/43[63] and transposing legislation in the various Member States – provides robust protection against discrimination based on racial or ethnic origin.

Apartheid

The situation in South African sports during the apartheid era can be characterized as follows:[64] in contrast to other areas of life, apartheid in South African sports was not based on specific laws, but rather on tradition and general rules of apartheid. In any event, white and non-white athletes did not participate in sporting competitions together or against each another. Other countries were expected to respect this practice, and on this basis non-white athletes from abroad were also prohibited from competing against white athletes in South Africa. Invitations from abroad directed at non-white South African athletes were ignored. Thus, it was impossible for non-whites to represent South Africa on the sporting field, irrespective of their achievements.

International sports organizations, which responded with all measures at their disposal including the suspension and exclusion of South African teams, can claim to have played a significant part in abolishing apartheid. Of particular note were the exclusion of the South African Table Tennis Association from the International Table Tennis Federation (ITTF) in 1956, the suspension (1961) and finally the exclusion (1976) of the whites-only Football Association of South Africa (FASA) by the Federation of International Football Associations (FIFA) and, above all, the exclusion of the South African Olympic Committee and, hence, South African athletes, from participation in the Olympic Games in line with the Olympic Charter. In 1976, many African countries boycotted the Olympic Games after the New Zealand Rugby National Team competed in South Africa.

The United Nations was instrumental in fighting apartheid, including its application to sports in South Africa. From 1968 to 1984, the UN General Assembly passed several resolutions that appealed to Member States to cancel any sporting relations with South Africa and with South African sports associations practicing apartheid. Beginning in 1971, this request was addressed not only to countries and sports associations, but also to individual athletes. Countries were requested in particular to exert influence on their national sports associations in order to achieve the exclusion of South African sports associations from international sports organizations. In their annual resolutions from 1979 to 1984, the UN General Assembly called on countries and sports organizations to give effect to a 1977 international declaration against the practice of apartheid in the sports arena. The media were also called upon to refuse to provide a platform for the aggrandizement of South African sports. The names of the athletes who maintained sporting relations with South Africa were published on a so-called "Blacklist" (secondary boycott). Between 1986 and 1993, the UN General Assembly passed annual resolutions to combat apartheid in sports.

In addition to these resolutions, an international agreement sponsored by the IOC against apartheid in sports was opened for signature in 1985 and came into force in 1988. No Western country signed the agreement, however. The parties agreed, among other things, to suspend sporting relations between their associations, teams, and single athletes with South Africa; that entry be denied to South African teams and athletes; that apartheid sports associations be excluded from international sports organizations; and, as a secondary boycott, that entry be denied to all associations, teams, and athletes that had participated in competition in South Africa insofar as this was compatible with the statutes of the pertinent organizations. The various worldwide boycott measures led to South Africa's isolation in international sports. This finally proved an effective means to achieve the abolition of race discrimination in sports – in a peaceful manner for the most part. Consequently, from 1986 onwards, South Africa allowed an increase in the number of mixed-race teams and spectators. As apartheid vanished, the return of South Africa to international sports was possible. The South African National Olympic Committee was readmitted to the Olympic Movement in time for the 1992 Games in Barcelona.

In the course of abolishing apartheid in South Africa, quotas were introduced that regulated the racial composition of national teams. These quotas were based on the overall racial composition of the South African population. Due to a resulting loss of quality, however, the quota rule was abolished for cricket in 2002 after several top white players had emigrated because of the quotas. The debate continued, however, with many speaking out in favor of reintroducing a quota system, although some labelled the system as mere "window-dressing."[65] Consequently, in 2013 a quota system was indeed reintroduced for cricket according to which each of the country's six teams must field at least one black African player in their starting line-up: any team fielding more than one black player is to receive a cash bonus.[66]

The South African government abolished the overall quota regime for rugby after the South African "Springboks" won the World Championship with 13 whites on a team of 15.[67] There has been no change in respect of the national team, the Currie Cup, or the Super Rugby competition, but a quota was reinstated for the third-tier Vodacom Cup competition at the beginning of the 2014 season.[68]

Religion

The attitudes of the various world religions toward sport differ. It is true that none of the major religions imposes a blanket ban on sports. Nor do the regulations of the main sporting organizations exclude any athletes from participating in sporting events on the basis of their religion. Indeed, the articles of association of the major national and international sporting organizations emphasize their neutrality in religious matters. The IOC even regards discrimination on the basis of religion as an infringement of the fundamental principles of the Olympics.[69] Religious obligations, however, can conflict with the exercise of sport, particularly in the professional arenas.

An early example of discrimination for religious reasons involved the 1960 Olympic boxing champion, Cassius Clay. In 1964 he converted to Islam and, during the Vietnam War, refused to comply with his draft into military service. As a priest of the religious society "Nation of Islam," he argued that he was entitled to refuse to perform military service[70] under his new name of Muhammad Ali. He was then stripped of his title as world champion in 1967, and his boxing license was revoked. Another conflict between sport and religion involved the Indian gymnast, Daldschit Singh, who participated in the 1970 World Championships. As a Sikh, Singh was forbidden from cutting his hair. But the regulations of the international association, the Fédération Internationale de Gymnastique (FIG), provided that points must be deducted from the performance of a competitor with long hair. Singh therefore had no other option but to compete with his hair covered by a turban.[71]

Muslim Athletes

The religious obligations and proscriptions which apply to Muslim athletes can interfere with their sporting performance or even result in their being unable to compete.[72] Particularly in professional sports, the observance of religious obligations, such as regular prayer and fasting during Ramadan, can make it very difficult if not impossible for Muslim athletes to carry out the obligations outlined in their contracts of employment.[73] Sports associations and teams may then avoid concluding contracts with Muslim athletes in order to escape any related hassle, or athletes may be sanctioned or possibly face termination of their contracts if they abide by their religious duties, thereby violating their professional duties. Whether contracts of employment can give rise to a duty on the part of Muslim athletes to advise their clubs that they must observe certain religious obligations, in particular the duty to fast, is a contentious issue.[74]

The regulation of clothing by sports associations may also cause problems. The applicable rules generally provide that the athletes' attire should facilitate the specific type of movement necessitated by the sport in question and that it should convey a uniform image. The adage of "sex sells" also encourages attractive clothing for the benefit of spectators and sponsors, for example, in beach volleyball.[75] By contrast, according to the precepts of Islam, female Muslims should cover their hair and bodies in public, excluding face and hands and, in some cases, forearms.[76] This explains why Muslim women seldom participate in international competitions in which the required clothing does not correspond with the precepts of the religion, either for reasons of practicality or because of binding association rules.[77] The imposition of Muslim clothing requirements in the sports arena is clearly a difficult problem with serious possible consequences of gender discrimination. Another problem involves a woman's engagement in sports in the presence of men (for example, spectators, trainers, or referees), even in clothing which is unobjectionable on a religious basis, if these men could possibly come into physical contact with the female athlete.[78]

FIFA forbids the display of religious symbols during football matches.[79] The Federation of Olympic Committees of Asia imposes sanctions upon athletes who use their clothing for the purpose of disseminating religious beliefs.[80] There are also countertrends, however. For example, the German Football Association is trying to water down FIFA's ban on religious symbols in order to render it possible for young Muslim girls to play football/soccer. The football association of the Australian state of Victoria has also anchored in its rules of competition the right of female Muslim footballers to wear a headscarf.[81]

A third area of possible conflict involves the prohibition of demonstrations of faith on the playing field, particularly of prayers. Thus, the Brazilian football team was cautioned by FIFA because its members prayed as a group on the soccer pitch. The Egyptian team, on the other hand, was not sanctioned when, in accordance with Muslim tradition, the players turned toward Mecca to pray in the middle of the football field. In this vein, it has been of interest how football associations reacted to David Beckham when he removed his shirt during play to reveal a tattoo, which appears on the right side of his body and portrays a grief-stricken Jesus Christ.[82]

Judo Observances

In Judo, a sport which has its roots in Shintoism, bowing is customary and, according to the rules, compulsory for all participants. The bowing takes place before stepping into the competition area and later before stepping onto the mat. Before competing, all contestants must bow en masse. In two cases brought by the same plaintiffs, courts in the United States and in Canada had to decide whether a judoka who refused to perform the bowing ritual could take part in competition. The plaintiffs, James and Leilani Akiyama and Jay Drangeid, were members of a club which did not practice bowing. When a Seattle tournament refused to allow the plaintiffs' team to participate without bowing, however, they filed a suit in a federal court, where they obtained a preliminary injunction in 1997 that prohibited the International Judo Federation and the national governing body from requiring them to bow. In a full hearing, the court ruled, however, that the plaintiffs must observe the ritual while participating in competitions.[83] In dismissing the 1997 injunction, the court wrote that "virtually any restriction or regulation imposed by a public accommodation could impinge on a person's religious beliefs."

The Akiyamas also sought relief in the British Columbia Human Rights Tribunal[84] in which they objected to the claims of Judo B.C. that contestants should bow to various areas and persons. The result was the same as in the United States. The Tribunal found that, contrary to the plaintiffs' claims, bowing in Judo was a cultural ritual and not a religious gesture. Furthermore, bowing to one's opponent was a gesture of courtesy and respect arising out of the philosophy of the sport. As such, it was a bona fide sporting requirement. Because bowing was not a religious practice, there was no need for Judo B.C. to accommodate the plaintiffs on grounds of religion.

CONCLUSION

Issues of discrimination in the sports arena and on the playing field are both important and vexing. On the one hand, discrimination on the basis of athletic merit or prowess is the essence of competition. Moreover, in international competition some discrimination on the basis of criteria other than athletic merit or prowess is not only acceptable, but essential to sports organization. Nationality is the prime example. On the other hand, discrimination on the basis of such generally immutable characteristics as gender, race, religion, and disability has become unacceptable.

As this study has shown, the trend toward equality of opportunity has been long and is still incomplete. Today, significant cultural norms and requirements still inhibit full equality of opportunity. Clubs and sports associations must help provide the impetus for greater equality and corresponding rules and requirements. To be sure, national and international laws are gradually providing the tools for reconciling cultural traditions with mandatory assurances of equality of opportunity for athletes. Above all, the sports-minded public must assume a central role in undertaking further reforms. Cultural factors will continue, of course, to be significant in determining their context and pace.

Ultimately, fairness is the core principle for addressing issues of discrimination, in the sense of both procedure and substance. The definition of fairness can, of course, be elusive and judgmental. But it is not so unsettled as to be ineffective. Quite the contrary is true in practice. On the basis of accepted attributes of fairness – impartiality, equity, good faith, coherence, and so on – the principle can be readily adapted to claims of unacceptable discrimination against athletes. Fairness will therefore be essential in the growth of a creditable regime of international sports law. The challenge is simply to take the principle seriously as guidance in further developing a viable framework for combating unacceptable discrimination in the sports arena.

NOTES

1. "Sport has the power to change the world. It has the power to inspire, it has the power to unite people in a way that little else does. It speaks to youth in a language they understand. Sport can create hope, where once there was only despair. It is more powerful than governments in breaking down racial barriers. *It laughs in the face of all types of discrimination.*" Nelson Mandela, Speech at the Inaugural Ceremony, Laureus Lifetime Achievement Award in Sports, Monte Carlo, Monaco (May 25, 2000) (emphasis added).
2. See generally James A.R. Nafziger, International Sports Law 121–126 (2d ed. 2004). The text draws upon Klaus Vieweg and Saskia Lettmaier, Anti-discrimination Law and Policy, in James A.R. Nafziger and Stephen F. Ross, Handbook on International Sports Law 258 (2011).
3. Fundamental Principles of Olympism, Olympic Charter, para. 5.
4. *Id.*, para. 7.
5. *Id.*, art. 43.
6. *Id.*, art. 2 (6).
7. Klaus Vieweg, Verbandsrechtliche Diskriminierungsverbote und Differenzierungsgebote, in Wuerttembergischer Fussball Verband E.V., Minderheitenrechte im Sport 71, 83 (2005).
8. 42 U.S.C. §12101–12213 (2012).
9. Disability Discrimination Act 1995 (Eng.).
10. Council Directive 2000/78, 2000 (establishing a general framework for equal treatment in employment and occupation).
11. 532 U.S. 661 (2001).
12. ADA, supra note 8, at § 12182(b)(2)(A)(ii).
13. 532 U.S. at 661, 682.
14. *Id.* at 683.
15. *Id.* at 690, quoting Martin v. PGA Tour, Inc., 994 F. Supp. 1242, 1252 (D. Or. 1998).
16. PGA Tour, Inc. v. Martin, 532 U.S. 661, 703–704 (2001) (Scalia, J., dissenting).
17. Pistorius was the gold medalist in the 200 meter run as well as the bronze medalist in the

100 meter run at the 2004 Summer Paralympics in Athens. In addition, he is the double amputee world record holder in the 100, 200, and 400 meter events. See, e.g., P. Charlish and S. Riley, Should Oscar Run?, 18 Fordham Intell. Prop., Media and Ent. L.J. 929 (2008).

18. M. Pryor, Oscar Pistorius Is Put Through His Paces to Justify His Right to Run, The Times (London), Nov. 20, 2007.

19. Some have suggested that this rule was introduced specifically to deal with the threat posed by Pistorius, an allegation vehemently denied by IAAF Council member Robert Hersh. Charlish and Riley, supra note 17, at 930.

20. IAAF Competition Rule 144.2(e) (2008).

21. See J. Longman, An Amputee Sprinter: Is He Disabled or Too-Abled?, N.Y. Times, May 15, 2007.

22. G-P., Brüggemann, A. Arampatzis, F. Emrich, and W. Potthast, Biomechanics of Double Transtibial Amputee Sprinting Using Dedicated Sprinting Prostheses, Sports technol., 1, No. 4–5, at 220, 226 (2008); BBC Sport, Blade Runner Handed Olympic Ban, Jan. 14, 2008.

23. Studie beendet Olympiatraum von Pistorius, Welt Online, Dec. 19, 2007.

24. See IAAF Call Time on Oscar Pistorius' Dream, Daily Telegraph, Jan. 10, 2008.

25. The evidential burden of proving the "advantage" in terms of IAAF rule 144.2(e) is on the sports association which imposed the suspension. The applicable standard the association must apply to prove that the user of a prosthesis has an overall net advantage over other athletes not using such devices is the "balance of probability." Pistorius v. IAAF, CAS 2008/A/1480, para. 92.

26. The IAAF did not ask Professor Brüggemann to determine whether the use of the prosthesis provided an overall net advantage or disadvantage. Pistorius v. IAAF, CAS 2008/A/1480, para. 85. The only purpose of the determination was the question of whether Pistorius' use of the prosthesis provided him with any kind of advantage.

27. Studie beendet Olympiatraum von Pistorius, Welt Online, Dec. 19, 2007.

28. It was observed that Pistorius was slower than other able-bodied runners off the starting blocks and during the acceleration phase, but faster during the second and third 100 meters. Pistorius v. IAAF, CAS 2008/A/1480, at 41.

29. Another advantage of a prosthesis is the mental impact on the other athletes who have to start a race next to an amputee. It is an open question whether this is so and whether a possible psychological obstacle of the able-bodied athletes may be considered, given the principle of non-discrimination.

30. The tests conducted on Pistorius cost about €30,000. See Charlish and Riley, supra note 17, at 939. If funding such tests is left to the individual athlete, challenges are unlikely to be brought. If sports governing bodies are left to pick up the tab, on the other hand, the financial burden on them might also be immense. The respective sports association should, however, regulate the process by which a disabled sportsperson who uses a prosthetic device can take part in competitions for able-bodied sportspeople in a way that guarantees safety and saves money. Thus, the sports association should compile a list of all institutions to be considered in the necessary studies, enumerate all factors to be investigated, and set out the procedure to be followed in the event that a disabled sportsperson makes an administrative appeal. A. Chappel, Running Down a Dream: Oscar Pistorius, Prosthetic Devices, and the Unknown Future of Athletes with Disabilities in the Olympic Games, 10 NC JOLT Online Ed. 1, at 16, 26 (2008).

31. Kuketz v. Petronelli, 821 N.E. 2d 473 (Mass. 2005).

32. See Maske Besiegt Hill, Süddeutsche Zeitung, May 17, 2010.

33. 29 U.S.C. §§ 621–634 (2012).

34. Werner Mangold v. Rüdiger Helm (2005), Case C-144/04, All E.R. (D) 287.

35. Allgemeines Gleichbehandlungsgesetz, Aug. 14, 2006 (F.R.G.).

36. Especially in gymnastics an argument in favor of a minimum age is lost insofar as prepubertal physical conditions are optimal.

37. Udo Steiner is one of Germany's leading sports lawyers. For selected works, see Peter J. Tettinger and Klaus Vieweg, Gegenwartsfragen des Sportrechts (2004).
38. Udo Steiner, Kinderhochleistungssport in Deutschland – Thesen Zur Verfassungslage, in Peter J. Tettinger and Klaus Vieweg, Gegenwartsfragen Des Sportrechts 154, 176 (2004).
39. This practice sparked off a lawsuit in 1984, when a group of women runners sued the IOC, the United States Olympic Committee (USOC), and the International Amateur Athletics Federation (IAAF), basing their claim on a violation of their constitutional right to equal protection. Martin v. International Olympic Committee, 740 F.2d 670 (9th Cir. 1984). The bid to force the 1984 Olympic organizers to include these two women's track events failed. It was not until the Barcelona Olympic Games in 1992 that these events were added to the Olympic menu. See J. Little, Running Against the Wind: Sex Discrimination in High School Girl's Cross Country, 76 UMKC L. Rev. 711 (2007–2008).
40. In Dodson v. Arkansas Activities Ass'n, 468 F. Supp. 394 (D. Ark. 1979), the court struck down this rule, reasoning that paternalistic tradition alone was insufficient justification for the different rules.
41. Case C-519/04P, July 18, 2006.
42. See Hayden Opie, Medico-Legal Issues in Sport: The View from the Grandstand, 23 Sydney L. Rev. 375, 396 (2001).
43. Frankfurter Allgemeine Zeitung, August 21, 2009, at 30.
44. See Alice Dreger, Seeking Simple Rules in Complex Gender Realities, N.Y. Times, Oct. 25, 2009, at SP8; Alice Dreger, Swifter, Higher, Stronger? Science Adds a Variable, N.Y. Times, Sept. 13, 2009, at 10.
45. See IAAF Adopts New Testing Rules, Statesman Journal (Salem, OR.), April 13, 2011, at 2B.
46. See Dreger, supra note 44, Sept. 13, 2009.
47. See Samiha Dabholkar, A Need to Intercede? The International Olympic Committee and Intersexuality, 13 Int'l Sports L.J., April 2013, at 55.
48. Sagen v. Vancouver Org. Comm [2009] B.C.C.A. 522.
49. Sagen v. Vancouver Org. Comm [2009] B.C.J. 1393.
50. Michael Cozzillio and Robert L. Hayman, Jr., Sports and Inequality 845 (2004); Klaus Vieweg, supra note 7, at 87 et seq.
51. See earlier text in the introduction of the section "Gender and Gender Identity."
52. Title VII of the Civil Rights Act of 1964, for example, only applies to race, color, religion, sex, or national origin (42 U.S.C. § 2000e et seq.), with the term "sex" held to refer only to membership in a class delineated by gender, not by sexual affiliations. Simonton v. Runyon, 232 F.3d 33, 36 (2nd Cir. 2000).
53. J. Pilgrim, D. Martin, and W. Binder, Far from the Finish Line: Transsexualism and Athletic Competition, 13 Fordham Intell. Prop. Media & Ent. L.J. 495, 544 (2003).
54. Id. at 499.
55. Y.L.A. Shy, "Like Any Other Girl": Male-to-Female Transsexuals in Professional Sports, Sports Law J. 95, 105 (2007).
56. Id. 108–109.
57. Gender Recognition Act 2004 (Eng.).
58. [2004] ch. 7, § 19.
59. For discussion, see Klaus Vieweg, Gleichschaltung und Führerprinzip – Zum recht-lichen Instrumentarium der Organsiation des Sports im Dritten Reich, Recht und Unrecht im Nationalsozialismus, at 244, 252 (P. Salje ed. 1985).
60. See Judith Holmes, Olympiad 1936: Blaze of Glory for Hitler's Reich 39–42 (1971).
61. Frankfurter Allgemeine Zeitung, Sept. 10, 2009, at 34; id. Nov. 28, 2009, at 31; The German Mädel, 35 Der Spiegel 112 (2009).
62. Titles VI (federally funded programs) and VII (employment) of the Civil Rights Act of 1964, 42 U.S.C. §§ 2000d, 2000e-2(a); 42 U.S.C. § 1981 (contracting).
63. Official Journal L 180, 19/07/2000 P. 0022–0026.

64. See Andreas Wax, Internationales Sportrecht – Unter besonderer Berücksichtigung des Sportvölkerrechts (2009); Andreas Krumpholz, Apartheid und Sport – Rassentrennung und Rassendiskriminierung im südafrikanischen Sport sowie Sportboykott Südafrikas, passim (1991).
65. See Lee Rodganger and Sapa, Sport quota debate in spotlight, Daily News, Nov. 25, 2011; BBC Sport, South Africa remove racial quotas, Nov. 7, 2007.
66. See Susan Njanji, Tackling Race Issues in White-dominated Cricket, Rugby, Mail & Guardian, Oct. 29, 2013.
67. Frankfurter Allgemeine Zeitung, Nov.10, 2007, at 33.
68. Accordingly, each team representing all or part of a South African province must have a minimum number of black players: seven on each match-day 22-player squad, two of which must be forwards, and seven of which must be among the starting 15. See Njanji, supra note 66.
69. See Olympic Charter, para. 5, supra note 3.
70. See Harald Krämer and Fritz K. Heering, Muhammad Ali 52 (2001).
71. 22 Der Spiegel 129 (1971).
72. See Niloufar Hoevels, Rechtsprobleme muslimischer Sportler in Deutschland, in Perspektiven des Sportrechts 63, 67 (K. Vieweg ed. 2005).
73. For an instructive overview, see Niloufar Hoevels, Islam und Arbeitsrecht 248 (2003).
74. Frankfurter Allgemeine Zeitung, Oct. 15, 2009, at 32 (FSV Frankfurt).
75. Official Beach Volleyball Rules, no. 5.1.
76. Hoevels, supra note 72, at 74.
77. A striking example was provided by the Bahrain track and field athlete, Rakia Al Gassra, who, in the heats of the 100 meter run in the Sydney Olympic Games, wore a long-sleeved shirt, long trousers, and a headscarf. Photographs of female Muslim athletes are printed in Hoevels, supra note 72 at 263.
78. The Vice-president of the Iranian National Olympic Committee, Abdolreza Sayar, provided as an example the Olympic combat sport, Taekwondo. In one match, the referee grabbed and raised the arm of an Iranian athlete as a sign of her victory, see Frankfurter Allgemeine Zeitung, Jan. 3, 2008, at 27.
79. FIFA Equipment Regulations, no. 10.2. See also the decision of the International Football Association Board: "The team of any player whose compulsory basic equipment displays political, religious or personal messages will be penalised by the host of the competition in question or by FIFA."
80. Frankfurter Allgemeine Zeitung, Dec. 12, 2006, at 37.
81. Frankfurter Allgemeine Zeitung, March 5, 2008, at 32.
82. See Frankfurter Allgemeine Zeitung, Jan.1, 2010, at 26.
83. Akiyama v. U.S. Judo Inc., 181 F.Supp.2d 1179 (W.D., 2002).
84. Akiyama v. Judo B.C. (No. 2) [2002] 43 C.H.R.R., D/425, 2002 BCHRT 27.

13. Hiding in plain sight: sexual harassment in sport
Terry Engelberg and Stephen Moston

INTRODUCTION

Sexual harassment is a social issue that can evoke highly polarized attitudes (Engelberg & Moston, 1997). To some it is a serious problem, requiring draconian actions with implications for all personal relationships within the workplace. Yet to others, it is an issue that is both trivial and humorous. These differing positions are, in part, due to the different ways in which we understand what is meant by sexual harassment. Over the last few decades, the media have compounded this confusion, with stories being featured more for their titillation value rather than their actual significance or representativeness. While these problems are characteristic of many other social issues, they are especially significant within the context of sexual harassment since it is still a relatively new phenomenon.

In this chapter we examine the issue of sexual harassment in sport. To date, there has been limited research on sexual harassment in the context of sport. This is particularly troubling as the extensive body of research from other settings, such as the workplace and within academia, suggests that the sporting world has many of the features that promote a culture where sexual harassment can occur (Fasting, Chroni, & Knorre, 2014; Tomlinson & Yorganci, 1997). For example, skewed gender ratios (e.g., an absence of women in managerial positions), sexualized atmospheres (e.g., scantily clad cheerleaders), and organizational power (e.g., the power held by coaches) have all been found to influence the incidence of sexual harassment. The problem of sexual harassment in sport runs so deep that even students of sporting disciplines (e.g., sports sciences) are at a greater risk of experiencing sexual harassment than students from other disciplines (Fasting, Chroni, Hervik, & Knorre, 2011).

THE ORIGINS OF SEXUAL HARASSMENT AS A SOCIAL ISSUE

Sexual harassment has been described as an issue with a long past, but only a short history (Engelberg & Moston, 1997). For example, modern audiences would recognize the experiences of Fantine in Victor Hugo's 1862 novel "Les Misérables," who is driven to the streets after rejecting the advances of a foreman, as sexual harassment. Although this is a fictionalized account, similar experiences have been the reality for many workers for centuries. However, before sexual harassment was defined, such behaviors were more likely to be accepted as simply part of working life, particularly for women.

To understand sexual harassment requires an examination of the changing patterns of workforces and education settings within industrialized countries over the last century. An increasing number of women have entered the workforce and higher education and have gradually moved towards equality in employment conditions. This has caused friction with the established (male) workforce, who, threatened by change, have begun to discriminate against newcomers. Sex is the most salient dimension by which we categorize people – there is evidence that children become aware of sex differences and start behaving in a sex-typed way before they are even able to speak (Ruble, Martin, & Berebaum, 2006). Consequently, when threatened by a new influx of workers, the male workforce began to discriminate against newcomers on the basis of their sex.

Within most historical frameworks sexual harassment is seen as an aspect of sexual discrimination against women, and parallels can be drawn with other forms of discrimination, such as racial or religious discrimination. With all such discrimination a single salient characteristic of the newcomer is identified and used as a basis for distinguishing between "us" and "them". These considerations mean that sexual harassment has been conceptualized, at least originally, as a problem for women. However, because within legal frameworks sexual harassment is construed as a form of discrimination, women as well as men can be victims of sexual harassment. This is applicable in every context, including sport (Title IX in the USA: US Department of Education, 1979).

The term sexual harassment was first employed in the 1970s, coming to widespread attention after the publication of the books *Sexual Shakedown* (Farley, 1978) and *Sexual Harassment of Working Women* (MacKinnon, 1979). These two publications were to prove highly significant, elevating the topic to that of a serious social problem. MacKinnon's book is particularly significant because it provided not only an early definition of the term, but also an important distinction between two main types of sexual harassment: *quid pro quo* (where a threat or bribery are implied) and *hostile environment*. This distinction shaped future guidelines on sexual harassment, such as those of the US Equal Employment Opportunity Commission (EEOC) and Australia's Human Rights and Equal Opportunity Commission (HREOC), renamed the Human Rights Commission in 2008.

Defining Sexual Harassment

Despite three decades of legislation and some well-publicized cases, there is still no clear consensus as to what sexual harassment is. Even though the term is widely used, interpretations of what is meant by sexual harassment vary considerably. Some of the various interpretations can be observed at three main levels.

First, at the national and cultural level, there are differences in how sexual harassment is defined across countries. Differing perspectives on the topic, as well as different legal systems, inevitably determine that a definition from one country is unlikely to be wholly endorsed in another. Most importantly, cultural variations will also have an important influence on acknowledging whether sexual harassment exists as a social or organizational problem or is seen as part of the normal courtship process (Fasting et al., 2011; Fasting et al., 2014).

Second, there are also differences between organizations: behavior that is tolerated in one workplace, educational institution, or sport setting is unacceptable in another. This may be evident in several ways, such as differing policies between organizations in the same geographical region or the same type of industry. Even within a single organization, inconsistencies can be found. For example, language that is permitted on the field or the oval is not acceptable in the offices of management or the boardroom.

Third, there are differences at the individual level. One person may find a behavior undesirable and distressing, but to another the same behavior may be regarded as harmless fun. Psychological research on attitudes towards sexual harassment has shown that in interpreting and defining behaviors as sexual harassment, individuals take into account a large number of factors that are not stipulated in governmental or organizational policies, such as prior relationships between the parties concerned.

Definitions of sexual harassment in sport are usually based on definitions in the workplace, and these in turn are generally framed within sex discrimination policy and legislation. For example, in the USA, the Women's Sports Foundation (2011) offers the following definition:

> Sexual harassment consists of unwelcome sexual advances, requests for sexual favors and other verbal or physical conduct of a sexual nature and can occur separately or be a part of abuse. Romantic and/or sexual relationships between coaches and athletes are regarded as an abuse of professional ethics, status and power.

Despite its implicit acknowledgement that sexual harassment can happen to both males and females and between those of equal organizational power, the Women's Sport Foundation highlights sexual harassment's effect on females and those of lower power (athletes). A similar but broader definition is provided by the Australian Womensport and Recreation Association (AWRA) (2009).

> Discrimination can take the following forms:
>
> a.   Direct Discrimination – This means treating someone less favorably than you would treat others in the same circumstances.
> b.   Indirect Discrimination – This occurs when a job requirement or condition is applied equally to all, which has a disproportionate and detrimental affect [*sic.*] on one sector of society, because fewer from that sector can comply with it and the requirement cannot be justified in relation to the job.
> c.   When decisions are made about an individual, the only personal characteristics taken into account will be those which, as well as being consistent with relevant legislation, are necessary to the proper performance of the work involved.
>
> Harassment is described as inappropriate actions, behavior, comments or physical contact that is objectionable or causes offence to the recipient. It may be directed towards people because of their gender, appearance, race, ethnic origin, nationality, age, sexual preference, a disability, or some other characteristic. AWRA is committed to ensuring that its employees and volunteers are able to conduct their activities free from harassment or intimidation.

Not surprisingly, there is a considerable overlap between organizational and legislative definitions. Generally, most definitions feature the terms unwanted, unsolicited, and of a sexual nature and a clause stating that a reasonable person would consider the behavior to be sexual harassment. This means that a reasonable person would find the behaviors objectionable or offensive. This is intended to prevent abuses of legislation on the part of the recipient. As the EEOC (1990) compliance manual states: ". . . the law should not serve as a vehicle for vindicating the petty slights suffered by the hypersensitive."

Many also address the distinction between *quid pro quo* (such as a coach making sexual demands of an athlete in return for privileges) and *hostile environment* harassment (such as a coach's crude behavior). However, not all organizational definitions are equivalent. Some organizations may adopt a more stringent policy than is required by law, perhaps as part of a wider policy on harassment and inappropriate behaviors. For example, the Women's Sports Foundation (2011) definition addresses what appear to be consensual relationships between coaches and athletes as problematic: these relationships are seen as an abuse of ethics, status, and power.

Most clubs and sporting organizations have adopted definitions of harassment (which may include sexual harassment specifically). As previously noted, inconsistencies between definitions do exist, and this has implications for the assessment of the extent of sexual harassment.

How Common Is Sexual Harassment?

Sexual harassment is still a persistent and widespread concern regardless of how it is defined. However, determining just how persistent and widespread is a challenging task. Even though there have been a large number of surveys and studies in various contexts, a true incidence figure is still lacking.

There are two main survey methodologies available to examine the extent of sexual harassment. First, researchers can use questionnaires or surveys. These may specifically address sexual harassment or contain questions on this topic which may form part of a wider ranging study, for example, on other issues such as general discrimination or abuse.

The reliability of incidence surveys is highly questionable, and comparisons between organizations, associations, and even within a single club are usually not possible. To compound the problem, many surveys start with the single question: "Have you been sexually harassed?" This is clearly an unreliable way to obtain much needed incidence data. For example, a person may freely admit they experienced unwanted sexual attention, such as suggestive comments, but decline to label it as sexual harassment (Engelberg & Moston, 1997).

Other forms of self-report research include telephone surveys and interviews or focus group discussions. Qualitative methods provide a clearer picture of how the recipient frames and perceives the behaviors.

Second, researchers may examine archival records, such as records of formal complaints or grievances. Such a procedure is less intrusive than a questionnaire based study or an interview, but it is prone to a number of major shortcomings, not least of which is the possibility that those responding under-report sexual harassment.

One further problem in attempting to determine the frequency of sexual harassment is that organizations may be reluctant to discuss such a sensitive issue. If a study were to show a high incidence of sexual harassment in a particular organization, despite a commitment to eliminating the problem, bad publicity could still be generated for the organization concerned. Consequently, when organizations conduct in-house incidence studies, the results may not be made public.

Such concerns greatly hinder the efforts of researchers. The extent to which organizations avoid the issue of sexual harassment was noted by US researcher Sandroff (1988), who found that only 9 percent of the Fortune 500 companies included questions about sexual harassment on employee surveys and only 4 percent raised it during exit interviews. There is no evidence available to establish whether this has changed in the intervening years.

In the context of sport, research into sexual harassment is very limited. Although sporting regulatory bodies provide guidelines (e.g., the Australian Sports Commission, UK Sport, and others), there is both a paucity of systematic collection of incidence data and a lack of systematic academic research into both sexual harassment and other forms of sexual abuse in sport. This situation could be due to inertia in the sport and recreation industry regarding the establishment of regulatory practices for a problem that many are reluctant to acknowledge (Brackenridge, 1997; Volkwein-Caplan, Schnell, Devlin, Mitchell, & Sutera, 2002).

Fasting et al. (2014) report that prevalence rates of both sexual harassment and sexual abuse in sport settings fluctuate between 2 and 50 percent. In part, this reflects the specificity of samples featured in studies (Fasting, Brackenridge, & Walseth, 2007). For example, some studies have focused on male harassment of females, while others have been even more restrictive, such as harassment of female athletes by male coaches or female–female harassment (Sand, Fasting, Chroni, & Knorre, 2011; Volkwein-Caplan et al., 2002).

As with studies of sexual harassment in the workplace, studies of sexual harassment in sport have found strong differences in the perceptions of males and females. For example, in 1998 the Australian Sports Commission (2001) surveyed the opinions and experiences of approximately 300 athletes and administrators. The study found that there was a dramatic difference in how males and females perceived harassment. In general, 20 percent more males than females considered harassing behavior as part of sport. One of the most dramatic differences between males and females was with respect to uninvited touching: 100 percent of females considered this behavior as harassment, while only 22.5 percent of males did. Further, nearly one in four males considered it acceptable to touch others (uninvited) and more than one in two males considered sexually explicit language as a normal part of sport. Another worrying finding was that one in ten female athletes perceived sexual propositions as part of sport and therefore acceptable, which lends support to the contention that females may be more accepting of such behaviors in a sport context. While there has not been any recent empirical research in Australia on this issue, anecdotal evidence suggests that (once again) little has changed in the intervening years. For example, in September 2014, a female journalist from *The Age* attended the Australian Football League (AFL) final, where she witnessed the crowd display racist, homophobic, and sexist comments (Lane, 2014).

> When I complained to a security guard, he told me that all fans do it and there was nothing they could do. Another person who'd complained shortly before me had been told the same thing, and was visibly distressed. While this is not the first time I've heard comments like this at AFL games, it was certainly the worst I've experienced personally. Inevitably, after I described the incidents on Twitter, suggestions flooded in that I was being overly sensitive. More than a few said I needed to "harden up, princess". It's all part of the fun, they said, part of the game.

Fasting, Brackenridge, and Sundgot-Borgen (2004) examined the prevalence of sexual harassment among 553 Norwegian female athletes by sport type. Their study included 56 different sport disciplines which were further subdivided into team and individual sports, whether revealing clothing was required for competition, gender structure, and gender culture. They found that, although women in masculine environments were more likely to report experiencing sexual harassment, it is participation in sport itself that is more important than sport type. The authors concluded that gendered structural relations in sport persist and that these are connected to females' experience of sexual harassment.

In the USA, Volkwein-Caplan et al. (2002) assessed the experience of sexual harassment of women in athletics, finding that about 20 percent of athletes had been exposed to threatening behavior, such as sexist comments and physical advances.

Other sexual harassment research in sport settings has focused on sports science students (Fasting et al., 2014) and females in sports writing (Pedersen, Lim, Osborne, & Whisenant, 2009). Fasting et al. (2014) explored the experiences of sexual harassment of women in two settings (organized sport and education) in three countries: Czech Republic, Norway, and Greece. Respondents in the Czech Republic and Greece were more likely to be recipients of sexual harassment than respondents in Norway. Overall, however, sexual harassment (from male peers or supervisors/coaches) occurred more in education than in the sport setting. One possible interpretation of this finding was that women in sport were more accepting of these behaviors, which is consistent with the Australian findings.

302 *Research handbook of employment relations in sport*

Pedersen et al. (2009) examined the experiences of 112 females who were sport print media professionals. They found that 50.9 percent had been recipients of sexual harassment (over the previous year) from a variety of individuals including supervisors, coaches, athletes, and members of sports media with whom they came into contact as part of their work. Although these women were negatively affected by such behaviors, they generally adopted a "you just grin and bear it" (p. 349) approach to the problem and that "harassment in our own offices is often as bad as it is in the locker rooms . . ." (p. 349). A similar feeling of acceptance of these behaviors as part of the job was among the findings of Hardin and Shain (2005), who found that women in sports media not only seem to accept discrimination and harassment as part of their jobs but also "see such treatment almost as 'routine' – not as deviant" (p. 814).

The organizational characteristics of the setting where the harassment takes place may explain why women, in particular, may see these behaviors as normative. Dellinger and Williams (2002) note that organizational culture shapes people's meanings of sexual harassment and influences how they deal with sexualized behavior. Consequently, and as argued earlier, incidence data based on simply asking workers whether they have been sexually harassed will invariably yield misleading results.

In sum, the existing research indicates that sexual harassment (and sexual abuse in general) appears to be prevalent in sport and that it is likely to be experienced by female athletes, although females in other spheres of sport (such as sport science students or sport journalists) seem to experience harassing behaviors as well. Although women in sport consider such behaviors as sexual harassment, they appear to be more accepting of such behaviors than women in other contexts, such as the workplace or academia. Most of the research has focused on coach–athlete interactions; however, there is evidence that suggests that peer athlete harassment is just, if not more, prevalent. Although female athletes in masculine and male dominated sports are more likely to experience sexual harassment, no sport is immune from sexual harassment and abuse in general.

What Do We Know About the Harassers?

Several studies have attempted to identify the perpetrators of sexual harassment. For example, in a study by Fasting, Brackenridge, and Sundgot-Borgen (2003), it was found that athletes experienced more sexual harassment from support personnel in sport (15 percent) than non-athletes did from a teacher at school or a supervisor/manager at work (7 percent). One reason for this may be that authority figures in sport exhibit behaviors towards athletes that are not exhibited or accepted at work or in education. Despite the focus on the coach as initiator of harassment, there is some evidence that other males also commit sexual harassment in a sport context. For example, a UK study found that harassment originated more from male peer athletes than from coaches (Tomlinson & Yorganci, 1997).

Surveys and incidence studies provide, at best, a sketchy picture of the perpetrators of sexual harassment. There is very little actual information about these individuals other than they are more likely to be male and that they are more likely to be in a position of formal power. To further compound this lack of knowledge, surveys tend to focus on (and get information from) the recipients of sexual harassment, rather than the offenders. This is not surprising. Zalk (1990) states that given the sensitivity of the topic, those who sexually harass are reticent to volunteer in research studies, for who would not only recognize their behavior as harassment and admit to being a harasser, but also volunteer to aid researchers?

The purpose of classifying or profiling those who sexually harass is to assist with an understanding of the kinds of behavioral patterns that may occur in a particular setting, rather than pathologizing or profiling the harasser. Profiling is problematic in that not only is it an inaccurate "science" (Trager & Brewster, 2001), but it also ignores the contextual characteristics that may facilitate or condone such behavior. Instead, as Brackenridge (1997) and Fasting and Brackenridge (2009) note, the purpose of such classifications is to aid in the development of interventions.

Most of what is known about the harassers derives from research in academic settings (Benson & Thomson, 1982; Dziech & Weiner, 1990) and from a handful of studies in sport contexts (Fasting & Brackenridge, 2009). Benson and Thomson (1982) argue that the combination of formal and situational power, together with long-entrenched misogyny held by lecturers, facilitates sexual harassment in academic settings. In a fascinating chapter filled with observations and insights into life on campus, "A portrait of the artist," Dziech and Weiner (1990) contend that there are two types of male harasser: the public harasser and the private harasser. The former is typically a young and friendly lecturer who behaves and dresses informally. This lecturer enjoys spending time with students, both in his office and in places like the student union or bars. Dziech and Weiner describe this individual as articulate and funny; his behavior is seldom coercive, but seductive. The private harasser is described in very different terms. This lecturer fits the stereotypical academic: he is a formal and conservative dresser, has a formal demeanor and manner, and presents himself as an authority figure that must be respected and obeyed. This individual shields himself in the sanctuary of his office, where he may, if the opportunity arises, coerce or bribe his students into inappropriate behavior of the *quid pro quo* type.

In addition to their analysis, Dziech and Weiner (1990) argue that male harassers adopt certain roles when dealing with female students. These are: the *counsellor-helper*, who behaves like a nurturer or caretaker but is also likely to exploit the vulnerabilities of his student; the *confidante*, who acts as friend to the student while developing a bond the student cannot get free from; the *intellectual seducer*, who gains personal information from the student while blinding the student with his knowledge; the *opportunist*, who takes advantage of situational power or opportunities; and the *power broker*, a private harasser who has the power to control grades, references, or job opportunities.

Little is known about sexual harassment initiated by those in positions of formal power in sport contexts, such as coaches. However, as the power dynamics of academia do not differ markedly from those in sports contexts, it has been proposed (Fasting & Brackenridge, 2009) that the relationship between a coach and an athlete is based on power and that the coach has power over the athlete and the athlete's self-esteem. Further, Fasting and Brackenridge note that athletes often accept a coach uncritically.

A conceptual framework that Fasting and Brackenridge (2009) draw on is that of Pryor and Whalen (1997), where it was proposed that there are two psychological functions served by sexual harassment behaviors: the expression of sexual feelings and the expression of hostility. Within these two categories, there are further subcategories: first, sexually motivated harassment may involve sexual exploitation and the expression of male over female power. Second, sexual attraction/miscommunication results from misunderstandings and misjudgments in interpersonal encounters that may be particularly prevalent in sexualized environments such as sport.

To further understand the dynamics of sexual harassment behaviors by coaches towards athletes, Fasting and Brackenridge (2009) conducted 19 semi-structured interviews with elite female Norwegian athletes (aged 15 to 33 years) who had experienced sexual harassment from a coach. Altogether, these athletes reported 59 incidents of sexual harassment, some of which had started when the athletes were as young as 13. Most of the behaviors reported were of a physical nature such as unwanted physical contact and unwanted sexually suggestive glances and looks. Verbal comments and sexist comments about athletes' body parts were also common. From the analysis of the behaviors reported and the characteristics of the coach (as portrayed by the athletes), the following typology was created: the *flirting-charming coach* is one who constantly flirts, jokes, and engages in playful physical contact such as pinching and wrestling; the *seductive coach* is described as constantly trying to hit on everyone and trying to get everyone in bed; and the *authoritarian coach*, who is a powerful individual displaying degrading and negative views about women in general, including the opinion that women should not participate or compete in sport. The researchers found that the behaviors displayed by the three types of harassers differed. While the flirting-charming coach and the seductive coach were more likely to initiate unwanted physical contact and engage in sexual comments, the authoritarian coach was more likely to treat athletes in a humiliating manner which undermined the athletes' self-respect.

There are clear parallels with the Dziech and Weiner (1990) classifications and patterns of behavior: the flirting-charming coach and the seductive coach are similar to the confidante and the opportunist lecturer, while the authoritarian coach is akin to the power broker. Most worryingly, the patterns of inappropriate, sexualized, and sexist behaviors described in both settings bear a remarkable resemblance.

In sum, most of what we know about those who commit sexual harassment in any setting is garnered from recipients' accounts. Research indicates that most of the harassers are male, that many of these are in positions of formal power, and that most recipients are female, although this is an oversimplification because not all men in positions of power sexually harass. There have been attempts to classify perpetrators into categories or typologies of sexual harassers, such as Dziech and Weiner (1990) in academia and Fasting and Brackenridge (2009) in the context of sport. However, classifications are problematic in that they tend to pathologize the initiator of behavior, rather than taking into account the societal or contextual variables that may lead to such behavior. Instead of identifying a typical harasser, this research serves to illustrate the patterns of behavior that reinforce power differentials or emphasize sexualized contexts.

Suggestions for Research and Practice

It is clear that in a context where sexual harassment behaviors are considered "part of sport" (Australian Sports Commission, 2001) and where there is inertia regarding the establishment of regulatory practices, combatting sexual harassment is not going to be an easy task. The following are some practical and research recommendations.

1.   Acknowledge the existence of the problem
Although public and organizational awareness of sexual harassment has increased, sporting organizations have lagged behind. As Lyons (2002, p. 113) notes: "Sport has long suffered from an antiseptic sense of its own

importance. The inability of a patriarchal system to enter into a critique of its dominant ideology has been chronicled by a number of authors, particularly those challenging the gendered basis of sport." Sport must drag sexual harassment out of hiding and into the light. Acknowledge that it happens and fight against it.

2.   Conduct meaningful and sustained research

While we applaud the work conducted by academics such as Fasting and her colleagues, there is still a dearth of research on sexual harassment in the context of sport. Related to the first point, there is a need to conduct regular and well-designed incidence surveys. It is rather disturbing to see that, in Australia at least, there has only been one major survey of sexual harassment in sport (Australian Sports Commission, 2001), which was conducted as long ago as 1998. Further research should attempt to formulate much needed theory on why sexual harassment happens in sport. This should incorporate an examination of psychological as well as contextual factors. There is also a need to know more about the (possible) initiators themselves. For example, what do males in positions of power think of sexual harassment? How do coaches perceive and deal with potentially contentious sexual relationships with those they coach?

3.   Develop and implement policy and guidelines

Although harassment-free sport guidelines adopted by many countries are a welcome step, what seems to be lacking is a commitment to ensuring these are followed through by all those involved in sport (coaches, athletes, administrators, instructors, support staff, board members, etc.) and constantly updated and monitored. As Lyons (2002) argues, "short-term moral panics and individual coach demonization cannot bring about lasting behavioral change" (p. 115).

Under the guidance of an overarching governing body, sporting organizations should develop training and materials that include the following steps. First, undertaking a needs assessment. This would identify whether sexual harassment happens in the particular organization, association, or club. Such assessment could be part of a larger assessment of general discrimination, ill-treatment, or bullying. Second, training should be delivered. This training should ideally include some form of role playing (Engelberg & Moston, 1997). All parties should be encouraged to discuss the topic with peers (such as other athletes) or with independent trainers. Feedback sessions should be encouraged. Third, training must be evaluated. Sporting organizations should see some positive change over time and this can only be assessed reliably by conducting regular needs assessments some weeks or months after the delivery of training. Evaluation need not be a costly or an intrusive exercise and may highlight shortcomings or areas for improvement in future training.

CONCLUSIONS

While sexual harassment serves many purposes (to its perpetrators at least), probably the most salient is to keep women out of sport. In many sporting clubs and organizations the predominantly male coaches and managers engage in behaviors that reinforce their authority over their female athletes. For example, an independent inquiry into the conduct of coaches and administrators from Swimming Australia showed that they had, until as recently as 2009, engaged in "bonding nights" involving strippers and porn parties (Halloran, 2014). Regrettably, to many in sport, inquiry into sexual harassment is dismissed as an irrelevance that interferes with their core business: winning (Fasting & Brackenridge, 2009). This position is highly prevalent and ultimately damaging to the integrity of sport.

REFERENCES

Australian Sports Commission (2001), *Australian research on harassment in sport. A snapshot in time: Athlete's perceptions of harassment*, accessed 29 September 2014 at http://fulltext. ausport.gov.au/fulltext/2001/ascpub/research_snapshot.asp.

Australian Womensport and Recreation Association (2009), *Australian Womensport and Recreation Association (AWRA) Equality Policy*, accessed 29 September 2014 at http:// www.australianwomensport.com.au/files/47474/files/Policies/AWRAEqualityPolicy2009. pdf.

Benson, D. J., and G. E. Thomson (1982), 'Sexual harassment on a university campus: The confluence of authority relations', *Social Problems*, **29** (3), 236–251.

Brackenridge, C. (1997), 'He owned me basically: Women's experiences of sexual abuse in sport', *International Review for the Sociology of Sport*, **32**, 115–130.

Dellinger, K., and C. L. Williams (2002), 'The locker room and the dorm room: Workplace norms and the boundaries of sexual harassment in magazine editing', *Social Problems*, **49** (2), 242–257.

Dziech, B. W., and L. Weiner (1990), *The lecherous professor: Sexual harassment on campus*, Urbana, Illinois, USA: University of Illinois Press.

Engelberg, T., and S. Moston (eds) (1997), *Sexual harassment in the workplace*, Sydney, Australia: Business & Professional Publishing.

Equal Employment Opportunity Commission (1990), *Policy guidance on current issues of sexual harassment. N-915-050*, accessed 29 September 2014 at http://www.eeoc.gov/policy/ docs/currentissues.html.

Farley, L. (1978), *Sexual shakedown: The sexual harassment of women on the job*, New York, NY, USA: Warner Books.

Fasting, K., and C. Brackenridge (2009), 'Coaches, sexual harassment and education', *Sport, Education and Society*, **14** (1), 21–35.

Fasting, K., C. Brackenridge, and J. Sundgot-Borgen (2003), 'Experiences of sexual harassment and abuse amongst Norwegian elite female athletes and non-athletes', *Research Quarterly for Exercise and Sport*, **74**, 84–97.

Fasting, K., C. Brackenridge, and J. Sundgot-Borgen (2004), 'Prevalence of sexual harassment among Norwegian female elite athletes in relation to sport type', *International Review for the Sociology of Sport*, **39**, 373–386.

Fasting, K., C. Brackenridge, and K. Walseth (2007), 'Women athletes' personal responses to sexual harassment in sport', *Journal of Applied Sport Psychology*, **19** (4), 419–433.

Fasting, K., S. Chroni, S. E. Hervik, and N. Knorre (2011), 'Sexual harassment in sport toward females in three European countries', *International Review for the Sociology of Sport*, **46** (1), 76–89.

Fasting, K., S. Chroni, and N. Knorre (2014), 'The experiences of sexual harassment in sport and education among European female sports science students', *Sport, Education and Society*, **19** (2), 115–130.

Halloran, J. (2014), 'Swimming Australia investigates coaches involved in a dirty pool of strippers and porn at bonding sessions in the Gold Coast', accessed 14 September 2014 at http://www.couriermail.com.au/sport/more-sports/swimming-australia-investigates-coaches-involved-in-a-dirty-pool-of-strippers-and-porn-at-bonding-sessions-in-the-gold-coast/story-fnp3ipql-1227057702722.

Hardin, M., and S. Shain (2005), 'Strength in numbers? The experiences and attitudes of women in sports media careers', *Journalism and Mass Communication Quarterly*, **82** (4), 804–819.

Lane, E. (2014), 'AFL has a problem with racism, sexism and homophobia', accessed 29 September 2014 at http://www.theage.com.au/comment/afl-has-a-problem-with-racism-sexism-and-homophobia-20140928-10n7pm.html#ixzz3EgGKNVMS.

Lyons, K. (2002), 'Review essay: Confronting sexual exploitation in sport', *Journal of Sexual Aggression: An international, interdisciplinary forum for research, theory and practice*, **8** (2), 111–117. doi: 10.1080/13552600208413344.

MacKinnon, C. (1979), *Sexual harassment of working women*, New Haven, CT, USA: Yale University Press.

Pedersen, P. M., C. H. Lim, B. Osborne, and W. Whisenant (2009), 'An examination of the perceptions of sexual harassment by sport print media professionals', *Journal of Sport Management*, 23, 335–360.

Pryor, J. B., and N. J. Whalen (1997), 'A typology of sexual harassment: characteristics of harassers and the social circumstances under which sexual harassment occurs', in W. Donohue (ed.), *Sexual harassment: Theory, research and treatment*, London, UK: Allyn & Bacon.

Ruble, D. N., C. L. Martin, and S. A. Berebaum (2006), 'Gender development', in W. Damon, R. M. Lerner, and N. Eisenberg (eds), *Social, emotional, and personality development* (6th ed., Vol. 3), Hoboken, NJ, USA: Wiley.

Sand, T. S., K. Fasting, S. Chroni, and N. Knorre (2011), 'Coaching behavior: Any consequences for the prevalence of sexual harassment?', *International Journal of Sports Science and Coaching*, **6** (2), 229–241.

Sandroff, R. (1988), 'Sexual harassment in the Fortune 500', *Working Woman*, **13** (12), 69–73.

Tomlinson, S., and I. Yorganci (1997), 'Male coach/female athlete relations: Gender and power relations in competitive sport', *Journal of Sport and Social Issues*, **21**, 134–155.

Trager, J., and J. Brewster (2001), 'The effectiveness of psychological profiles', *Journal of Police and Criminal Psychology*, **16** (1), 20–28.

US Department of Education (1979), *A policy interpretation: Title IX and intercollegiate athletics. Federal Register, 44(239)*, accessed 30 September 2014 at http://www2.ed.gov/about/offices/list/ocr/docs/t9interp.html.

Volkwein-Caplan, K., F. Schnell, S. Devlin, M. Mitchell, and J. Sutera (2002), 'Sexual harassment in athletics vs. academia', in C. Brackenridge and K. Fasting (eds), *Sexual harassment and abuse in sport: international research and policy perspectives*, London, UK: Whiting & Birch.

Women's Sports Foundation (2011), *Sexual harassment and sexual relationships between coaches, other athletic personnel and athletes: The Foundation position*, accessed 29 September 2014 at https://www.womenssportsfoundation.org/en/home/advocate/title-ix-and-issues/title-ix-positions/sexual_harassment.

Zalk, S. R. (1990), 'Men in the academy: A psychological profile of harassment', in M. A. Paludi (ed.), *Ivory power: Sexual harassment on campus*, New York, NY, USA: SUNY Press.

14. The evolution of anti-doping policy: workplace implications for athletes
James Skinner, Terry Engelberg and Stephen Moston

INTRODUCTION

This chapter begins by presenting a brief history of doping in sport. It was found that throughout history athletes have been known to seek advantages over their competitors and this has included doping practices. Societal trends occurring during the mid-nineteenth century saw an increase in doping practice and drug-related deaths in sport. It was during this time that governments and sporting organisations began to see the need for comprehensive action against drugs in sport. During this period, the policy developments of governments and sporting organisations did not lead to reductions in doping in sport. This is underpinned by the rationales for anti-doping policy being out of touch with the nature of contemporary sport as well as the ambiguity that surrounds the focus of anti-doping policies.

Second, the chapter provides a background to the establishment of the World Anti-Doping Agency (WADA), and segments policy developments into two main sections. The first section covers the successes in policy development, including the acceptance by governments and the sporting community of the need for an independent agency to lead the anti-doping agenda; the speed of which the agency was established; and the speed of which the agency secured legitimacy as the world leader in anti-doping policy. The second section covers the tensions in policy development, including harmonisation of anti-doping policies; the goals of harmonisation and implications for implementation; tensions regarding the implementation of policy that is underpinned by flawed rationales; and tensions regarding the marginalisation of athletes in the development of anti-doping policy.

The chapter concludes by providing insights into how policy changes have created a "work environment" that requires the athlete to accept unique employment conditions. It details how policy developments have created an era of employment surveillance techniques that ultimately shape and regulate the workplace to normalise the conduct and decisions of athletes to achieve the desirable doping policy objectives (Miller & Rose, 1990).

Background to Doping in Sport

Doping in sport was considered broadly as the:

> use by athletes of drugs that are banned by their federations and usually include stimulants (commonly used in endurance events such as long distance cycling), anabolic steroids (used by many athletes to increase bulk, in weightlifting for example, and/or to enable more intensive training), narcotic analgesics (used as painkillers), diuretics (used to flush other drugs out of the body or to help reduce weight in weight-related events such as boxing or judo), and hormone-based drugs whose use is similar to that of steroids. (Houlihan, 1999a, pp. 311–312)

Since Houlihan's (1999a) definition, doping legislation has broadened to include the use of recreational drugs (referred to as illicit drugs) by sports people, both in and out of competition times (WADA, 2009b). With the increasingly global nature of sport, doping in sport has become established as an issue to be considered at both national and international levels (Houlihan, 1999a). While doping in sport has attracted much public debate and policy development over recent decades, the very idea of anti-doping policy is a relatively new concept in the policy landscape, and there is still much to learn about the phenomenon (Houlihan, 1999a).

History of Doping in Sport

Understanding the history of doping is important to an understanding of why doping is currently banned. Consequently, many of the most keenly debated issues in the field of research centre on the interpretation of historical data, where it has been claimed (with some considerable degree of justification) that history has been rewritten to serve modern needs (Engelberg, Moston & Hutchinson, 2014).

Engelberg et al. (2014) suggest publications on doping often begin by outlining how ancient athletes used performance enhancing substances. For example, Verroken (2000, p. 1) writes:

> ... in the third century BC Galen reported that ancient Greek athletes used stimulants to enhance their physical performance; at the ancient Olympic Games, athletes had special diets and were reported to take various substances to improve their physical capabilities. The winner of the 200 m sprint at the Olympic Games of 668 BC was said to have used a special diet of dried figs! The Ancient Egyptians used a drink made from the hooves of asses, which were

ground and boiled in oil before being flavoured with rose petals and rose hips, to improve their performance. In Roman times, gladiators used stimulants to maintain energy levels after injury. Similar behaviour by medieval knights has also been noted.

The narrative then typically fast forwards to more recent times and continues to provide evidence of doping in sport (Houlihan, 1999b; Verroken, 2005; Waddington, 2000). In the late nineteenth century, substances such as caffeine, cocaine, strychnine, alcohol, and oxygen were linked with athletes in European countries seeking to gain advantages in sporting events (Verroken, 2005). The first reported drug-related death in sport occurred in 1896, when cyclist Arthur Linton died after reportedly being administered strychnine by his coach (Verroken, 2005). Strychnine is known for its stimulant qualities, but is also commonly used in rat poison (Bull, 2008). Although the reason for Linton's death was debated at the time, his coach was banned from cycling (Verroken, 2005). At the 1904 Olympics, marathon runner Thomas Hicks came close to death after being administered a cocktail of strychnine and brandy (Houlihan, 1999b; Verroken, 2005). Hicks claimed the gold medal, and there were no ramifications regarding his use of drugs (Bull, 2008). During the 1920s, stimulants, known as "pep pills," were known to be used by football teams in the UK (Mazanov & McDermott, 2009; Waddington, 2000). The use of drugs to enhance performance was based on the hope of improved performance, rather than robust empirical evidence that drugs did improve performance (Houlihan, 1999b). Furthermore, although several high-profile drug-related incidents had occurred, this did not dissuade athletes from using drugs (Houlihan, 1999b).

Verroken (2005) outlines that before the mid-twentieth century there was limited "documentary evidence available to substantiate the hypothesis that drugs had been used in sport" (p. 30). In explaining this dearth of documentation, others have argued that up until the 1950s the use of drugs in sport was largely ignored, and it is only since then that drug use in sport has been considered unacceptable (Houlihan, 1999a; Waddington, 2000).

The content of these potted histories has been expertly critiqued by several authors (e.g., Beamish & Ritchie, 2006; Dimeo, 2007; Gleaves, 2014; Yesalis & Bahrke, 2002), who suggest that history has largely been adapted and rewritten to meet current perspectives on the topic of doping. Moreover, historical accounts of doping generally agree that current attitudes towards doping are a modern creation (Engelberg et al., 2014).

Societal Trends in Doping

Waddington (2000) highlights that an understanding of doping in sport must therefore seek to understand why drugs have recently become an issue in contemporary society. Since the mid-twentieth century, there have been several shifts including an increase in societal drug use generally and the changing nature of contemporary sports that has become increasingly conducive to the increased use of performance enhancing drugs.

First, the Second World War (WWII) saw amphetamine-like substances becoming increasingly available. Initially intended for combat troops to enhance alertness and delay fatigue (Houlihan, 1999b; Verroken, 2005; Waddington, 2000), these drugs filtered into sports during the 1940s and 1950s to enhance sports performance (Verroken, 2005). Several drug-related deaths in sport during the 1960s demonstrated just "how wide-spread drug abuse had become" (Verroken, 2005, p. 30). This increasing propensity for athletes to take drugs was in line with broader societal trends, including liberal approaches to drug experimentation, particularly during the 1960s (Houlihan, 1999b; Lippi, Franchini, & Guidi 2008; Verroken, 2005); the development of specific drugs during the "pharmaceutical revolution" to alter the functions of the body, delivering a far greater choice of drugs for athletes to choose from (Verroken, 2005); and increased social acceptance of pharmaceutical application in the day-to-day lives of people, as well as for use in sport (Verroken, 2005; Waddington, 2000).

Second, post-WWII, sport has played an increasingly important political role in building national identity. Competition and winning have been emphasised through modern sports, as winning offers national prestige and contributes to the nation's psyche (Waddington, 2000). As a result, the pressure on athletes to perform is immense (Waddington, 2000). From the 1980s, the globalisation and commercialisation of sport have also influenced drug taking in sports. Sport has become a business where athletes' livelihoods rest on their athletic performance (Waddington, 2000). As a result of this fact, athletes fear failure and seek to avoid it (Houlihan, 1999b). The use of banned doping substances and practices therefore becomes attractive, not only for rehabilitation, but to win (Houlihan, 1999b; Stewart, Nicholson, Smith & Westerbeek, 2004; Waddington, 2000).

However, most Western societies have not been accepting of these changes. Trends of increasing drugs use in society, changes in the nature of sport, and increasing drug use in sport have occurred alongside increased expectations regarding the quality of life experienced in Western countries from the mid-twentieth century (Waddington, 2000). An increasing awareness and concern for health and wealth, coupled with several high-profile doping-related deaths during the 1960s, contributed to calls for sports to keep themselves free from drugs (Houlihan, 1999a). This saw the health of the athlete and potential risks of performance-enhancing drugs become a rationale for policy development. Other rationales included the notion that doping undermines the level playing field in competition and is a form of cheating, and that drug use has the potential to "undermine the credibility of sport" in the eyes of governments and other interested organisations (Houlihan, 1999b, p.108), as well as providing poor role models for young sports participants.

The various anti-doping policies that have developed in the latter half of the twentieth century and beginning of the twenty-first century have seen a range of planned and unplanned outcomes (Smith & Stewart, 2008; Waddington, 2000). The implementation of anti-doping policy has not necessarily curbed the use of performance enhancing drugs in sport. In some cases, it has encouraged the development of new drugs which are not detectable, therefore encouraging athletes to participate in increasingly dangerous practices (Smith & Stewart, 2008; Waddington, 2000). One factor contributing to these unplanned policy outcomes is the romanticised notions of sport that underpins the rationales for anti-doping policies (Kayser & Smith, 2008; Smith & Stewart, 2008). What is clear, however, is that these rationales created the impetus for policy development that fundamentally changed the work environment for athletes.

Rationales for Anti-Doping Policy

There are a number of rationales that are used to justify anti-doping policy. First, there is a need for anti-doping policy to protect the health of the athlete. This is primarily based on the assumption that drug use is dangerous to the health of the athlete. However, some sports, by their very nature, can be dangerous to athletes' health, highlighting a contradiction with this health-based rationale (Houlihan, 1999b; Kayser & Smith, 2008; Smith & Stewart, 2008). Smith and Stewart (2008) criticise the paternalistic nature of this particular rationale, arguing: "given that athletes are free to engage in sports with substantial risks, why are they not also free to utilise performance enhancements that are, in some cases, less risky than the sports in which they engage?" (p. 125). Waddington (2000) has suggested that under such circumstances it would make sense to ban performance enhancing drugs for junior athletes, but allow adults to make their own decision. Contradictions to the rationale also exist where drugs are banned out of concern for athletes' health on the one hand, but then, on the other hand, sponsorship agreements are signed to use sports as a marketing tool for tobacco and alcohol products, which are evidenced to cause immense amounts of harm to athletes and communities (Smith & Stewart, 2008; Waddington, 2000).

Second, anti-doping policy is needed to ensure a level playing field in competition. This argument is based on the assumption that a "drug code is essential to the maintenance of a level playing field" (Smith & Stewart, 2008, p. 124). The level playing field has become increasingly important in contemporary sport due to the importance of spectators in the business of sport, as well as the need to ensure a fair chance of winning to maximise unpredictability for gambling in sport (Waddington, 2000). However, it is argued that athletes and teams will have access to varying types and extents of resources that will differentiate them from other teams across a range of variables (Kayser & Smith, 2008; Smith & Stewart, 2008; Waddington, 2000). Houlihan (1999b) argues that "sport is all about seeking an advantage over other competitors" (p. 110), while Smith and Stewart (2008) argue that "sporting competitions are inherently unbalanced" (p. 125). However, no other factors that contribute to competitive advantage in sport (access to resources, coaching expertise, facilities, etc.) have been given as much attention as performance enhancing drugs, thus setting this second rationale as another contradiction in anti-doping policy.

Third, the rationale that anti-doping policy is needed to preserve the integrity of sport is based on the assumption that drug use impacts on the ethics of sport, thus tarnishing its image (Houlihan, 1999b; Smith & Stewart, 2008). Supporters of anti-doping policy agree that "drug use in sport is contrary to the very principles upon which sport is based" (Verroken, 2005, p. 53). However, this rationale has been criticised for romanticising the structures and nature of sport, particularly the contemporary notion of sport that values winning and performance. As Tamburrini (2007) argues:

> what seems to be the case is that sport has evolved into a highly competitive, professional activity in which agents try their best to perform at their highest possible level. Unlike recreational sports – whose main traits (to have a good time and promote health) still marked competitive sport at the beginning of the twentieth century – professional sport is now driven by a desire to expand the boundaries of what hitherto was considered to be humanly possible, even by jeopardising one's own health. In that sense, professional elite sport does not differ from other professional activities in which individuals are granted the right to freely choose the level of sacrifice and risk-taking they are willing to accept in order to achieve success. (p. 27)

From this point of view, the contradiction of this third rationale is highlighted, and it can be argued that "doping is not only compatible with, but also incarnates, the true spirit of modern competitive elite sports"

(Tamburrini, 2007, p. 24). This perspective argues that the social construction of sport has valued athletic performance, winning, and continual improvement as key benchmarks (Beamish & Ritchie, 2006; Houlihan, 1999b; Tamburrini, 2007). As outlined by Houlihan (1999b), "the pattern of sport that develops in a society is the product of that society" (p. 13).

Further, support for this rationale based on the importance of sport role models has also been criticised (Smith & Stewart, 2008). This notion is based on the inherent social good that sport is assumed to offer. However, as Smith and Stewart (2008) have argued, "sport can just as easily act as a catalyst for socially dysfunctional behavior" (p. 124). There is limited evidence that positive sport role models elicit positive behaviour, or that negative role models elicit negative behaviour, in relation to drug use (Smith & Stewart, 2008).

Smith and Stewart (2008) sum up their critique of the rationales:

> The realities of sport are that, even in drug-free situations, athletes do not set particularly good examples, sport is not a level playing field, attempts to protect an athlete's health are often no more than token gestures and the integrity of sport is determined just as much by its structures, management systems and culture as it is by the behaviour of its players. As a result, it is fanciful to think that a selective and punitive anti-doping policy will, of itself, ensure the social and moral progress of sport. Indeed, draconian policies that are embedded with heavy penalties can just as easily force players to take even greater risks in the quest for sporting stardom. (p. 127)

The contradictions in policy justification highlighted here illustrate significant issues at the core of anti-doping policy. While each rationale may have some intuitive plausibility, the literature argues that none of these are capable of justifying the significant policy commitment that has been met by governments and sporting organisations around the world in the pursuit of drug-free sport (Houlihan, 1999b; Waddington, 2000).

Ambiguity of Anti-Doping Policy

Another factor that is considered to contribute to the mixed outcomes for anti-doping policy is the ambiguity of policy focus and implementation (Houlihan, 1999b; Smith & Stewart, 2008). The ambiguity of policy focus has three main considerations. First, there has been limited consensus in defining the issue of drug use in sport and determining what the policy outcomes should be (Houlihan, 1999b). Second, there has been varying degrees of commitment to the anti-doping agenda across the sport and government stakeholders (Houlihan, 2014). Third, there have been tensions between sports and governments regarding who should provide leadership for anti-doping policy. Each of these is discussed below.

First, in defining the issue of drugs in sport, the types and practices need to be considered, as well as who is responsible for the issue. The anti-doping issue has come to address legal and illegal drugs, therapeutic and performance enhancing uses, and recreational and social uses (Mottram, 2005). The literature highlights that there are blurred boundaries between these types of drugs and their applications (Houlihan, 1999b; Waddington, 2000). These blurred lines are also influenced by "the steady development of new drugs, the constant exploration of the wealth of existing drugs for those with as yet undiscovered ergogenic properties, and the constant refinement of existing preparations" (Houlihan, 1999b, p. 81). Such advancement in ways to enhance performance has also seen genetic enhancement come to be considered in anti-doping policy, albeit to a limited extent (Miah, 2004; Edwards & Skinner, 2006). Various stakeholders and ideologies influence the policy debate, and these debates take place at both international and national levels (Houlihan, 1999b). As a result, defining the issue of drugs in sport is subject to multiple perspectives and takes place in a highly politicised context (Houlihan, 1999b).

Second, the ambiguity around the policy agenda has led to some organisations operating with limited commitment to the anti-doping agenda (Houlihan, 2014). During the late 1980s, a number of high-profile incidents have prompted formal inquiries into sports doping in Australia, the UK, and Canada (Houlihan, 1999b; Stewart et al., 2004). These inquiries revealed a poor culture in the sports community towards anti-doping. Some governments were acting subversively and allowing cover-ups of doping practices (Houlihan, 1999a).[1] Some sporting organisations had little incentive to control and monitor drug use, as performance of athletes is tied to government funding of their sports (Houlihan, 1999b). These revelations, however, demonstrated to some countries that non-compliance was not worth the shame if they were found out. As such, government involvement was increased and countries such as Australia, the UK, and Canada established specific agencies to deal with the policy development, implementation, and the testing of athletes (Houlihan, 1999b).

Third, tensions between sports and governments regarding whether the drug issue should be dealt with within the sports, or whether there is a need for government intervention, have contributed to the ambiguity and complexity of anti-doping policy (Houlihan, 1999b). The sports consider doping in sport to be a matter that should be regulated at the sport level, perceiving government intervention to undermine the ability of sporting organisations to control their sports. However, since the 1980s, governments have become increasingly critical of the limited action taken by sports to control the increasingly pertinent issue of doping in sport (Houlihan, 1999a).

The sports movement has struggled to maintain a position of power in the anti-doping agenda, as governments around the world have not been satisfied that sports have taken adequate action to address the issue (Houlihan, 1999a). The International Olympic Committee (IOC) maintained its list of banned substances since it was established in 1971 (Houlihan, 1999b), and was involved in the drafting of the Council of Europe's Anti-Doping Charter, in an attempt to maintain a position of power in a context where there was an increasing presence of specialist doping forums and multi-lateral agreements between countries (Hanstad, Smith & Waddington, 2008; Houlihan, 1999a). In 1993, the IOC secured the agreement of organisations involved with the committee to move towards policy harmonisation across the sports; however, the IOC was unwilling to partner with non-sport bodies in this agreement (Verroken, 2005). The scale of the problem of doping in sport and inaction taken by sporting organisations were the major reasons that governments gained the position of power, as the resources required were more than the sports movement could commit alone (Houlihan, 1999a).

As a result, a situation has occurred where sporting organisations and governments exist as two sources of anti-doping policy with very different focuses (Houlihan, 1999b). In the context of sport, the majority of policy has been aimed at reducing demand, as many of the drugs used are legal (Houlihan, 1999b). Sporting organisations have focused on both legal and illegal drugs through regulation, to varying extents. Governments have focused mainly on illegal drugs through a variety of approaches. This fragmentation of sport and government interests sees a policy context where:

> The IOC is concerned with the elimination of doping at competitions organised under the auspices of the Olympic movement in order to be able to ensure the probity of results. The international federations may vary considerably in the application of anti-doping policy, with some limiting testing to established elite athletes, others to elite and near elite, and still others extending coverage to include juniors and veterans. While some governments see doping in sport as part of a broader anti-drugs policy, others tend to treat doping as a minor problem best left to sports authorities. Thus, doping in fringe sports such as body building is often ignored as it falls outside the mainstream concerns of sports organisations and government. Overall there is little evidence of consistency and stability regarding objectives of sports anti-doping policy. (Houlihan, 1999b, pp. 97–98)

The late 1990s and early 2000s saw concerted efforts towards harmonisation of policy, setting international standards, and encouraging commitment to these standards by domestic governments and sporting organisations (Houlihan, 2002, 2004, 1999b).[2] Issues of harmonisation will be elaborated in the next section.

World Anti-Doping Agency: Successes in Anti-Doping Policy Development

The need to establish an organisation focused on the anti-doping agenda was highlighted due a series of high-profile doping issues in the late 1990s (Houlihan, 2004). Issues included the alleged cover-ups in the 1996 Atlanta Olympics and the high-profile doping cases of the 1998 Tour de France (Foschi, 2006; Houlihan, 2004; Waddington, 2000);[3] both were seen to be a catalyst for the anti-doping conference convened by the IOC in 1999 (Hanstad et al., 2008; Stewart & Smith, 2010; Verroken, 2005).[4] Governments who attended the conference were extremely critical of the IOC. Verroken (2005) explains that "the debate demonstrated the strength of feeling among the governments to require the sports movement to clean up their sports or face government intervention" (p. 61). The IOC had originally proposed an international anti-doping body governed by a council responsible to the IOC President (Hanstad et al., 2008). However, this was rejected due to arguments that this would amount to a conflict of interest, as there were suspicions regarding the credibility of the IOC to take such a role (Hanstad et al., 2008; Verroken, 2005).[5] The conference saw those athletes and sporting organisations present support the establishment of an independent world agency to pursue the anti-doping policy agenda (Hanstad et al., 2008; Verroken, 2005). As a result, an agreement was made to form the WADA, with the objective of being operational by the 2000 Sydney Olympics (Verroken, 2005).

WADA was established in 1999 as an international and independent agency to provide "scientific research, education, development of anti-doping capacities, and monitoring of the World Anti-Doping Code" (WADA, 2011a). WADA was founded in Lausanne, Switzerland, in 1999 and opened its headquarters in Montreal, Canada, in 2002 (Verroken, 2005). WADA was structured to be governed equally by the sports movement and governments around the world (WADA, 2011a). The sports movement referred to in WADA documentation is the IOC, who make up half of the WADA Foundation Board and Executive Committee (WADA, 2011b, 2011c). The aim was for WADA to be funded equally by the sports movement and governments around the world (WADA, 2011a). In practice, the IOC provided funding initially, then in 2002 some government funding was provided, and by 2008, the government contribution matched the IOC's dollar for dollar (WADA, 2011e). Across the range of policy priorities, WADA strives for harmonisation of policy and practice at all levels of sport and across all organisations involved in sport (WADA, 2011d). As part of this harmonisation process, WADA took full control of the IOC's prohibited substances list in 2004 (Verroken, 2005).

The success of WADA in establishing itself as the legitimate leader in the anti-doping agenda has been attributed to several factors (Smith & Stewart, 2008). First, the equal partnership between the sports movement and governments of the world for the governance and funding of WADA (WADA, 2011b, 2011c) is considered to have contributed to the legitimacy of WADA through both capital and influence (Smith & Stewart, 2008). Second, WADA has "secured international declarations that have commended and ratified the policy code it has developed" (Smith & Stewart, 2008, pp. 123–124). This includes the Copenhagen Declaration on Anti-Doping in Sport (2003), which was drafted and agreed to by governments in attendance at the Second World Conference on Doping in Sport held in Copenhagen, Denmark, in March 2003 (Verroken, 2005; WADA, 2003). This declaration was "the political document through which governments signaled their intention to formally recognize and implement the World Anti-Doping Code" (WADA, 2003). Third, the World Anti-Doping Code has been approved by the United Nations Educational, Scientific and Cultural Organization (UNESCO) under the International Convention on Doping in Sport (Smith & Stewart, 2008). The Convention has implications for governments around the world. The Code is a "non-governmental document that applies only to members of sports organizations" (UNESCO, 2011b). The Convention goes beyond the Code to provide "the legal framework under which governments can address the specific areas of the doping problem that are outside the domain of the sports movement" (UNESCO, 2011b). The Convention came into effect on 1 February 2007 and is considered to be "the most successful convention in the history of UNESCO in terms of speed of development and entry into force" (UNESCO, 2011a).

Houlihan (2014), however, points to a number of weaknesses of the Convention in supporting the objectives of the World Anti-Doping Code. In particular, he points to the 2012 WADA Executive Report on the effectiveness of testing programs that suggests there is "no general appetite to undertake the effort and expense of a successful effort to deliver doping-free sport" (p. 267).

These three factors, however, are considered to have consolidated WADA's position in the anti-doping agenda (Smith & Stewart, 2008; Stewart, Adair & Smith, 2011). These factors have constructed a policy framework whereby sport bodies must enact WADA policy to be able to access funding from their relevant governments or sanctioning of competitions from their relevant international governing body (Smith & Stewart, 2008).

Anti-Doping Policy Development and Tensions

Despite the success of WADA in establishing its legitimacy as the leading international player for anti-doping policy, there have also been a series of tensions regarding policy harmonisation. Underpinning the need for policy harmonisation is the "recognition of the global character of elite sports circuits and the high level of international mobility of athletes" (Houlihan, 1999b, p. 154). Houlihan (2004, 1999b) argues that there is little point in only some governments and sport governing bodies adopting anti-doping policy if athletes train or compete in other countries where there is limited anti-doping policy. High-profile cases during the 1990s highlighted this issue when athletes appealed punishments for testing positive on the grounds that testing procedures were not followed when testing was being conducted in another country on behalf of the athletes' country of residence (Houlihan, 1999b). Prior to WADA, it was fairly "easy for sports organisations and governments . . . to pay lip service to the goal of harmonisation as it was rarely defined and rested comfortably in the realm of policy aspiration rather than in the scope of practical policy" (Houlihan, 2002, p. 183). The goal of harmonisation gained momentum under WADA's main mandate for the harmonisation of anti-doping policy (WADA, 2009a).

The priority of harmonisation has come under scrutiny as there have been limited attempts to define and clarify the goals and processes for harmonisation, which contributes to the ambiguity of the policy space (Houlihan, 2002; Stewart & Smith, 2010). There have been concerns for the duplication of testing authorities, including those situated in the International Federations as well as the National Agencies (Verroken, 2005). There are also concerns over the role of WADA in harmonising the regulation of both performance enhancing drugs and illicit drugs, and regulating these in and out of competition.[6] Further, the intention of WADA was to be an "equal partnership between sport and governments"; however, in practice, there have been struggles to find a way forward that ensures "mutual ownership" but does "not surrender control to either sport or government" (Verroken, 2005, p. 61).[7]

Beyond these issues, there has been debate within the sports movement, with arguments against harmonisation abounding from various sport stakeholders (Houlihan, 2002), including:

- professional sport argues they should not be subject to policy regarding amateur sports;
- professional sportspeople argue they deserve leeway with certain drugs as sport is their way of making a living;

- non-Olympic sports argue they should not be subject to IOC standards;
- some Olympic sports argue that harmonisation of anti-doping policy undermines their autonomy.

Other arguments have been based on the danger of harmonising a flawed policy. The policy that is to be harmonised has not yet addressed the contradictions of the rationales underpinning the anti-doping agenda that were outlined in the previous section (Kayser & Smith, 2008; Smith & Stewart, 2008). Moreover, it is argued that the same policy has not acknowledged the social construction of modern sport (Beamish & Ritchie, 2006; Tamburrini, 2007); has continued to be based on limited empirical evidence regarding the effects of drug taking in sport (Stewart et al., 2011); and has continued to marginalise the voice of athletes (Beamish & Ritchie, 2006; Foschi, 2006; Houlihan, 2004).

In terms of the contradictions in the rationales, limited acknowledgement of the nature of modern sport, and limited evidence base for policy, there has been some limited theorising in the literature that seeks to understand how these policy agendas have been established and maintained (Houlihan, 1999a; Stewart et al., 2011; Stewart & Smith, 2010). It is argued that political processes of networks (Houlihan, 1999a) and power plays (Stewart et al., 2011) have contributed to an anti-doping agenda which is based on dominant ideologies and value judgments, more so than empirical evidence (Stewart et al., 2011) or neutral debates as to how best to manage the realities of modern sport (Tamburrini, 2007). These commentators argue that it is unlikely that athletes in contemporary sport are going to be discouraged from using performance enhancing drugs by punitive anti-doping policies (Houlihan, 1999a, 1999b; Kayser & Smith, 2008; Smith & Stewart, 2008; Stewart et al., 2011; Stewart & Smith, 2008; Tamburrini, 2007; Waddington, 2000). Instead policy makers are encouraged to consider the advantages of harm minimisation approaches where the emphasis is on reducing harm rather than eliminating drug use (Kayser & Smith, 2008). Harm minimisation approaches are underpinned by the notion that there are more factors influencing athletes' compliance, or non-compliance; the decision is not only influenced by potential punishment for non-compliance.[8] Recent research supports such a shift in policy approach, as it demonstrates athletes' attitudes towards drug taking are influenced by a range of factors.[9]

Anti-Doping Policy: Implications for Athlete Work Practice

In terms of employment conditions, Kuipers and van Bottenburg (2015) suggest "that existing anti-doping measures seriously impact the lives of elite athletes and their immediate entourage, which imposes a moral burden to evaluate these measures in the best possible way" (p. 57). Shortfalls do exist with regard to the input of the athlete perspective on how anti-doping policy has an impact on their work environment. The noted lack of athlete participation in international anti-doping policy development is not unusual (Moston, Engelberg & Skinner, 2015a; Skinner, Moston & Engelberg, 2011). Some would suggest it reflects a lack of athlete participation in decision-making processes affecting their work lives more generally. Houlihan (2004) summarises the literature on international world-class anti-doping policy when he writes that "anti-doping policy is generally made for, or on behalf of, athletes, rarely in consultation with athletes, and almost never in partnership with athletes" (pp. 421–422).

The importance of the athlete's perspective has been highlighted due to the civil rights of the athlete and to what extent the WADA Code protects these rights, or impinges on them (Houlihan, 2004). In Houlihan's discussion of the Code, he concluded that the increased recognition of the WADA Code across countries and sports serves to protect the rights of the athlete by ensuring that sporting organisations follow the good practice set out by WADA.[10] However, the major issue concerning WADA policy and the WADA Code is that little effort has been made to recognise athletes as a significant stakeholder in the process that shapes their work practice. WADA did establish an Athlete Committee in 2005 to incorporate the perspectives of clean athletes across WADA's policy priorities (WADA, 2011e). There continues, however, to be criticism of the premise upon which the anti-doping policy is based. That is, that the athlete is responsible for ensuring adherence to the policy does not take into account that there are many scenarios which athletes cannot control despite the utmost care (Foschi, 2006).

The WADA Code has also been criticised due to the implication of athletes inadvertently agreeing to a range of expectations through their participation in sport (Horvath, 2006). Further, cases where positive tests have occurred have demonstrated that "in such situations athletes are consistently left with no recourse" (Foschi, 2006, p. 485). As such, it is argued that the WADA Code has the potential to violate certain rights by not ensuring "each athlete a fair and *real* opportunity to prove their innocence" (Foschi, 2006, p. 485, original italics). Similarly, Stewart and Smith (2014) point to the views of civil libertarian groups who suggest there are:

> Excessively zealous strategies for exposing athletes who, while at first glance might have been labeled "drug cheats", had, on further investigation, done nothing more than consumed amino acids, taken herbal stimulants, ingested caffeine, and used home grown cannabis to escape the competitive pressures of elite sport. (p. 116)

In their current work environment athletes must agree to conditions that those in the general workforce may see as an infringement of their privacy and workplace rights. Anti-doping campaigners seeking to identify and prosecute drug users have devised surveillance measures such as the Athlete Whereabouts Scheme. The logic behind the scheme is that effective out-of-competition testing programs are essential to the fight against doping in sport regardless of the personal circumstances of athletes. If an athlete is at another location other than where they identified they can be sanctioned (Mazanov, 2014). The case of Belgian cyclist Kevin van Impe, who was asked to provide a sample while attending the cremation of his baby son Jayden, not only provided a focal point for those opposed to such doping controls, but also highlighted the intrusion into the rights of athletes. As such, Mazanov suggests that the Whereabouts scheme appears to place priority on administrative integrity rather than recognising its implications for athletes. Similarly, Houlihan (2014) points to the selective compliance of some countries to the scheme and carelessness in collecting whereabouts information.

The Athlete Biological Passport (ABP) can also be considered a workplace regulation that athletes have to accept as part of their employment contract. Introduced in 2009, its primary purpose was to monitor changes to selected biological variables over time that indirectly reveal the effects of doping, rather than attempting to focus on the detection of a doping substance or a doping method (Stewart & Smith, 2014). The ABP provides an individual electronic record of the blood chemistry of athletes. Any change or movement in hormone levels would be detected through the prior data recorded in the ABP. The ABP was seen as a way to combat the increased use of erythropoietin (EPO). The use of EPO in endurance events in particular had become a major concern for anti-doping authorities. The ABP was essentially developed to convey a clear and concise message to athletes that drug cheats would not be tolerated (Stewart & Smith, 2014). This policy initiative was formulated without consultation or consideration of the workplace implications for athletes and, in turn, had the potential to create tensions between anti-doping authorities and athletes.

The supplements scandal that surrounded the Australian Football League (AFL) club Essendon also raised tensions and concerns surrounding the employment contracts of professional players. Essendon was investigated from early 2013 by the Australian Sports Anti-Doping Authority

(ASADA) over whether its supplements program was compliant with the WADA Code. An outcome of the investigation was the concern raised around duty-of-care failures relating to the players allegedly being injected with the banned peptide Thymosin beta-4. It was suggested that the players were unaware that the peptide being administered was not compliant with the Code. This claim raised the issue of whether Essendon had failed to provide the players with a safe workplace. Under these circumstances, it was suggested that the players could exercise their right to terminate their contracts with the club and enter the trade or pre-season draft market (Niall, 2013).

AFL player contracts are different and more complicated than normal employment contracts in that they are a "tripartite agreement" between the AFL, the club, and the player (Niall, 2013). In each standard AFL contract, however, there is a clause that states:

> The AFL club shall provide a playing, training and working environment which is, so far as is practicable, free of any risk to the health, safety and the welfare of the player. Without limitation, the AFL club shall observe and carry out its obligations under the applicable Occupational Health and Safety Act or its equivalent. (Clause 7.3 of the AFL/Essendon/Player Contract)

The repudiation of the contract would not require the players to have taken WADA banned substances, and it could be based upon the fact that the players had been either given "harmful substances" or if "there is inadequate information about whether a substance is harmful." As such, a case could be made that due to welfare, health, and safety breaches, players could say their contract has been "repudiated," thereby allowing players to "terminate" the contract (Niall, 2013). Although a tribunal hearing found the players not guilty of doping offences,[11] the Essendon doping scandal highlighted that players were willing to accept the direction provided by coaches as to supplements they should use, and to a large extent were powerless to challenge this direction.

The numerous attempts to create a more robust anti-doping system in recent times have been based on strategies consistent with the tenets of deterrence theory (Moston, Engelberg, & Skinner, 2015b). This approach has created a set of workplace criteria that are unique and a workplace regulatory environment that can change quickly. The 2007 anti-doping policy initiatives in Australia illustrate the extent to which this trend has emerged. George Brandis, the then Minister for Arts and Sport, launched a zero tolerance approach to drug use in sport. This policy initiative extended beyond performance enhancing drug use to the use of illicit drugs, captured in the "Illicit Drugs-in-Sport Policy" (IDSP). The new measures in this policy could include out of competition illicit drug testing to be carried out by national sporting organisations (Stewart & Smith, 2014). Although this policy initiative was not fully implemented, it did signal the extent to which the government was willing to intervene in the working lives of athletes. This was further highlighted in 2013 when the President of the Australian Olympic Committee stated that it would be mandatory for future Olympians to sign a statutory declaration that their past was drug free. A false statement would carry possible imprisonment, a fine, or a combination of both (Stewart & Smith, 2014). Recent research, however, that interviewed athletes who have been sanctioned for doping violations, suggests that "neither career (e.g., bans or suspensions) nor financial (e.g., fines) sanctions were seen as effective deterrents" (Engelberg, Moston & Skinner, 2014, p. 275). This research brings into question whether political motivations were influencing anti-doping policy decisions. These policy initiatives do, however, highlight how quickly the workplace environment of athletes can change.

CONCLUDING COMMENTS

This chapter has shown how attempts to eliminate or reduce both performance enhancing and illicit drug use in sport has created a unique and, some may suggest, overly regulated work environment for athletes. Even when anti-doping policies of sporting organisations are positioned in the interests of athletes, some suggest that these policies are aimed more at protecting the brand and image of the organisation. Stewart, Smith, and Dickson (2008) suggest that AFL's drug management policies may initially suggest that the primary goal is to "preserve the health and well being of players [as discussed in the Essendon case above], but in fact turns out to be a paternalistic tool for controlling the behaviour of players to protect the AFL brand" (p. 69). The "third strike policy" names and shames the players after they have tested positive to a drug test on the third occasion. This is done because the AFL suggests "the player has engaged in conduct which is unbecoming or is likely to prejudice the reputation of the AFL and bring the game into disrepute" (Stewart et al., 2008, pp. 69–70). Contrary to this, Stewart et al. (2008) argue that after their "third strike" the player's name and drug taking behaviour is made public at the price of "brand protection."

While doping is considered a major threat to the integrity of sport, and drug use needs to be addressed, the workplace implications of strategies used to eliminate and/or reduce the use of drugs in sport seem to be a secondary consideration. The key challenge when establishing a policy framework to combat drug use is to protect the workplace rights of athletes while ensuring that their welfare is a core element of any anti-doping policy.

The establishment of the Athlete Whereabouts Scheme and the ABP, the Essendon doping scandal, the Australian government's attempt to legislate for national sporting organisations to test in and out of competition for performance enhancing and illicit drug use, and the introduction of criminal prosecution as the ultimate deterrence approach in countries such as Italy, Germany, and France, highlight how the workplace environments of athletes have primarily been driven by policy objectives aimed at drug detection with very limited, if any, consideration of how this agenda could impact on the workplace environment of athletes.

NOTES

1. The 2015 revelations surrounding the alleged state supported doping practices in Russia is a recent example of this.
2. Houlihan (2002, p. 177) gives a comprehensive overview of the evolution of anti-doping policy over the last 60 years.
3. For a detailed case study of the 1998 Tour de France, see Waddington (2000).
4. For further detail on the background to the IOC conference, see Hanstad et al. (2008).
5. For further detail on issues regarding the credibility of the IOC taking responsibility for the anti-doping body, see Hanstad et al. (2008).
6. For further discussion on the regulation of illicit drug use, see Horvath (2006).
7. For further discussion regarding the power struggles surrounding WADA, see Hanstad et al. (2008).
8. For further information on harm-minimisation approaches, see Bessant (2008), Kayser & Smith (2008), Tamburrini (2007), and Waddington (2000).
9. For further information on athletes' attitudes towards drug taking, see Dunn, Thomas, Swift, Burns & Mattick (2010), Gucciardi, Jalleh & Donovan (2011), Petróczi (2007), and Smith & Stewart (2008).
10. Houlihan, in his 2014 paper, moves beyond a discussion of recognition of the Code to examine the ways in which compliance to the Code has been measured by WADA. He suggests there is significant concern with inadequate compliance among some event organisers and some participating countries.
11. Since the writing of this chapter, WADA appealed the Australian Football League's Anti-Doping Tribunal decision that the Players were to be cleared of any wrongdoing. The Court of Arbitration for Sport upheld WADA's appeal to sanction 34 current and former players (Players) of the Australian Football League's Essendon Football Club who played for Essendon during the 2012 season.

REFERENCES

Beamish, R., and I. Ritchie (eds) (2006), *Fastest, highest, strongest: A critique of high-performance sport*, New York, NY, USA: Routledge.
Bessant, J. (2008), 'From "harm minimization" to "zero tolerance" drugs policy in Australia: How the Howard government changed its mind', *Policy Studies*, **29** (2), 197–214.
Bull, A. (2008), 'Cheats sometimes prosper', *The Guardian: The Sport Blog*, 30 May 2008

accessed 10 May 2012 at http://www.guardian.co.uk/sport/2008/may/30/drugsinsport.
olympicgames.
Dimeo, P. (2007), *A history of drug use in sport: 1876–1976: Beyond good and evil*, New York,
NY, USA: Routledge.
Dunn, M., J. Thomas, W. Swift, L. Burns, and R. Mattick (2010), 'Drug testing in sport:
The attitudes and experiences of elite athletes', *International Journal of Drug Policy*, 21,
330–332.
Edwards, A., and J. Skinner (2006), 'Matrix empire', in Allan Edwards and James Skinner
(eds), *Sport Empire*, Oxford, UK: Meyer and Meyer, pp. 114–125.
Engelberg, T., S. Moston, and B. Hutchinson (2014), *A review of the social science anti-
doping literature and recommendations for action*, Australian Government Department
of Regional Australia, Local Government, Arts and Sport: Anti-Doping Research
Program.
Engelberg, T., S. Moston, and J. Skinner (2014), 'The final frontier of anti-doping: A study
of athletes who have committed doping violations', *Sport Management Review*, 18 (2),
268–279, http://dx.doi.org/10.1016/j.smr.2014.06.005.
Foschi, J. (2006), 'A constant battle: The evolving challenges in the international fight
against doping in sport', *Duke Journal of Comparative and International Law*, 457–486.
Gleaves, J. (2014), 'A global history of doping in sport: Drugs, nationalism and politics',
International Journal of the History of Sport, 31 (8), 815–819, doi:10.1080/09523367.201
4.909621.
Gucciardi, D., G. Jalleh, and R. Donovan (2011), 'An examination of the sport drug control
model with elite Australian athletes', *Journal of Science and Medicine in Sport*, 14 (6),
469–476.
Hanstad, D., A. Smith, and I. Waddington (2008), 'The establishment of the world anti-
doping agency: A study of the management of organizational change and unplanned
outcomes', *International Review for the Sociology of Sport*, 43 (3), 227–249.
Horvath, P. (2006), 'Anti-doping and human rights in sport: The case of the AFL and the
WADA Code', *Monash University Law Review*, 32 (2), 357–386.
Houlihan, B. (1999a), 'Anti-doping policy in sport: The politics of international policy
co-ordination', *Public Administration*, 77 (2), 311–334.
Houlihan, B. (ed.) (1999b), *Dying to win: Doping in sport and the development of anti-doping
policy*, Germany: Council of Europe Publishing.
Houlihan, B. (2002), *Dying to win* (2nd ed.), Germany: Council of Europe.
Houlihan, B. (2004), 'Civil rights, doping control and the World Anti-Doping Code', *Sport
in Society*, 7 (3), 420–437.
Houlihan, B. (2014), 'Achieving compliance in international anti-doping policy: An analysis
of the 2009 World Anti-Doping Code', *Sport Management Review*, 17, 265–276.
Kayser, B., and A.C.T. Smith (2008), 'Globalisation of anti-doping: The reverse side of the
medal', *British Medical Journal*, 337, 85–87.
Kuipers, H., and M. van Bottenburg (2015), 'Prevalence of doping use in elite sports: A
review of numbers and methods', *Sport Medicine*, 45 (1), 57–69.
Lippi, G., M. Franchini, and G. Guidi (2008), 'Doping in competition or doping in sport?',
British Medical Bulletin, 86, 95–107.
Mazanov, J. (2014), 'Drug control in sport: What, how and by whom?', in B. Stewart and
M. Burke (eds), *Drugs and sport: Writing from the edge*, Victoria, Australia: Dry Ink Press,
pp. 31–72.
Mazanov, J., and V. McDermott (2009), 'The case for a social science of drugs in sport',
Sport in Society, 12 (3), 276–295.
Miah, A. (ed.) (2004), *Genetically modified athletes: Biomedical ethics, gene doping and sport*,
London, UK and New York, NY, USA: Routledge.
Miller, P., and N. Rose (1990), 'Governing economic life', *Economy and Society*, 19 (1), 1–31.
Moston, S., T. Engelberg, and J. Skinner (2015a), 'Perceived incidence of drug use in
Australian sport: A survey of athletes and coaches', *Sport and Society: Cultures,
Commerce, Media, Politics*, 18 (1), 91–105.

Moston, S., T. Engelberg, and J. Skinner (2015b), 'Athletes' and coaches' perceptions of deterrents to performance-enhancing drug use', *International Journal of Sport Policy and Politics*, **7** (4), 623–636.

Mottram, D. (2005), 'An introduction to drugs and their use in sport', in D. Mottram (ed.), *Drugs in sport* (4th ed.), London, UK: Routledge, pp. 1–28.

Niall, J. (2013), 'Essendon players can walk out: Experts', accessed 1 June 2015 at http://www.theage.com.au/afl/afl-news/essendon-players-can-walk-out-experts-20130822-2sekq.html.

Petróczi, A. (2007), 'Attitudes and doping: A structural equation analysis of the relationship between athletes' attitudes, sport orientation and doping behaviour', *Substance Abuse Treatment, Prevention, and Policy*, **2**. doi: 10.1186/1747-597X-2-34.

Skinner, J., S. Moston, and T. Engelberg (2011), *Athletes' and coaches' attitudes about drugs in sport*, Report prepared for the Department of Health and Ageing. Gold Coast: Griffith University, Australia.

Smith, A.C.T., and B. Stewart (2008), 'Drug policy in sport: Hidden assumptions and inherent contradictions', *Drug and Alcohol Review*, **27**, 123–129.

Stewart, B., D. Adair, and A.C.T. Smith (2011), 'Drivers of illicit drug use regulation in Australian sport', *Sport Management Review*, **14**, 237–245.

Stewart, B., M. Nicholson, A.C.T. Smith, and H. Westerbeek (eds) (2004), *Australian Sport: Better by Design? The evolution of Australian sport policy*, London, UK and New York, NY, USA: Routledge.

Stewart, B., and A.C.T. Smith (2008), 'Drug use in sport: Implications for public policy', *Journal of Sport and Social Issues*, **32** (3), 278–298.

Stewart, B., and A.C.T. Smith (2010), 'The role of ideology in shaping drug use regulation in Australian sport', *International Review for the Sociology of Sport*, **45** (2), 187–198.

Stewart, B. and A.C.T. Smith (2014), 'Sport, drug-use regulation and human rights: An Australian case study', in B. Stewart and M. Burke (eds), *Drugs and sport: Writing from the edge*, Victoria, Australia: Dry Ink Press, pp. 101–124.

Stewart, B., A.C.T. Smith, and G. Dickson (2008), 'Drug use in the Australian Football League: A critical survey', *Sporting Traditions*, **25** (1), 57–74.

Tamburrini, C. (2007), 'Are doping sanctions justified? A moral relativistic view', in A. Schneider and F. Hong (eds), *Doping in sport: Global ethical issues*, New York, NY, USA: Routledge, pp. 23–35.

UNESCO (2011a), *Background to the convention*, accessed 7 June 2011 at http://www.unesco.org/new/en/social-and-human-sciences/themes/sport/anti-doping/international-convention-against-doping-in-sport/background/.

UNESCO (2011b), *International convention against doping in sport*, accessed 7 June 2011 at http://www.unesco.org/new/en/social-and-human-sciences/themes/sport/anti-doping/international-convention-against-doping-in-sport/.

Verroken, M. (2000), 'Drug use and abuse in sport', *Baillière's Best Practice and Research. Clinical Endocrinology and Metabolism*, **14** (1), 1–23.

Verroken, M. (2005), 'Drug use and abuse in sport', in D. Mottram (ed.), *Drugs in sport* (4th ed.), London, UK: Routledge, pp. 29–63.

WADA (2003), *Copenhagen declaration on anti-doping in sport*, accessed 13 June 2011 at http://www.wada-ama.org/Documents/World_Anti-Doping_Program/Governments/WADA_Copenhagen_Declaration_EN.pdf.

WADA (2009a), *Constitutive instrument of foundation of the World Anti-Doping Agency*, Lausanne.

WADA (2009b), *World Anti-Doping Code*, accessed 12 September 2014 at http://www.wada-ama.org/Documents/World_Anti-Doping_Program/WADP-The-Code/WADA_Anti-Doping_CODE_2009_EN.pdf.

WADA (2011a), *About WADA*, accessed 6 April 2011 at http://www.wada-ama.org/en/About-WADA/.

WADA (2011b), *Finance*, accessed 7 April 2011 at http://www.wada-ama.org/en/About-WADA/Funding/.

WADA (2011c), *Governance*, accessed 7 April 2011 at http://www.wada-ama.org/en/About-WADA/Governance/.
WADA (2011d), *President's welcome message*, accessed 7 April 2011 at http://www.wada-ama.org/en/About-WADA/Presidents-Welcome-Message/.
WADA (2011e), *WADA history*, accessed 7 April 2011 at http://www.wada-ama.org/en/About-WADA/History/WADA-History/.
Waddington, I. (ed.) (2000), *Sport, health and drugs: A critical sociological perspective*, London, UK and New York, NY, USA: E & FN Spon.
Yesalis, C., and M.S. Bahrke (2002), 'History of doping in sport', *International Sports Studies*, **24** (1), 42–76.

PART IV

THE ECONOMICS OF PROFESSIONAL SPORTS

15. Player trades, free agents and transfer policies in professional sport
Simon Gardiner and Roger Welch

INTRODUCTION

For a typical employee the relationship with the employer, including how and when that relationship can be terminated, is regulated by the contract of employment. Employment contracts also have an important role to play for professional sportsmen and women, but in some team sports, internal sporting rules operate to act as a player restraint and provide significant control on the part of the employer over the employee player. These restraints act essentially by not allowing a player to sign a contract with or be allocated to a new club without the existing club's agreement. This control by a player's club (and employer) promotes contract stability between teams and players. This stability is justified on the sporting grounds of ensuring competitive balance between teams (in that no one club can acquire all the top players) and the unpredictability of outcome in the result of a match. However, the contract stability that player restraints boost is inevitably at the expense of player mobility, resulting in an inherent tension that sports bodies and sports regulators have had to grapple with.

Player restraints can be characterized firstly as those that specifically restrict freedom of movement from one club to another. This includes, in US professional sports, the reserve clause, where a club acquired exclusive rights over a contracted player to prolong the contract upon its expiry. This has effectively prevented players becoming free agents at the end of their contracts so as to be able to negotiate with a potential new employer club. The effect of the reserve clause has been challenged in the professional leagues in the US, notably in litigation that led to the successful challenge to the anti-trust law exemption in baseball and introduced free agency.[1] In Europe, the transfer and registration system, most notably in professional football, has historically operated similarly as a restriction on the movement of players and the attainment of free agency. The legal challenge to the restraints provided by the transfer and registration system will be the focus of this chapter.

Player restraints on movement can occur secondly, and indirectly, by restraints on wages through mechanisms such as salary caps that operate in US professional leagues and increasingly in professional teams sport in Europe. European football does not operate a salary cap, but the Financial Fair Play rules introduced by the Union of European Football Associations (UEFA) requires that player wages and other club expenditure do not exceed club income.

In the context of the focus on football, it is necessary to understand how contractual relationships interrelate with transfer systems and the requirement for a player to be registered with a specific club. This chapter will explain how transfer systems work, their relationship with European law – in particular the role that has been played by the European Commission and rulings of the Court of Justice of the European Union (CJEU, formerly the ECJ) – and international sporting bodies such as FIFA (Fédération Internationale de Football Association), and will discuss how transfer systems may be further regulated in the future. Inevitably, the main focus is on professional football, but transfer systems also operate in other professional sports such as rugby league, basketball and handball. Rugby union does not currently operate a transfer system, but there have been calls for it to adopt one.[2] Effectively, as transfer systems are sporting rules which act as restraints on players' freedom of contract and movement, any ruling or decision by the CJEU concerning one sport will have ramifications for all other relevant sports. The major issues of discussion are the circumstances in which a player can be prevented from moving to another club, when a player becomes a free agent and is able to move at will, prohibitions on the 'tapping up' of players and the impact of transfer windows.

LITERATURE REVIEW

The following sources inform this chapter and can be regarded as further reading.

Primary Sources

FIFA Regulations for the Status and Transfer of Players, http://www.fifa.com/mm/document/affederation/administration/01/06/30/78/statusinhalt_en_122007.pdf.

These rules regulate international transfers where a player moves to a club in a different national association to that of his current club. This chapter provides detailed explanation and critical analysis of these rules.

English Premier League Rules 2013/14, http://www.premierleague.com/

content/dam/premierleague/site-content/News/publications/handbooks/
premier-league-handbook-2013-14.pdf.

Sections T, U and V of these rules provide the model for the regulation of player transfers and contracts, approaches to and by players and the operation of transfer windows for all the domestic leagues in Britain. The rules therefore provide a detailed exemplar of how a transfer system actually operates and the basis for the critique of transfer systems contained in this chapter.

Opinion of Advocate General Lenz in ASBL Union Royale Belge des Societes de Football Association & others v Jean-Marc Bosman [1996] 1 CMLR 645 (Case C-415/93).

This landmark ruling provides the major basis for legal modification of the transfer system in Europe, and indeed throughout the world as a whole. This illustrates the role of Europe as a power base of football in a global context. This chapter and many of the sources cited in it focus on the Bosman ruling and its ongoing ramifications.

Secondary Sources

R. Blanpain and R. Inston (1996), *The Bosman Case: The End of the Transfer System?*, London: Sweet & Maxwell; Leuven: Peeters.

A. Caiger and J. O'Leary (2000), 'The end of the affair: *"The Anelka Doctrine"* – the problem of contract stability in English professional football', in A. Caiger and S. Gardiner (eds), *Professional Sport in the EU: Regulation and Re-regulation*, The Hague: Asser Press.

J. O'Leary and A. Caiger (2000), 'The re-regulation of football and its impact on employment contracts', in H. Collins, P. Davies, and R. Rideout (eds), *The Legal Regulation of the Employment Relation*, London: Kluwer.

These works provide comprehensive and seminal critiques of the transfer system, and argue that transfer systems constitute a form of slavery and should be replaced by regulation through normal contractual mechanisms.

S. Gardiner, R. Parrish and R. Siekmann (2009), *EU, Sport, Law and Policy: Regulation, Re-regulation and Representation*, The Hague: Asser Press.

The essays contained in this text critically examine and discuss the relationship between EU policy and law with particular focus on how the traditional system of self-regulation in sport has increasingly become subject to re-regulation through the juridification of sporting rules – including transfer systems – particularly through rulings of the CJEU concerned with freedom of movement and competition law. The essays also provide detailed commentary on the central EU policy document, the European Commission's White Paper on Sport.

S. Weatherill (2006), 'Anti-doping revisited – the demise of the rule of "purely sporting interest"?', *European Competition Law Review*, **27** (12), 645–657.

This article analyses rulings of the CJEU which have drastically restricted the notion of what constitutes a 'pure' sporting rule outside the scope of legal regulation. Consequently, there can be no doubt that the issues discussed in this chapter are all subject to legal regulation and that such regulation overrides traditional systems of self-regulation by sporting bodies.

R. Welch (2012), 'Sport and contracts of employment', in S. Gardiner, J. O'Leary, R. Welch, S. Boyes and U. Naidoo, *Sports Law*, London: Routledge, Chapter 9.

This chapter contains in-depth analysis of employment contracts in professional sport and of the Bosman ruling with regard to freedom of movement. It discusses how contractual mechanisms that can be applied to a number of different types of employment contracts could also be used in contracts between clubs and players.

S. Gardiner and R. Welch (2007), 'The contractual dynamics of team stability versus player mobility: Who rules "the beautiful game"?', *Entertainment and Sports Law Journal*, **5** (1).

This article sets out in detail our perspectives on the transfer system in football and on the FIFA rules on international transfers. We argue that a modified form of the transfer system should be permitted as it provides the most efficient and certain mechanism for striking a balance between club stability and the right of players to terminate their employment contracts. It argues that transfer systems are best regulated through a system of reflexive law based on social dialogue and/or an EU Directive setting out minimum standards whilst leaving detailed regulation in the hands of sporting bodies.

G. Pearson (2015), 'Sporting Justifications under EU Free Movement and Competition Law: The case of the football "transfer system"'. *European Law Journal*, **21** (2), 220–238.

This article provides a comprehensive critique of the FIFA rules and their failure to bring the transfer system into line with EU law.

There is a full list of the other sources cited in the text at the end of this chapter.

THE TRANSFER SYSTEM IN BRITISH FOOTBALL AND THE BOSMAN RULING

Normally, when an employee's current contract comes to an end that employee has complete freedom to seek employment with a new employer.

Except in relatively special cases where employers can rely on clauses contained in an employment contract imposing some restrictions of this freedom of contract, the former employer has no control over the former employee's choice of a new employer. This is so even when the latter is a competitor of the former employer. The essence of a transfer system in sport is that at the end of his contract a player is not free to negotiate a move to a new club unless he is permitted to do this by his current club. In this case he is literally a free agent who can move to a new club on whatever terms he (or his agent) can negotiate. Otherwise he is only permitted to move to another club if that club pays a transfer fee. If the two clubs cannot agree on the amount of this fee then the player remains an employee of his current club and is thus tied to it. Rules requiring professional players to be registered with clubs provide the mechanism for the operation of a transfer system, as a player can only be registered permanently with one club and that club can refuse to release a player's registration unless a transfer fee is agreed.

In Britain, the football transfer that operates in professional football has been regarded as compatible with British law since the decision of the English High Court in *Eastham v Newcastle FC* (1963).[3] This transfer system continues to apply in its entirety to players who are under 24 and out of contract. When such a player's contract comes to an end the club can retain him as a registered player through offering a new contract on terms no less advantageous than the expired contract. This offer must be made by the third Saturday in May, which is just after the end of the domestic season. The player is permitted to reject this offer and thereby become 'free' to negotiate a move to another club, but this is subject to the clubs agreeing a transfer fee. If a fee cannot be agreed between the two clubs the player's registration can be transferred to the new club providing that club agrees to pay a fee as determined by the Professional Football Compensation Committee. In practice, a player's desire to move may be frustrated if the other club is not prepared to pay the required fee or accept that the amount of the fee should be determined by the Compensation Committee. Moreover, a player may submit to pressure to sign a new contract with a club to regain some security of employment.

However, where a player's contract comes to an end after his 24th birthday then that player is free to reject any offer made to him by his current club and to commence negotiations with other clubs with a view to joining one of them. If a contract is successfully concluded with another club then the player's registration passes to his new club. This freedom of contract enjoyed by players over the age of 24 is the consequence of the landmark ruling in 1996 by the CJEU (when it was still the European Court of Justice) in the *Bosman* case.

The European Court's ruling in this case is based on its interpretation of what is now Article 45 of the Treaty on the Functioning of the European Union (TFEU),[4] which provides for the right of EU nationals to work and reside in any Member State on equal terms with the nationals of that State. This Article is directly applicable, which means it is enforceable in national courts and tribunals. The Article takes precedence over any conflicting national laws. Under Article 267 of the TFEU, at the request of either party, or at its own discretion, a national court may decide to request a preliminary ruling from the European Court on the meaning of Article 45 (or any other aspect of EU law). The European Court is not deciding the case on appeal but is answering the questions put to it by the national court. This court will then decide the case by applying the interpretation of the Article contained in the European Court's ruling, and any relevant national law which does not conflict with it, to the facts of the case. The opinion of an Advocate General to the European Court is highly influential, but not binding, on any ruling (or decision) that the Court gives.

This is the process through which Bosman, a Belgian footballer, was able to challenge traditional transfer systems then operating in European leagues. Bosman was placed on the transfer list by his club, RC Liege, once he refused to accept a new contract at a lower wage. Bosman wished to move to a French club, US Dunkerque, but RC Liege ultimately refused to process the transfer as it doubted US Dunkerque's ability to pay the agreed fee. Subsequently, the Belgian Football Association and UEFA became parties to the case as both bodies argued that their respective rules requiring transfer fees were lawful. The Cour d'Appel, Liege requested a preliminary ruling from the European Court. One question put to the European Court was whether what is now Article 45 TFEU is to be interpreted as: '... prohibiting a football club from requiring and receiving payment of a sum of money upon the engagement of one of its players who has come to the end of his contract by a new employing club.'

The Opinion of Advocate General Lenz was in the affirmative on the basis that:

> ... the transfer rules directly restrict access to the employment market in other Member States ... under the applicable rules a player can transfer abroad only if the new club (or the player himself) is in a position to pay the transfer fee demanded. If that is not the case, the player *cannot* move abroad. That is a *direct* restriction on access to the employment market. (para 10 of the Opinion)

This aspect of Lenz's Opinion was subsequently accepted by the European Court in its ruling in Bosman's favour.

As a general principle of EU law it is possible to justify restrictions on or interference with rights granted by EU law. However, any such justification must meet the requirement of proportionality. Justification will fail if the adverse impact of the restriction on a person or organization outweighs the benefits secured by it, or any legitimate objectives secured by the restriction can be achieved by other means. In reaching his conclusion the Advocate General considered and rejected the need to protect smaller clubs and provide compensation to clubs for training players as constituting grounds for justifying the retention of the transfer system. In so far as these objectives were legitimate, they did not meet the requirement of proportionality as they could be achieved through a redistribution of income from larger to smaller clubs. In short, any legitimate interests could be achieved by means other than a transfer system impeding rights of freedom of movement.

A second limb of the Bosman ruling concerned the compatibility with EU law of national rules which imposed quotas on the number of foreign players that could be fielded in a match. The European Court ruled that in so far as players who were EU nationals were concerned such quota systems were unlawful. This aspect of Bosman and its ongoing ramifications will be fully considered in Chapter 17.

CONSEQUENCES OF BOSMAN

It is interesting to reflect with the benefit of hindsight on the fact that many of the initial responses to the *Bosman* ruling concentrated on the extent to which it would still be business as usual. The essence of the ruling is that an out of contract player must be permitted to move to a club in a different EU Member State, and therefore there was an argument that the ruling would not affect the transfer system then operating *within* domestic leagues as the ruling did not explicitly cover the situation where a player wishes to move to another club within the same country. It was assumed by almost everyone (including ourselves) that *Bosman* had no implications for players who wished to secure transfers whilst still under contract.

On the other hand, whilst the actual legal position has not been and in practice never may be clarified, there were arguments (Morris, Morrow & Spink, 1996; Gardiner & Welch, 1998) that *Bosman* did impact on transfers within Member States. Hence the decision by the regulatory bodies in Britain to make voluntary changes to the domestic transfer system by restricting it to players under the age of 24, as detailed above. In making these changes the threat of legal challenge was pre-empted.

The *Bosman* ruling did not and does not directly apply to players recruited from outside of the European Union and European Economic

Area (EEA). Players from, as examples, European States outside of the EU/EEA, the Americas, most African countries, Asia and Australia are not protected by Article 45 TFEU. As a matter of historical record it should be noted that FIFA decided with effect from 1 April 1997 to change its rules to permit any player to move to other clubs within the EU on free transfers once their contracts expire. Thus a British club still has to pay a transfer fee to import a player from, for example, an Australian club. However, if it retains that player until his contract expires a transfer fee cannot be claimed unless that player negotiates a move to a club outside of the EU.

The view that *Bosman* had no implications for players who were still under contract was challenged by the European Commission. The initial background to intervention by the Commission was the announcement by Nicolas Anelka in the summer of 1999 that he no longer wanted to honour his contract to play for Arsenal FC. Anelka wished to leave the UK and play for the Italian club, Lazio. At the time of this announcement Anelka had another four years of his contract to run. The problem for Anelka was that Arsenal was not prepared to release him from his contractual obligations, and Lazio was not prepared to pay the sizeable transfer fee that Arsenal required.

This situation generated legal debate (initiated by Jean-Louis Dupont, the Belgian lawyer who advised Bosman) around whether to prevent a player from terminating his employment contract, as the transfer system does, is as much a restraint on a player's freedom of movement as where a player is prevented from moving to another club on the expiry of that contract. The argument on behalf of Anelka was that he should have the right to break his contract providing he was prepared to pay compensation to Arsenal by reference to the normal contractual principles for calculating damages (Caiger & O'Leary, 2000; cf. Tsatsas, 1999). The position with respect to Anelka was ultimately resolved when Arsenal accepted a transfer bid submitted by Real Madrid. However, the incident cast doubt on the original assumption, in the aftermath of *Bosman*, that Article 45 only applied to out of contract players. The case certainly illustrated the power possessed by star players with an international reputation to challenge the restrictions on them imposed by transfer systems.

The legal situation was further complicated by a complaint to the Commission by the Italian club Perugia. The basis of the club's complaint was that it wished to recruit an Italian player, Massimo Lombardo, from the Swiss club, Zurich Grasshoppers. Although Lombardo was at the end of his contract with Grasshoppers, *Bosman* did not directly apply to his situation, as Switzerland is not covered by EU law. In December 1998 the Commission ruled that the then existing transfer system in its entirety, not just on expiry of a player's contract, violated EU competition law. This resulted in FIFA coming under considerable pressure to formulate proposals for reform, although the Commission had also emphasized it was not seeking the complete abolition of the transfer system as it recognized the 'specificity of sport'.

FIFA REGULATIONS FOR THE STATUS AND TRANSFER OF PLAYERS

This threat of litigation by the European Commission led to FIFA adopting new rules for the regulation of the international transfer system. These first came into force on 1 September 2001, and an amended version applied from 1 July 2005. It must be emphasized that the FIFA rules apply only to international transfers where a player has negotiated a move to a club in a different national association to the one in which he currently plays.

Essentially, the FIFA rules modify the international transfer system by restricting its full operation to players under the age of 23. Even with regard to such players the intention was that negotiated transfer fees would be replaced by compensation calculated by applying criteria set out in Annex 4 to the rules. The transfer system is loosened up for players over 23 by enabling a player to terminate his contract and move to another club once the protected period of his contract has expired. This protected period is three seasons in the case of a contract signed by a player before his 28th birthday, and two seasons in the case of a contract signed after a player's 28th birthday. The rules specify that a player's contract may not last for longer than five years.

Under Article 17 of the FIFA rules, once the protected period has expired, a player is able to terminate his contract in order to join a new club provided compensation is paid to his current club. This compensation should be at least equal to the remaining value of the player's contract plus any transfer fee that the club paid for the player (the value of this fee decreases over the period of time that the contract has lasted). If there is unilateral breach without just cause during the protected period his club will again be entitled to claim compensation, but sporting sanctions will also be applied against the player. Sporting sanctions may also be applied where contracts are terminated outside of the protected period but such termination is not in accordance with the strict requirements of Article 17 (see the *Webster* case, below). Under Article 23, a player is prevented from participating in any official football match, except for the club to which he was contracted, for up to an effective period of four months as from the beginning of the next season. This period can be extended to a maximum period of six months in cases of aggravating circumstances, such as failure to give notice or recurrent breach.

If a club has induced a player to act in breach of contract the ban may continue until the expiry of the second transfer window following the date the breach of contract was committed. However, any such ban cannot last for longer than 12 months. Where appropriate, sporting sanctions may also be imposed against the player's agent and the club inducing the breach. Sanctions against the latter may include fines, bans on participating in the transfer market, deduction of points and exclusion from competitions.

The FIFA rules further enhance player mobility by enabling players to terminate their contracts if they have due or a 'sporting just cause'. The former position is in accordance with general contract law principles to be found in common law countries if a club has committed a serious breach of contract which enables the player to establish constructive dismissal, so that it is the club that, in law, is deemed responsible for terminating the contract. However, there is no automatic correlation between the notion of a 'sporting just cause' and a club acting in breach of contract. For the purposes of international transfers only, Article 15 of the FIFA rules stipulates that sporting just cause includes failure to involve an 'established Professional' in less than 10 percent of a club's official matches. However, the meaning of sporting just cause is otherwise not defined, and there is clearly scope for different interpretations at the level of national courts where national associations have embraced the concept of contract termination for 'sporting just cause'. It is of interest to note that the English Premiership and Football League rules have yet to do this even though the FIFA rules specify that all national associations should make provision for such termination in their national rules.

THE FIFA RULES IN PRACTICE

As is so often the case the devil is in the detail, and even when the protected period has expired, or the player wishes to terminate for sporting just cause, he may not terminate his contract during a season. Indeed, a player only has 15 days after the last official match of the season to notify his club that he has decided to terminate his contract with it. The practical significance of these restrictions is demonstrated by the findings of FIFA's Dispute Resolution Chamber (DRC) in the *Webster* case. Andy Webster terminated his contract with the Scottish football club, Hearts FC, at the end of the 2005–06 season and then agreed to move to Wigan FC. Hearts successfully argued that Article 17 did not apply, even though the protected period of Webster's contract had expired, as he had failed to give the requisite 15 days' notice. In fact, Webster gave notice within 15 days of the Scottish Cup Final, which he argued by custom and practice constituted the last match of the Scottish season. The DRC disagreed but, on the basis that this constituted a minor breach of the rules, only banned him from the first two matches of the following season.

With respect to compensation, the DRC rejected Hearts' claim of £5 million and awarded the club £625 000. This figure was arrived at by reference to the residual value of Webster's contract with Hearts which, because his salary in the first year of his contract with Wigan was also taken into account, was then multiplied with a 1.5 coefficient (this being the permitted maximum). The basis for awarding this lower amount of compensation was approved by the Court of Arbitration for Sport (CAS).[5]

The *Webster* case was initially hailed as the 'new Bosman' in so far as it confirms the right of a player to change clubs irrespective of whether his current club is prepared to release him from his contract. However, the case also demonstrates the narrow nature of the freedom of movement provided by Article 17 in that it limits the window of opportunity for contract termination to 15 days. This is particularly problematic given prohibitions on under-contract players from talking to or being approached by other clubs. The FIFA rules do not permit players to negotiate contracts with new clubs until they are in the final six months of their contract and are therefore in the process of becoming free agents. Moreover, these rules only apply where a player is seeking to move to a club in a different national association. By way of contrast, and as discussed further below, in Britain, players can only approach clubs in domestic leagues after their contracts have expired.

The way in which the FIFA rules have not led to the intended relaxation of the transfer system is particularly illustrated by the decision of the CAS in *Matuzalem*.[6] The CAS granted Shakhtar Donetsk compensation of €11 258 934 plus interest in circumstances where it accepted that the player had terminated his contract in accordance with Article 17 of the FIFA rules outside the protected period of his contract. In calculating this compensation, the CAS took into account a number of factors including the conduct of the player in accepting a salary increase at a time when he knew he was looking to move to another club.

The CAS's approach to Article 17 is encapsulated by para 63 of its judgment where it states:

> ... a termination of a contract without just cause, even if this occurs outside of the Protected Period and following the appropriate notice period, remains a serious violation of the obligation to respect an existing contract and does

trigger the consequences set out in art. 17 para. 1 FIFA Regulations. In other words, art. 17 FIFA Regulations does not give to a party, neither a club nor a player, a free pass to unilaterally breach an existing agreement at no price or at a given fix price.

It is clear from this dictum that the CAS does not perceive Article 17 as providing for the right of a player to buy out his contract as this concept would be commonly understood. Rather, the Article does enable a player to secure his release from being registered as a player with a particular club, but only if the relevant compensation is paid, and this may well be a very substantial sum of money which is in excess of the direct financial loss suffered by a club as a result of the player's termination of his contract.

FIFPro, the footballers' international trade union, has criticized the *Matuzalem* ruling on the basis that it operates as a significant restraint on a player's ability to move to a new club once the protected period of his contract has expired, and this contradicts the enhanced mobility which it was intended should be given to players under Article 17 of the FIFA Regulations. Thus, in FIFPro's view, the only basis for compensation should be the residual value of a player's contract. However, *Matuzalem* has been followed by the CAS in subsequent case law.[7]

The cumulative effect of this case law is that it is much more complicated and expensive than originally envisaged for a player under contract to terminate that contract in order to effect a move to a new club. Indeed, even without these interpretations, it has never been absolutely clear whether the FIFA rules conform with EU law, as, to date, the CJEU has never been called upon to rule on this issue, and litigation challenging the rules could still occur in the future. Moreover, there has been academic criticism of the FIFA rules. For example, John O'Leary and Andrew Caiger (O'Leary & Caiger, 2000) have provided a particularly intriguing argument supporting the contention that *Bosman* applies to players denied a mid-contract transfer. They argue that any player who unilaterally breaks his contract should be considered to be out of contract. Thus, in line with *Bosman*, the employing club has no option other than to release his registration. The club's only remedy is to seek damages for breach of contract. Caiger and O'Leary also stress that to permit professional footballers to act in this way is simply to allow them to act as any other employee under any other contract of employment is able to do.

These arguments are certainly cogent. However, they fail to take into account whether sporting rules which act as a form of restraint should nevertheless be regarded as justifiable. Moreover, as mentioned above, there are circumstances, which logically could be applied to footballers' contracts, whereby courts can grant injunctions to prevent employees from acting in breach of contract, or from working for a competitor on termination of an existing contract, even though such contractual provisions constitute restrictive covenants in restraint of trade (see McCutcheon, 1997; Gardiner & Welch, 2007; Welch, 2012). Thus it is not always the case that an employee is free to walk away from a job by unilaterally breaking the contract of employment. It is also debatable whether a player who terminates a contract through committing a unilateral breach can be regarded as being 'out of contract' in the sense that that concept was used in *Bosman*. The general tenor of the ruling was that an 'out of contract' player is a player whose contract has run its course and thus expired. It remains to be seen whether the correct legal position will ever be clarified by a ruling from the CJEU.

Further restrictions on the ability of players under contract to move to other clubs are provided by the imposition of 'transfer windows' and prohibitions on players and their agents talking to other clubs before their contracts have expired. The latter rules, designed to prevent the 'tapping up' of players, are particularly problematic in the British domestic leagues.

TRANSFER WINDOWS

Both FIFA and UEFA rules require the establishment of transfer windows. These are specified periods during which transfers of players are permitted. With the exception of temporary transfers where a club loans a player to another club, transfers may not take place outside of these windows. In the British domestic leagues the transfer windows are specified as commencing at midnight on the last day of the season and ending on 31 August, with a second window opening at midnight on 31 December and ending on 31 January.

It is the case that transfer windows do exist in other sports and were accepted as valid for basketball by the European Court in its ruling in *Lehtonen*.[8] However, the fact that transfer windows have been objectively justified as having sporting benefits connected with team stability and 'regularity' of sporting competition in one sport does not automatically mean that this must also be the case in all other sports (McAuley, 2003).

Indeed, it can be argued that the transfer windows, as they operate in European football, would fail the test of proportionality in that they are too restrictive. The suspicion is that they essentially favour the larger richer clubs who can afford to assemble large squads and spend significant sums on transfers in a concentrated period of time. FIFPro has issued a statement that supports the view that transfer windows in the UK constitute an invalid restraint of trade.[9] Although the Premier League has essentially accepted their legitimacy, the Football League has led an orchestrated campaign against them. It has argued: 'League clubs have traditionally relied on the flexibility to buy, sell or loan players whenever needed for either football or financial reasons. If this freedom is restricted clubs' financial health will suffer'.[10] Moreover, such criticisms are not restricted to League clubs. For example, during Portsmouth FC's first season in the Premiership (2003–04), Harry Redknapp, the manager, claimed that the club's fortunes on the field of play were unduly hampered by injuries in circumstances where new players could not be brought in.[11]

'TAPPING UP'

Under rules that operate in the British domestic leagues (for example, Rules T2, T6 and T8 of the Premier League), unless a player is out of contract and therefore a free agent, a club may not, without the consent of his current club, directly or indirectly approach a player with a view to signing him. Moreover, this applies even to a player who will be out of contract at the end of the season. Such a player may only be approached once the season has finished after the third Saturday in May, and then only if that player has not received a new offer from his current club, or he has declined such an offer. Players and their agents are also prohibited from making similar approaches to clubs without the permission of the player's current club. It should be noted that indirect approaches include a statement made publicly by or on behalf of a club expressing interest in acquiring the registration of a player under contract, or by such a player expressing interest in transferring his registration to another club.

The operation of these rules is exemplified by a well-documented incident involving Arsenal, Ashley Cole and Chelsea FC. Both Cole and Chelsea were fined by the English Football Association for breach of what was then Rule K5, through discussing Cole moving to Chelsea without first seeking Arsenal's permission for such talks to take place. Cole did subsequently move to Chelsea, and it is the case that this specific incident did not result in litigation – indeed the CAS declined on jurisdictional grounds to review the case. Nevertheless, the validity of the rules is still open to challenge and thus litigation in the future cannot be ruled out. It can be argued that the rules constitute unreasonable restraints of trade and/or violate a player's freedom of movement under EU law. It may also be that they are in breach of EU competition law on the basis that the English Premier League occupies a dominant position in the European market and the rules are an abuse of this position.

The essential question is what makes footballers different to other

employees, including those on fixed term contracts, who may seek to negotiate with a prospective employer either on entering into an employment
contract with that employer on the expiry of the current contract or with
a view to the buying out of that contract. In short, it may be argued that
Rules T2, T6 and T8 constitute an illegal restraint of trade. Additionally, it
could be argued that these rules are unjustifiable constraints on a player's
freedom of movement under Article 45. Indeed, legal advice provided to
FIFPro by its lawyer Wil van Megen suggests that the rule is contrary to
EU law.[12] This contention is reinforced by the fact that other leagues in
Europe do not have equivalents to these rules.

It should be taken into account that Rule T6 also constitutes a term in
a player's contract, and, in counter position to the above, it can be argued
that other mechanisms to prevent valuable employees from acting in
breach of contract, such as the use of garden-leave provisions and post-
employment restraints, have been upheld as valid by the courts. Moreover,
players enjoy significantly high salaries and untypical security of employment during the currency of their contracts. Footballers are paid handsomely even when injured or when not selected. In short, players are major
business assets and thus clubs have a proprietary interest in holding them
to their contracts. Overall, there is an analogy between the operation of
the Rule and using contractual mechanisms to protect other proprietary
interests such as trade secrets and goodwill. With respect to proportionality, the Premier League has argued that the Rule is necessary for competitive integrity, contractual stability, team stability and competitive balance
(for further discussion see Shear & Green, 2005; Goldberg & Pentol, 2005).

In our view, the arbitrary nature of the Rule does seem invidious. As the
Rule stands, no distinction is made between a player whose contract has
several years to run and a player who is in the last year of his contract and
is free to move on expiry of that contract. The latter needs to ascertain his
prospects, both with his current club and prospective new clubs, as far as
the signing of a new contract is concerned. It is hard to see how preventing
a player from doing this until his current contract has expired can be anything other than an unreasonable restraint, or disproportionate restriction
on his freedom of movement. This is particularly the case given that the
FIFA rules do permit players, wishing to negotiate international transfers,
to talk to clubs in other countries with a view to concluding a pre-season
contract during the last six months of their current contracts.

It should be noted that similar rules apply to clubs and players in English
rugby league. For example, the Rugby Football League (RFL) decided to
suspend Paul Cooke, after its Operational Rules Tribunal found that the
player had broken its rules by approaching Hull Kingston Rovers whilst
still under contract to local rivals Hull FC. Whilst the same argument set

out above applies with respect to restraint of trade, it is less likely that a rugby league player could succeed in challenging the rules under EU law. This is because it would be difficult to establish that the English RFL has a dominant position in the European market and/or its rules affect trade between Member States contrary to Article 102 TFEU (Sandlant & Silkin, 2007).

CRITIQUING THE TRANSFER SYSTEM

As we have seen neither the *Bosman* ruling nor the FIFA rules have led to substantial changes to, let alone the abolition of, transfer systems as they operate within domestic leagues in professional football. Moreover, even with regard to international transfers it has proved much harder than anticipated for players under contract to move to other clubs outside of the protected period of their contracts. It is also the case that transfer fees remain highly inflated, despite the FIFA rules seeking to restrict fees to the costs of developing a player's abilities; and the transfer system continues to have its murky side with regard to the activities of agents and deals allegedly concluded through the handing over of payments as sweeteners to facilitate them (Gardiner, 2006), and ongoing controversies concerning third party 'ownership' of players whereby an agent, rather than a club, holds a player's registration.

It can be argued that the transfer system should simply be abolished. One such argument is based on the view that the transfer system is a form of slavery, and that players should be freed from the shackles it provides to enable clubs to tie players to them for the entire period of their contracts, or, in the case of younger players, even after their contracts have expired (Blanpain & Inston, 1996). If clubs were no longer able to hold on to a player by refusing to release that player's registration, a footballer would be in the same position as employees in general.

On the other hand, we have argued that even if clubs were no longer able to hold on to a player's registration, the commodification of professional football is such that there would still be an informal transfer system in that clubs would still wish to avoid litigation by negotiating sums of compensation where a player is seeking to move to a new club in breach of contract. Essentially, footballers would be in the same position as that currently occupied by their managers and coaches. Therefore, the solution lies not so much in the abolition of the transfer system as in putting in place a workable system of regulation which recognizes the valid concerns of regulatory bodies, players, clubs and, indeed perhaps most importantly of all, long-suffering football fans (Gardiner & Welch, 2007).

The failure of the FIFA rules to result in a significant relaxation of the transfer system has led to renewed calls from both FIFPro and EU bodies for further external intervention. FIFPro has criticized how the enhanced player mobility, which the FIFA rules were intended to bring about, has in practice been circumvented by restrictive interpretations and the levels of compensation that a player or his new club are required to pay if a player decides to terminate his contract outside of the protected period. Consequently, FIFPro warned FIFA and UEFA that it is seriously contemplating mounting a legal challenge to the transfer system in the CJEU. In the wake of this warning, in September 2015, FIFPro lodged a formal complaint to the European Commission with specific reference to the FIFA rules on the basis that they violate EU competition law.[13] FIFPro also supports the findings of a new EU report, published on 7 February 2013, which urges the overhaul of the football transfer system.[14]

According to the report, the current system mostly benefits the wealthiest clubs, superstar players and their agents. With respect to the perspectives of Advocate General Lenz in *Bosman* on the redistribution of money generated by the transfer system, it is interesting that the report has found that football clubs spend around €3 billion a year on player transfers but very little of this trickles down to smaller clubs or the amateur game. The number of transfers in European football more than tripled in the period 1995–2011, whilst the amounts spent by clubs on transfer fees increased seven-fold. But most of the big spending is concentrated on a small number of elite clubs which have the largest revenues, or are backed by very wealthy investors. This is despite fair play rules, introduced by UEFA and implemented in the English Premier and Football Leagues, which seek to limit the amount of a debt that a club may incur so that it must substantially operate within the income generated by its gate receipts and other commercial activities. The report concludes that the level of redistribution of money in the game, which should compensate for the costs of training young players and developing new talent, is insufficient to allow smaller clubs to develop and to break the stranglehold that the biggest clubs continue to have on the sport.

The report's proposals include:

1. FIFA and national football associations to ensure stronger controls over financial transactions.
2. Introduction of a 'fair-play levy' on transfer fees beyond an amount to be agreed by the sport's governing bodies and clubs to ensure fund redistribution from rich to less wealthy clubs.
3. Better publicizing of the movement of players to ensure that solidarity compensations are paid to clubs and that the latter are aware of their rights.

4. Establishing a limit on the number of players per club.
5. Regulating the loan transfer mechanism.
6. Addressing the issue of 'third-party ownership' where a player is effectively leased to a club by an agent.
7. Ending contractual practices which inflate transfer fees, such as where a club extends the protected period during which players cannot be transferred without its consent.

The report also calls for full implementation of UEFA's Financial Fair Play rule and stronger solidarity mechanisms to enhance youth development and the protection of minors. The authors of the report urge sports bodies to improve their cooperation with law enforcement authorities to combat money laundering and corruption.

It is perfectly possible that, in the not too distant future, the findings of this report could result in renewed intervention by the European Commission and/or, as evidenced by FIFPro's warning to FIFA and UEFA, to further litigation before the CJEU. For us, the essential problem has been that the traditional system of self-regulation by sporting bodies is clearly no longer viable and, indeed, was further undermined by the CJEU's position that there is rarely such a thing as a pure sporting rule which is beyond the scope of litigation. The Court's arguments are expounded in its rulings in the *Meca-Medina* and *Motoe* cases, which will be discussed in Chapter 17 (also see Weatherill, 2006).

Even without these rulings it cannot be doubted that the transfer system and related rules on 'tapping up' and the restriction of transfers to specified transfer windows are susceptible to challenge on the basis of Article 45 TFEU and EU competition law. However, systematic, clear and reasonably certain legal rules have not been put in place because challenges to the transfer system have been piecemeal. The fate of the transfer system and its related rules have been and remain subject to the vagaries of litigation both in terms of whether such litigation takes place and what decision a relevant court – notably the CJEU – chooses to reach.

The root of the problem is that the ongoing commodification of professional football has resulted in increasing juridification so that self-regulation continues to be replaced by external legal regulation. As Foster has argued, when talking about juridification:

> ... at a simple level, it merely reproduces the traditional idea of private and public realms, with private areas increasingly being subject to public or judicial control, a move from voluntarism to legalism. But it offers also a more complex version which stresses the interaction as legal norms are used to reorder the power relations within the social arena. (Foster, 1993)

The central issue to be resolved is that once juridification becomes inevitable, and constitutes an ongoing process, what form of juridification will provide the most appropriate basis for external regulation?

FIFPro still favours resolution through collective agreement, and this accords with our own contentions (Gardiner & Welch, 2007) that the best mechanism for resolving all of the problems identified above lies in the adoption of the methodology of reflexive legal regulation.[15] The advantage of reflexive law is that it enables a set of principles to be provided, which must be adhered to as a minimum, but the detailed implementation of a system of regulation is delegated to relevant bodies be they (as examples) national legislators or governing bodies of particular sports. A system of reflexive law can provide a compromise between ensuring that particular standards are complied with and respecting the autonomy of those concerned with operating a particular system or activity and who understand the specificities involved. This presents a symbiotic relationship between normative rules within and without the particular activity in question (Wynn, 2000).

In the context of transfer systems, we have contended that the best basis for resolving the potential for conflict in advance is by moving to a system of reflexive law using the method of EU social law as a paradigm (Gardiner & Welch, 2007). The advantage of EU social law is that it requires the involvement of the relevant social partners. Under Article 154 TFEU, the European Commission must engage in dialogue with the social partners as to the content of any proposed Directive. Moreover, Article 155 TFEU permits the relevant social partners to conclude their own collective agreements, which, if the social partners so request, may then be given legal force through an EC Directive.

FIFPro has agreements with both FIFA and UEFA for social dialogue and thus there is the possibility that a collective agreement regulating football could be entered into in the future (for further discussion see Branco-Martins, 2003; Gardiner, Parrish & Siekmann, 2009). Specifically, we have argued that through such a collective agreement, or in its absence a directive derived from social dialogue, EU law could require national football associations to adopt a modified and more flexible version of the FIFA transfer rules which would be incorporated into their more detailed national rules reflecting national preferences. A collective agreement or directive could also contain provisions providing for minimum standards relating to the use and operation of transfer windows, and for rules regulating the rights of players under contract to talk to other clubs about their future.

Similarly, the concept of contract termination for sporting just cause, as contained in the FIFA rules, should be incorporated into any collective

352 Research handbook of employment relations in sport

agreement or directive. This could be defined as including circumstances in which a player (whilst fit) has not been selected for x number of first team games, and where a player is informed, or has good reason to believe, that he is no longer wanted by his current club.

One possible variation to the current FIFA rules would be, on the expiry of a contract's protected period or where the contract is terminated for sporting just cause, to permit a player to terminate his contract during a season if a player has negotiated a move to a club which is in a different league, and which is thus not in competition with his current club. The normal rules relating to such a player being cup-tied could continue to apply as far as domestic or European cup competitions are concerned. Such a change should also reduce the complexities involved in the implementation of Article 17 of the FIFA rules, as demonstrated by the *Webster* case (see above). Another change to the current rules could be to place an absolute limit on the compensation that is to be paid to a club, where a player exercises a right to buy out his contract, to the actual financial loss incurred by that club. By analogy with the way that a sum of damages is calculated under English contract law the club would then be in the financial position it would have enjoyed had the player allowed his contract to complete its course.

CONCLUSIONS

It may well be the case that the failure of the FIFA rules to bring about a significant relaxation of the transfer system, combined with the failure by the big European clubs to institute a process whereby the money secured by transfer fees is redistributed throughout domestic leagues, will lead to further regulation of the transfer system along the lines set out in the EU report. It remains our view that reflexive law provides the best mechanism for effective regulation.

In addition to fleshing out the proposals contained in the EU report, we suggest that the essential principles underlying such regulation, either through collective agreement or EU legislation, should include:

1. Provision *within* all European Associations for unilateral termination of a contract by a player after the expiry of a protected period, or for 'sporting just cause'.
2. Permitting players to approach other clubs in any domestic or European Association in the latter stages of their contracts, or towards the end of a contract's protected period.
3. The abolition (or extensive liberalization) of transfer windows – both within and between European Associations.

NOTES

1. *Flood v Kuhn*, 407 US 258 (1972).
2. See 'Andrew Hore backs IRB's global transfer system', http://www.bbc.co.uk/sport/0/rugby-union/17568661 – last accessed 25/03/2014.
3. *Eastham v Newcastle United FC* [1963] 3 All ER 139 Ch D.
4. At the time of the Bosman ruling this was Article 48 of the EU Treaty which, through renumbering, subsequently became Article 39 of the EU Treaty and now is Article 45 of the Treaty on the Functioning of the European Union (TFEU).
5. *CAS 2007/A/1298/1299/1300 Wigan Athletic FC/Heart of Midlothian/Webster*.
6. *CAS 2008/A/1519-1520 Matuzalem/Shakhtar Donetsk/Real Zaragoza/FIFA*.
7. See, for example, *CAS 2009/A/ 1880 Essam El-Hadaray v FIFA & Al-Ahly Sporting Club*.
8. Case C-176/96 *Jyri Lehtonen & Castors Canada Dry Namur-Braine v Fédération Royale Belge des Sociétés de Basketball ASBL*.
9. This view is based on advice provided by Paul Golding QC – see FIFPro press statement, 'International transfer windows could fail if challenged nationally', 21 December 2004.
10. Football League Press Release – statement by Chairman Sir Brian Mawhinney, 23 September 2004.
11. 'Window gets the thumbs down from the pros' *The Guardian*, 1 February 2003.
12. See FIFPro press statement 'Fines in "tapping up" case may be contrary to European law', 7 June 2005.
13. 'Players' union FIFPro to take transfer system to European courts', http://www.theguardian.com/football/2013/dec/17/players-union-fifpro-transfer-system-european-courts – last accessed 25/03/2014; 'Football transfer system must change, says world players' union', http://www.bbc.co.uk/sport/0/football/25418135 – last accessed 25/03/2013.
14. See http://ec.europa.eu/ireland/press_office/media_centre/feb2013_en.htm#28 – last accessed 25/03/2014. For details of FIFPro's formal complaint see http://www.fifpro.org/en/news/fifpro-takes-legal-action-against-fifa-transfer-system; http://www.theguardian.com/football/2015/sep/18/fifpro-transfer-fees-could-go-fifa-brussels – last accesssed 08/03/2016.
15. The origin of this term lies in legal sociology, and its essence is that intervention through external regulation should both reflect the norms established by those historically involved in the internal regulation of the activities in question and impose modifications to those norms which can be enforced by legal means.

REFERENCES

Blanpain, R. and R. Inston (1996), *The Bosman Case: The End of the Transfer System?*, London, UK: Sweet & Maxwell; Leuven: Peeters.
Branco-Martins, R. (2003), 'European sport's first collective labour agreement EFFC', *International Sports Law Journal*, 1.
Caiger, A. and J. O'Leary (2000), 'The end of the affair: "*The Anelka Doctrine*" – the problem of contract stability in English professional football', in A. Caiger and S. Gardiner (eds), *Professional Sport in the EU: Regulation and Re-regulation*, The Hague, Netherlands: Asser Press.
Foster, K. (1993), 'Developments in sporting law', in L. Allison (ed.), *The Changing Politics of Sport*, Manchester, UK: Manchester UP.
Gardiner, S. (2006), 'Football bungs and brown paper bags revisited', *Sport and the Law Journal*, **14** (3), 6–10.

Gardiner, S., R. Parrish and R. Siekmann (2009), *EU, Sport, Law and Policy: Regulation, Re-regulation and Representation*, The Hague, Netherlands: Asser Press.

Gardiner, S. and R. Welch (1998), 'The winds of change in professional football: The impact of the Bosman ruling', *Contemporary Issues in Law*, **3** (4), 289–312.

Gardiner, S. and R. Welch (2007), 'The contractual dynamics of team stability versus player mobility: Who rules "the beautiful game"?', *Entertainment and Sports Law Journal*, **5** (1).

Goldberg, M. and S. Pentol (2005), 'Football "tapping up" rules – anachronism or necessity?', *Sport and the Law Journal*, **13** (1), 15–16.

McAuley, D. (2003), 'Windows, caps, footballs and the European Commission. Confused? You will be', *European Competition Law Review*, 394.

McCutcheon, P. (1997), 'Negative enforcement of employment contracts in the sports industries', *Legal Studies*, **17** (1), 65–100.

Morris, P.E., S. Morrow and P.M. Spink (1996), 'EC law and professional football: Bosman and its implications', *Modern Law Review*, **59** (6), 893–902.

O'Leary, J. and A. Caiger (2000), 'The re-regulation of football and its impact on employment contracts', in H. Collins, P. Davies and R. Rideout (eds), *The Legal Regulation of the Employment Relation*, London, UK: Kluwer.

Pearson G (2015), 'Sporting justifications under EU free movement and competition law: The case of the football "transfer system"', *European Law Journal* 21(2), 220–38

Sandlant, D. and L. Silkin (2007), 'Player contracts: Paul Cooke: RFL tribunal findings and European Law', *World Series Law Reports*, **5** (12).

Shear, G. and A. Green (2005), 'Footballers and fixed term contracts', *Sport and the Law Journal*, **13** (2), 16.

Tsatsas, N. (1999), 'Anelka's costly walk-out case has a hole in it', last accessed 16/02/2016 at http://www.theguardian.com/football/1999/jul/23/newsstory.sport1.

Weatherill, S. (2006), 'Anti-doping revisited – the demise of the rule of "purely sporting interest"?', *European Competition Law Review*, **27** (12), 645–657.

Welch, R. (2012), 'Sport and contracts of employment', in S. Gardiner, J. O'Leary, R. Welch, S. Boyes and U. Naidoo, *Sports Law*, London: Routledge, pp. 393–459.

Wynn, M. (2000), 'European social dialogue: Harmonisation or new diversity', in H. Collins, P. Davies and R. Rideout (eds), *The Legal Regulation of the Employment Relation*, London, UK: Kluwer.

16. Similarities and differences between competitive balance and uncertainty of outcome: a simple comparison of recent history in the NBA and NFL
Rodney Paul and Andrew Weinbach

INTRODUCTION

The concept of evenly matched teams being important to the overall success of a sports league has received much attention by economists and the sports media. In his excellent and highly influential work on sports, Rottenberg (1956) noted that for firms to compete, they must be of equal size. For team sports as an industry this is not necessarily true. Key city attributes, such as income per capita and population, differ greatly across the country and around the world.

Economic theory dictates that teams in sports leagues attain market power through restricting entry to their leagues. Even with restricted entry, however, some cities offer greater opportunity for success and profits than others. Given these substantial differences in potential revenues, it is important to consider what attributes of league competition will keep fans interested over longer time horizons. Honeymoon effects exist upon expansion or relocation to a city, but generally the luster wears off quickly in the eyes of fans if teams do not achieve some level of successful performance on the field, court, rink, or pitch.

The concept of competitive balance and the uncertainty of outcome hypothesis attempt to deal with these pivotal issues. Rottenberg (1956) introduced the uncertainty of outcome hypothesis, suggesting that poor performing teams will not only hurt their local market, but will hurt the profitability of the league as a whole. As fans of the local team stop watching the sport, due to poor performance and little hope of future success, this impacts the other teams in the league as it reduces interest overall in the product, for both the regular season and the postseason. Having non-competitive teams in a league will likely lead to lower interest in attending games and lower interest in watching games on television. This, in turn, reduces the revenues from ticket sales and television rights.

There are exceptions to the strong relationship between on-field and team financial success, however, with one such example being the Chicago Cubs of Major League Baseball. The Cubs have a long history of futility, but are loved and accepted by local fans (and many around the country). Despite their long losing history, the Cubs draw very well in terms of home attendance and the team remains popular with fans. Overall, these are exceptions to the issue raised by Rottenberg (1956), with the financial success of most teams being dependent upon their performance.

Empirical measures of competitive balance are typically defined as ex-post figures of how closely matched teams are in a given league, conference, division, or match-up. Some of the key variations of these measures are discussed in this chapter. Uncertainty of outcome is typically discussed as an ex-ante figure, reflecting expectations of how close fans (consumers) expect given games, divisions, or leagues to be. Both terms embody the same general idea, but there are some key differences in ways these notions are measured, and there often appears to be some confusion between the terms, especially in the minds and words of the media and of the fans themselves.

Although sports economists attempt to define these terms clearly and measure and debate their individual merits, definitions of these terms may differ quite substantially across individuals. Some may say competitive balance when they mean uncertainty of outcome or vice versa. In some cases it is likely that the terms are truly interchangeable as fans may take the terms to mean the exact same thing. In other cases, the differences between the terms may be very important as they relate to understanding fan behavior or making decisions at the team or league level.

Sanderson and Siegfried (2003) explain in great detail why competitive balance issues are important and why they differ across cities in sports leagues. Income and population are extremely important as wealthier and more populated areas have a distinct advantage in earning substantial revenues, allowing them to attract greater talent than other teams. Apart from these variables, Sanderson and Siegfried (2003) discuss why factors such as local resident preferences, differences in tastes of players, and impact of the game itself can play important roles. In some cities, due to the opportunity cost of alternative forms of entertainment, residents may be more inclined to pay for winners than residents of other locales. In terms of the players, some players may choose to locate in a city with a nice climate or to increase their chance of winning a championship, forgoing more lucrative financial offers for these amenities. With some sports, the game experience may be just as important to the fan as the competition on the field. Having side entertainment, excellent food and drink, and a friendly atmosphere may be more important to fans in some cities than in others. All of these factors may play a key role in talent distribution and differing degrees of competitive balance across sports and leagues.

League policy can also play a big role in the degree of competitive balance across leagues. Institutional arrangements such as restrictions on free agency (not allowing the best players to sign in the biggest markets), reverse-order drafts (where the worst teams in the league get to draft the top players in the following season's entry draft), salary caps (limits on team spending), luxury taxes (imposing costs for spending more than a set limit), and revenue sharing (redistribution of income from more success-ful markets to less successful markets) may play a key role in securing a desired level of competitive balance and/or uncertainty of outcome within a league.

Although commonly considered to play a big role in keeping leagues competitive, factors such as salary caps, luxury taxes, reverse-order drafts, and so on, may not be effective in maintaining competitive balance, given the implications of the Coase Theorem (Coase, 1960). The Coase Theorem notes that under zero transactions costs the allocation of resources is invariant to the assignment of property rights. In other words, resources will always flow to their highest value use.

For example, whether a league has free agency or not, the Coase Theorem implies that the best players will eventually play for the city and team where they are valued the most. In open free agency the player will sign with this team as they will offer him the largest contract. In a closed market, where the team has exclusive rights to the player, the player will still end up in the best market for them as this team will trade for the player, making the other city an offer that exceeds the value of that player to their market. Many researchers have investigated the Coase Theorem as it relates to team sports and have investigated how the market for talent has changed with major institutional changes such as free agency and salary caps. Some excellent examples of this research include Depken (1999), Eckard (2001), Maxcy and Mondello (2006), and Szymanski (2007).

The key factors described by Sanderson and Siegfried (2003) generally influence both competitive balance and uncertainty of outcome. When a league suffers from a lack of competitive balance, as perhaps a few big markets dominate the landscape, the games are likely to suffer from a distinct lack of uncertainty of outcome in terms of the individual contests. Teams with greater amounts of talent generally have a big advantage over teams with lesser talent (although coaching and other factors could mitigate in these circumstances), leading to expectations of blowouts when these teams play. Therefore factors which lead to uncertainty of outcome will generally also lead to a lack of competitive balance.

Fort (2012) clearly describes four ways of thinking about measures of competitiveness in leagues. There is game uncertainty, which describes the closeness of scores of individual games. Another version is end-of-season uncertainty, which describes how tightly bunched teams are in the regular season of play. Fort also notes the importance of postseason access uncertainty (which teams will make the playoffs?) and season-to-season uncertainty (relating to the turnover of successful teams – in other words, are there dynasties in the league?). While the first measure appears to be more of the classic uncertainty of outcome (measured before the game is actually played), the other three measures are alternative (or complementary) ways that competitive balance has typically been defined. It is important to note, from our point of view, that game uncertainty is typically measured ex-ante, while the other three measures are calculated ex-post.

In terms of different types of competitive balance measures, the standard in the field has generally been the use of the standard deviation of wins percentages of teams in a league which dates back to Noll (1988) and Scully (1989). The Herfindahl–Hirshman Index was used to calculate the percentage of time a team has been a champion (Depken, 1999), while Schmidt and Berri (2001) introduced the use of Gini coefficients as a measure of competitive balance. Eckard (2001) suggested the use of variation in team performance as a measure and Humphreys (2002) introduced the competitive balance ratio, which is the average of the standard deviation of win percentage over many seasons compared to the league average standard deviation. These measures (and others) have been used to study the impact of competitive balance on attendance, its impact due to league policy measures, and many other factors in the literature.

For the uncertainty of outcome hypothesis, on the other hand, a common measure that has been suggested and used in the sports economics literature stems from the betting market. Betting market odds or point spreads, depending upon the sport, serve as an excellent measure of uncertainty of outcome as these prices from simple financial markets have been shown to generally be unbiased predictors of the outcome of games. This does not mean they are accurate from game to game, of course, because noisy outcomes are the norm in sports and are part of the reason fans are so interested in spending their time watching and following these games. In the aggregate these prices have been shown to serve as excellent game forecasts and therefore offer information as to the anticipated level of closeness within a game.

Betting market odds and point spreads also offer a distinct informational advantage over common ex-post measures of competitive balance due to the inclusion of factors such as injuries, suspensions, and weather conditions into these prices. A simple binary ex-post figure such as a win-loss record or a calculation of whether the team made the playoffs cannot account for times when a star player was injured or a coach was suspended. Betting market odds and point spreads account for these changes in real time and are assumed to reflect full information about a game by the time of market close (with studies of market efficiency supporting this notion).

Using betting market odds to measure uncertainty of outcome first appeared in studies of English soccer in studies by Peel and Thomas (1988, 1992). Studies of European soccer leagues have also described the link between betting market odds and attendance (Forrest and Simmons, 2002) and have made the case for betting market odds as the best measure of match uncertainty for soccer matches in Spain (Buraimo et al., 2006).

Odds were also used as a measure of uncertainty of outcome in Major League Baseball in studies by Knowles et al. (1992) and Rascher (1999). Lemke et al. (2010) used betting market odds to estimate the influence of uncertainty of outcome on baseball attendance. Paul et al. (2009) compared uncertainty of outcome (as measured by betting market odds) to competitive balance to discuss fan perceptions of competitive imbalance in Major League Baseball during the 1990s and early 2000s. Coates and Humphreys (2012) used betting market odds to study uncertainty of outcome in the National Hockey League and noted distinct links to attendance at hockey games.

Betting market prices as a measure of uncertainty of outcome has also been used to study television ratings. Forrest et al. (2005) studied the English Premier League and found that more uncertainty of outcome increased television ratings. Similar findings were found for the Spanish Football Premera Division (Buraimo and Simmons, 2009). Using very detailed television rating data (minute-by-minute), Alavy et al. (2010) showed that television ratings for European soccer was also positively influenced by uncertainty of outcome. Berkowitz et al. (2011) showed that uncertainty of outcome positively impacted television ratings and attendance in NASCAR. It has recently been argued in the literature that betting market odds should be considered as a measure of competitive balance, rather than just uncertainty of outcome (Bowman et al., 2013).

Given the relationship of competitive balance and uncertainty of outcome to studies of fan interest as measured by attendance and television ratings, it is important to note the similarities and differences, if any, between the information provided by the calculated measures of these terms. If there is no discernable difference between competitive balance and uncertainty of outcome measures, then they will be simply interchangeable and ease of data availability may be the only reason to choose one over the other. If these measures reveal conflicting estimates about competitiveness or outcome uncertainty in leagues over time, it becomes important to understand the source of these differences and identify situations where one measure may be preferable to the other.

To illustrate situations where simple measurements of competitive balance and uncertainty of outcome are either similar or vastly different, we choose to use two simple measures to compare and contrast recent history in the National Basketball Association (NBA) and the National Football League (NFL). Both leagues are major sports in North America and around the world and they offer the apples-to-apples comparison on the uncertainty of outcome front as both sports use point spreads in their respective wagering markets. Through a comparison of two well-known, yet simple, measures of competitive balance and uncertainty of outcome, we attempt to show how the calculated figures can clearly mimic each other in some circumstances, yet be very different in others.

COMPARING SIMPLE MEASURES OF COMPETITIVE BALANCE AND UNCERTAINTY OF OUTCOME: NBA AND NFL

To illustrate the similarities and differences between simple measures of competitive balance and uncertainty of outcome we choose to investigate two popular leagues in North America, the NBA and the NFL. From our perspective, these sports are useful in comparison because they both use point spreads in the betting markets for their sports, instead of odds. Given that both sports use point spreads, a simple measure of the uncertainty of outcome of games in these sports is the average of the absolute value of the point spread for the individual season of interest.

The absolute value of the point spread is used as a measure of how closely matched the teams are in a given contest. Although it may be very important for some applications of the uncertainty of outcome hypothesis (i.e. attendance modeling) to specify the home team in the contest, for our purposes we only wish to determine how closely contested games are expected to be without regard to if the home team or road team is expected to win. Therefore, we calculate the average of the absolute value of the point spread for each season as our measure of the uncertainty of outcome for the NBA and NFL. Higher values of the absolute value of the point spread translate into less uncertainty of outcome as one team is more heavily favored in the contest. Lower values of the absolute value of the point spread imply that there is more uncertainty of outcome in the contests.

To compare what is happening with competitive balance in each sport, we also calculate the simple standard deviation of win percentage for each season in our sample of the NBA and NFL. We then used this figure to calculate the Noll–Scully ratio of standard deviations (RSD). Following Fort (2011, 2012), the RSD is calculated by taking the actual standard deviation (ASD) of win percentages and dividing it by the idealized standard deviation (ISD). ISD is calculated as given in Fort and Quirk (1995), which is 0.5 divided by the square root of N, where N is the number of games in the season. If ASD = ISD, then the Noll–Scully ratio is equal to one. Competitive imbalance occurs as RSD gets further away from one in a given sample. Other measures such as Gini coefficients could also be used to measure competitive balance in a situation such as this, but we defer to the findings and discussion of Utt and Fort (2002), where it was concluded that the simple standard deviation of win percentage tends to work very well as it overcomes some potential flaws in other measures.

We compare and contrast what has happened in recent years in both leagues as it relates to the NBA and NFL. We will discuss the results for the NBA first and then discuss the NFL results. After going through each sport individually, we will then discuss the similarities and differences between the measures in the two sports.

NBA

For the NBA we have win-loss records and betting market point spread data from www.covers.com from the 1995–96 to 2010–11 seasons. We stopped our sample at the conclusion of the 2010–11 season due to the NBA lockout and shortened season of 2011–12. From the win-loss records we calculated the standard deviation of win percentage for each season in the sample and then proceeded to calculate the Noll–Scully RSD. From the point spread data, we calculated the absolute value of the average point spread for each game played in each season within our sample. Our measure of competitive balance is the Noll–Scully RSD, and its relationship over time is shown in Figure 16.1. Our measure of the uncertainty of outcome is derived from the absolute value of the point spread and is shown in Figure 16.2.

As can be seen from Figures 16.1 and 16.2, the time paths of both the Noll–Scully RSD and the average of the absolute value of the point spread per season are strikingly similar. The linear trend in each chart notes the decrease over time of both of these variables, implying that competitive balance has generally improved in the NBA at the same time the uncertainty of outcome has increased in this sport. The relative spikes in the variables appear about the same time (1996–97/1997–98 and 2007–08/2008–09) for both variables. Although there are some slight differences between the peaks and troughs of the time series for both variables, it

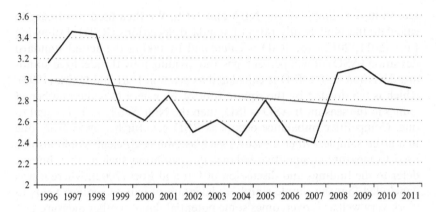

Figure 16.1   Noll–Scully RSD: NBA 1996–2011

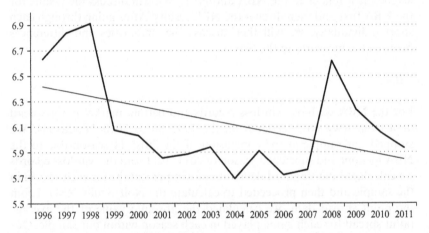

Figure 16.2   Average of the absolute value of the point spread: NBA 1996–2011

visually appears that both the measures for competitive balance and uncertainty of outcome move together with respect to the NBA.

To illustrate the relationship between the two variables, we note the correlation coefficients in both levels and first differences in Table 16.1.

The correlation coefficient between the two measurements is high, both in levels and in first differences. This confirms the visual evidence in the figures above that these simple measurements of competitive balance and uncertainty of outcome appear to be very closely related in the NBA.

To further illustrate the relationship between the two variables,

Table 16.1   Correlation between competitive balance and uncertainty of outcome: NBA

Relationship between:	Correlation coefficient (levels)	Correlation coefficient (first diff)
RSD and average of the absolute value of the point spread	0.9062	0.8100

Table 16.2   Four-year interval measurements of competitive balance and uncertainty of outcome: NBA

Years	4-year RSD	4-year average of the absolute value of the point spread
1996–1999	3.1984	6.6159
2000–2003	2.6424	5.9294
2004–2007	2.5328	5.7732
2008–2011	3.0091	6.2113

Table 16.3   Eight-year intervals and test for differences in means: NBA

Years	8-year RSD	8-year average of the absolute value of the point spread
1993–2002	2.9204	6.2727
2003–2012	2.7709	5.9923
Probability value of t-test: samples have same mean	0.4896	0.2754

Table 16.2 breaks the NBA sample into four-year intervals and notes the average values of the measures of competitive balance and uncertainty of outcome.

By looking at the four-year intervals, it is clear that the Noll–Scully RSD has fallen over time, but did increase in the last years of the sample. The four-year averages for the absolute value of the point spread mirrors the movements of the Noll–Scully ratio as it relates to uncertainty of outcome.

Table 16.3 notes the averages when breaking the sample in half (eight-year intervals) and shows the probability value of the t-test of the null hypothesis that the two samples have the same mean.

Both the Noll–Scully RSD and the absolute value of the point spread fell when comparing the eight-year averages of each time series. Although the averages are lower in each of the later periods in the sample, the t-test cannot reject the null that the samples have the same mean.

In general it can be seen that the measures of competitive balance and uncertainty of outcome move in the same general fashion in the NBA. In each measure the moves between the variables are highly correlated and show that competitive balance has improved while more uncertainty of outcome has occurred. Although there are some slight differences that could be meaningful in certain settings, these measures of competitive balance and uncertainty of outcome are likely interchangeable over this time frame for the NBA as they both appear to capture the same relevant information about competitive balance and outcome uncertainty.

NFL

For the NFL we were able to obtain a slightly longer sample of point spread data and were able to compare this information to the win-loss records of teams for the 1993–2012 seasons. We chose to start in 1993 as with this season both free agency and the salary cap were part of NFL rules involving team rosters and player movement, which may have led to a substantial change in both variables due to transitional factors and poor/effective cap management by individual teams (Paul and Weinbach, 2012). The competitive balance measure (Noll–Scully RSD) for the NFL is shown in Figure 16.3 while the uncertainty of outcome measure (average of the absolute value of the point spread) is illustrated in Figure 16.4.

Substantial differences between the measures of competitive balance and uncertainty of outcome are readily apparent from the graphs for the NFL. The plot of the Noll–Scully RSD illustrates a clear and steady increase in the value of this variable over time from 1993–2012. The linear trend is upward sloping which highlights the fact that in the last ten years of the sample, none of the values for the standard deviation of win percentage were below 1.44. As a comparison, the standard deviation of win percentage was around 1.26 at the sample minimum for the 1995 NFL season.

When comparing the graph for competitive balance to uncertainty of outcome, the differences between the time plots of the variables are quite striking. The average of the absolute value of the point spread has a slight downward relationship during the sample period, as illustrated by the linear trend plotted on the chart. The average absolute value of the point spread shows variance from season to season (as would be expected), but the mean value of this variable appears to fluctuate around 5.5 points throughout the sample.

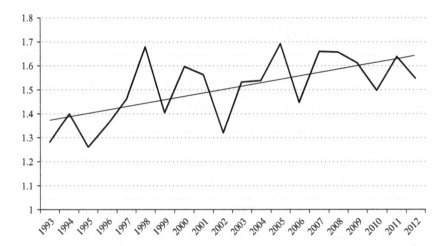

Figure 16.3 Noll–Scully RSD: NFL 1993–2012

Figure 16.4 Average of the absolute value of the point spread: NFL 1993–2012

To further illustrate these differences we note the correlation coefficients between the variables in Table 16.4.

Unlike the NBA sample, in the NFL there is a decided lack of correlation between our measures of competitive balance and uncertainty of outcome. As seen in the graphs and noted by the correlation coefficients, there appears to be little similarity between the standard deviation of win percentage and the average of the absolute value of the point spread for the NFL.

Table 16.4   Correlation between competitive balance and uncertainty of outcome: NFL

Relationship between:	Correlation coefficient (levels)	Correlation coefficient (first diff)
RSD and average of the absolute value of the point spread	0.2144	0.2969

Table 16.5   Five-year interval measurements of competitive balance and uncertainty of outcome: NFL

Years	5-year RSD	5-year average of the absolute value of the point spread
1993–1997	1.3531	5.5273
1998–2002	1.5135	5.4860
2003–2007	1.5756	5.5027
2008–2012	1.5906	5.5620

Table 16.6   Ten-year intervals and test for differences in means: NFL

Years	10-year Average Standard Deviation of Win Percentage	10-year Average of the Absolute Value of the Point spread
1993–2002	1.4333	5.5067
2003–2012	1.5807	5.5323
Probability Value of t-test: samples have same mean	0.0117	0.8947

To further illustrate these differences, we show the five-year averages for each variable (Table 16.5) and the ten-year averages coupled with the probability value of the t-test that the samples have the same mean (Table 16. 6).

The five-year averages show how the competitive balance has decreased over time in the NFL, but the measure of uncertainty of outcome has changed little over the course of the sample. In a curious result, where the Noll–Scully RSD showed a large average increase from the 1993–97 to 1998–2002 period, the average of the absolute value of the point spread actually decreased slightly during this time frame.

By comparing the sample means over ten-year periods for both variables, it is clear that competitive balance was reduced by a statistically significant margin in the second half of our sample. The probability value of the t-test that the ten-year samples have the same mean for the Noll–Scully RSD can clearly be rejected at the 5 percent level. The ten-year samples for the measure of uncertainty of outcome, however, show little change between the two time frames. The t-test cannot reject the null that the two ten-year periods have the same mean for the average of the absolute value of the point spread.

For the last two decades in the NFL, measures of competitive balance and uncertainty of outcome are drastically different. While competitive balance has appeared to substantially decline, the uncertainty of outcome has remained generally unchanged. The choice of which variable to study – the ex-post measure of competitive balance or the ex-ante measure of uncertainty of outcome – may affect the results and lead to incorrect conclusions and improper policy decisions.

Specifically for the NFL it appears that the fans and the media are more likely to pay attention to the measure of uncertainty of outcome, as there has been little outcry or notice of the deterioration of competitive balance over the past two decades. Perhaps this is due to competitive balance still being better than it may have been in the more distant past, but we happen to believe it is more likely due to individual game uncertainty remaining mostly constant during this time frame.

CONCLUSIONS

Although similar in nature and often confused in general conversation, competitive balance and uncertainty of outcome have some distinct differences as they relate to the study of sports. Competitive balance is typically measured in an ex-post manner, taking some form of the standard deviation of win percentage or indexes of which teams made the postseason. Uncertainty of outcome, on the other hand, is typically measured ex ante and is often proxied by betting market prices (odds or point spreads) which are assumed to incorporate all available information about the game prior to the game actually being played.

The two concepts and their respective measures are often used to investigate attendance and television ratings, and in analysis of league policy decisions. Each measure provides information about the state of the league and how it has changed over time, but the question remains of how similar these figures truly are. Although competitive balance is often thought of as backward-looking and uncertainty of outcome as forward-looking, the lines blur when uncertainty of outcome measures (odds/point spreads) are aggregated over time. This measurement certainly provides information on expectations of how competitive a game is expected to be. In addition, it also contributes information that typical measures of competitive balance will not represent on a game-by-game basis such as the effect of injuries, suspensions, and weather conditions. Through its aggregation and after the fact inspection, this ex-ante figure becomes another possible avenue to study competitive balance over many seasons for a league, rather than just a measure of individual game outcome uncertainty as it relates to fan decisions.

To investigate the similarities and differences between competitive balance and uncertainty of outcome, we chose two simple measures of these concepts to explore across two major North American sports: the NBA and the NFL. For competitive balance we chose to use the simple measure of the standard deviation of win percentage converted into the Noll–Scully RSD by comparing actual standard deviations to their idealized values. For uncertainty of outcome we chose to use the average of the absolute value of the point spread for all games in each season studied. The leagues are easily compared as both sports use point spreads in their respective betting markets.

In relation to how similar these measures are in relation to conveying information about the degree of competitiveness and/or outcome uncertainty, the answer from our simple study reveals a common economic moniker: it depends. In the NBA the two measures appear to be very closely related. There was a high degree of correlation between the two figures over time, as evidenced visually by the similar shapes of the plots of the values of these figures over time. Both competitive balance and uncertainty of outcome, as measured, improved over the recent sample as the RSD figure substantially decreased (the standard deviation of win percentage fell over time) and the average of the absolute value of the point spread became smaller over the course of the sample. It appears that both measures capture the same information, and it is likely that using either figure will help to explain key relationships of fan interest, such as attendance and television ratings.

The NFL, on the other hand, shows a dramatic difference between the two measures. While competitive balance in the NFL was shown to have worsened since 1993, uncertainty of outcome has remained mostly unchanged. The Noll–Scully RSD has steadily increased in the past two decades, while the average of the absolute value of the point spread does show year-to-year volatility, but the overall average has remained near 5.5 over the course of the years studied. In looking only at the Noll–Scully RSD, one may conclude that the NFL has become less competitive over the past two decades. When focusing on the average of the absolute value of the point spread there does not appear to be a problem, as this measure appears to be generally steady over the period.

In relation to personal preference between the concepts of competitive balance and uncertainty of outcome and their respective measures, we have to admit that we tend to favor toward the use of wagering market based prices. We find the availability of these measures before the game is played as particularly useful, but also appreciate the pieces of information that betting market prices provide that measures of wins and losses (or indices of playoff appearances or playoff turnover) cannot, such as short-term and long-term injuries, suspensions of players or coaches, or the impact of weather conditions on given teams. We also believe that these market based measures may more closely tie to fan perceptions of teams and game quality and may offer substantial insights into which games they choose to attend or view and which games they do not.

This said, the traditional measures of competitive balance also provide key pieces of information and may be better measures as it relates to macro policy decision making on the part of sports leagues and owners. The very simple comparison that we provide in this research as it relates to the NBA and NFL illustrates that sometimes measures of competitive balance and uncertainty of outcome will provide the same information, but in other cases they may be substantially different. Research on baseball (Paul et al., 2009) found a similar result to the NFL, where competitive balance and uncertainty of outcome measures were quite different. Further research into other sports that use odds in the betting market as it relates to uncertainty of outcome (soccer, hockey, etc.) and those that use point spreads (college football, college basketball, etc.) will help to deepen our understanding of where competitive balance and uncertainty of outcome measures diverge.

For researchers and those that will use the research, it is likely that different measures will need to be compared and contrasted to determine the best measure to use for the given circumstance. For some purposes (i.e. attendance modeling, television rating modeling, analysis of policy, etc.), one measure may be clearly superior, while in others the result may prove to be indifferent to the use of competitive balance or uncertainty of outcome (or any of their possible measures). Theoretical modeling and empirical testing of competitive balance and uncertainty of outcome measures may help to reveal why differences between the two measures exist. Some differences may have to do with the length of schedule of the season, units of scoring (i.e. 6 points for a touchdown in the NFL, 2-point vs. 3-point shots in basketball, single runs or goals in baseball and soccer), or style of play of particular teams (more offensive vs. a more defensive approach). As shown in this chapter for the NBA and NFL, it might not just depend upon the purpose of the research, but it might depend upon the league itself. For instance, in relation to the study of television ratings, fan demand for different sports may unveil itself in different manners based upon the instrument used for measurement. Just because betting market odds may better describe consumer choices for one sports league, it may not mean that it is the best measure for all sports leagues.

Although the use and comparison of multiple measures of competitive balance and uncertainty of outcome may prove tedious and could yield conflicting results in some instances, these challenges provide an exciting opportunity for researchers in the field of sports economics. To be able to better understand subtle (and not-so-subtle) differences between these measures and how they relate to fan demand is extremely important not only to the sports economics field, but also to league executives, owners, ticket offices, television networks, and many others. Understanding what fans desire in terms of competitiveness or outcome uncertainty will provide more efficiency and easier implementation in providing what these consumers truly hope to see. This will provide the opportunity for leagues and teams to better implement policies to improve their product and ultimately will lead to mutually beneficial gains to fans, owners, league personnel, and players alike.

REFERENCES

Alavy, K., A. Gaskell, S. Leach, and S. Szymanski (2010), 'On the edge of your seat: Demand for football on television and the uncertainty of outcome hypothesis,' *International Journal of Sport Finance*, **5**, 75–95.

Berkowitz, J. P., C. A. Depken II, and D. P. Wilson (2011), 'When going in circles is going backward: Outcome uncertainty in NASCAR,' *Journal of Sports Economics*, **12** (3), 253–283.

Bowman, R., J. Lambrinos, and T. Ashman (2013), 'Competitive balance in the eyes of the sports fan: Prospective measures using point spreads in the NFL and NBA,' *Journal of Sports Economics*, **14** (5), 498–520.

Buraimo, B., D. Forrest, and R. Simmons (2006), 'Outcome uncertainty measures: How closely do they predict a close game?' in J. Albert and R. Koning (eds), *Statistical Thinking in Sports*, Boca Raton, FL, USA: Chapman and Hall.

Buraimo, B. and R. Simmons (2009), 'A tale of two audiences: Spectators, television viewers, and outcome uncertainty in Spanish football,' *Journal of Economics and Business*, **61**, 326–338.

Coase, R. (1960), 'The problem of social cost,' *Journal of Law and Economics*, **3**, 1–44.

Coates, D. and B. Humphreys (2012), 'Game attendance and outcome uncertainty in the National Hockey League,' *Journal of Sports Economics*, **13**, 364–377.

Depken, C. (1999), 'Free agency and the competitiveness of Major League Baseball,' *Review of Industrial Organization*, **14**, 205–217.

Eckard, E. W. (2001), 'Free agency, competitive balance, and diminishing returns to pennant competition,' *Economic Inquiry*, **39**, 430–443.

Forrest, D. and R. Simmons (2002), 'Outcome uncertainty and attendance demand in sport: The case of English soccer,' *The Statistician*, **51**, 229–241.

Forrest, D., R. Simmons, and B. Buraimo (2005), 'Outcome uncertainty and the couch potato audience,' *Scottish Journal of Political Economy*, **52** (4), 641–661.

Fort, R. (ed.) (2011), *Sports Economics*, 3rd Edition, Upper Saddle River, NJ, USA: Prentice Hall.

Fort, R. (2012), 'Competitive balance in the NFL,' in K. Quinn (ed.), *The Economics of the National Football League: The State of the Art*, New York, NY, USA: Springer.

Fort, R. and J. Quirk (1995), 'Cross-subsidization, incentives, and outcomes in professional team sports leagues,' *Journal of Economic Literature*, **23**, 1265–1299.

Humphreys, B. (2002), 'Alternative measures of competitive balance,' *Journal of Sports Economics*, **3**, 133–148.

Knowles, G., K. Sherony, and M. Haupert (1992), 'The demand for Major League Baseball: A test of the uncertainty of outcome hypothesis,' *American Economist*, **36**, 72–80.

Lemke, R. J., M. Leonard, and K. Tlhokwane (2010), 'Estimating attendance at Major League Baseball games for the 2007 season,' *Journal of Sports Economics*, **11**, 316–348.

Maxcy, J. and M. Mondello (2006), 'The impact of free agency on competitive balance in North American professional team sports leagues,' *Journal of Sport Management*, **20**, 345–365.

Noll, R. (1988), 'Professional basketball', Stanford University Studies in Industrial Economics Paper no. 144.

Paul, R. A. and A. Weinbach (eds) (2012), *Competitive Balance in the NFL? The Economics of Excellence in International Sport*, Hamburg, Germany: Hamburg University Press.

Paul, R., A. Weinbach, R. Borghesi, and M. Wilson (2009), 'Using betting market odds to measure the uncertainty of outcome in Major League Baseball,' *International Journal of Sport Finance*, **4**, 225–263.

Peel, D. A. and D. A. Thomas (1988), 'Outcome uncertainty and the demand for football,' *Scottish Journal of Political Economy*, **35**, 242–249.

Peel, D. A. and D. A. Thomas (1992), 'The demand for football: Some evidence on outcome uncertainty,' *Empirical Economics*, **17**, 323–331.

Rascher, D. (1999), 'A test of the optimal positive production network externality in Major League Baseball,' in J. Fizel, E. Gustafson, and L. Hadley (eds), *Sports Economics: Current Research*, Westport, CT, USA: Praeger.

Rottenberg, S. (1956), 'The baseball players' labor market,' *Journal of Political Economy*, **64**, 242–258.

Sanderson, A. and J. Siegfried (2003), 'Thinking about competitive balance,' *Journal of Sports Economics*, **4**, 255–279.

Schmidt, M. B. and D. J. Berri (2001), 'Competitive balance and attendance: The case of Major League Baseball,' *Journal of Sports Economics*, **2** (2), 145–167.

Scully, G. (1989), 'The fans demand for winning,' in G. W. Scully (ed.), *The Business of Major League Baseball*, Chicago, IL, USA: University of Chicago Press.

Szymanski, S. (2007), 'The Champions League and the Coase Theorem,' *Scottish Journal of Political Economy*, **54** (3), 355–373.

Utt, J. and R. Fort (2002), 'Pitfalls to measuring competitive balance with Gini coefficients,' *Journal of Sports Economics*, **3**, 367–373.

17. Playing quotas
Simon Gardiner and Roger Welch

INTRODUCTION

Professional sport is subject to complex patterns of migration. These shift over a period of time, with different sports in specific countries importing playing talent from a variety of countries and regions. As greater distinctions have emerged between the commercial value of markets in a range of sports between countries, sporting rules providing player quotas based on nationality have emerged as a 'protectionist' mechanism to restrict supply and demand of players. These are of course in addition to legal rules that restrict immigration on the basis of nationality through visa requirements.

Historically, UEFA's (the Union of European Football Associations) 3+2 rule, which operated in the early 1990s, provided a good example of the imposition of a player quota system in professional football. This rule restricted the number of foreign players, that is, players who were not nationals of the domestic leagues in which they played, who could be included on a team-sheet in a UEFA competition to three. An additional two foreign players could be included if they had played in a country for an uninterrupted period of five years. Such players were deemed to be assimilated into the relevant domestic league.

In this chapter we set out how the *Bosman*[1] case resulted in major changes to the football transfer system. The second limb of the ruling has had a significant impact on the legality and operation of playing quotas. Both limbs of the *Bosman* ruling were based on what is now Article 45[2] of the Treaty on the Functioning of the European Union (TFEU) establishing the rights of European Union (EU) nationals to work on a non-discriminatory basis in any EU Member State. *Bosman* successfully argued that the 3+2 rule restricted the freedom of movement of players who are EU nationals as clubs with their full quota of foreign players were likely to restrict new contracts to indigenous players. What is now the Court of Justice of the European Union (CJEU, but at the time of the ruling was the ECJ, that is, the European Court of Justice) agreed the rule offended the fundamental principle of EU law that all European Community (EC) nationals must be treated on an equal basis.[3] The increased mobility of labour generated by the ruling has led to new patterns of migration on the part of professional sportsmen.

This chapter will chart the response to the *Bosman* ruling within football and the continuing use of player quotas for non-EU players. The focus of the chapter will be the reintroduction of player quotas within Europe as a result of UEFA's 'home grown player rule', which requires a specified number of players in a squad to have been developed by the club, or within the same football association, for a specified number of years as youth players. We will also discuss the proposal by FIFA (Fédération Internationale de Football Association) for a 6+5 rule which, if ever implemented, would apply throughout the world. These specific regulatory regimes provide a case study of the operation of sporting rules providing player quotas which potentially could inform the operation of and the legality of quota systems in other team sports. As examples, quota systems are used or have been proposed in basketball, cricket, handball, both codes of rugby and volleyball.[4]

The chapter will discuss why player quotas have been incrementally reintroduced into football and other team sports and evaluate their legality in the context of the *Bosman* ruling and EU discrimination law. The underlying debate is the extent to which regulation of professional sports by sporting authorities should be subordinate to external legal regulation. These are issues which have been subject to developments in and challenges posed by EU law.

Our central contention is that both the UEFA and FIFA rules are in violation of EU law on freedom of movement. If this contention is correct then this will have repercussions for all quota systems used in professional sports where such sports are played in EU Member States. Quota systems will only be lawful if they can be justified, and we will seek to demonstrate that the reasoning on justification which is set out in the *Bosman* ruling continues to be applicable, and therefore it remains very difficult for justification to be pleaded successfully. The chapter will conclude by considering and discussing alternatives to the use of quota systems.

In developing the arguments contained in this chapter we have drawn on the following key primary and secondary sources. The primary sources set out the relevant law and the UEFA regulations. The secondary sources assess the impact of the UEFA rule and contain in-depth arguments on the compatibility of both the UEFA and FIFA rules with EU law.

Primary Sources

Case C-415/93, *Union Royale Belge des Societes de Football Association & others v Jean-Marc Bosman* [1995] ECR I-4921.

Case C-438/00, *Deutscher Handballbund e V v Maros Kolpak* [2003] ECR I-4135.

www.uefa.com/multimediafiles/download/regulations/uefa/
    others/82/68/51/826851_download.pdf.

Secondary Sources

S. Miettinen and R. Parrish, 'Nationality Discrimination in Community
    Law: An Assessment of UEFA Regulations Governing Player Eligibility
    for European Club Competitions (The Home-Grown Player Rule)',
    (2007) 5(2) *Entertainment and Sports Law Journal*.
S. Gardiner and R. Welch, 'Bosman – There and Back Again: The
    Legitimacy of Playing Quotas under European Union Sports Policy',
    (2011) 17(6) *European Law Journal* 828.
Study on the Assessment of UEFA's 'Home Grown Player Rule'
    Negotiated procedure EAC/07/2012.

NATIONALITY QUOTAS POST-*BOSMAN*

In the years since the *Bosman* ruling was delivered, clubs within EU
Member States have had a wide number of nationalities to select a team
from. There is an obvious interface here with the ongoing relaxation of
transfer rules as required first by the *Bosman* ruling and more recently
by the European Commission. Indeed, the only real restrictions will be
derived from a Member State's individual immigration rules. For example,
European footballers, who are not nationals of EU Member States (and
the European Economic Area (EEA) states of Liechtenstein, Iceland and
Norway), and players from outside of Europe are still required to be in
possession of a work permit if they are to play for a club in the Premier and
Football Leagues. Similarly, the regulations of national sporting associations may still impose quotas on the fielding of non-EU foreign players.
The latter position is widespread in Europe, although it does not apply in
the English Leagues.[5]

  However, with respect to such quotas, yet further player mobility was
generated by the ECJ ruling in *Kolpak*.[6] The facts of *Kolpak* are straightforward. Kolpak was a Slovakian goalkeeper for the German Handball
club, TSV Ostringen eV Handball. According to the rules of Deutscher
Handballbund (DHB), the German Handball Federation clubs were
prohibited from fielding more than two non-EU nationals. The ECJ was
asked to give a preliminary ruling on whether, under Article 38 of the
Europe Agreement between Slovakia and the EU, Slovakian workers were
entitled to general equality of treatment with nationals of the relevant
Member State.

Applying its reasoning in *Bosman*, the ECJ ruled that nationals of third countries who were parties to Europe Agreements were entitled to be treated in the same way as national players for the purposes of a sport's rules. In short, they could not be considered ineligible for team selection because there was already the specified quota of non-EU nationals selected for the game. Similarly, in *Simutenkov*,[7] a case involving a Russian national playing professional football in Spain, the ECJ ruled that he was protected by a non-discriminatory provision contained in an agreement on partnership and cooperation signed between the EU and the Russian Federation in 1994.

Essentially, nationals of a number of countries, which have entered into agreements with the EU containing non-discrimination clauses which can be interpreted as taking direct effect, must be treated on an equal basis with nationals of the Member State in which they have secured employment. Thus quota restrictions on foreign players do not apply to them as such restrictions constitute working conditions for the purposes of non-discrimination clauses in relevant agreements. Not all agreements between individual countries and the EU will contain such provisions, but, in addition to football, the *Kolpak* case has had an effect on sports such as cricket and both codes of rugby; games which *Bosman* has only minimally impacted upon as they are not widely played professionally in Europe. Such players have become commonly known as 'Kolpak' players.

The 'Cotonou Agreement' between the EU and the African, Caribbean and Pacific Group of States (ACP) concerning the objectives of sustainable development and poverty reduction has had a significant impact. For example, a number of players have been signed by rugby league sides from countries such as Fiji, Tonga and Samoa. In rugby union and cricket, a significant number of South Africans have taken advantage of the ruling to play for professional clubs in England. In English county cricket, in comparison to say Australian players, South African cricketers can no longer be subject to rules which restrict the number of overseas players that can play for a county to one in any given season. As a response to a concern that many county teams are fielding a significant number of players not eligible to play for the England national team, the governing body for cricket, the England and Wales Cricket Board (ECB), has linked the central payments made to counties to the number of English qualified players who represent the county. This in effect means that in every game a 'Kolpak' player plays instead of an English qualified player, a county receives over £1000 less from the ECB.[8]

Prior to the ruling in *Kolpak*, there had been some speculation that the ECJ was going to extend Article 45 TFEU to nationals of associate countries. Such radical change was not given effect and Article 45 TFEU remains inapplicable to such nationals. Thus, they have no rights to enter a Member State to take up employment, or to move from Member State to Member State in order to do so.[9] A transfer to a club in another Member State will still be subject to that country's immigration rules. Presumably, national laws requiring work permits, on the expiry of a non-national's contract, still apply to nationals of countries with associate status. Moreover, a number of the European countries to which *Kolpak* applied, are now EU Member States, and their nationals will be protected fully by Article 45 TFEU.

WHY ARE QUOTAS BACK ON THE AGENDA?

Whilst *Kolpak* has not had the dramatic effect that some anticipated, its consequences combined with those of *Bosman* have resulted in ongoing and significant controversy. As is not unusual in the context of discrimination law, there has been a backlash, with arguments at various levels in football that the legacy of *Bosman*, compounded by *Kolpak*, is to damage the fortunes of national teams and prevent the emergence of home grown talent. In a range of professional team sports within the EU, the player squads have become increasingly cosmopolitan, with newly emerging patterns of player migration developing. However, it should be stressed again that professional sport has been an employment sector that has historically involved complex patterns of international migration.[10]

In the last few years, a number of sports, and in particular football, have moved to reintroduce player quotas. In April 2005, UEFA introduced its 'home grown players' rule for European cup competitions and recommended that national associations adopt similar rules for their own domestic leagues.[11] In May 2008, FIFA formally proposed a '6+5 rule' based on a quota of six national players in any given team.[12] Although the UEFA rule predates the FIFA proposal, we shall consider the two rules out of chronological order on the basis that, on the face of it, FIFA's proposals are more problematic legally. But first it is necessary to address the major question as to why there has been increasing concern from the football authorities over the impact of *Bosman* and the subsequent case law of the ECJ. The following can be identified as the *perceived* problems that European law has created for football.

Firstly, aggregation of top playing talent within a small elite of clubs in European football, notably those who have been able to qualify for participation in the UEFA Champions League on a regular basis, has led to a real challenge to the crucial sporting characteristic of unpredictability of outcome as a distortion of sporting competition. These clubs have dominance due to their control of the top playing talent, whose nationality is largely irrelevant.

Secondly, the freedom of movement provisions have led to the top talent from EU Member States moving to the economically powerful leagues in European football, notably England's Premier League, Spain's La Liga and Italy's Serie A. This influx into the economically powerful leagues has resulted in diminished opportunities for young emerging indigenous talent within those Member States. This can be supported by research that demonstrates that foreign players employed by English, Spanish, Italian, German and French clubs in each country's top league made up 42.4 per cent of all players during the 2007–2008 season rising to 46.59 per cent of all players in the 2013–2014 season. In the English Premier League, the number of foreign players in these two respective seasons has moved from 59.5 per cent to 62.9 per cent.[13]

Thirdly, this migration has been at the expense of young domestic talent. Contrary to the view expressed by Attorney General Lenz in *Bosman*, that it was unlikely that the migration of foreign players would increase to the extent that the chances of domestic players would be seriously diminished,[14] it is argued that, in fact, this is just what has occurred.[15] It is also argued that young domestic players have also been unable or unwilling to move to other Member States in meaningful numbers as a balancing tendency to differing degrees in different countries.

Fourthly, this migration has manifested itself in a smaller pool of eligible players to pick for the national teams of Member States. Consequently, national teams throughout Europe have been weakened. This is a widely held belief. However, one research study suggests that over a 30-year period from 1977 to 2007, the performance of the England national team has improved in the post-*Bosman* years.[16]

Fifthly, Member States from which playing talent has migrated are increasingly impoverished in terms of the performance of their club teams. Beyond the new dynamic that has emerged since *Bosman* within the EU, the *Kolpak* and *Simutenkov*[17] cases have applied non-discrimination provisions to a wider range of countries beyond the EU's borders. Moreover, Europe, as the powerhouse of world football, has also become a focus for migration patterns of player talent into Europe from around the world. Subject to any quota system operated by a particular football association and national immigration rules, significant foreign non-EU national players have been able to secure employment within European football leagues. This has both caused impoverishment in national leagues worldwide and impacted adversely upon national sides. It has also created exploitation and the trafficking of playing talent away from many, mainly developing, countries.[18]

Lastly, in the context of the pan-European UEFA competitions, especially the Champions League, economic impact includes less competitive balance in competitions, an increased link between money and sporting success and fewer opportunities for locally trained players to play.[19]

The above arguments are regarded as undermining the rationales of *Bosman* and *Kolpak*, and, essentially, the reintroduction of playing quotas in some guise is seen as righting the wrongs of the effects of the rulings. With reference to these arguments, the chapter will now examine the legality of FIFA's and UEFA's proposals for player quotas.

FIFA 6+5 RULE

This proposal, agreed at the FIFA Congress in May 2008, essentially provides that at the beginning of each match, each club must field at least six players who are eligible to play for the national team of the country of the club.[20] However, there are no restrictions proposed on the number of non-eligible players under contract with the club (although restrictions on size of squads that may be permitted in individual leagues will have to be taken into account).[21] This restriction applies to the starting line-up of the team, and coaches will be able to modify the ratio of national players in the team during the game with up to three permitted substitutions all of whom can be non-eligible players.

It should be noted, that at the time of writing, the 6+5 proposal appears to have been abandoned.[22] However, given FIFA's insistence that it is both preferable to UEFA's rule and compatible with EU law it can be anticipated that the 6+5 rule or something akin to it will resurface in the future. It is also the case that the proposal both reflects and feeds current political debates concerning the pros and cons of economic migration – in particular, perspectives that see economic migration as a problem which has a damaging impact on indigenous populations. Thus it remains pertinent to examine the history of the proposed rule and legal arguments for and against its compatibility with EU law.

FIFA claims the proposal is needed for all the reasons stated above, but, additionally, because 'the universal development of football over the last century would not continue if there were increasing inequalities between continents, countries and protagonists in football'.[23] There has been political support for FIFA's proposal[24] and significant support for it within the football family.[25] However, most academic evaluation has been that within Europe such player quotas would clearly be contrary to Article 45 TFEU in terms of being a form of discrimination ruled unlawful by the ECJ decisions in *Dona*,[26] *Bosman*, *Kolpak* and *Simutenkov*.[27]

An alternative analysis is presented by a FIFA commissioned report by the Institute for European Affairs (INEA).[28] As with the partly UEFA funded, Independent European Sport Review (the Arnaut Report),[29] the INEA Report exemplifies a recognised way of presenting a lobbying position on the development of the EU's sports policy. However, unlike the Arnaut Report, which was the culmination of significant consultation amongst a range of stakeholders in European sport and which provides a well-argued and constructed case for greater recognition of the 'specificity of sport' by the EU, the INEA Report is somewhat more limited. Arguably, it provides a badly structured, repetitive and somewhat simplistic justification for the 6+5 proposal. Most football fans understand the significance of the 'hand of God' in determining an outcome – it is not difficult to identify the 'hand of FIFA' in the Report's recommendations.

The argument presented by the INEA Report is as follows. The 6+5 proposal is portrayed as being axiomatically for the good of football as a response to the detrimental impact of the *Bosman* ruling in the years subsequent to it. The major problems the ruling has created for football, as perceived by the authors of the Report, have been summarised above. The 6+5 proposal is consequently presented as being a purely sporting rule outside the 'soft law' regulatory involvement of the EU in sport and a 'sporting response' to the perceived current ills within football and thus not contrary to European competition law. This argument is very unlikely to succeed given the ECJ rulings in *Meca-Medina* and *Motoe*.[30] Taken together these rulings enable the European Court to consider the compatibility with EU law of any rules, which a sport's regulatory body have deemed 'pure' sporting rules, that impact on a person's ability to participate in that sport or have other economic consequences.[31]

Similarly, the INEA Report contends that the proposal is not discriminatory under Article 45 TFEU. However, the central legal barrier to the implementation of FIFA's proposal is that it is clearly likely to constitute direct discrimination. As held by the ECJ in *Commission v Italy*,[32] direct discrimination cannot be justified and can be legitimated only by reference to one of the express derogations in Article 45(3) TFEU on grounds of public policy, public security or public health or through secondary legislation. It is difficult to see how the 6+5 rule, any more than the original pre-*Bosman* 3+2 rule, could permit derogation under any of these headings and therefore should be ruled as inherently unlawful.

There are arguments, developed initially in the *Cassis de Dijon* case,[33] that there can be an 'unwritten justification' of direct discrimination in circumstances of 'pressing reasons of public interest', and that the 6+5 rule should be regarded in this light by the ECJ.[34] However, it is debatable whether the interests of sport could ever be seen in this way. By way of analogy, it is useful to have regard to the ECJ rulings in *Viking*[35] and *Laval*.[36] These cases concern conflict between national law on rights to strike and the freedoms of establishment and to provide services. In these rulings, despite accepting that rights to strike have the status of fundamental rights within the EU, the ECJ gave priority to protecting the freedoms established by the EU Treaty.[37] If a similar approach is taken to freedom of movement under Article 45 TFEU, and the symbiotic relationship this has with EU discrimination law then, even if the 6+5 rule does genuinely further the interests of professional football (and potentially other sports), it is unlikely to pass the test of 'pressing public interest'. The needs of sport are surely of less significance to the public interest than the exercising of *fundamental* rights to strike by trade unions and their members to protect pay, conditions and job security.

The INEA Report also argues that the 6+5 rule should be seen as indirect rather than direct discrimination and thus can be justified as a proportionate means to deal with the above problems. The Report argues that the rule is not based on the nationality of the player but to the 'entitlement to play for the national team concerned'.[38] This seems a very weak argument. Whilst nationality is the primary requirement for eligibility for the national teams, it does not give an automatic right to be able to play for such teams. For example, some players who have become naturalised in a certain country based on a stipulated period of residency, but who have previously played for another national team, are not eligible due to FIFA restrictions.

One sporting rule that the EU Commission has consistently seen as legitimate is the right to select national athletes for national team competitions.[39] Therefore, it is clear that a non-national cannot play for a national side. So given that the 6+5 rule will disadvantage all non-nationals it would appear to be directly discriminating against that group. Whilst it is true there is no formal restriction on the number of non-nationals a club can employ, in practice it is likely that clubs will adopt the view that it is less commercially viable to employ any more non-nationals. Applying the classic test for direct discrimination used in English law, the point (albeit one that cannot be pre-determined) will be reached when it can be said that 'but for' a player's nationality he would have been seen as a suitable player for a club to recruit.[40]

If the 6+5 rule is not directly discriminatory, but can correctly be seen as indirect discrimination, then justification is available. However, it is argued below that justification of the rather less discriminatory UEFA rule should fail on the basis of proportionality. If this view were to coincide with that adopted by the courts then justification of the FIFA rule must surely be impossible. In this respect, the view that the FIFA rule should be supported because the UEFA 'proposal to ensure that a certain number of home-grown players are included in a squad of 25 simply does not go far enough'[41] is rather ironic in that it is being favoured as more effective because it operates in a more discriminatory manner. A basic tenet of European law is that the more discriminatory a policy is, the more difficult it becomes to justify it as a proportionate response.[42]

Ultimately, it is difficult to discern any fundamental difference between the 6+5 rule and the 3+2 rule rejected in *Bosman* – the later rule is really the earlier rule in a new guise. Similarly, the problems that *Bosman* is regarded as having created were entirely predictable and indeed intended consequences of the ruling. It was always clear that the best leagues attract the best players and will continue to do so. This is part of the logic of EU social law that workers can move to other Member States where they can enjoy the best rewards for their labour. There is no rational basis for excluding footballers from this. In a sense it is a case of *Bosman* there and back again. As is substantiated below, in examining the arguments advanced for justifying both the FIFA and UEFA rules, the reasons for rejecting these as identified by Advocate General Lenz in *Bosman* remain pertinent and cogent.

Moreover, the philosophical basis of EU law on freedom of movement is that EU nationals are able to move between Member States irrespective of the perceived problems this causes for national economies or the job security of national workers. If reducing unemployment is (correctly) not regarded as justifying national quotas it is difficult to see how invoking the specificities of sport will be seen as anything other than an attempt at special pleading. On a global basis, the FIFA proposal underestimates the barrier to the international mobility of footballers erected by national immigration laws. In Britain, for example, work permits are effectively only available to top internationals from top national teams, and even where a player has a work permit he is still required to obtain a new one before he can transfer to another club.[43] The idea that foreign players are swamping the English and other European Leagues seems a peculiarly European case of xenophobia.

It should be noted that the international players union, FIFPro, although supporting the sporting aims behind the FIFA proposal, accepts that, as professional players are employees, both national and EU law provisions will be infringed.[44] The European Parliament and the European Commission have indicated clearly that they regard the 6+5 rule as directly discriminatory and contrary to Article 45 TFEU. This is within the development of a European sports law policy that has applied the values of equality and equal treatment that have been generally and expressly determined by the ECJ.[45]

HOME GROWN PLAYER RULE

However, both FIFPro and the European Commission have indicated some approval for UEFA's rules on home grown players, though FIFPro has emphasised the need to protect young players, including those from Africa, in that the rule could have the unintended consequence of an influx of trainee players between 14 and 16 into the major European leagues.[46] Alternatively, Miettinen and Parrish have argued that the UEFA rules may offend EU law in that they cannot be justified by reference to normal principles 'on the grounds that they are disproportionate, unfit for the purposes they are relied upon or pursue economic as well as legitimate and justifiable non-economic objectives'.[47]

The UEFA plan was first proposed in 2005. The rule requires clubs participating in the Champions League and the UEFA Cup to have a minimum number of home grown players, that is players who, regardless of their nationality, have been trained by their club or by another club in the same national association for at least three years between the age of 15 and 21. This was set at four players in a maximum squad of 25 in the first season of application – 2006–2007. This rose to eight out of the maximum squad of 25 players in the 2008–2009 season.[48]

The perceived legitimacy of this policy has led to a number of domestic leagues introducing similar restrictions to their playing squads. In England, the Football League introduced restrictions, which started in the 2009–2010 season, which require four players in the match day squad to have been registered by a domestic club for three years before their 21st birthday.[49] In fact, for most Football League clubs this will merely be reflecting the status quo that has existed for many years, with clubs already complying with this requirement. More significantly, in terms of the potential practical impact, the Premier League has adopted similar rules with effect from season 2010–2011.[50]

Any policy or rule that is intrinsically liable to affect migrant workers more than national workers and thus impede access to the labour market and freedom of movement constitutes indirect discrimination. It is clear that UEFA's rule falls into this category but, as such, will be lawful if it can be justified. Justification of the UEFA rule requires it to be established that the rule does further the objective needs of football and meets the criterion of proportionality. For this to be the case the objectives secured by the rule must not be outweighed by the discriminatory impact of it and there must be no other means by which these objectives can be met just as effectively.

With respect to potential justification, it is important to take into account that the rule has received a positive response from a number of quarters. Like the European Commission and FIFPro, the European Parliament has been supportive and:

> expresses its clear support for the UEFA measures to encourage the education of young players by requiring a minimum number of home-grown players in a professional club's squad and by placing a limit on the size of the squads . . . [It] believes that such incentive measures are proportionate and calls on professional clubs to strictly implement this rule.[51]

The Arnaut Report contended that the measure would: encourage training programmes in order to promote, develop, nurture and educate new talents; promote the local nature of clubs, so fans identify more with their team; maintain competitive balance by reducing the importance of money; reduce the tendency towards 'hoarding' of players; widen the pool of talent within an association eligible to represent the national team.[52]

The Report went on to suggest that, 'the purpose and nature of this rule is such that it would qualify for an exemption under EU competition law'.[53] Equally, however, if this is not the most appropriate legal instrument to provide security for this system, the authors also consider that Guidelines could be very useful on the matter to confirm the compatibility of the rule with EC law.

The White Paper on Sport reaffirms this position:

> acceptance of limited and proportionate restrictions (in line with EU Treaty provisions on free movement and European Court of Justice rulings) to the principle of free movement in particular as regards: the right to select national athletes for national team competitions; the need to limit the number of participants in a competition; the setting of deadlines for transfers of players in team sports . . . rules requiring that teams include a certain quota of locally trained players could be accepted as being compatible with the Treaty provisions on free movement of persons if . . . indirect discrimination effects resulting from them can be justified as being proportionate to a legitimate objective pursued, such as to enhance and protect the training and development of talented young players.[54]

The White Paper highlighted the need for further consideration and, in 2008, the Commission published a report accepting that the home grown player rules 'seem to comply with the principle of free movement of workers . . . [E]ven though they might lead to indirect discrimination on the basis of nationality, the UEFA rules have been endorsed by the Commission, subject to a review of their practical consequences by 2012.'[55]

The assessment of the home grown player rule published in April 2013 provides an extensive legal and economic analysis. There is an acceptance that the rule 'amounts to an indirectly discriminatory rule because even though the Rule is neutral in terms of nationality, national workers are placed at an advantage over migrant workers'.[56] The report also accepts UEFA's claim that there is a sporting justification for the rule promoting competitive balance but that '[The] neutrality or very limited positive effect of the Rule in terms of improving competitive balance and the training and development of young European Union players must be balanced against the impact the Rule has on restricting a player's freedom of movement.'[57] Two main recommendations are made.

Firstly, the impact of the home grown player rule needs continued monitoring, and the position should be reviewed in three years' time. Secondly, 'rather than adopting a negative position on the Rule, the European Commission should extend an invitation to UEFA to consult with key stakeholders on whether alternative measures, that do not carry discriminatory effects, can deliver more substantial benefits for European football.'[58]

ALTERNATIVE SPORTING MEASURES

The focus on alternative measures is a key issue in this area. The authors' view is that the reality of the home grown player rule, like the 6+5 rule, is that it is protectionist in nature. Most fundamentally, even if the rule is seen as justifiable in political and footballing contexts, it still has to satisfy the legal requirement of proportionality, and the above arguments fail to take into account that there are alternative ways of securing the legitimate interests of professional football.

As made clear by Advocate General Lenz in *Bosman*, redistribution of income provides the most effective and fairest way of ensuring that the vast sums of money secured by large clubs are shared with their smaller brethren.[59] This both increases the potential for competitive balance and provides income for the development and enhancement of youth academies and the establishment of national scouting networks. Rather than preventing clubs from fielding foreign players, is it not much better to encourage the provision of the requisite financial and physical resources for the identification and development of young local talent?[60]

It may be the case at present that it is commercially more attractive to attract youth talent from other clubs who are classified as 'home grown' rather than investing in potentially costly infrastructure. Indeed, in the context of post-*Bosman* transfer systems, youth academies are increasingly seen as not commercially viable.[61] This is because once a player has reached the age of 23 or 24 and is out of contract, free agency applies with no right for a transfer fee or compensation from the former employing club. This is despite the money that club may have invested in training that player in his youth. However, in this regard it could be possible for clubs to enter into a collective agreement with one another to reserve a share of the income from broadcasting rights and the like for clubs that agree to invest in youth academies. Such an agreement would also meet the aspirations of football fans who, typically, enjoy seeing their club field a mixture of international stars and players with local connections and thus a genuine commitment to the club.

Rather than this focus on restrictions on the labour market, other approaches which focus on the product market may constitute a more proportionate response to solve the perceived problems in football include salary caps, though these have been rejected by FIFPro and operate artificially to restrict the income that professional players can earn. It may be only the big stars who can become millionaires through playing the 'beautiful game', but this is a dream that many young footballers from working class backgrounds have, and why should it be denied to them. Such restrictions do not exist in other parts of the entertainment industry such as music and acting, so why should they in professional sport.[62] It is also important to take account of UEFA's 'Financial Fair Play Plan', which is designed to equalise the financial muscle of clubs around Europe.[63] This does not impose a formal salary cap but should restrain clubs from paying salaries to players that they cannot afford.

FIFPro has suggested as an alternative that there be a cap on transfer fees.[64] This seems rather more attractive: it will contribute to the restoration of competitive balance and prevent the richer clubs gazumping attempts by smaller clubs to sign star players. Admittedly, it will reduce the signing on fee that such players will earn, but this is preferable to a permanent restriction on their incomes.

Arguably the weakest argument for the UEFA rule, and indeed FIFA's 6+5 rule, is the view that it will increase the number of players eligible for national teams by increasing the pool of national talent. The best clubs will always recruit the best national players and there should always be sufficient numbers of these to provide the squads for international competitions. As Advocate General Lenz observed, the fortunes of the Scottish team are hardly affected by the fact that their best players often choose to play in the English Premier League. Indeed, as he also commented, the importing of foreign internationals into a domestic league has a tendency to improve the skills of domestic players rather than have a negative impact on their development.[65] Moreover, any player, whether or not a national of the country where the club is located, can become a 'home grown player' after playing in a domestic league for a three-year period between the ages of 15 and 21.[66]

As well as the issue of proportionality, it is also necessary to take into account the unintended effect the home grown player rule could have on the supply and trafficking of young players from developing countries, particularly Africa, largely carried out by un-licensed agents and outside of regulatory frameworks.[67] As things stand, FIFA has estimated that there are around half a million transfers of minors in football per year.[68] This is movement of young people on a very significant scale, and the home grown player rule could exacerbate the problem. The rule may be designed to encourage the development of young local talent, but in practice it could lead to abuse of the notion of what a home grown player actually is.

FIFA has recently modified its transfer regulations so that young players under 18 can now move to a club in a different region or country as long as the family relocates to it for non-football reasons, such as a parent changing jobs.[69] There is evidence that in the past, parents have in fact been provided with 'manufactured' jobs by clubs in the local area.[70] The new regulation does, however, require a sub-committee of the FIFA Players' Status Committee to vet all transfers of minors,[71] but it can be anticipated that new circumventions of the system will be devised. Thus, it is at least feasible that clubs will manipulate the nature of the home grown player and the UEFA rule will contribute to rather than prevent exploitative trafficking.

SIMILAR RULES IN OTHER SPORTS

Team sports other than football have of course been subject to the same issues around how to respond to EU law challenges provided by the *Bosman* ruling to sporting rules that operate as player restraints. Different sports have a variety of player quotas in national and pan-European competitions, and a number of sports have moved to introduce rules requiring playing squads containing a number of locally trained players. For example, in April 2014 the European Commission issued a 'Reasoned Opinion' that requires the Spanish Association of Basketball Clubs to 'change its rules on the composition of basketball teams, as the current quotas for locally trained players lead to indirect discrimination towards players from other Member States'.[72] The EU Commission established that in some competitions, rules required that up to 88 per cent of the players needed to be locally trained and that the sporting justifications of encouraging the recruitment and training of young players and the promotion of competitive balance, did not pass the test of 'appropriateness and proportionality'.[73]

CONCLUSIONS: THE REGULATORY FUTURE

We have sought to substantiate through the above arguments that tensions between the traditional autonomy of sporting regulatory bodies and external legal intervention, particularly through rulings of the ECJ and the resultant juridification of sporting rules, has generated uncertainty and, in the context of discrimination law, renewed resistance – particularly in professional football. Similar tensions have existed, and to some extent continue to do so, in the context of transfer systems – particularly on the part of those who regard any transfer system as a form of slavery which should be rendered completely invalid under European law. With respect to the latter, our proposed solution has been the adoption of a collective agreement or directive based on the methodology of reflexive labour law (as discussed in Chapter 15).

Perspectives on national quotas are inevitably coloured by attitudes to the international mobility of labour in general. In the case of the authors, for example, we see football as a global sport with a global audience and would like to see footballers being able to play for any club in the world irrespective of their nationalities. This is of course subject to the need to protect young players from trafficking or exploitation, but again we are of the view that these sorts of abuses are more the product of immigration rules rather than being prevented by them. Our preferred solution to problems such as maintaining a competitive balance between clubs and encouraging local talent would be through a combination of a cap on transfer fees and redistribution of income to assist clubs in establishing and maintaining effective local academies.

However, personal political perspectives notwithstanding, if something like the home grown player rule was the result of a collective agreement involving FIFPro, UEFA and FIFA, or at least EU legislation based on dialogue between these social partners, then this would put such a rule on a legitimate basis, with the detail of the rule and the justifications for it being the product of rigorous bargaining replacing or underlying legislative processes. This would reflect the appeal from sports bodies for legal certainty and greater precision of the regulatory environment. Most importantly, as any such rule would then have a clear legal foundation, it would pre-empt, or at least limit, the impact of the vicissitudes of litigation before the European Court.

NOTES

1. Case C-415/93, *Union Royale Belge des Societes de Football Association & others v Jean-Marc Bosman* [1995] ECR I-4921.
2. This was previously Article 39 of the EC Treaty and at the time of the Bosman ruling was Article 48.
3. For more see R. Blanpain and R. Inston, *The Bosman Case: The End of the Transfer System?* (Sweet & Maxwell; Peeters, 1996).
4. Indeed, similar proposals have been mooted in other team sports. See, for example, 'FIVB ready to fight EU labor laws on "4+2" player rule', International Volleyball 21 May 2008, www.fivb.ch.
5. See M. Colucci, 'Quota for foreign football players allowed to play in a club: A comparative analysis at national level', (2008) (available at www.rdes.it/FOREIGN_PLAYERS36.pdf).
6. Case C-438/00, *Deutscher Handballbund eV v Maros Kolpak* [2003] ECR I-4135.
7. Case C-265/03, *Igor Simutenkov v Abogado del Estado, Real Federacion Espanola de Futbol and Ministerio Fiscal* [2005] ECR I-2579.
8. For more, see S. Boyes, 'Caught behind or following-on? Cricket, the European Union and the "Bosman effect"', (2005) 3(1) Entertainment and Sports Law Journal, http://www2.warwick.ac.uk/fac/soc/law/elj/eslj/. Note a stricter interpretation by the EU Commission of the Cotonou Agreement has lead to narrower work permit criteria based on need for past international record of recipients, see 'ECB wins overseas player battle', 26 October 2009, http://news.bbc.co.uk/sport1/hi/cricket/counties/8325975.stm.
9. See S. Boyes, 'In the shadow of Bosman: The regulatory penumbra of sport in the EU', (2003) 12(2) Nottingham Law Journal 72; F. Hendrickx, 'The European non-EU player and the Kolpak case', (2003) International Sports Law Journal 12; S. van den Bogaert, 'And another uppercut from the European Court of Justice to nationality requirements in sports regulations', (2004) 29(2) European Law Review 267.
10. See, for example, P. Lanfranchi and M. Taylor, *Moving with the Ball: The Migration of Professional Footballers* (Berg, 2001).
11. See the current UEFA 'Regulations for the Champions League Competition', www.uefa.com/multimediafiles/download/regulations/uefa/others/82/68/51/826851_download.pdf.
12. 'Fifa backs Blatter on quota plan', http://news.bbc.co.uk/sport1/hi/football/europe/7421348.stm, 30 May 2008.
13. Professional Football Players' Observatory (PFPO) 'Annual review of the European football players', www.football-observatory.com/. This research identified that European wide, non-European players now represent 50 per cent of the total number of foreign players. Also see 'Fewer club-trained players, more expatriate footballers in the big five European leagues 2009', www.fifa.com/worldfootball/clubfootball/releases/newsid=1096497.html#fewer+club+trained+players+more+expatriate+footballers+f ve+european+leagues.
14. Case C-415/93, n. 1 supra, para. 145.
15. This argument is fundamentally the basis of recent proposals of the FA Chairman's England Commission (May 2014), available at www.thefa.com/. . ./england/the-fa-chairmans-england-commission-report. For analysis see D. Winne, 'Limiting non-EU players entering English football', (2014) 12(10) *World Sports Law Report*.
16. F. Huxtable, 'Player quotas: The good, the bad and the illegal', (2008) September, *Soccer Investor*.
17. Case C-265/03, *Igor Simutenkov v Abogado del Estado, Real Federacion Espanola de Futbol and Ministerio Fiscal* [2005] ECR I-2579, involved a Russian national playing professional football in Spain, where the ECJ ruled that he was protected by a non-discriminatory provision contained in an agreement on partnership and cooperation signed between the EU and the Russian Federation in 1994.

18. L. Backe Madsen and J. M. Johansson, *Den Forsvunne Diamanten* (The Lost Diamond) (Tiden Norsk Forlag, 2008).
19. M. Daziel et al. 'Study on the assessment of UEFA's "home grown player rule"', Negotiated procedure EAC/07/2012, 30 April 2013.
20. 'Yes in principle to 6+5 rule', www.fifa.com/aboutfifa/federation/bodies/media/newsid=684707.html.
21. The English Premier League has been criticised on squad sizes operated by many clubs. For example, it is reported that in the 2008–2009 season, Liverpool FC had a first team squad of 62 players, see 'Uefa slam "ridiculous" Big Four squad sizes', www.guardian.co.uk/football/2009/mar/29/uefa-liverpool-squad-sizes-premier-league, 29 March 2009.
22. BBC sport reported that the FIFA congress in June 2010 decided to abandon the proposal, see http://news.bbc.co.uk/sport1/hi/football/8733164.stm. However, there has been no official confirmation of this by FIFA or indeed by other interested parties such as the Fédération Internationale des Associations de Footballeurs Professionnels (FIFPro).
23. 'FIFA Congress supports objectives of 6+5', www.fifa.com/aboutfifa/federation/bodies/media/newsid=783657.html, 30 May 2008.
24. UK All Party Parliamentary Football Group, 'English football and its governance', www.allpartyfootball.com/APFG_Report_on_English_Football_&_Its_Governance_April_2009%5b1%5d.pdf.
25. 'Mourinho voices support for FIFA's "6+5" rule', http://soccernet.espn.go.com/news/story?id=632412&cc=5739.
26. Case 13/76, *Donà v Mantero* [1976] ECR 333.
27. P. Boucher, 'Kicking off', (2007) Employment Law, November, 18–19; C. Anderson, 'Player contracts: New FIFA regulations on the transfer of minors', (2009) 7(11) World Sports Law Reports; F. Majani, 'An excavation into the legal deficiencies of the FIFA 6 Plus 5 rule and the UEFA home-grown players rule in the eyes of the European Union law', (2009) 1–2 International Sports Law Journal 19; R. Williams and A. Haffner, 'FIFA quotas ruled offside?', (2008) 158 New Law Journal 1017.
28. Institute for European Affairs, 'Expert opinion regarding the compatibility of the "6+5 rule" within European Community law', (INEA, 2008).
29. J. Arnaut (2006), 'Independent European sport review', www.independentfootball review.com/.
30. Case C519/04P, *Meca-Medina v Commission of the European Communities* [2006] ECR 1-6991; Case 49/07, *Motosyklesistiki Omospondia Ellados NPID (MOTOE) v Elliniko Dimosio* [2008] ECR I-0000.
31. For further discussion see S. Weatherill, 'Anti-doping revisited – the demise of the rule of "purely sporting interest"?', (2006) 27(12) European Competition Law Review 645, pp. 647, 652, 657; and 'Article 82 EC and sporting "conflict of interest": The judgment in MOTOE', (2008) 3–4 International Sports Law Journal.
32. Case C-283/99, *Commission v Italy* [2001] ECR I-4363.
33. Case 120/78, *Rewe-Zentrale AG v Bundesmonopolverwaltung für Branntwein* [1979] ECR 649.
34. See R. Conzelmann, 'Models of the promotion of home grown players for the protection of national representative teams', (2008) 3–4 International Sports Law Journal 26, who cites Case C-2/90, *Wallonian Garbage* (1992) ECR I-4431 and Case C-379/98, *PreussenElecktra* (2003) ECR I-2099 in support of position.
35. Case C-438/05, *International Transport Workers' Federation and Finnish Seamen's Union v Viking Line ABP and OÜ Viking Line Eesti* [2007] ECR I-10779.
36. Case C-341/05, *Laval v Svenska Byggnadsarbetareförbundet* [2007] ECR I-11767.
37. For a full discussion of these cases see A. C. L. Davies, 'One step forward, two steps back? The Viking and Laval Cases in the ECJ', (2008) 37(2) Industrial Law Journal 126.
38. INEA, op. cit. n. 28 supra, 136.
39. European Commission, 'White Paper on Sport', (2007) COM (2007) 391, para. 4.2; re-affirmed in European Commission, *Communication on Sport: Developing the European*

Dimension in Sport (2011). However, note the continued interest of restrictions of access to individual competitions within Member States for non-nationals, see Tender No. DG EAC/19/2009.

40. This test was first formulated by the House of Lords in *James v Eastleigh Borough Council* [1990] 2 AC 751.
41. UK All Party Parliamentary Football Group, op. cit. n. 24 supra.
42. See, for example, the principle of proportionality as propounded by the ECJ in Case 170/84, *Bilka-Kaufhaus Gmbh v Weber von Hartz* [1986] ECR 1607.
43. For current position see www.ukba.homeoffice.gov.uk.
44. For FIFPro's view on the 6+5 rule and the home grown players rule see www.fifpro. org/index.php?mod=one&id=16627, 5 June 2008.
45. See joined Cases 117/76 and 16/77, *Albert Ruckdeschel & Co. and Hansa-Lagerhaus Ströh & Co. v Hauptzollamt Hamburg-St. Annen; Diamalt AG v Hauptzollamt Itzehoe* [1977] ECR 1753.
46. Conzelmann, op. cit. n. 34 supra.
47. S. Miettinen and R. Parrish, 'Nationality discrimination in community law: An assessment of UEFA regulations governing player eligibility for European club competitions (the home-grown player rule)', (2007) 5(2) Entertainment and Sports Law Journal.
48. UEFA, 'Regulations of the UEFA Champions League 2008/2009', www.uefa.com/ multimediafiles/download/regulations/uefa/others/70/22/60/702260_download.pdf.
49. 'Clubs vote for "home-grown" rule', http://news.bbc.co.uk/sport1/hi/football/7789808. stm, 18 December 2008.
50. D. Conn, 'Homegrown doesn't mean English but rule will help', *The Guardian*, 2 September 2010. Premier League squads may be up to 25 senior players and must include no more than 17 players who are not home grown. A player is home grown if he has spent three seasons with any English or Welsh club. However, there are no restrictions on the number of players in a squad below the age of 21.
51. European Parliament, 'Resolution on the Future of Professional Football in Europe', 29 March 2007, at 34.
52. Arnaut Report, op. cit. n. 29 supra, para. 6.58.
53. Ibid, para. 6.59.
54. White Paper on Sport, op. cit. n. 39 supra, action 9 of the Pierre de Coubertin Action Plan, 6.
55. 'UEFA's rules on home-grown players receive green light from the Commission', http:// ec.europa.eu/sport/news/news270_en.htm, 14 August 2008.
56. Executive Summary para. 6 op. cit. n. 19 supra.
57. Executive Summary para. 11 op. cit. n. 19 supra.
58. Executive Summary conclusion op. cit. n. 19 supra.
59. Case C-415/93, op. cit. n. 1 supra, para. 233.
60. I. Lynam, 'Player contracts: "6+5": Analysis of whether the proposal is "fit for purpose"', (2009) 7(5) World Sports Law Report.
61. D. Conn, 'Clubs leave lost youth behind as academies fail English talent', www.guard ian.co.uk/football/david-conn-inside-sport-blog/2009/sep/09/chelsea-fifa-premier- league-academies, 9 September 2009.
62. R. Fort and J. Quirk, 'Cross-subsidization, incentives, and outcomes in professional team sports leagues', (1995) 33(3) Journal of Economic Literature 1265; P. Harris, 'Salary caps', (2002) Sport and the Law Journal 120.
63. 'Uefa introduces tough penalties for spendthrift clubs', http://news.bbc.co.uk/sport1/hi/ football/europe/8709871.stm.
64. R. Parrish and S. Miettinen, *The Sporting Exception in European Union Law* (TMC Asser Press, 2008).
65. Case C-415/93, op. cit. n. 1 supra, paras. 145 & 146.
66. The Spanish national, Cese Fabregas, whilst he played for Arsenal, can be cited as an illustration. The link therefore between being a home grown player and being eligible for the national side is not certain. Conversely, and somewhat ironically, some

nationally eligible players, such as the former English international Owen Hargreaves, who was an apprentice player at Bayern München, are not 'home grown players'.

67. Note the recent CAS case concerning the upholding of FIFA Players' Status Committee judgment against the Danish FA and FC for registering minor players from Nigeria 06.03.2009 – Final Award – CAS 2008/A/1485 *FC Midtjylland v FIFA*; also see Backe Madsen and Johansson, op. cit. n. 18 supra.

68. 'Fifa cracks down on child transfers', www.guardian.co.uk/football/2009/sep/05/uefa-fifa-child-footballer-transfers.

69. See 'FIFA regulations on the status and transfer of players', Article 19, www.fifa.com/mm/document/affederation/administration/66/98/97/regulationsstatusandtransfer%5fen%5f1210.pdf.

70. 'Chelsea facing legal threat over signing boy of 11', www.guardian.co.uk/football/2009/sep/05/chelsea-legal-threat-alleged-player-poaching, 5 September 2009. Chelsea FC were put under a FIFA imposed transfer ban over Chelsea's illegal recruitment of the teenage forward Gaël Kakuta from Lens, overturned by agreement between the parties before a formal appeal hearing by CAS, www.tas-cas.org/d2wfiles/document/3947/5048/0/2010.02.04%20PR%20Eng%20_Final_.pdf.

71. 'FIFA tighten minor player transfer regulations', www.eufootball.biz/Legal/6470-fifa_minor_player_transfer_regulations.html, 8 December 2008.

72. 'Spanish basketball clubs call for reform after EC Opinion', (2014) 12(4) World Sports Law Reports.

73. Ibid.

Index